W9-CNX-193

Second Edition

LATIN AMERICA

Political Culture
and Development

Russell H. Fitzgibbon

Julio A. Fernandez
State University of New York
Cortland, New York

PRENTICE-HALL, INC. Englewood Cliffs, New Jersey 07632

Library of Congress Cataloging in Publication Data

FITZGIBBON, RUSSELL HUMKE (date)
　　Latin America: political culture and development.

　　Bibliography: p.
　　Includes index.
　　1. Latin America—Politics and government—1948-
I.　Fernandez, Julio A. (date)　　II. Title.
JL953 1980.F57　　　320.98　　　80-12035
ISBN 0-13-524348-3

Editorial/production supervision and interior
　design by Linda Schuman
Cover design by Zimmerman & Foyster
Manufacturing buyer: Edmund W. Leone

This book is for Irene and Doris.

© 1981, 1971 by Prentice-Hall, Inc., Englewood Cliffs, N.J. 07632

All rights reserved. No part of this book
may be reproduced in any form or
by any means without permission in writing
from the publisher.

Printed in the United States of America

10　9　8　7　6　5　4　3　2　1

PRENTICE-HALL INTERNATIONAL, INC., *London*
PRENTICE-HALL OF AUSTRALIA PTY. LIMITED, *Sydney*
PRENTICE-HALL OF CANADA, LTD., *Toronto*
PRENTICE-HALL OF INDIA PRIVATE LIMITED, *New Delhi*
PRENTICE-HALL OF JAPAN, INC., *Tokyo*
PRENTICE-HALL OF SOUTHEAST ASIA PTE. LTD., *Singapore*
WHITEHALL BOOKS LIMITED, *Wellington, New Zealand*

CONTENTS

PREFACE

The Latin American political scene is one of infinite variety. It is elementary that political systems in Latin America are not what the respective constitutions purport to establish and that it is consequently necessary to look beyond the basic laws and documents to government and political life in action. Hence, armies and parties, labor unions and the Church, and a number of other groups and factors need to be considered before the totality of Latin American political culture assumes its true proportions.

Two convictions have helped shape the nature of the volume: First, it is important to have some familiarity with the political culture of both the area as a whole and of the individual countries, and, second, it is essential to take on a concern for the overall development of the various political systems.

To the credit of the topic approach, it can be said that political systems in the Latin American family have much in common. And yet, the governments and politics of the several Latin American systems grow more dissimilar as time passes. Each political system develops its own political individuality, practices, responses, and structures, and these diverge from each other more and more with successive years and decades. Latin American structures are peculiarly the heirs of earlier centuries, and to a greater degree than is true for the United States, one must know the conditioning effects of the past in order to understand the existing political culture and the many faces of development in Latin America.

It is perhaps appropriate to conclude this preface with a few words of acknowledgment for assistance rendered. Wives of authors are of course not unhonored, but they are too often unsung. Ours are named in the dedication of the book, but we must add our deep gratitude to them both for the many generous and unselfish things wives do for husbands in the throes of book-birth.

We also want to add our thanks to Mrs. Anna Totoritis for an excellently completed task of typing, under deadline pressures, the final draft of the manuscript.

Finally, we extend our thanks to officials of Prentice-Hall, Inc. for assistance and courtesies of many kinds, especially to Mr. Stan Wakefield, Political Science editor, and to Mrs. Audrey Marshall, his assistant.

R.H.F.
J.A.F.

ADDENDUM

Dr. Russell H. Fitzgibbon, coauthor of this volume, died on January 8, 1979. At the time of his death, we had completed the final draft of the manuscript, including the dedication page and the preface. Professor Fitzgibbon was my mentor and friend, as well as coauthor. His passing has been a deep personal loss to me. It is my hope that this book will be a lasting memorial to this great scholar.

I should like to express my appreciation to Mr. Alan L. Fitzgibbon for his valuable comments and moral support during the final stages of the publication of this book.

J.A.F.

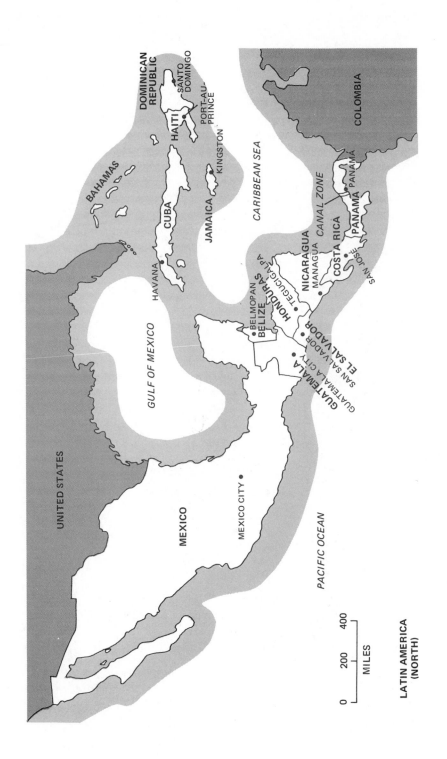

UNITED STATES

MEXICO

MEXICO CITY •

GULF OF MEXICO

BAHAMAS

CUBA

HAVANA •

JAMAICA

KINGSTON •

HAITI

DOMINICAN REPUBLIC

PORT-AU-PRINCE

SANTO DOMINGO

CARIBBEAN SEA

BELIZE

BELMOPAN •

GUATEMALA

GUATEMALA CITY •

HONDURAS

TEGUCIGALPA •

EL SALVADOR

SAN SALVADOR •

NICARAGUA

MANAGUA •

COSTA RICA

SAN JOSE •

PANAMA

CANAL ZONE

PANAMA •

COLOMBIA

PACIFIC OCEAN

MILES

0   200   400

LATIN AMERICA
(NORTH)

CARACAS

VENEZUELA

GEORGETOWN
PARAMARIBO

SURINAME

GUYANA

FR. GUIANA

BOGOTÁ

COLOMBIA

CAYENNE

QUITO •

ECUADOR

PERU

BRAZIL

LIMA

BOLIVIA

• LA PAZ

• BRASÍLIA

PARAGUAY

ASUNCIÓN •

CHILE

PACIFIC OCEAN

ARGENTINA

URUGUAY

SANTIAGO •

BUENOS AIRES •

MONTEVIDEO

ATLANTIC OCEAN

FALKLAND IS.

| 0 | 300 | 600 |

MILES

LATIN AMERICA
(SOUTH)

Part One

THE OVERALL VIEW

1

POLITICAL CULTURE
AND DEVELOPMENT
IN LATIN AMERICA

POLITICAL CULTURE

Latin American political culture has certain significant features which represent traditional and modern themes of Latin American nation building. Without doubt, contemporary political culture in Latin America has been shaped by its rich heritage. Contemporary Latin Americans reflect Indian and Hispanic cultural traditions which have produced cultures that are neither wholly Hispanic nor Indian. In cultural affinities, what black Africa is to Brazil and the Caribbean nations, Western Europe is to Chile, Argentina, and even Peru.

Latin Americans have learned from the past to better understand the present. Such important developments as the Spanish-Portuguese conquest, miscegenation, and Euro-American fusion help explain the evolution of certain Latin American sociopolitical structures and ideologies which are peculiarly the heirs of an earlier era: The land tenure arrangements, the prevalence of force, the importance of the family, the social status order, the influence of the Catholic church, the stress on personalism, and the lure of the *caudillo*-type leader have all been deeply involved in the disquieting shifts of the process called modernization.[1]

There is a strong tendency in both academic and nonacademic circles in the United States to think and speak of Latin America as a single geographical

[1]Peter Ranis, *Five Latin American Nations: A Comparative Political Study* (New York: Macmillan, 1971), p. 153.

3

and cultural unit. But we should be aware and forewarned of the diversity within the area and the distinct character of the societies and institutions of the component political systems of the region. This discussion of political culture in Latin America takes a broad conceptual approach; its emphasis on leading ideas, acknowledged by Latin Americans themselves, will provide a theoretical framework allowing a greater degree of flexibility in appraising the relative merits of political culture as a heuristic concept in the study of Latin America.

The Political Dimension of Culture

The political scientist assumes that the concept of culture has a political dimension that suggests a special analytical category in which a political system can be studied. In this framework of political culture, the student of politics examines problems and processes associated with the socialization of the individual within a given political setting.

It has been asserted that culture is an important variable of the political environment, shaping the kinds of demands entering the political system. David Easton makes the point that the members of every society act within the limits of a continuing culture that shapes their general aims, specific objectives, and the procedures they feel ought to be employed. This suggests that culture embodies societal value standards and consequently indicates possible conflict areas if demands for "valued things" are not satisfied by the political system.

Some political specialists on Latin America (Martin Needler, for one) feel that the term *political culture* has definite persuasive value when employed to encompass the wide range of nonpolitical variables (such as traditions, attitudes, thought, and behavior patterns) which help shape various kinds of political activity and legitimacy. In fact, it is generally agreed that to understand the issues which cause conflict in Latin American systems, one must first know the aggregate political behavior of the Latin American people. This is indeed a large order for the political scientist because it involves intense study of the area's political culture; it means that the totality of expectations and attitudes shared by the Latin American population toward political decision making must be understood.

A widely discussed determinant of Latin American political culture is the colonial heritage, manifested in the attitudes of the Latin American people toward both the decision-making role of government and their participation in it. The strong tendency toward personalism and authoritarianism in political culture is well known. Simón Bolívar took it into account when he wrote: "The President of the Republic, in our Constitution becomes the sun, which, fixed in its orbit, imparts life to the universe. This supreme authority must be perpetual." To date, attempts to deemphasize the authoritarian and personalistic nature of government as decision maker have not been successful in the Latin American region.

Political participation in the decision-making process means very little to average Latin Americans. They are more concerned with the benefits that emanate from the national political process rather than with insuring their participatory role in it. The typical Latin American will react with suspicion or mistrust to the activities of national government, especially to such formal institutions as the courts, political parties, and legislatures. One could say that the Latin American's social and political behavior is governed by the cultural trait of *personalismo,* which encourages loyalty only to close friends and relatives and not to impersonal aggregates. Still, the mysticism in their culture allows the majority of Latin American people to identify with the abstract concepts of liberty, nationalism, and democracy.

The Alienation Motif in Latin American Political Culture

There is clear evidence of a pattern of alienation from governmental authority in Latin American political culture. The alienation syndrome that characterizes Latin America cannot be simply explained. Scholars do know, however, that feelings of alienation do exist among the Latin American citizenry, perhaps caused by the disrupting stages of modernization which the Latin American countries are experiencing.

In trying to achieve modernization, Latin Americans may work against such formidable problems as high illiteracy, archaic socioeconomic structures, and racial discrimination. These problems only deepen the frustrations of the underprivileged who, because of their circumstances, cannot play a meaningful role in the industrialization of their nation-states.

In such a situation, the vast modernization differential that exists between the haves and have-nots is accentuated. The have-nots are the majority of *olvidados,* or forgotten groups, without access to economic or political power, without any future whatsoever. They are forced to eke out a miserable existence in the *barriadas, villas miseria, callampas, ranchitos, colonias de paracaidistas,* and *favelas* (as the wretched slums are called in, respectively, Lima, Buenos Aires, Santiago, Caracas, Mexico City, and Rio de Janeiro). Where so many live in abject poverty, guerrilla activity or violent revolution appears an easy outlet for pent-up frustrations and a sure way to secure a better and more independent way of life.

Simply stated, the alienated masses in Latin America are seeking respect and identity in a world they see as governed by a privileged sector made up of oligarchic groups who control not only the main sources of wealth but also the political power. The question is, How can the impoverished masses in Argentina and Brazil, the alienated Indians in Peru and Guatemala, the miners in Bolivia, and the farmers in Ecuador be incorporated into the mainstream of decision making in their respective national systems?

The problem for politics in Latin America, in view of the alienation which characterizes the political culture of the area, might best be described as certain cultural disparities that affect the 50 percent to 95 percent of the submerged masses of the region who, like the bulk of an iceberg, remain unnoticed. The cultural disparities between rich and poor and between urban and rural areas negatively affect the political education process. Illiterates have no appreciation of politics; they participate only intermittently in outbursts of practical activity.

It should be stressed that *latifundismo,* or ownership of huge estates, also works against the political education of the submerged masses. A brief analysis of this kind of agricultural practice in Latin America reveals that it is arbitrary and oppressive to the peasant masses who are striving to improve their bargaining power and political participation in matters affecting their welfare. In a *latifundio* agriculture the peasant is imprisoned in a system which requires blind obedience to a landed elite. The totalitarian character of the system discourages freedom of choice and socializes the peasant to believe in total submission and unquestioned loyalty to the will of the power elite.[2]

The problem of alienation, triggered by the forces of modernization, deserves careful study because of its political import for the process of nation building in developing Latin American polities. It is arguable that the alienation syndrome appears from country to country and, in Latin America, may manifest itself in varying degrees by powerlessness, meaninglessness, isolation, and lawlessness on the part of the citizenry. It is not, however, the purpose of this analysis to explore in depth this particular theme of alienation in Latin American political culture but rather to recommend it as an area for further study by interested students.

Looking briefly at two major powers in Latin America, Argentina and Mexico, one can observe a manifest incidence of alienation in their respective political cultures. In Argentina, the alienation phenomenon operates as a stumbling block to the legitimization of the political system because of a "quality of withdrawal . . . a passive value orientation . . . toward causes and one's fellow man."[3] Certain isolative attitudes indicative of frustration, disorder, aggression, and a general negative orientation toward things political seem to characterize many Argentine citizens. The average Argentine is thus de-

---

[2]Ernest Feder, *The Rape of the Peasantry: Latin America's Landholding System* (New York: Doubleday, 1971), p. 111.

[3]Thomas F. McGann, *Argentina: The Divided Land* (New York: D. Van Nostrand, 1966), p. 102.

scribed as a marginal, alienated person without political guidance or reference points, and this seems to be the political predicament.[4]

In Mexico, the theme of alienation implicit in the works of Samuel Ramos, Víctor Alba, and Oscar Lewis is of special significance for evaluating psychocultural aspects of the transitional Mexican personality. In the Mexican political culture, such variables as apathy, distrust, passivity, disillusionment, fatalism, collectivism, afamilism, personal frustration, and marginality contribute to the alienation syndrome.

In *La democracia en México,* Pablo González Casanova comments on the plight of the "marginal Mexican" who lives in the rural sector and does not fully participate in the benefits of society. Those who fall in the marginal category, the Mexican Indian, for example, tend to be deprived in many areas —nutrition, education, life style, and overall political mobility. Among the marginal population the potential for violence is high, a concern to Mexican leadership. The demands of excessive population with spiraling inflation can only worsen the problem of the marginal Mexican. It is argued that a politics of national unification for development and modernization will continue to aggravate alienative tendencies in the Mexican political culture.

Pluriculturalism and Nation Building

Students of nation building are very much aware of the Pandora's box of difficulties developing in political communities that cannot achieve solidarity based on ethnic identity, race, caste, religion, language, or region. Pluriculturalism (or cultural pluralism) poses a serious threat to the majority of the developing systems of the Third World, whether in Asia, Africa, or Latin America.[5]

A major problem of nation building is how to cope with the cultural tensions generated by differing value systems among the people in states seeking a sense of national identity. Multiple loyalties are known to be legion in polities where plural cultural networks of social solidarity exist. In Latin America a novel formula has been developed to change the challenge of cultural pluralism into a positive symbol of national identification—through, for example, the Guaraní myth in Paraguay and the ideology of *Indigenismo* in Mexico.

Several policy alternatives have been proposed to enable Latin America

[4]Julio A. Fernández, *The Political Elite in Argentina* (New York: New York University Press, 1970), p. 22.

[5]The terms *pluriculturalism* and *cultural pluralism* are used interchangeably. For specific use of the concept of cultural pluralism on which we rely for the purposes of discussion, see Charles W. Anderson, Fred R. von der Mehden, and Crawford Young, *Issues of Political Development* (Englewood Cliffs, N.J.: Prentice-Hall, 1967), p. 17.

to cope with the problem of multiple loyalties. Among them are federalism as a form of therapy for regionalism; an integrative ideology such as *Aprismo* (deriving from the Aprista party in Peru) or *Indigenismo* (underscoring one's Indianism) as in Mexico; assimilation through intermarriage; and separation of certain differentiated groups, such as the unintegrated Indians in Central America and the Andes, from the rest of the population.

The authoritarian formula is another possible alternative for dealing with differences that may arise in a culturally plural environment.[6] This trend toward authoritarian forms of rule has been observed in varying degrees in such Latin American states as Brazil, Cuba, and Peru. In those states controlled by military-bureaucratic regimes, the military is sometimes commended for its nation-building efforts, even though they tend to fall short of providing culturally alienated sectors with full institutionalized access and representation in the major policy-making circles.[7]

So far in our discussion, certain ideas have been presented to interest the student of Latin America in the important concept of political culture. Political culture relates not only to nation building and modernization but also to the delicate process of political socialization; that is, the way political sentiments towards politics are learned—for better or worse—by the average citizen.

Contemporary political culture in Latin America is characterized by a certain ambivalence described as "a competition, a strain, and an intellectual battleground between the old order with its aristocratic weave and the new with its popular thrust and national banners."[8] To this broad characterization of Latin American political culture must be added certain stereotypic traits. These include a propensity toward personalistic and highly emotional politics, a stress on intellectuality and dogmatism in public administration, and the tendency to identify with and take pride in national historical and contemporary symbols.

Revolution, for example, has acquired symbolic value in contemporary Latin America. There is special emotional attachment to the revolutions of Mexico in 1910, Bolivia in 1952, Cuba in 1959, and Peru in 1968. In general military and civilian governments in Latin America use the symbol of revolution to win support for their regimes and reformist policies. Latin American states will often pay lip service to their revolutionary heritage, recalling with pride their revolution that brought independence from Spain. Even rebel groups used the rhetoric of revolution to legitimize their struggle against established authorities. To provide ideological vitality to his revolt against the Cuban government of Fulgencio Batista, Fidel Castro invoked the memory of

---

[6]See Crawford Young, *The Politics of Cultural Pluralism* (Madison: University of Wisconsin Press, 1979), pp. 519–520.

[7]Young, *Cultural Pluralism*, pp. 519–528.

[8]Ranis, *Five Latin American Nations*, p. 154.

José Martí (Cuba's most revered patriot, killed in the Independence War of 1895–1898). The Nicaraguan Sandinista Front of National Liberation found it helpful to be named after a foe of President Somoza Garcia, Augusto César Sandino, who opposed the presence of U.S. Marines in that country during the 1930s.

One could argue that Latin America is not a culture of political participation. At best Latin America's people are still largely a client population yearning to receive benefits from government but unable, short of rebellion, to modify local conditions. Any effort to create a Latin American participant citizenry would seem to be essentially an attitudinal problem. If one can solve the attitudinal problems in Latin America, the argument states, a workable form of cultural nationalism will likely ensue. This, of course, is easier said than done; obvious and engrained cultural tensions of regionalism, sectionalism, and multiple loyalties pervade the area and are in fact detrimental to the processes of Latin American nation building.

In Latin America distrust remains a basic attitude not only between regions but also between leadership structures in the various political systems. The Latin American paradox is that, concomitant with the attitude of distrust, the citizenry has strong expectations and aspirations for national development.

Although average Latin Americans may claim to favor the state's playing a leading role in modernization, at the same time they seem to lack the motivation or real commitment to action in this direction. Herein lies the problem.

LATIN AMERICAN DEVELOPMENT

The Peninsular focus on political culture implies a necessity to concentrate on the conditioning factors of Latin American development, which are crucial for understanding the possibilities and limitations of the various political systems to be discussed later.

To understand the nature and extent of Latin America's political and social inheritance from the peninsular mother countries, the student should note how political structures and attitudes developed in Spain and Portugal. The geography of the peninsula that became Spain and Portugal influenced these two countries' internal politics. Mountain ranges made transportation and communication difficult. The unnavigable rivers became barriers rather than ties. Despite the unifying impact of Rome, deeprooted and tenacious localism and separatism existed, which even today are reflected in the politics of many contemporary Latin American systems. Localism and cosmopolitanism seem contradictory, but their parallel presence is undeniable both in the Hispanic peninsula of two thousand years ago and in Latin America today.

The ethnic composition of ancient and medieval Spain represented the melange that its geographic factors would lead one to expect. The original Iberians received racial contributions from Celts, Phoenicians, Greeks, Carthaginians, Romans, Vandals, Suevi, Visigoths, Berbers and other Moslems from Africa, and blacks. Intermarriage, then in Spain and now in Latin America, came to be viewed with greater tolerance than in the countries growing out of the British empire.

Roman governmental forms were not imposed in Spain until almost three-quarters of a century after the first penetration because of the difficulty of reducing the peninsula militarily, a difficulty which even at that early date revealed the ethnic and political particularism so characteristic of the country. The early unit of Roman administrative control was the town. This reinforced Spain's rudimentary emphasis on urbanism that can be credited to the Phoenicians, Greeks, and Carthaginians, even though the Romans' purpose was military and political and that of their predecessors was commercial. The town, and later the city, came to be the major unit in demographic-social organization. Urbanism was a persistent objective throughout the long centuries of peninsular development—in Spain, then in the overseas colonies, and subsequently in the independent Latin American systems. Latin American urbanism was of great importance long before industrialism could contribute to it. It is no accident that Latin America now has almost no units of local rural government—Latin America inherited its governmental system from the Spain and Portugal of many centuries ago, which in turn had inherited their system from Roman and even earlier periods. The Roman influence provided the strong thread of centralism that runs through the political panorama in all succeeding centuries.

To understand Latin American politics, one should also note the tremendous development from the early eighth century to the end of the fifteenth century. During those centuries the primary motif was the struggle of Christian against Moslem, the religious-political crusade called the *Reconquista* or Reconquest. The Moslem epoch accounts for the glorification of the warrior class in Spain, for the development and rigidifying of social divisions and classes, for the advancement of the Catholic church as an omnipotent structure politically as well as spiritually, for the ultimate growth of religious and social intolerance, for the entrenchment of conflict almost as a way of life, and for the magnification of executive authority and languishing of incipient democracy. The immense impact of the Reconquest can be traced at almost every point in the political profile of contemporary Latin America, sometimes even in the details of structure.

Moslem Spain's long resistance to the expanding Christian states enabled their opponents to develop the attitudes, practices, and structures that were transmitted to and in part transmuted into the fabric of contemporary Latin American politics and government. The emergence of such governmental structures as the monarchy, clergy, nobility, and bureaucracy left an indelible mark on contemporary political life.

Hereditary rather than elective monarchy was gradually established in Castile, Aragon, and Portugal. Theoretically the king in the various Hispanic states—most notably Castile and Aragon—was absolute. In the eyes of the law he was the supreme legislator, judge, and administrator for his whole realm. The resemblance of this office to the later presidency in many Latin American systems is more than coincidental. It is no real qualification of the comparison when we reflect that the presumed limitation of tenure of the Latin American executives did not seriously handicap such hardy perennials as Juan Manuel de Rosas of Argentina, Rafael Leonidas Trujillo of the Dominican Republic, Juan Domingo Perón of Argentina, or Alfredo Stroessner of Paraguay.

The clergy in Castile were a privileged class less powerful only than the nobility. Especially in the closing decades of the Reconquest, the clergy took full advantage of the fact that they symbolized the extramundane nature of the religious crusade. They gained a more practical benefit from their virtual monopoly on literacy—they became the secretaries and accountants of the increasingly important bureaucracies. Both medieval Spain and modern Latin America made a subtle but important distinction between the Church as a religious-spiritual and as a political-economic institution.

Relations between government and Church were complicated; they were at once mutually supportive and antagonistic. The Catholic rulers staunchly supported the Church, granting it many concessions and much influence. They never permitted their devotion to the Holy Faith to obscure their goal of supreme and centralized royal authority, however. The gain by the crown of the *patronato real* (the authority given by the pope to Spanish rulers to make specified ecclesiastical appointments) made the ruler practically the administrative head of the Church in Granada and the Colonies. Crowns have vanished in Latin America, but a number of executives still retain major authority in filling high Church posts.

The nobility in medieval Spain held its position partly through tradition, partly through circumstance. The power of the nobles, coupled with the lack of effective control over them by the kings, resulted in a large degree of irresponsibility. At times the Spanish nobles became petty despots or glorified highwaymen. In various parts of more than one Latin American republic, their psychic heirs were found in the small-scale *caudillos,* irresponsible local politicos who were virtually immune to central regulation or control.

Changes in the Spanish social structure, especially the slow growth of a middle class, presaged a decline in the fortunes of the nobility. Various kings in all three of the major Hispanic states increasingly tended to vest administrative functions in persons of lower social rank, appointed on an individual rather than a hereditary basis. This left the greater nobles more and more a decorative role only. Later, Latin American presidents would find that development of a civil service, dependent on themselves, would decrease the effectiveness of the purely political elements with which they vied.

As representative units at the local, regional, and national level deteriorated in the various Spanish states, the bureaucratic behavior patterns that emerged were characterized by a sterile formalism still present in Latin America today. This was particularly evident in the so-called conciliar system—such bodies as the *Consejo Real* (Royal Council), the Council of Castile, the *Consejo de Hacienda* (Finance Council), and others. The several councils illustrated quite early what was to become a fundamental characteristic of Spanish and Spanish-American political organization: a tendency away from any separation of the governmental powers either of collective bodies or single officials.

The chief defects of the Spanish colonial administrative system were, probably in order, ponderousness, venality, and lack of a democratic or representative foundation. Almost from the beginning, the system was paternalistic and bureaucratic. Officials at all levels were required to render minute reports to superiors and detailed instructions to subordinates. The sheer time involved in writing all these documents, usually in numerous copies, fostered a mental attitude that enthroned the routine, the traditional, and the orthodox. Earnest and enterprising officials might forge ahead on their own initiative, but if they had a very human concern for their own tenure in office, they would be inclined to follow all the minute detail of their instructions at the sacrifice of getting things accomplished. *"Obedezco pero no cumplo"* ("I obey but do not execute") was a common response attributed to administrators on receiving instructions from superiors.

Materialistic and often cynical attitudes made graft, bribery, nepotism, and official corruption almost inevitable. Instances of officials who were poor when appointed then wealthy when they retired a few years later were common. It was often said that a high colonial official needed three fortunes: the first to buy his administrative post, the second to maintain himself ostentatiously while in it, and the third to bribe his superior for clearance on leaving it. Justice was often sold almost openly. Customs officials were frequently "approachable." The government often winked at such flouting of its laws to avoid unrest, if not actual revolt, by aggrieved officials. Privilege was hallowed. Genuine representative government, or any form of popular control, was nonexistent. Creation of a titled nobility, concessions to powerful leaders, continued centralization of functions, and most important, discrimination against the *criollos*[9] robbed the Spanish system of any sound and solid foundation.

Notwithstanding, the student of Latin American development can ill afford to minimize the Spanish and Portuguese contribution to the Americas. Spain's administrative hand was held far more firmly over the development of

---

[9]A *criollo,* or creole, is a person of full Spanish blood or ancestry, born in the Americas.

its colonies than Portugal's was over its empire. Portugal's attitude towards its huge Brazilian colony was relatively casual and indifferent; as a result governmental structures in that vast territory developed haphazardly. Political agencies were in many cases patterned after those which Spain had adopted more systematically, however, and consequently what has been written about Spanish development applies at least in part to Portuguese evolution. On the whole Spanish America was probably quite as well governed as Spain itself. It was not so much the administrative defects of the colonial system, serious though they were, that introduced the revolutionary ethos in the developmental process in Latin America; rather, a highly unintelligent Spanish commercial policy coupled with ideological factors constituted the revolutionary syndrome in Latin America.

The Development of Revolution
in Latin America

Students of Latin American political behavior have already witnessed the revolutionary overthrow of more than one hundred Latin American governments in the twentieth century. The phenomenon of revolution so endemic in Latin American political culture has expressed itself in both systemic instability and systemic evolution aimed at improving the overall social and economic system of the polity. Of course, any revolution that is at all widespread or profound will inevitably have its roots in the past. The early revolutions in Spanish America were no exception. Oppression and the monopolizing of high office by Spanish colonial administrators were increasingly felt by the creoles just as the creoles began to be stimulated by imported French ideas. The egalitarian influences of the frontier affected creole attitudes in the Spanish colonies. In some Spanish colonies the increasing tendency of creoles and upper-level mestizos to think of themselves as *americanos* unconsciously fed their dissatisfaction with their psychological, economic, and political subordination; an identical reaction subtly characterized many eighteenth-century English colonists far to the north.

During the later colonial period the influence of the Church was in general overwhelmingly conservative and repressive. The Inquisition, the virtual Church monopoly over education, and the privileged economic position of the clergy all tended to mold a submissive and conforming colonial mind.

Economic grievances were important. Taxation was often oppressive but even more irritating was its inequality and erratic administration. The traditional Spanish trade monopoly was irksome and strangling and could not be maintained in the face of growing colonial demands for goods that the mother country could not supply in quality and variety. Hence Spain's hold on colonial commerce deteriorated, and smuggling grew so rapidly as to become almost a way of economic life in some areas. Bribery was commonplace. The wide-spread belief that Spain was unconscionably milking its colonies whetted the revolutionary appetites of the Spanish Americans.

The wide penetration of foreign, especially French, ideas was also signifi-cant. Many wealthy young creoles were educated in Spain and France, and they could not escape exposure to the ideas of the Encyclopedists. Among the more outstanding leaders in the independence movements who were suckled on French revolutionary philosophy were Bolívar, O'Higgins, and Nariño. The low literacy level, possibly not more than 5 percent, was of less importance in assessing the impact of imported ideas and materials than might be thought. It was the literate creole minority, or even just a fraction of it, that was responsible for crystalizing the revolutionary movements; the large mass was still politically inert. Rousseau's *Social Contract* became a political bible for the nucleus of revolutionaries; Montesquieu's *The Spirit of the Laws* was widely read among the creoles. The success of the first Latin American revolu-tions in the nineteenth century was hardly conclusive in a developmental sense, for the result was merely independence with practically no fundamental social change. There was in fact no blueprint for change attending the severance of the political umbilical cord of Spanish America with the mother countries.

What was the nature of the Latin America that embarked on indepen-dence roughly a century and a half ago? Perhaps the word *independence* should be put in quotes. Although nominal political independence was estab-lished, economic, cultural, and psychological freedom from Europe was many decades in being confirmed—and in some ways has not yet been entirely achieved. The penetration of foreign ideas, whether they be Marxism or demo-cratic socialism, Soviet communism, Maoism, Titoism, fascism, corporativism, Nasserism, or third-world nationalism, continue to find expression in the ideological milieu of the Latin American culture. Apart from the political manifestations discussed earlier, the general foundation on which politics was laid posed many difficulties.

It is worth noting that both military exigencies and widespread theoriz-ing about the merits of monarchical or republican forms of government con-tributed to producing a void. The general lack of civilian political experience and a tradition of administrative responsibility led to polarized leaders as "strongmen" *(caudillos)* or philosophers *(pensadores)*. The types persisted long after independence was won and only gradually lost their sharply defined characteristics.

The *caudillo* was a chieftain, usually with military experience, a practical man of action, impatient with discussion and deliberation. Often he was a saber-rattling man on horseback, such as Argentina's Juan Manuel de Rosas and Mexico's Antonio López de Santa Anna. Personal appeal and dominance explained him; he held his followers by inner force and charisma, and their allegiance was to him as an individual, not to an area or a set of principles. The sword and the gun weighed heavily in the *caudillo's* political armament, and he was often adaptable enough to fit himself to a large or a small stage in his political-military adventuring. He left a long and bitter legacy to Latin American politics, but to his credit it can be said that he sometimes helped reduce the anarchy and turbulence of the time. If at times his peace was praetorian, still it permitted seeds of constitutionalism and democracy to germinate slowly and often held centrifugal forces in check.

At the opposite end of the political spectrum was the equally interesting *pensador,* or philosopher. Bolívar once described *pensadores* as "gentle visionaries who, dreaming of republics in the air, have endeavored to achieve political perfection presupposing the perfection of mankind." The *pensadores,* best fitted by formal education to succeed to political power, had been forced by circumstances into an intellectual environment of sterility and often frustration. Hence, they tended to become introspective and, when faced with the exigences of practical politics during the revolutions, often doctrinaire. They could find ideas in the *Social Contract* which they felt should be applied to the Latin American political scene, but Rousseau offered no solutions of concrete governmental and administrative problems. In the competition between ideas and actions it was obvious that *caudillo* and philosopher scarcely spoke each other's language. Each was generally contemptuous of the other, although at times they were curiously respectful and even envious of each other.

In Latin America today it is not unusual to characterize political leadership in terms of the *caudillo-pensador* dichotomy to differentiate between the intellectual leadership of, say, an Arturo Frondizi and the strongman flair of a Juan Perón.

Indeed the Latin American developmental scene is complex and fraught with crises of legitimacy, national integration, social and political participation, and the equal distribution of material benefits. Understandably agricultural, commercial, and industrial pursuits had been much neglected during the years of the revolutions, resulting in bankrupt treasuries and the need for diligent political and economic application. Thus economic and often diplomatic vassalage to more developed countries beyond the oceans continued.

The revolutions established new sovereignties, but they did not create, at least immediately, new nations or democracies. It is little wonder that many of the Latin American states long experienced vicious political cycles of revolution, anarchy, and dictatorship. One must judge contemporary Latin American politics not according to what has been achieved in Western Europe or Anglo-America but according to what the Latin American states had to begin with. In such terms, they are often found not wanting.

The Latin American revolution is not dead: At best, it can be described in the words of Gustavo Lagos and Horacio Godoy as a continuing "revolution of being."[10] The overall aim of this kind of revolution is to surmount depen-

---

[10]Gustavo Lagos and Horacio H. Godoy. *Revolution of Being: A Latin American View of the Future* (New York: Free Press, 1977), pp. 97–98, 167–177.

dency and underdevelopment in a complex international environment. Analysis in the ensuing chapters is intended to evoke empathic appreciation of the political development and to provide a clearer and deeper understanding of the problems as well as the intricate pattern of forces that shape the national development of the twenty Latin American countries discussed in this book. In each of the chapters the material will be organized into broad categories of political culture and environment, governmental and political structures, and developmental prospects.

REFERENCES

ADAMS, RICHARD NEWBOLD. *The Second Sowing: Power and Secondary Development in Latin America.* San Francisco: Harper & Row, 1967.

ADIE, ROBERT F., and GUY E. POITRAS. *Latin America: The Politics of Immobility.* Englewood Cliffs, N.J.: Prentice-Hall, 1974.

ALBA, VICTOR. *Nationalists without Nations.* New York: Holt, Rinehart & Winston, 1968.

ALMOND, GABRIEL. *Political Development: Essays in Heuristic Theory.* Boston: Little, Brown, 1970.

ALMOND, GABRIEL, and G. BINGHAM POWELL. *Comparative Politics: A Developmental Approach.* Boston: Little, Brown, 1966.

ALMOND, GABRIEL, and SIDNEY VERBA. *The Civic Culture.* Boston: Little, Brown, 1965.

ANDERSON, CHARLES. *Politics and Economic Change in Latin America.* New York: D. Van Nostrand, 1967,

ANDERSON, CHARLES, FRED R. VON DER MEHDEN, and CRAWFORD YOUNG. *Issues of Political Development.* Englewood Cliffs, N.J.: Prentice-Hall, 1967, pp. 45–56.

ARCINIEGAS, GERMAN. *Latin America: A Cultural History.* New York: Knopf, 1967.

AYRES, ROBERT. "Development Policy and the Possibility of a 'Liveable' Future for Latin America." *American Political Science Review* 69:2 (June 1975), 507–525.

BINDER, LEONARD, JAMES S. COLEMAN, JOSEPH LA PALOMBARA, LUCIAN W. PYE, and MYRON WEINER. *Crises and Sequences in Political Development.* Princeton, N.J.: Princeton University Press, 1971.

BLACK, CYRIL E. *The Dynamics of Modernization: A Study in Comparative History.* New York: Harper & Row, 1966.

BURNETT, BEN G., and KENNETH F. JOHNSON. *Political Forces in Latin America: Dimensions of the Quest for Stability.* Belmont, Calif.: Wadsworth, 1970.

BURNS, E. BRADFORD. *Latin America: A Concise Interpretive History.* 2nd ed. Englewood Cliffs, N.J.: Prentice-Hall, 1977.

CALVEZ, JEAN-YVES. *Politics and Society in the Third World.* New York: Orbis Books, 1973.

CLISSOLD, STEPHEN. *Latin America: A Cultural Outline.* New York: Harper & Row, 1965.

COCKROFT, JAMES D., ANDRÉ GUNDER FRANK, and DALE L. JOHNSON. *Dependence and Underdevelopment.* New York: Doubleday Anchor Books, 1972.

DENTON, CHARLES F., and PRESTON L. LAWRENCE. *Latin American Politics: A Functional Approach.* San Francisco: Harper & Row, 1972.

DUNCAN, W. RAYMOND. *Latin American Politics: A Developmental Approach.* New York: Holt, Rinehart & Winston, 1976

EINAUDI, LUIGI, RICHARD MAULIN, ALFRED STEPAN, and MICHAEL FLEET. *Latin American Institutional Development: The Changing Catholic Church.* Santa Monica, Calif.: Rand Corporation, October 1969.

FAGEN, RICHARD, and WAYNE CORNELIUS. *Political Power in Latin America: Seven Confrontations.* Englewood Cliffs, N.J.: Prentice-Hall, 1970.

FARLEY, RAWLE. *The Economics of Latin America: Development Problems in Perspective.* New York: Harper & Row, 1972.

FEDER, ERNEST. *The Rape of the Peasantry: Latin America's Landholding System.* New York: Doubleday Anchor Books, 1971.

FERNÁNDEZ, JULIO A. *The Political Elite in Argentina.* New York: New York University Press, 1970.

FURTADO, CELSO. *Economic Development of Latin America.* Cambridge: Cambridge University Press, 1970.

———. *Obstacles to Development in Latin America.* New York: Doubleday, 1970.

GLASSMAN, RONALD M. *Political History of Latin America.* New York: Funk & Wagnalls, 1969.

GONZÁLEZ CASANOVA, PABLO. *La democracia en México.* Mexico City: Ediciones ERA, S.A., 1965.

GRIFFIN, KEITH. *Underdevelopment in Spanish America.* London: Allen & Unwin, 1969.

HALPER, STEFAN A., and JOHN R. STERLING, eds. *Latin America: The Dynamics of Social Change.* New York: St. Martin's Press, 1972.

HAMILL, HUGH M., JR., ed. *Dictatorship in Latin America.* New York: Knopf, 1965.

HARRIS, LOUIS K., and VÍCTOR ALBA. *The Political Culture and Behavior of Latin America.* Kent, Ohio: Kent State University Press, 1974.

HEATH, DWIGHT B., and RICHARD N. ADAMS, eds. *Contemporary Cultures and Societies of Latin America.* New York: Random House, 1965.

HENRÍQUEZ UREÑA, PEDRO. *A Concise History of Latin American Culture,* trans. by Gilbert Chase. New York: Holt, Rinehart & Winston, 1966.

HIRSCHMAN, ALBERT O. *Journeys Toward Progress.* New York: Twentieth Century Fund, 1963.

HOPKINS, RAYMOND. "Aggregate Data and the Study of Political Development." *Journal of Politics* 31:1 (1969), 71–94.

HOROWITZ, IRVING L., ed. *Masses in Latin America.* New York: Oxford University Press, 1970.

HUIZER, GERRIT J. *The Revolutionary Potential of Peasants in Latin America.* Lexington, Mass.: Heath-Lexington Books, 1973.

HUNTINGTON, SAMUEL P. *Political Order in Changing Societies.* New Haven, Conn.: Yale University Press, 1968.

JAGUARIBE, HELIO. *Political Development: A General Theory and a Latin American Case Study.* New York: Harper & Row, 1973.

KEITH, ROBERT, ed. *Haciendas and Plantations in Latin American History.* New York: Holmes & Meier, 1977.

KLING, MERLE. "Toward a Theory of Power and Political Instability in Latin America." *Western Political Quarterly* 9:1 (March 1956), 21–40.

LABELLE, THOMAS J. *Education and Development: Latin America and the Caribbean.* Los Angeles: Latin American Center, University of California, 1972.

LAGOS, GUSTAVO, and HORACIO H. GODOY. *Revolution of Being: A Latin American View of the Future.* New York: Free Press, 1977.

LAMBERT, JACQUES. *Latin America: Social Structures and Political Institutions.* Berkeley and Los Angeles: University of California Press, 1967.

LANDSBERGER, HENRY A., ed. *Latin American Peasant Movements.* Ithaca, N.Y.: Cornell University Press, 1969.

———. *Rural Protest: Peasant Movements and Social Change.* New York: Macmillan, 1974.

LEWIS, OSCAR. *Five Families.* New York: John Wiley, 1963.

LIPSET, SEYMOUR MARTIN. "Values, Education, and Entrepreneurship." Chapter 1 in *Elites in Latin America,* ed. by Seymour Martin Lipset and Aldo Solari. New York: Oxford University Press, 1967.

LISS, SHELDON B., and PEGGY LISS, eds. *Man, State and Society in Latin American History.* New York: Holt, Rinehart & Winston, 1972.

McGANN, THOMAS F. *Argentina: The Divided Land.* New York: D. Van Nostrand, 1966.

MALLOY, JAMES M., ed. *Authoritarianism and Corporatism in Latin America.* Pittsburgh: University of Pittsburgh Press, 1977.

MARTZ, JOHN D., ed. *The Dynamics of Change in Latin American Politics.* 2nd ed. Englewood Cliffs, N.J.: Prentice-Hall, 1971.

MEIER, GERALD M. *Leading Issues in Economic Development: Studies in International Poverty.* New York: Oxford University Press, 1970.

MORENO, FRANCISCO JOSÉ, and BARBARA MITRANI, eds. *Conflict and Violence in Latin American Politics.* New York: Harper & Row, 1971.

NEEDLER, MARTIN C. *An Introduction to Latin American Politics: The Structure of Conflict.* Englewood Cliffs, N.J.: Prentice-Hall, 1977.

———. *Political Development in Latin America: Instability, Violence, and Evolutionary Change.* New York: Random House, 1968.

———, ed. *Political Systems of Latin America.* 2nd ed. New York: Van Nostrand Reinhold, 1970

ODELL, PETER R. *Economies and Societies in Latin America: A Geographical Interpretation.* New York: John Wiley, 1973.

O'DONNELL, GUILLERMO A. *Modernization and Bureaucratic-Authoritarianism: Studies in South American Politics.* Berkeley: Institute of International Studies, University of California, 1973.

OLIEN, MICHAEL D. *Latin Americans: Contemporary Peoples and Their Cultural Traditions.* New York: Holt, Rinehart & Winston, 1973.

ORGANSKI, A. F. K. *The Stages of Political Development.* New York: Knopf, 1965.

PAZ, OCTAVIO. *The Labyrinth of Solitude,* trans. by Lysander Kemp. New York: Grove Press, 1956.

PIKE, FREDERICK B. *Spanish America 1900–1970: Tradition and Social Innovation.* London: Thames and Hudson, 1973.

PREBISCH, RAÚL. *The Economic Development of Latin America and Its Principal Problems.* New York: United Nations, 1950.

———. *Change and Development: Latin America's Great Task.* Washington, D. C.: Inter-American Development Bank, 1970.

PYE, LUCIAN W., ed. *Communications and Political Development.* Princeton, N.J.: Princeton University Press, 1963.

PYE, LUCIAN W., and SIDNEY VERBA, eds. *Political Culture and Political Development.* Princeton, N.J.: Princeton University Press, 1965.

RAMOS, SAMUEL. *El perfil del hombre y la cultura en México.* Mexico City: Espasa-Calpe Argentina, 1951.

RANGEL, CARLOS. *The Latin Americans: Their Love-Hate Relationship with the United States,* trans. by Ivan Kats. New York: Harcourt Brace Jovanovich, 1977.

RANIS, PETER. *Five Latin American Nations: A Comparative Political Study.* New York: Macmillan, 1971.

ROSENBAUM, WALTER A. *Political Culture.* New York: Holt, Rinehart & Winston, 1975.

ROSTOW, W. W. *Politics and the Stages of Growth.* Cambridge: Cambridge University Press, 1971.

————. *The Stages of Economic Growth.* Cambridge: Cambridge University Press, 1960.

SCHMITTER, PHILIPPE. "The New Strategies for the Comparative Analysis of Latin American Politics." *Latin American Research Review* 4:2 (Summer 1969), 83–110.

SHAPIRO, SAMUEL, ed. *Integration of Man and Society in Latin America.* Notre Dame, Ind.: University of Notre Dame Press, 1967.

SIGMUND, PAUL E., ed. *Models of Political Change in Latin America.* New York: Holt, Rinehart & Winston, 1970.

SILVERT, KALMAN H. *Expectant Peoples, Nationalism and Development.* New York: Random House, 1963.

————. *The Conflict Society: Reaction and Revolution in Latin America.* New York: American Universities Field Staff, 1966.

SMITH, T. LYNN. *Studies of Latin American Societies.* New York: Doubleday, 1970.

SNOW, PETER, ed. *Government and Politics in Latin America.* New York: Holt, Rinehart & Winston, 1967.

STAUFFER, ROBERT B. "The Biopolitics of Underdevelopment." *Comparative Political Studies* 2 (October 1969), 361–388.

STEIN, STANLEY J., and BARBARA STEIN. *The Colonial Heritage of Latin America: Essays on Economic Dependence in Perspective.* New York: Oxford University Press, 1970.

STEPAN, ALFRED. "Political Development Theory: The Latin American Experience." *Journal of International Affairs* 20:2 (1966), 223–234.

TANNENBAUM, FRANK. *Ten Keys to Latin America.* New York: Knopf, 1962.

THURBER, CLARENCE E., and LAWRENCE S. GRAHAM, eds. *Development Administration in Latin America.* Durham, N.C.: Duke University Press, 1973.

TOMASEK, ROBERT D., ed. *Latin American Politics: Studies of the Contemporary Scene.* 2nd ed. New York: Doubleday Anchor Books, 1970.

TORRES, JAMES F. "Concentration of Political Power and Levels of Economic Development in Latin American Countries." *Journal of Developing Areas* 7 (April 1973), 397–410.

United Nations Economic Commission for Latin America. *Development Problems in Latin America.* Austin, Texas: Institute of Latin American Studies, University of Texas Press, 1970.

URQUIDI, VICTOR. *The Challenge of Development in Latin America.* New York: Holt, Rinehart & Winston, 1964.

VELIZ, CLAUDIO, ed. *Obstacles to Change in Latin America.* New York: Oxford University Press, 1965.

VON LAZAR, ARPAD. *Latin American Politics: A Primer.* Boston: Allyn & Bacon, 1971.

WAGLEY, CHARLES. *The Latin American Tradition: Essays on the Unity and Diversity of Latin American Culture.* New York: Columbia University Press, 1968.

WELTY, PAUL T., ed. *Latin American Cultures.* Philadelphia: Lippincott, 1974.

WIARDA, HOWARD. "Toward a Framework for the Study of Political Change in the Iberic-Latin Tradition." *World Politics* 25 (January 1973), 206–235.

WILCZYNSKI, J. *Socialist Development and Reforms.* New York: Holt, Rinehart & Winston, 1972.

WILLIAMS, EDWARD J. *Latin American Political Thought: A Developmental Perspective.* Tucson: University of Arizona Press, 1974.

WILLIAMS, EDWARD J., and FREEMAN WRIGHT. *Latin American Politics: A Developmental Approach.* Palo Alto, Calif.: Mayfield, 1975.

WOLF, ERIC R., and EDWARD C. HANSEN. *The Human Condition in Latin America.* New York: Oxford University Press, 1972.

WORCESTER, DONALD E., and WENDELL G. SCHAEFFER. *The Growth and Culture of Latin America,* 2 vols. 2nd ed. New York: Oxford University Press, 1971.

WYNIA, GARY W. *The Politics of Latin American Development.* New York: Cambridge University Press, 1978.

YOUNG, CRAWFORD. *The Politics of Cultural Pluralism.* Madison, Wisc.: University of Wisconsin Press, 1979.

ZEA, LEOPOLDO. *The Latin American Mind.* Norman, Okla.: University of Oklahoma Press, 1963.

Part Two

MEXICO
AND
CENTRAL AMERICA

2

MEXICO

The Institutionalization
of a Socio-Political
Revolution

POLITICAL CULTURE AND ENVIRONMENT

Compared to other large Latin American countries, Mexico has had a tortured political development. With Argentina, Brazil, and Chile, it has emerged as one of the quartet of what are generally considered the major states of the area, but the road that brought it to that eminence was indeed a winding and rocky one.

Mexico's 760,000 square miles make it the third largest country of Latin America, but less than half its land is arable. One fifth of the land is forested, and a quarter is officially unaccounted for. Hence, the food (apart from meat) for more than sixty million people must be raised on only fifty million acres.

Lacking navigable rivers, Mexico has had to rely on railroads and high-ways for its basic transportation. Because Mexico is a mountainous country, this has created great engineering and financial problems. Until quite recently the country has not been well linked by internal transportation. It was not coincidence, then, that caused the remote and relatively inaccessible north to become a breeding ground for revolution on more than one occasion; its people have at times felt like stepchildren in the Mexican family.

The Valley of Mexico, containing the national capital, is the heartland, or the "core region," of the country. The Federal District, which is for practical purposes identical with Mexico City, contains almost a seventh of the country's population. The District's demographic superiority and Mexico's long tradition of political centrism help explain why more remote parts of the country feel slighted.

The ethnic pattern of Mexico's population differs significantly from the other major countries of Latin America. Mexico has an overwhelmingly Indian and mestizo-inclined-toward-Indian population. It is estimated that almost three-tenths of its people are Indians, seven-tenths are mestizo, and only a very small fraction white. Since 1910 the policies of Mexico have reflected as much "Indianization" as those of any country in Latin America. It is estimated that an appreciable number of Mexico's people primarily speak Indian languages, although a substantial number are bilingual. Assimilation of Indians and the Indian-oriented segments of the mestizos into the economic, social, and political fabric of Mexico has been a major problem. Sheer population growth has also had serious political consequences, especially in recent decades.

The character of the population has another important political implication. In many instances the Indian has an almost mystical attachment to the land. A feeling of possession through a spiritual or psychic uniting with the soil helps explain the *ejido* (communally held land farmed by a village) and other programs of the government. At the same time the hacienda (a large estate or landholding) has been not only an important unit of landholding but also a symbol of a way of life in competition with the *ejido.*

Postindependence Mexican Political Development

Since independence Mexico's political development has proved to be a difficult, though exciting, process of national self-determination.

In examining these early phases of political development, one notices that Mexican independence came in reverse, as it were. Hidalgo and Morelos had led an impassioned but futile rebellion. The liberal revolution in Spain in 1820 convinced Mexican conservatives that they must cut the ties with the mother country to be certain of maintaining their vested interests. Augstín de Iturbide took the lead and by September 1829 succeeded in establishing a conservative regime. This, however, was soon toppled by a greater opportunist, General Antonio López de Santa Anna. Santa Anna, a *caudillo* par excellence, had sufficient charisma to appeal mightily to the immature Mexican political mentality. He dominated and blighted Mexican politics well into the 1850s. From 1846 to 1848 a war with the United States cost Mexico about half its territory and brought home to Mexicans the sorry bequest of a generation of chaotic and undisciplined politics.

The two decades of the Reform, from the middle 1850s to the middle 1870s, presented Latin America with as much of a social revolution (except for the undisciplined Haitian action of the 1790s) as the area had yet seen. There was the rise of a new generation of revolutionary elites—above all,

Benito Juárez—and the resurgence of the twin concepts of liberalism and federalism, both to be triumphant in the Reform's great document, the Constitution of 1857.

The constitution definitely returned the country to federalism, though little real power was granted to the states. To preclude unintentional establishment of a stronghold of conservative power in a senate, the constituent assembly set up a unicameral legislative branch—a chamber of deputies based on population. The constitution said nothing about basic land reform. Although the constitution would later be revered in many Mexican eyes, when viewed objectively as a realistic reflection of Mexican needs and problems of the day, it probably left much to be desired.

Juárez

A spin of the political wheel of fortune brought Benito Juárez to the presidency. Juárez, a full-blooded Zapotec Indian, championed the cause of the Indian underdog. Whether in power or out, in Mexico or out, Juárez became the leader, spokesman, idol, and symbol of the liberal forces for the next two decades. Juárez was stubborn and uncompromising, even dictatorial in his later years, but his memory as a champion of the Reform grew almost into a legend in Mexico.

Juárez's leadership of the Reform was interrupted by European intervention. With French support, Archduke Maximilian of Austria assumed the Mexican throne in 1864, as Emperor of Mexico. In well-intentioned but futile ways Maximilian tried to act like a liberal and hence soon alienated his conservative supporters. A combination of internal and foreign forces brought Maximilian to his final defeat; he was executed in 1867. The Reform was now able to return to the main track, but its momentum was largely gone. Juárez, facing increasing frustrations, was reelected in 1871, but he died soon afterwards. His vice-president, Sebastián Lerdo de Tejada, completed the term and was reelected in 1876. He was soon ousted by one of Juárez's generals, Porfirio Díaz. The Reform came to an end.

Díaz

The Díaz era might best be characterized as a period of *Dies Irae* (days of wrath). Once in power late in 1876, Díaz continued to speak like a liberal, but he soon allowed his conservatism to show. He was to rule Mexico for almost three and a half decades, longer than any other Latin American dictator. It was a praetorian era, a *pax porfiriana,* a time in which the efficient *rurales* (militia) suppressed the long prevalent banditry, though some bandits were given the ironic choice of joining the *rurales* or facing a firing squad.

Through coercive mobilization efforts, Díaz rapidly turned Mexico from a state of virtual anarchy into a nation of peace and security. With an advisory staff of *"científicos"* (the self-designated "scientific ones") who favored the rich at the expense of the poor, he encouraged the tendency toward *latifundismo* (large estates). The concentration of landholding was almost unbelievably great; in some states as many as 99.5 percent of the heads of families were landless; numerous haciendas included more than 250,000 acres each. The hacienda system as a way of life provided a static element in the Mexican social and economic scene, and it was the pillar of the Mexican *ancien régime* first toppled after the Revolution.

The regime also encouraged foreign economic investment, to the point where some opponents of Díaz complained bitterly that Mexicans were stepchildren in their own country. Foreign interests were generally able to monopolize much of the country's economic activity and wealth.

It was primarily power, political power, that Díaz sought; he was content to leave economic exploitation largely to others and did not unduly enrich himself. Still, Díaz's political system generated sufficient resentment to precipitate the Revolution of 1910 and his resignation a year later. Francisco I. Madero, the mystical, naive, politically unrealistic son of a great landowning family soon took over the presidency. He was ill prepared for it; though an excellent catalyst of resistance to the old regime, he lacked the strong will or political insight needed to deal with the hard realities of chaotic politics and was eventually assassinated. In various parts of Mexico armed resistance arose, led by such revolutionary notables as Pancho Villa, Emiliano Zapata, and Venustiano Carranza. Carranza proved capable of consolidating his political position to adopt the famous 1917 Querétaro Constitution.

The Querétaro Constitution was a flaming banner of political and economic nationalism. Its predecessor six decades earlier had established a milestone of political independence and advancement; the new document added a declaration of economic freedom.

Although Carranza was unenthusiastic about the new basic law, so quickly and firmly did it become a symbol of the new Mexican nationalism that he could not escape the necessity of paying it lip service from time to time. His political position was deteriorating, however; he was forced to flee early in 1920 and was assassinated before reaching Veracruz and foreign safety.

The bloody decade of the Mexican Revolution was ended. For a time revolutionary politics was dominated by "the Triumvirate of Agua Prieta": Generals Alvaro Obregón, Plutarco Elías Calles, and Adolfo de la Huerta (not related to Victoriano Huerta).

Calles

From 1917 to 1934 a host of revolutionary leaders reigned, including Obregón and Calles, who tried to stabilize governmental structures. Friction between Church and government became the most spectacular aspect of callista politics. The feud between the two institutions was renewed early in 1926 and pursued bitterly through and beyond the term of Calles. In futile imitation of Henry VIII, the government briefly attempted to set up a national Catholic church in Mexico. For a time the *"cristero* war" in 1926–1927 seemed to spell a revival of the War of the Reforma seventy years earlier, but the government ruthlessly crushed the fanatical armed resistance of young Catholics. An uneasy truce, essentially a government victory, was negotiated in 1929.

It was Calles who proposed that all elements espousing revolutionary principles join to form a single "revolutionary" party. A later call to scores of such groups to send delegates in March 1929 to a convention in Querétaro, hallowed birthplace of the constitution, brought more than nine hundred delegates representing virtually all "revolutionary" groups in Mexican life. They created the National Revolutionary Party (Partido Nacional Revolucionario, or PNR).

Calles succeeded in making the new entity his personal vehicle for continuing to dominate the political scene. But local *caudillos,* mostly military, were too strong to be ignored. Hence the initial organization of the PNR was more a federation of local political components under a national executive committee. Calles became the *jefe máximo* of the organization and found it a weapon whose potential even he did not fully realize. Local centers of authority were gradually eroded, and the party organization became increasingly institutionalized. The PNR and its successors long outlasted and ultimately transcended any single person, but the incumbent president would always play a major role in its operation.

Cárdenas

In 1934 General Lázaro Cárdenas was elected president. Cárdenas was also an heir of the revolutionary tradition, but, unlike many others, he took the Revolution seriously. During the years of Cárdenas, the Revolution was thrown into high gear, a higher gear, in fact, than any in which it moved before or since his time. In many respects Cárdenas became the personification of the Revolution.

For six years Cárdenas led a high-pressure crusade to achieve the goals of the Mexican Revolution. Cárdenas's first problem was to consolidate his position in power politics. The obvious stumbling block was Calles, but Cárdenas had the last word. In the spring of 1936, he forced Calles into exile in the United States, where he remained for the rest of Cárdenas's term; thus he eliminated the most threatening challenge. Long-standing friction with the Church was eased. The high point of support for Cárdenas was reached in mid-March of 1938. As the climax of a long-standing friction with United States and British oil interests, Cárdenas decreed the expropriation of virtually all foreign-owned petroleum properties. A few weeks later a single dissenter, the ambitious and neglected General Saturnino Cedillo, sought to win United States backing by starting a revolt in the remote parts of San Luis Potosí. The action was quickly crushed; Cedillo was killed. It was the last formal attempt at a military uprising against an incumbent president.

In domestic politics Cárdenas was preoccupied with land and labor. He was able to keep the myth of the Mexican Revolution alive, especially because of his interest in the land problem and his empathy with the Mexican peon. During his six years in office far more land was distributed to *ejido* organizations than during all preceding administrations. In the labor field Cárdenas encouraged an able and ambitious young intellectual, Vicente Lombardo Toledano, to establish the Mexican Confederation of Workers (Confederación de Trabajadores de México, or CTM). It immediately took the center stage of labor politics from the moribund Mexican Regional Labor Confederation (Confederación Regional Obrera Mexicana, or CROM) headed by Luis Morones. For a time Lombardo was the second most powerful man in Mexico.

To consolidate his gains against the entrenched callista forces, Cárdenas reorganized the party structure. Under Calles's control, the core of PNR membership had been the bureaucracy. Cárdenas encouraged vastly expanded party membership from among the labor and agrarian sectors. The result of the reorganization was the Party of the Mexican Revolution (Partido de la Revolución Mexicana, or PRM). The most obvious structural change was the division of the party into four functionally based sectors—labor, agrarian, military, and "popular." All four sectors were given prominent roles in the nomination of party candidates for office. The labor and agrarian sectors had close ties to the dominant labor and agrarian organizations. The "popular" sector became a catchall refuge for those not included elsewhere, but the bureaucracy continued to be its backbone. Organization of a military sector seemed to be a retrogressive step in that the "political generals" were now given a formal voice in politics. But other factors, which ultimately would deflate the role of the military in politics, were subtly at work. Cárdenas, late in 1940, dissolved the military sector, throwing its remaining interested membership into the popular sector; this action alone did not, of course, remove the military from politics.

The Cárdenas regime ushered in an era of marked political stability in Mexican politics. The revolutionary party was rechristened the Institutional Revolutionary Party (Partido Revolucionario Institucional, or PRI). Under its aegis, all successive presidents have completed their constitutional six-year terms and have pursued in varying degrees the lofty ideals of the Mexican Revolution: General Manuel Avila Camacho (1940–1946); Miguel Alemán Valdéz (1946–1952); Adolfo Ruiz Cortines (1952–1958); Adolfo López Mateos (1958–1964); Gustavo Díaz Ordaz (1964–1970); Luis Echeverría Alvarez (1970–1976); José López Portillo (1976—). The function of the president in the Mexican system will be discussed later, but it may be useful at this point to focus briefly on the recent administrations of Echeverría Alvarez and López Portillo.

Echeverría

Echeverría, another Cárdenas-like leader, assumed the presidency of Mexico on December 1, 1970. In his inaugural address he made it quite clear that his administration would be a progressive one, based on economic necessity as much as social justice. The rallying cry of his program of social and economic reforms was *"arriba y adelante"* ("upward and forward"), which was intended to indicate the developmental commitment of his administration to accelerate Mexico's already phenomenal growth over the past decades and to insure wider sharing in the fruits of national progress for all Mexican people.

In political circles Echeverría has been characterized as a technician. He believed strongly in a no-nonsense approach to Mexican politics. This was clearly brought out in his inaugural address, when he declared that his government would be a rule of law devoid of any "false defeatist solutions" to social problems and forever on guard against "simulators, revolutionary dreamers, anarchists, provocateurs, and agitators moved by foreign interests."[1] He further expressed his willingness to welcome foreign investment to complement Mexican capital within the general guidelines of the Mexicanization principle. This was to assure United States and other foreign investors that his government would not be guided by an "expropriation mentality" but that pragmatism in the Mexican national interest would be duly exercised.

Echeverría had his share of political and economic problems. Disadvantaged citizens, who exist either totally outside or only on the edge of the consumer society, made clear their disenchantment with the government and called for improvements in their lot. Mexico's rich also registered their concern for what was described as the lukewarm commitment to Mexico's business interests. In sum Echeverría found himself the target of both the rich and the poor, of both the Right and the Left, who did not view government thinking on socioeconomic and political development as compatible with their respective interests. The problems of the regime were further compounded by widespread anomie, which took the form of scattered violence in the rural areas.

The regime was noticeably shaken by the militaristic activities of such guerrilla groups as Movimiento Acción Revolucionaria (Revolutionary Action Movement) and others that surfaced in the political environment, instilling fear and disrupting support for the government. To curb the violence the Echeverría regime initiated rigorous antiterrorist campaigns. This was indeed a period of political stress and strain for Mexico, what with the rampant kidnappings (including Echeverría's own father-in-law) and murders commit-

---

[1] *The Times of the Americas,* December 9, 1970, p. 3.

ted by extremist groups bent on creating chaos in the most stable country in all Latin America.

Before his inauguration Echeverría was depicted by both Mexican and foreign observers as a messianic technocrat whose administration would enable the economic horse to pull the social cart, thereby insuring domestic stability. Once in power Echeverría found himself unable to cope satisfactorily with the acute economic problems of the country, and social complaints intensified. In his efforts to deal with inflation, which worsened during his regime, Echeverría incurred the displeasure of the powerful private sector. This sector viewed his antiinflation policies—substantial wage increases and plans to open state-run shops to control rising prices—as much too leftist. However well-intentioned his motives may have been, Echeverría's abortive domestic economic policies simply intensified the existing polarization between Left and Right which has pervaded Mexican politics since 1936.

On balance it can be said that President Echeverría saw himself as a man with a mission: to provide a Cárdenas type of leadership bringing to the country's have-nots genuine social reform and freedoms, which he felt were lacking during the tenure of his rightwing predecessor, Díaz Ordaz. But unlike the great reformist president of the 1930s, Echeverría fell short of his goals. He could not achieve substantive improvements for Mexico's marginal groups, despite the fervor of his brand of economic nationalism. He failed to give national priority to the attainment of social goals while reducing Mexico's dependence on foreign loans without lessening the country's overall productive capacity to provide more new jobs for a growing population. This was indeed a large order. It can be said in retrospect that the chief executive did the best he could, given the fact that among other things Mexico, like the United States, was experiencing the side effects of a worldwide recession which exacerbated uncertainties for both the private and public sectors. Allegations that President Echeverría merely followed a policy of "make-believe development" which produced the "stabilization of misery" in Mexico are debatable, to say the least. It is perhaps more accurate to say that Echeverría, deliberately or not, intensified alienative tendencies in the culture by what has been called his program of *"apertura democrática"* (a democratic opening) between left-wing and right-wing elements in Mexico. This was clearly visible in the presidential politics of succession, which culminated in the selection of Finance Minister José López Portillo.

Third Worldism

In foreign affairs, Echeverría's actions spoke louder than his words. His internationalism, or better yet "Third Worldism," was designed to secure for Mexico a position of leadership among the developing nations in order to help improve their social and economic stature in the international community. To this end, Echeverría played a highly active, if not militant, role both in and outside the hemisphere—to the discomfiture of both Washington and foreign investors. It is known, for example, that Echeverría led the movement to bring Castro back into the inter-American family, and Echeverría made it clear to the United States government that it should not rely on Mexico's oil to break the OPEC (Organization of Petroleum Exporting Countries) cartel.

To register Mexico's strong opposition to the violation of human rights by repressive regimes, the chief executive boycotted the sixth general assembly of the OAS (Organization of American States) held in Santiago, Chile, and broke off relations not only with the Chilean military junta responsible for the overthrow of the constitutional government of Salvador Allende but also with the allegedly racist governments of South Africa and Rhodesia. Wherever the opportunity presented itself, Echeverría gave lip service to the idea that Latin America is an integral part of the Third World. During his state visit to Washington, the Mexican chief executive leveled criticism against United States policy of favoring military regimes at the expense of democracies for the leadership of Latin America in the Third World.

It is generally agreed that not since Lázaro Cárdenas has a Mexican president played such an active role in world politics; Echeverría championed his country's international role in all quarters. In such international forums as the United Nations and its various agencies, Echeverría vigorously spear-headed third-world policies and debates. He bequeathed to López Portillo an impressive record of international accomplishments essentially designed to assert Mexico's international role and to promote trade and development. To Echeverría's credit, he signed various lucrative agreements between Mexico and the European Economic Community, the Council for Economic Assistance, and the Communist economic alliance. He also negotiated the establishment of a mixed Mexico-Caribbean Community Commission and a mixed Mexican-Andean Commission. Through Echeverría's initiative, a United Nations Charter of Economic Rights and Duties of States was formulated. His leadership was visible in the establishment of an international sugar agreement and coffee cartel. He also took the bold step of establishing a two-hundred-mile exclusive economic zone to assert Mexican sovereignty over offshore fishing rights.

In all his international efforts President Echeverría expressed sincere concern for the underdeveloped, powerless countries of the world whose hope for global justice could be realized, as far as he was concerned, only through the establishment of a new international economic order. He thus used the United Nations Charter of Economic Rights and Duties of States as the framework for launching such multinational agencies as the Latin American Economic System (Sistema Económico Latinoamericano, or SELA) and NAMUCAR (Naviera Multinacional del Caribe), a multinational Caribbean shipping fleet, to foster broad collaboration and economic defense for the economies of Latin America.

Toward the end of his administration, President Echeverría further proposed a third-world economic system to coincide with the efforts of the nonaligned countries to guarantee their rights to international transactions and to explore avenues for promoting economic, financial, technological, and industrial cooperation.

To his hand-picked successor and close friend, José López Portillo, Echeverría bequeathed an economically vulnerable country beset with political uncertainties. Deliberately or not, Echeverría's reformist policies, designed to spread the nation's wealth more equitably over its increasing population and to broaden the political base of a revolutionary party, provoked anxiety, undermined confidence in the economy, and resulted in a flight of capital.

López Portillo

López Portillo took office on December 1, 1976, after receiving 17.5 million votes out of the 18.5 million cast. Before his election he had witnessed some of the drastic measures of his predecessor, such as land expropriations in northwest Mexico, wage concessions to organized labor, deficit spending to promote social programs, and major devaluation of the peso because of continuing high inflation and increasing balance of payments deficits. This was in marked contrast to the Mexico of the 1950s and 1960s, which had experienced real economic growth estimated at around 7 percent a year while maintaining a healthy balance of payments and a relatively low inflation rate in an environment of political stability which was most attractive to foreign investors.

López Portillo assumed the chief executive's office under great pressure to take immediate action against widespread unemployment, galloping inflation, and falling food production in a country whose population was expected to increase from 62 million to 74 million by 1980. It is not surprising that in his first state of the nation message on September 1, 1977, López Portillo made it clear that he had inherited a country that was in poor shape and that recovery would be slow. Among other factors, he emphasized that discoveries of significantly more oil and gas deposits had occurred and that monetary reserves had increased by 600 million to 2.93 billion dollars during his first ten months in office. He also stated that confidence in the economy had been restored, foreign borrowing curtailed, and the trade deficit considerably reduced.

López Portillo reminded the Mexican people that, despite some improvement in the economy, "Mexico is at the most difficult, most skeptical and darkest point of the crossroads." He cautioned the Mexican people not to expect his administration to perform an economic miracle that would eradicate almost insoluble social and economic problems. What his message clearly indicated was that in solving these problems his administration would "prefer to pay the price of wisdom even if it takes longer because," as the President put it, "it is very easy to be irresponsible." The chief executive gave special emphasis to the importance of the government's Alliance for Production. He made it clear that the alliance should be construed not as "a campaign slogan nor a temporary solution to an emergency" but as a viable agency in which all sectors of the economy, private and public, would be able to share the burden of national development. Rather than blaming the private sector for Mexico's problems, he exhorted business to collaborate with him through an alliance for production to stabilize the country's economy.[2]

Once the economic malaise subsided, the new administration hoped to be able to reap the benefits of Echeverría's great investment in industrial facilities. López Portillo inherited a country that in six years had doubled its capacities for steel, petrochemical, and electricity production. Known oil reserves had tripled.

Emboldened by Mexico's emergence as a potentially powerful nation with some of the world's largest energy reserves, López Portillo bluntly criticized the United States for being insensitive to Mexican dignity and interests during President Carter's February 1979 visit to Mexico. Although presidents López Portillo and Carter reached no concrete agreements on such major issues as energy, illegal Mexican immigration, U.S. trade barriers to Mexican agricultural products, and narcotics, their talks opened the way for negotiations which will influence the overall relationship between the two countries in these and other matters. President López Portillo emerged as a staunch defender of Mexican national pride and independence; President Carter acquired valuable insight into the sensitive feelings of the "new Mexico" with its increasing oil wealth and power.

The López Portillo administration walked a tightrope, striving on the one hand to regain the political ground lost by his militant predecessor with conservative elements while on the other trying hard not to incur the displeasure of reformist groups who viewed his political overtures to the Right with suspicion. President López Portillo was under considerable pressure not to see Pope John Paul II when he visited Mexico in January 1979 to inaugurate the third meeting of the Latin American Bishops' Conference (Conferencia Episcopal Latinoamericana, or CELAM). Despite Mexico's anticlerical constitution, the chief executive met the Pope at the airport and received him later in the presidential palace without any major political repercussions. In respect to liberals, López Portillo legalized the Mexican Communist party (to be discussed later) for the first time in forty years.

How far to the left or right the López Portillo administration turns out

[2] *New York Times,* September 2, 1977, Sec. IV, p. 1.

to be at this point seems less important than how the political sector perceives it to be. One might theorize that the chief executive's overall performance will be judged not so much on the ideological complexion of his administration or his policies as on his political ability to carry out his recovery program and to deal with political divisions among the many sectors of Mexican society.

GOVERNMENTAL AND POLITICAL STRUCTURES

In some ways Mexico's political development makes it unique among Latin American states. Mexico is largely a product of the peculiar interrelationship between government as government and the country's party system. In studying Mexico, the student of developmental politics is immediately intrigued by the overwhelming dominance of a monolithic presidentialism which permeates the political and administrative structures of the entire country.

The Imperial Presidency

In Mexico as elsewhere the principle of federalism would seem to involve only the relations between national authority and the country's subdivisions. In Mexico, however, federalism is subtly intertwined with another principle embodied in the United States constitutional system: separation of powers. Not only are the states subordinate to the central authority to a greater degree than in other Latin American countries, but among national governmental structures (at least in those Latin American states that are reasonably constitutionally ruled), the Mexican executive most extremely overshadows the "powers" of government. The student of Mexican politics is often intrigued by the symbolic relationship that exists between the president and the governing Mexican party—now the PRI, a party more thoroughly and broadly organized than any other in Latin America.

The president has always been the dominant figure in the party's operation and policy-making function. At one stage the party, or perhaps the president "wearing a party hat," exercised predominant influence in governmental matters; now, however, the president wears his own hat. Robert E. Scott put it well: The president's role has shifted "from primarily that of a personalistic party leader toward director of an increasingly powerful government bureaucracy that arbitrates among the reasonably well-adjusted functional interest associations which submit themselves to the discipline of the emerging governmental system."[3] Thus the party, qua party, cannot now challenge the president.

[3]Robert E. Scott, *Mexican Government in Transition* (Urbana: University of Illinois Press, 1959), pp. 244–245.

The Making of the Mexican President

How does this governmental superman obtain office? Over the passing years many conventions have developed to circumscribe the choice of Mexican presidents, so that the process has now become almost ritualistic. The process of selection first involves the concept of what Brandenburg calls "the Revolutionary Family." That "family" includes the president of the country, former presidents (in election years), the presidential nominee, a handful of national and regional political leaders (including the most prominent cabinet members), and a few wealthy persons and organized labor leaders. The Mexican president is normally head of the "family," but under special circumstances he may not be. (In the 1928–1934 period Calles, rather than the succession of puppet presidents, called the turns.) In the politics of succession, choice of a successor normally devolves upon the incumbent president, who consults with some but not necessarily all of his family of intimate advisers. Many considerations must be weighed: the person's residence, social and political antecedents, relationship to segments of the party (Center, Right, or Left), and attitudes toward the Church and foreign powers (especially the United States). Out of this careful examination comes a stereotype of the prospective nominee, one that is probably more sharply defined than is true of his opposite number in the United States at a similar stage of the process. The number of Mexicans who are "presidentiable" (*presidenciable*) is hence limited at any given time.

The candidate-to-be will probably reside in one of the central states of Mexico, be a cabinet member in the retiring administration (though the candidate must resign this post before accepting the nomination in order to meet the prescribed qualifications for the presidency), and be a political and philosophical middle-of-the-roader. The candidate will probably belong to the middle-class; he will appear dynamic and, if possible, *muy hombre* ("very much a man"), only a nominal Catholic, and perhaps a Mason (but not an atheist or a Protestant). The candidate is most apt to be uncommitted to either the labor or the agrarian sectors or the bureaucracy of the party, a strong nationalist but one who will neither curry nor antagonize foreign interests, and a civilian. No one, of course, possesses all of these qualifications; political assets must be balanced against liabilities.

The incumbent president refrains from announcing an ultimate choice as long as possible. To announce a preference too early would automatically decrease the president's own political influence from that moment and unduly encourage a bandwagon movement for the successor. The incumbent must also firmly discourage premature or too open activity by hopefuls looking to advance their own selection. At the psychologically appropriate time, the presidential hand will customarily be tipped by getting a large labor or agrarian union to announce itself in favor of the person the president has privately selected; this is part of the ritual. The bandwagon then starts rolling, and when the party convention meets late in the year preceding the election, its ratification of the predetermined choice is almost anticlimactic. Convention oratory is directed not toward support of rival candidates but to praise of the one who has received the presidential nod. The nominee does not need to worry about being elected; yet it is again a part of the ritual that the candidate "run scared," conducting a strenuous campaign and appearing in all parts of the country.

Election is by direct popular vote. The person elected must be a native-born Mexican of native-born Mexican parents. The president may not have any ecclesiastical status nor have occupied a cabinet post, a military rank, or a state governorship within the six months preceding the election. Once inaugurated, the president holds office for six years. For many years the Mexican president was the only Latin American chief executive who could not be reelected at any time even though he might first have held the presidency only temporarily or provisionally. If a vacancy occurs during the first two years of the term, it is temporarily filled by congress, which then sets up a special election to fill the balance of the term. If a vacancy occurs during the last four years, it is filled for the rest of the term by congress. In this event, there is no vice-president.

For all purposes, Mexican presidents function as the government and brook no serious challenge to their hegemony at the federal, judicial, state, or local levels.

Once in office the president must immediately take an active and dominant role, directing every aspect of the government. Some of the executive powers are constitutional, others are extraconstitutional or political; the latter are likely to be the more important. Probably most important is the subtle power and responsibility of conciliating, harmonizing, and balancing the many organized forces and currents that represent contemporary Mexican political dynamism. When interests and demands of the agrarian and labor sectors of the party clash, the president must arbitrate and satisfy them as best he can. When the army wants more perquisites, the president must weigh the request against the need for new schools, roads, or housing. The president must balance the insistence of one state or region for public improvements or economic development against equal insistence by other states or regions. When one manufacturing concern wants favorable financial deals, tax concessions, or other special considerations that may undercut its competitors, the president must moderate between the conflicting interests.

Of the president's more formal powers, the power of appointment is perhaps most important. It is estimated that the president has for personal disposal some fifteen thousand appointments to make. Many of these, of course, are handled as patronage at the direct disposition of other key figures. These appointments include executive and administrative, diplomatic, some military, and party positions.

The president totally controls Mexican foreign policy, limited only by the strongly established tradition that the principles of nonintervention and self-determination must be upheld.

The presidency is not only unchallenged by congress, the courts, and the states but has also reduced other potential competitive threats to power. Most notable is the near miracle accomplished in the political emasculation of the army. In Mexico, the army appears to be firmly subordinated to civilian— which is to say presidential—control.

Presidential influence in the legislative realm is awesome. The impact is both constitutional and extraconstitutional. Not only may the president introduce legislation in congress (and Article 71 of the constitution confers that power on the president before it does on members of congress) but the president also has a dominant, extralegal voice in selection of members of both chambers in the first place. In campaign years, selection of congressional candidates, especially designation of senatorial candidates, falls more to the presidential nominee than to the incumbent president, but in the hands of either it is so broadly applied that the legislators, though nominally elected, are actually little more than executive appointees.

Policy making, theoretically a legislative function, is assigned by politics and tradition almost entirely to the president. It is Mexico's de facto one-party system that greases presidential control over the legislative process.

It is probably safe to conclude that in none of Latin America's major governments does the legislature occupy a more abased position than in Mexico. "The legislative function," says Scott, "resides in the two chambers only in the most sterile, legalistic sense, depriving the senators and deputies of even this small pretense of independence with which to salve their bruised egos."[4] It is the president, state governors, regional political bosses, and a few other insiders—all members of PRI, of course—who virtually handpick candidates for senators and deputies. The candidates are consequently beholden to those who have tapped them for legislative seats; hence, a premium is put on party discipline and political docility. Congress becomes a rubber stamp; it affixes the imprimatur of "Approved by the Popular and Representative Branch" to policies the president alone has decided upon. The myth of free congressional action is a convenient fiction, and everyone recognizes it as such.

The judiciary, though subservient, is not as humiliatingly so as the legislature, for at least two reasons. The more specific reason is that, except for an interlude of a decade, Supreme Court judges have served for "good behavior," which is equivalent to saying for life. Hence the judiciary has far more continuity than the congress. Probably a more important if less tangible reason is that the judiciary carefully avoids infringing on policy decisions. Even in Mexico's approach to judicial review, the courts do not try to upset any presidential apple carts.

[4]Scott, *Mexican Government,* p. 262.

Without doubt the most important contribution that Mexican jurisprudence has made is the *juicio de amparo* (*amparo* means protection). This writ resembles an injunction in Anglo-American jurisprudence, but it also embodies certain features of the writs of habeas corpus, mandamus, and certiorari. The purpose of the writ of *amparo* is to provide protection to a person who is wronged by the application of a law. It does not pass on the unconstitutionality of the law involved; it simply renders redress to the individual. Hence, many *amparo* suits may arise under a single law; the only relief for the courts lies in the possibility that the president and congress may see fit to modify the law to remove the cause for the large number of *amparo* cases. *Amparo* does not apply to political or policy matters, hence there is little risk of stepping on presidential toes.

If the Mexican legislature and judiciary were more genuinely "separate but coordinate and equal" branches of the government, at least a theoretical balance would exist within the national government, thus permitting the states to assert themselves more effectively. But the president faces no real challenge to his power within the national government—indeed, the people expect and want no such challenge—and hence it would be virtually unthinkable for the states to offer a threat to the president. The Mexican states simply cannot pretend to be a source of real political power. Also important, the states lack any historical position or tradition that would give them the foundation of a "states-rights psychology" similar to that in the United States.

Obviously, the enormous and growing responsibilities of political control exercised by the president cannot be handled by a single individual. The president can rely on a subservient cabinet, but its members are not as closely attached to him as he might like. In response to this need, an almost unconscious process of institutionalizing the presidency began. In 1958 López Mateos took the most concrete step, establishing the secretariat of the presidency, a coordinating and controlling agency intended to undertake long-range comprehensive planning, effective supervision of the budget, and liaison functions, all of which previously had to be handled informally. The new office, staffed by a large, highly trained group of aides, greatly facilitated the process of constant consultation with representatives of organized group interests. Concurrent growth of a career bureaucracy also favors the institutionalization of the presidency. Emphasis is increasingly put on trained career personnel, and although the problem of transfer of subordinate loyalties from one president to a successor cannot be completely solved, the president's worry of ferreting out and removing "rotten apples," as it were, is correspondingly lessened.

Along with the formal cabinet portfolios are a considerable number of other positions, unintegrated with one another, that have great political and administrative importance. These positions are the directorship of Nacional Financiera (the government's development bank), the directorship of Pemex (the government petroleum corporation), the presidency of the Bank of Mexico, the directorship of the National Popular Subsistence Corporation (Compañía Nacional de Subsistencias Populares, or CONASUPO), a corporation charged with regulating the price and supply of many commodities, the directorship of the Social Security Institute, and numerous others. Such agencies illustrate Mexico's deep-rooted tendency to bureaucratize its administration. The president controls all such agencies, at least indirectly. Such a system has both advantages and disadvantages. While it develops a good deal of expertise and continuity and even considerable bureaucratic impact on the governmental process, it also encourages a tendency toward padding and ponderousness and increases the difficulty of internal communication.

Evolution of the Mexican presidency into what is relatively the most powerful single constitutional office in all Latin American government has led to extraordinarily involved nuances and implications that can only be suggested here. The Mexican president is Olympian in superiority over all other elements in the country. On the surface, this seems an unhealthy concentration of power in a single person or office. Yet subtle limitations are placed on the presidency, as a result of the institutionalization of the office. The president has, in a sense, become a prisoner—quite a willing one, it is true—of a trend that makes the operation of the office more constitutional and legal than political and personal. Although this somewhat restricts the president's flexibility, it also solidifies the base of the office. In practice the president must be moderative, conciliatory, and bland, no matter how nationalistic and inflammatory the public utterances may sound. The days of a charismatic president —a Juárez, a Madero, even a Cárdenas—seem to be past; the office, so to speak, has become bigger than the person who occupies it.

At the same time, growth of the presidential office has doubtless been a major factor in enabling Mexico to become the "matured Revolution" that Howard Cline has called it, to develop a more integrated population than most Latin American nations have achieved (certainly more so than in any other predominantly Indian-mestizo country), and to attain a degree of economic thrust probably greater than can be found elsewhere in Latin America. To the extent that these things can be credited to the expanded role of the chief executive, they are no mean achievements for the institutionalized presidency.

The Party Structure

Sometimes it is asked whether the one-party system in Mexico precludes the possibility of a democratic political context. Many authorities hold that it does not. The answer is probably to be found in determining just how far and how well a given country's party system permits aggregation and articulation of popular interests. If those processes do indeed take place within the framework of a single party, then we probably must conclude that democracy exists despite the traditional assumption that free and effective party competition is a sine qua non of democracy. The mere fact that Mexico's party format is unusual does not, by itself, invalidate the country's claim that it is indeed democratic.

Evolution of the party structure in Mexico can be traced through three phases of development. The first involved stabilization of the anarchic party politics in the 1920s; the PNR organization headed by Calles moved swiftly and forcefully to deflate the ambitions and power of the regional generals and civilian *caudillos* who had brought their petty sectional parties and interests into the new organization in 1929. In the second phase, the local interests and organizations were finally suppressed and supplanted by cross-regional functional groups. During the third phase strict personal control and the operation of party mechanisms slowly and subtly declined in favor of more institutionalized devices. Just as the presidency itself yielded to gradual institutionalization, so the president's relationship to the party followed a parallel path.

In a general way, these phases of party evolution corresponded with the succession of labels under which the party operated: PNR, PRM, and PRI. Although the new labels were pasted on at specific moments, the shifting development of the party was a continuing process that did not wholly yield to such clear timing.

Probably the most delicate and risky aspect of the guided evolution of party structure was the creation and then liquidation of the military sector during the second phase of party development. The other three sectors were civilian in composition and, given the state of political organization in the late 1920s and early 1930s, could not be ignored. Labor and the peasant farmers were both homogeneous groups, and Cárdenas took pains to make each of them more politically conscious and vocal. Sector organization was the obvious answer. Calles, before his ouster from politics, had come to place increasing reliance on the bureaucracy and, in turn, the bureaucracy was increasingly group conscious. Although the popular sector was in reality a catchall, its core was the Federation of State Service Workers' Unions (Federación de Sindicatos Trabajadores en Servicio del Estado, or FSTSE); in effect the popular sector was the institutionalized bureaucracy.

But the military, like labor and the peasants, was also a well knit and politically conscious group. The army was "the Guardian of the Revolution," a sonorous title that the more politically minded generals still cherished, either genuinely or hypocritically. Consequently in 1937 it would have been unrealistic—perhaps impossible—to deny the army parity with the other sectors. Cárdenas's rationalization for including the military was that it would be better to establish responsibility for the army's political activity by giving it regular status within the party structure.

But two broad trends altered the role of the army in politics: the gradual predominance of civilian political influence over militarism and the increasing professionalization of the army. The civilian sectors vigorously protested granting the military the dignity of sector status. And as the army became more professional, the removal of sector status was more palatable. Less than three years later the old generation of "political generals" was dying or retiring, and the professionally trained younger group of officers did not view politics in the same way as their elders. The action of 1940 did not make the military apolitical, but the army officers who wished to remain active in politics were enrolled into the popular sector.

The party became increasingly known as the "government" or the "official" party. Association of party and government was not as official or formal as it was under Mussolini in Italy or Hitler in Germany, but it was nonetheless effective.

Mexican election laws, dating in their present form primarily from 1953, are designed first, to rig the situation in favor of the government party and second, to concentrate party authority at the highest levels, both in PRI and the minor parties. There is an almost conscious disregard of anything like grass-roots control of party policy making, choice of candidates, and such. Given the still underdeveloped state of political consciousness and articulation of large numbers of Mexicans, even among members of groups that are parts of the extragovernmental mechanism of the country, this is not as callous as it might seem—it is at least realistic.

The entire authority over such matters as party organization, recognition, removal of recognition, scrutiny, adjustment, and certification of election returns is placed in the hands of the Ministry of Government or agencies controlled by it. It has been alleged that the ministry has at times consciously favored PRI in its actions and decisions and that cooperative minor parties are given breaks that are denied to uncooperative ones. The key to a minor party's activity, almost to its life, is the granting of registration by the Ministry of Government. To be eligible for registration, a party must meet a number of qualifications, chief of which is reasonably widespread party support in various parts of the country. This effectively precludes strictly local parties. Parties not granted official registration may not officially run candidates or take part in formal electoral activities.

Legal control over parties and their operation is much more complete and detailed in Mexico than in the United States. Inasmuch as the government has, since 1929, established a peculiarly intimate relationship with a single party, this means that the minor parties, and even PRI if the government so prefers, can be reduced to virtual impotence in the whole political process. Successive presidents had two basic alternatives: They could continue to allow an omnipotent government party to call the turns, or they could move the essential decision-making process out of party channels and into an institutionalized presidency. They chose the second alternative. The result has been that the party has become in considerable degree a façade—though a highly important one; actions are taken in its name which actually lie outside its mechanisms and control.

The PRI's organization is detailed and complex. Perhaps the only Latin American party to rival it in that respect was Argentina's Peronista party. Possibly the most significant difference between the two was the fact that the Peronista party failed to institutionalize itself, as Mexico's party has done. The circumstances of Perón's removal from power in 1955 made it impossible for the party, his creature, to survive for a long time in its erstwhile form, but there is not the slightest question of the continuance of Mexico's government party from one administration to another.

Since its establishment in 1929, Mexico's government party has been controlled on the national scene by three agencies at different levels. As they now exist, they are the National Assembly, the National Council, and the National Executive Committee. Theoretically, the Assembly is sovereign within the party structure and the other bodies are merely its agents; in reality the CEN is clearly predominant. The relationship is very roughly analogous to that prevailing within the British government. Theoretically the House of Commons is sovereign and the cabinet is subordinate to it; actually the House of Commons is normally controlled entirely by the cabinet.

It is obvious that the CEN and for that matter the entire party machinery are completely controlled by the president of the republic. If the president must have a more direct line of contact with the CEN, it comes through the president of the committee—who, political body and soul, is the national president's person—and through the two congressional representatives on the committee. An incoming national president will naturally want his own appointee in the party presidency and often makes the position available by "kicking upstairs" to high elective or appointive office the person already occupying the post. PRI organization at state and local levels roughly duplicates in miniature that at the national level. After more than three decades of existence, the sector structure of PRI has become almost revered. In the 1930s it was not illogical to base intraparty activity on the three homogeneous groups of *ejido* farm workers, organized industrial labor, and the military, using the popular sector as a catchall for remaining groups. With the economic maturing of Mexico, interest-group diversification has become greater, and it is questionable whether the agrarian, labor, and popular sectors (the three remaining sectors) can indefinitely continue to embrace, without too much artificiality, all the variant elements they now contain. Suggestions have been made, for example, that a fourth sector comprising large-business and heavy-industry interests should be established.

To the outsider the agrarian sector appears the best knit of the three. Its core is the National Peasants' Confederation (Confederación Nacional Campesina, or CNC) composed of two million or more *ejido* members. Development of the *ejido* program, especially in the 1930s, was accompanied by serious flaws that were only slowly removed. In his haste to get land into the hands of the peasants, Cárdenas neglected to give proper attention to such matters as extension of credit, provision of implements, development of adequate marketing channels, and introduction of better seed varieties and improved techniques. But gradually the program took shape. The CNC provides Latin America's best example of politicization of a large agricultural segment of the population.

The Minor Parties

With the overwhelming dominance of the government party, one may legitimately ask what role is left for minor parties. They do form part of the political picture in Mexico and probably will continue to do so. A preliminary question is, What has the course of minor parties been? In general, minor parties may be divided into two types, the transient and the permanent (or perhaps one should say quasi-permanent). The two kinds may be phased historically, although with some overlapping.

Transient Parties. In 1940, 1946, and 1952 the government party's presidential candidate received the most opposition from the nominee of a temporary grouping, bloc, or coalition. In 1940 it was the Revolutionary National Unification Party (Partido Revolucionario de Unificación Nacional, PRUN); in 1946, the Mexican Democratic Party (Partido Democrático Mexicano, or PDM); and in 1952, the Federation of Mexican Peoples' Parties (Federación de Partidos del Pueblo Mexicano, or FPPM). These were not ordinary personalistic parties. Each was thrown together around the person of a disgruntled leader of the government party who, finding himself blocked from the official nomination, took the path of frustration out of the party. In each case, he took with him as many dissatisfied interest groups as possible. The resulting parties were consequently oppositionist and negative and had so little cohesiveness that once they were defeated, as was inevitable, they disintegrated almost immediately. Given the pattern of presidential voting preceding the era of transient parties, the latter groups did reasonably well in garnering votes.[5] The increasing institutionalization of PRI made it progressively less likely that transient parties would be a continuing phenomenon in Mexican

[5]Percentages of votes cast for the government party candidate, or before 1929 one might say the favored or "inside" candidate, are illuminating. They were: 1917, Carranza, 98.1; 1920, Obregón, 96.0; 1924, Calles, 84.2; 1929, Ortiz Rubio, 93.6; 1934, Cárdenas, 98.1. Calles was opposed by a popular general, Angel Flores, and Ortiz Rubio by a man of great distinction, José Vasconcelos, which probably accounts for their lower percentages in those elections. Otherwise, the government party's percentage was only slightly less pure than Ivory soap and comparable to majorities obtained in various Nazi plebiscites. Consider the following three elections: In 1940 Avila Camacho won 93.5 and Almazán 6.4 percent; in 1946 Alemán won 79.1 and Padilla 19.6 percent; and in 1952 Ruiz Cortines won 74.3 and Henríquez Guzmán 15.8 percent.

politics. The role of minor parties, such as it is, is rather to be filled by the permanent small opposition groups.

Permanent Parties. The test of a "permanent" minor party is not whether it presents a candidate in at least two successive presidential elections —the oldest of the current minor parties did not offer a presidential candidate until it was thirteen years old—but rather whether it maintains a semblance of organization and activity between presidential elections and offers at least a scattering of candidates in interim elections for deputies, state legislatures, and local councils.

The first of the still existing groups is the National Action party (Partido de Acción Nacional, or PAN), established in 1939. PAN is often described as Catholic-oriented, but this is primarily because it, like the traditional Catholic church, is conservative. PAN's original membership was largely elitist professionals and intellectuals. PAN is by no means a member of the Christian Democratic family. It represents the most solidly organized rightist group in Mexico, though it does not monopolize all conservative opinion. Its socioeconomic moorings have been upper and upper-middle class and it has usually reflected more of an aura of dignity than most Mexican parties. Its campaign literature and other publications, for example, are normally more sedate than those of PRI.

In 1940 and 1946 PAN supported transient party presidential candidates, but in 1952 it decided to nominate its own candidate, an action that required its seeking broader popular support than had previously seemed necessary. It drew a reasonably satisfactory 7.8 percent of the presidential vote in 1952. The years following 1952 posed an important policy question, Should PAN repudiate and attack "the Revolution" and all it connoted, or should it accept the system and adopt a Mexicanized role of "His Majesty's loyal opposition"? The decision to espouse the second position caused the party considerable soul-searching and vacillation, but it did not result in schism. The question was made more pertinent by the fact that, as PRI came to be more moderate and to include a broader range of small, middle-class entrepreneurs, it could provide a congenial and obviously more rewarding party home for some persons who, because of their economic philosophy, had previously leaned toward PAN.

PRI's greater tolerance of the Church—perhaps one should say the Revolution's greater accommodation with Catholicism—helped cut part of the ideological ground from under PAN. But its fraction of the vote has slowly increased. In 1958 López Mateos won 90.4 percent and the PAN candidate 9.4 percent of the presidential vote; in 1964 Díaz Ordaz won 89 percent and PAN's nominee 11 percent of the vote; in 1970 Echeverría Alvarez won over 85 percent of the presidential vote and the PAN candidate won 14 percent. In 1976 when PAN failed to present its traditional opposition candidate because of an intraparty split, López Portillo received 94 percent of the votes.

Second oldest of the minor parties is the Popular Socialist party (Partido Popular Socialista, or PPS). It dates back to 1948 and was originally called simply the Popular Party. It was the creation of Vicente Lombardo Toledano, who found that his and Alemán's views as to PRI directions were irreconcilable. Until his death Lombardo remained the regular leader of PPS but, despite the fact that he radiated more charisma than most Mexican politicos, PPS was by no means entirely a personalistic party. It occupies a position on the Mexican Left roughly analogous to that of PAN on the Right.

A third legally recognized minor party—very minor indeed—is the Authentic Party of the Mexican Revolution (Partido Auténtico de la Revolución Mexicana, or PARM). It is essentially a party of nostalgia. A few old-line revolutionary generals and other leaders, dating back even to the time of Madero, became increasingly distressed at the way in which Alemán turned the government party toward the political luxuries and away from its earlier philosophical coloration. The result was their formation of PARM in 1957. The new party had very little weight to throw around, and both in 1958 and 1964 it supported PRI candidates for the presidency, although it nominated a few candidates for subordinate offices. The government gave PARM leaders occasional patronage crumbs from time to time, and in 1964 the party garnered enough votes to give it the smallest number of federal deputies allotted to any minor party. PARM's future on the Mexican party scene appears precarious. Both the PARM and the PPS supported López Portillo in his overwhelming victory at the polls in 1976.

A Christian Democratic party (Partido Demócrata Cristiano, or PDC) was organized in 1963. It is an orthodox member of the international Christian Democratic family, but it is as yet too new in Mexico to have made any mark or gain legal recognition. Before the 1976 presidential elections the Christian Democrats made an abortive attempt to seize control of the PAN.

For the first time in forty years the López Portillo government legalized the Communist party as well as the newly formed Socialist Workers party and the Mexican Democratic party. The most visible of these three authorized parties has been the Communist party. In the July 1979 congressional elections in which the ruling PRI won some 70 percent of the popular vote, the Communist organization received about 10 percent, which would qualify the party to be permanently registered—only 1.5 percent of the vote is needed—and to present a candidate in the 1982 presidential elections.

Recognition of the Communist party came as no surprise in light of its prevailing strength among trade unions, students, and intellectuals. The overall attractiveness of the Mexican Communist party was further enhanced by its establishing independence from Moscow and its display of Euro-Communist tendencies, which appealed to certain groups in the Mexican polity.

Communist activity in Mexico began as early as 1919 and was viewed sympathetically by many Mexican revolutionary leaders. The government extended diplomatic recognition to the Soviet Union in 1924 but severed relations in 1930 and did not renew them for a dozen years. Communist positions in the 1930s and 1940s were typically opportunistic and shifting. They never succeeded in getting government license to move legally, but such denial did not prevent the party from operating vigorously; it was only nominally underground. In the late 1930s the party was in an especially difficult position because of the presence of Leon Trotsky in Mexico (1937–1940). The fact that Diego Rivera, the famous muralist, had persuaded Cárdenas to give Trotsky asylum put the artist in disrepute with Communists almost until Rivera's death in 1957. Even though the assassination of Trotsky in 1940 removed a problem for the Communists, a deep schism between Stalinists and Trotskyists continued in labor organizations.

Complementing the Communist organization on the left is the Socialist Workers party. Another Marxist group, this party stresses independence from the International Communist movement and the Socialist International; it advocates the establishment of a popular revolutionary government by following a non-Castroite strategy of legal opposition in Mexico. The Movement of National Liberation (Movimiento de Liberación Nacional, or MLN) was for a time regarded as former President Lázaro Cárdenas's organization. This pro-fidelista group is relatively inactive in the political process.

At the right of the political spectrum, one finds the Mexican Democratic party, a conservative group that emerged from the Sinarquista movement; its major political tenets are based on papal encyclicals. The Sinarquista movement in which the Mexican Democratic party is rooted deserves brief mention. This political organization is formally called the National Sinarquist Union (Unión Nacional Sinarquista, or UNS) and to date remains unrecognized by the government.

The Sinarquistas were an allegedly mass-based, reactionary quasi-fascist group originating in Guanajuato in 1937. As with PAN the *raison d'être* for *sinarquismo* came as a reaction to the strong leftist trend of the Cárdenas administration, although the Sinarquistas inherited the psychology and perhaps some of the membership of the *cristero* movement of the late 1920s. Although PAN and the Sinarquistas had points of ideological similarity, they had important differences as well, chief of which was the considerably lower economic, social, and educational level occupied by most Sinarquistas. They represented a socially marginal group, unable or unwilling to take advantage of the *ejido* program and fanatically Catholic in religious affiliation. In its early years, *sinarquismo* had much rapport with the Spanish Falange and it also probably received moral and perhaps financial support from the Nazis. The movement bore a certain resemblance to Brazilian *integralismo*.

Sinarquistas took their political positions in sharply differentiated blacks and whites. Among the "saints" in Sinarquista political theology were Cortés, Iturbide, Maximilian, and Díaz; the "devils," as one might guess, included Hidalgo, Juárez, Madero, and Cárdenas. Communism, the "Protestant"

United States, and the Mexican Revolution were all anathema. Wholly praise-worthy were the Catholic church, Hispanicism, and the concept of orderly reform of Mexican life (*Orden* was the title of a Sinarquista magazine). Sinar-quista proposals for political, economic, and social action in Mexico were generally fuzzy, but many of the basic objectives were very similar to what the Revolution proclaimed as its goals. The difference was that the Sinarquistas would vest these ends with a Catholic rather than a revolutionary ethic and mystique.

The original position of the Sinarquistas had been to scorn organization or operation as an orthodox party. Everything moving within the revolution-ary context, even though ostensibly in opposition to the government, was inherently corrupt and *sinarquismo* would have none of it; it was a "move-ment," not a party. This stance changed in the postwar period. In 1947 the Sinarquistas gained party registration as the Fuerza Popular or Popular Force; they still did not like to call themselves a party. Life as a party was short. In 1948 in a downtown rally in Mexico City, the Sinarquistas draped the statue of Juárez in black. A protest by PRI that this was an insult to the memory of Juárez led to quick cancellation of Fuerza Popular registration by the Ministry of Government. Since 1952 the UNS has maintained a weak organ-ization, but it is no longer regarded as even an imaginary threat (as it was once construed) to the Revolution, the government, or PRI.

Mexico's permanent minor parties have not made for themselves an effective place in the political process of the country. Perhaps they cannot do so. It is claimed that they serve an educational function, but given the emo-tional and unsophisticated nature of much of Mexican political expression, the validity of that claim is dubious. To be truly educational, minor parties must work willingly within the framework of an accepted system. It is probable, and for good reason, that Mexico's minor parties work within the system only grudgingly at most. The concept of a "loyal opposition," criticizing but not rebelling, simply has not taken root in Mexican political soil. It is rumored that in certain electoral districts minor party candidates are even financially sup-ported by PRI or the government so that a democratic opposition to the dominant political machine will appear to exist.[6] If true, this is not a good groundwork for honest party opposition.

DEVELOPMENTAL PROSPECTS

There is indeed a grave concern in the higher echelons of the dominant revolutionary party that unless effective steps are taken to institutionalize the political opposition to enable it to give the ruling party more than a sterile

[6]Cf. L. Vincent Padgett, *The Mexican Political System* (Boston: Houghton Mifflin Com-pany, 1966), p. 63n.

challenge, the PRI will be forced to campaign against an *oposición de la apatía* (opposition of apathy). This actually happened in the 1976 election when López Portillo, minus an opponent and with millions abstaining, scored a predictable victory at the polls.

The López Portillo government has instituted a political reform designed to institutionalize and to strengthen the opposition to the PRI. Among other measures, it has called for enlarging congress to four hundred seats, one hundred of which would be reserved for minority opposition parties and would be filled by proportional representation.[7] Feelings about the intent of this ambitious political reform are mixed. Some political analysts believe that it reflects the pragmatism of the López Portillo administration and that if it works, it will serve to verify Mexican democracy by permitting minority parties to become majorities and thus challenge PRI hegemony. Others feel that only the ruling party stands to gain from this reform. In the Mexican political system, they argue, opposition groups are tolerated only because of the cybernetic or informational function they serve; that is, they keep the ruling party attuned to popular needs and social tensions which, if left unattended, could disrupt the existing system. Other analysts think that such a reform is intended to purge the existing system of its political shortfalls. Commenting on the reform measure, a deputy stated: "All of us are obliged to put to an end the incredibility of electoral results and strengthen our political goodwill in order that the people may have full faith in their parties and in the electoral authorities . . ."[8]

It is generally agreed that political reform, regardless of its motives, is a positive step on the part of the López Portillo administration, reflecting a strong commitment to continue the quest, begun under the Echeverría administration, for an *apertura democrática* (democratic openness) conducive to more pluralism in Mexican democracy. The likelihood that a minor party will grow into an effective challenger of PRI is, of course, almost nil as long as PRI fulfills reasonably well its function of aggregating and articulating interests and reactions and of providing channels of access to high executive officialdom.

Even granting the artificiality of the electoral changes of 1963, giving minor parties almost a guarantee of limited deputy representation in the national chamber may ultimately build up a responsible sense of the critical function of the minor parties. The distribution after seven successive elections (disregarding refusals to accept seats, etc.) is shown in Table 2–1.

In view of the generally low estate of the legislative branch, however, it is unrealistic to assume that minor parties will play a significant legislative role.

The problem of channeling views so as to generate and reflect consensus and contribute advice that will assist in governmental decision making has resulted in a greater degree of economic-interest organization in Mexico than

[7] *Latin American Report,* October 14, 1977, p. 318.
[8] *Hispano Americano,* August 15, 1977, p. 6.

TABLE 2-1   Distribution of Legislative Seats

	1958	1961	1964	1967	1970	1973	1976
PRI	153	172	175	174	178	188	190
PAN	6	5	20	20	20	25	20
PPS	1	1	10	10	10	10	12
PARM	1		5	6	5	7	8
PNM	1						
Totals	162	178	210	210	213	230	230

anywhere in Latin America. Economic organization has become almost a fetish with Mexicans; this attitude resulted years ago in the establishment of a streetwalkers' union in Mexico City. Two important points differentiate the Mexican situation from that in the United States: First, virtually all commercial or industrial enterprises in Mexico are required by law to join an appropriate association; and second, these associations have semiofficial relations with the government at the national level.

.. Much of the organizational-associational objective is attained through the sector structure of PRI, but important parts of it take place outside of PRI. The most notable extra-PRI examples are the Confederation of National Chambers of Commerce (Confederación de Cámaras Nacionales de Comercio, or CONCANACO) and the Confederation of Industrial Chambers (Confederación de Cámaras Industriales, or CONCAMIN). Laws going back to 1936 established compulsory membership in three hundred or more functionally or geographically based chambers united in one or the other of the national confederations. Theoretically the government deals only with the organized groups, although it is not unknown for a wealthy and politically powerful industrialist or entrepreneur to bypass organizational channels. Nonetheless, even though both organizations are outside the PRI framework, CON-CANACO and CONCAMIN are increasingly important in the Mexican political-economic power structure. Other interest representation is gained through associations representing such groups as bankers, insurance companies, importers, and exporters as well as many specialized trade associations.

Some students of the Mexican party system have felt that so all-embracing a group as the PRI, one that blankets so many diverse and even conflicting elements, cannot possibly continue indefinitely. (The party claims from five to seven times as many members as all other Mexican parties combined.) The usual suggestion is that one or more of the sectors may become sufficiently disgruntled to secede and form one or more separate parties. The possibility of such schism seems remote. It would be necessary for the element splitting away to gain recognition as a new party from the Ministry of Government. Ways could probably be found to deny such a party registration. Even if it succeeded in gaining recognition, the dissatisfied group would have to weigh its political chances against the remaining monolith of the party. Secessionist leaders would doubtless ponder the political fate of Vicente Lombardo Toledano, who in 1947, seven years after his waning sector and party fortunes had led to his "promotion" to the secretary generalship of the Confederation of Latin American Workers (Confederación de Trabajadores Latinoamericanos, or CTAL), left the CTM and PRI to form his own political party. Lombardo thereafter remained virtually in political limbo, and without doubt other PRI leaders contemplating the same step would think twice before emulating him. This does not rule out the possibility of a political maverick group within the PRI attempting to strike out on its own.

In April 1978 the Leandro Valle Association, founded within the ranks of the PRI in 1972 by the then Minister of National Defense, General Hermenegildo Cuenca Díaz, announced that it would seek "national political association status" from the Federal Electoral Commission. There is much speculation in political circles that the Leandro Valle Association is considering seceding from the PRI fold, especially if the latter veers too far to the Left in order to appeal to Marxist-Leninist elements in the country. General Luis R. Casillas, president of the association, which is described essentially as a military officers' group of 130,000 members, has indicated that for now the association will remain within the ranks of the PRI. But in PRI circles there appears to be cautious skepticism about the association's intentions.

A barely concealed function of the government party has been that of providing an overlay mechanism for making nominations for representative offices. One who only reads the constitution would assume that senators and deputies are elected from the states as units and that local officials are elected from subordinate geographic units. But as has been noted, the sectors and other agencies of the party actually control nominations (tantamount to election, of course), even though party choices are in turn controlled from above. Hence, the party serves an aggregating function that while necessary in some form in Mexico is provided only unofficially. Mexico extraconstitutionally superimposes functional representation on direct representation. It is one of the few states in the world outside of completely controlled political systems where such a situation can be found.

The political system of Mexico has now had more than half a century to achieve and consolidate the goals of the Revolution. This is longer than any other Latin American state has yet had to accomplish basic social reform. On balance, Mexico's record has been good. Still, the Sisyphean task of instituting the goals of the Mexican Revolution continues to challenge the leadership of each successive president. True, Mexico is modernizing through its highly successful exploitation of oil and natural gas reserves (which have further enhanced the nation's global influence), steel mills, power stations, and so forth, but the problems of social and economic inequities which exacerbate political and economic marginality in Mexican society are still festering.

The López Portillo administration is apparently committed to using the country's oil wealth to overcome Mexico's social and economic problems rather than to promote the international status of Mexico. Despite rumors that in the 1980s Mexico could become the greatest oil producer in the West, López Portillo stressed that oil production would not exceed national developmental needs. The López Portillo regime has made reasonable progress toward promoting private investment, reversing the flight of capital, stabilizing the peso, and curbing wages and public spending. The agrarian sector was neglected, however, as the Mexican government continued to develop its oil potential. López Portillo used the army to discourage illegal seizures of land; in February 1979 the army was put on alert when six oil wells were occupied near Villahermosa by peasants who blamed Pemex for inadequate compensation for expropriated land and damage to agricultural property.

The viability of Mexico's astonishingly stable development and its virtual one-party democracy may well depend on how successfully those who govern cope with the pressing problems of inflation, high unemployment and underemployment, and the widening gap between the powerful rich and the helpless poor. No one questions the enormousness of the challenge that confronts Mexican decision makers as they attempt to spearhead development without betraying the lofty ideals of the Mexican Revolution, which was supposed to have ended six decades ago.

One may surmise that the revolutionary façade is maintained by the political elites because it is good propaganda and provides a familiar and useful symbolism, but in reality the party is wholly practical and materialistic. Herein lies the rub of its political success. The word *revolutionary* has become as much a part of the formal vocabulary of Mexico's dominant party element as *democracy* could possibly be in the United States; yet as a guideline for actually determining PRI directions, the Revolution receives only lip service. Following this style of political pragmatism, it can be said that Mexico has indeed come a long way.

REFERENCES

ALBA,VÍCTOR.. *The Mexicans, the Making of a Nation.* New York: Holt, Rinehart & Winston, 1967.

ALMOND, GABRIEL A., and SIDNEY VERBA. *The Civic Culture: Political Attitudes and Democracy in Five Nations.* Boston: Little, Brown, 1965.

AMES, BARRY. "Bases of Support for Mexico's Dominant Party." *American Political Review* 64 (March 1970), 153–167.

BETETA, RAMÓN. *The Mexican Revolution: A Defense.* Mexico City: DAPP, 1937.

BRANDENBURG, FRANK. *The Making of Modern Mexico.* Englewood Cliffs, N.J.: Prentice-Hall, 1964.

CALLCOTT, WILFRID H. *Santa Anna: The Story of an Enigma Who Once Was Mexico.* Norman, Okla.: University of Oklahoma Press, 1936.

CLINE, HOWARD F. *Mexico: Revolution to Evolution, 1940–1960.* New York: Oxford University Press, 1962.

————. *The United States and Mexico.* (2nd ed.) Cambridge, Mass.: Harvard University Press, 1963.

CUMBERLAND, CHARLES. *Mexico: The Struggle for Modernity.* New York: Oxford University Press, 1968.

FAGEN, RICHARD R., and WAYNE A. CORNELIUS, JR., eds. *Political Power in Latin America: Seven Confrontations.* Englewood Cliffs, N.J.: Prentice-Hall, 1970.

FERNÁNDEZ, JULIO A. *Political Administration in Mexico.* Boulder, Colo.: Bureau of Governmental Research and Service of the University of Colorado, 1969.

FROMM, ERICH, and MICHAEL MACCOBY. *Social Character in a Mexican Village.* Englewood Cliffs, N.J.: Prentice-Hall, 1970.

FUENTES DÍAZ, VICENTE. *Los partidos políticos en México.* 2 vols. Mexico City: np., 1954.

GONZÁLEZ CASSANOVA, PABLO. *La democracia en México.* Mexico City: Ediciones Era, 1965.

GLADE, WILLIAM P., and CHARLES W. ANDERSON. *The Political Economy of Mexico.* Madison, Wisc.: University of Wisconsin Press, 1963.

GREENBERG, MARTIN H. *Bureaucracy and Development: A Mexican Case Study.* Lexington, Mass.: Heath, 1970.

GRIMES, C. E., and CHARLES SIMMONS. "Bureaucracy and Political Control in Mexico: Towards an Assessment." *Public Administration Review* 29 (January-February 1969), 72–79.

GRINDLE, MERILEE S. "Policy Change in an Authoritarian Regime: Mexico Under Echeverría." *Journal of Inter-American Studies and World Affairs* 19:4 (November 1977), 523–556.

————. *Bureaucrats, Politicians and Peasants in Mexico.* Berkeley: University of California Press, 1977.

HANSEN, ROGER. *The Politics of Mexican Development.* Baltimore.: Johns Hopkins University Press, 1971.

JOHNSON, JOHN J. *Political Change in Latin America: The Emergence of the Middle Sectors.* Stanford, Calif.: Stanford University Press, 1965.

JOHNSON, KENNETH F. "Ideological Correlates of Right Wing Political Alienation in Mexico." *American Political Science Review* 59 (September 1965), 656–664.

————. *Mexican Democracy: A Critical View.* rev. ed. New York: Holt, Rinehart & Winston, 1978.

JOHNSON, WILLIAM W. *Heroic Mexico.* New York: Doubleday, 1968.

KLING, MERLE. *A Mexican Interest Group in Action.* Englewood Cliffs, N.J.: Prentice-Hall, 1967.

KOSLOW, LAWRENCE, ed. *The Future of Mexico.* Tempe, Ariz.: Arizona State University Latin American Studies, 1978.

LEWIS, OSCAR. *Five Families.* New York: John Wiley, 1963.

LIEWEN, EDWIN. *Mexican Militarism: The Political Rise and Fall of the Revolutionary Army.* Albuquerque: University of New Mexico Press, 1968.

LOMNITZ, LARISSA A. *Networks and Marginality: Life in a Mexican Shantytown,* trans. by Cinna Lomnitz. New York: Academic Press, 1977.

MECHAM, J. LLOYD. "An Appraisal of the Revolution in Mexico." Chapter 14 in *The Caribbean at Mid-Century,* ed. by A. Curtis Wilgus. Gainesville, Fla.: University of Florida Press, 1951.

MIRANDA, JOSÉ. *Las Ideas y las Instituciones Políticas Mexicanas.* Mexico City: UNAM, 1952.

NEEDLER, MARTIN C. *Politics and Society in Mexico.* Albuquerque: University of New Mexico Press, 1971.

PADGETT, L. VINCENT. *The Mexican Political System.* Boston: Houghton Mifflin, 1976.

————. "Mexico's One-Party System: A Re-evaluation." *American Political Review* 51 (December 1957), 995–1008.

PAZ, OCTAVIO. *The Labyrinth of Solitude.* New York: Grove Press, 1961.

————. *The Other Mexico: A Critique of the Pyramid.* New York: Grove Press, 1974.

POITRAS, GUY E. "Mexico's 'New' Foreign Policy." *Inter-American Economic Affairs* 28:3 (Winter 1974), 59–78.

PURCELL, JOHN F. H., and SUSAN KAUFMAN PURCELL. "Mexican Business and Public Policy." Pp. 191–226 in *Authoritarianism and Corporatism in Latin America,* ed. by James M. Malloy. Pittsburgh: University of Pittsburgh Press, 1977.

RAMOS, SAMUEL *Profile of Man and Culture in Mexico.* Austin: University of Texas Press, 1967.

RUTHERFORD, JOHN D. *Mexican Society During the Revolution: A Literary Approach.* Oxford: Clarendon Press, 1971.

REYNA, JOSÉ LUIS, and RICHARD WEINERT, eds. *Authoritarianism in Mexico.* Philadelphia: Institute for the Study of Human Issues, 1977.

ROSS, STANLEY R. *Is the Mexican Revolution Dead?* New York: Knopf, 1967.

SCHMITT, KARL M. *Communism in Mexico: A Study in Political Frustration.* Austin: University of Texas Press, 1965.

SCOTT, ROBERT E. *Mexican Government in Transition.* 2nd ed. Urbana: University of Illinois Press, 1964.

SHAPIRO, YORAM. "Mexican Foreign Policy under Echeverría." *Washington Papers* 6:55 (1978), 7–70.

SILVA HERZOG, JESÚS. *Breve Historia de la Revolución Mexicana.* 2 vols. Mexico City: Fondo de Cultura, 1960.

SIMPSON, LESLEY B. *Many Mexicos* 4th ed. Berkeley and Los Angeles: University of California Press, 1966.

SMITH, PETER H. *Labyrinth of Power: Political Recruitment in Twentieth-Century Mexico.* Princeton, N.J.: Princeton University Press, 1979.

SOLÍS QUIROGA, HÉCTOR. *Los partidos políticos en México.* Mexico City: Orion, 1961.

SPAIN, AUGUST O. "Mexican Federalism Revisited." *Western Political Quarterly* 9 (September 1956), 620–632.

STEVENS, EVELYN P. *Protest and Response in Mexico.* Cambridge, Mass.: MIT Press, 1975.

TANNENBAUM, FRANK. *Mexico: The Struggle for Peace and Bread.* New York: Knopf, 1956.

VERNON, RAYMOND. *The Dilemma of Mexico's Development.* Cambridge, Mass.: Harvard University Press, 1965.

WILKIE, JAMES. *The Mexican Revolution: Federal Expenditure and Social Change Since 1910.* Berkeley: University of California Press, 1967.

ZAMORA MILLÁN, FERNANDO. *Mexico.* 1st ed. Mexico City: UNAM, 1964.

3

THE HISTORIC CENTRAL AMERICAN FEDERATION

The six isthmian countries between Mexico and South America constitute a politically complex and varied segment of Latin America, yet geographically and economically they are enough alike to group them under the title Central America. The history and politics of Panama, however, have differed so from that of the others that it is wiser to exclude that country from *Central America* and restrict the term to the historic Central American federation of Guatemala, Honduras, El Salvador, Nicaragua, and Costa Rica. Panama will be examined separately in Chapter 4.

The five states of the Central American federation vary greatly in area, population, urbanization, literacy, and other factors (see Table 3–1). If all five states were united as one, as they have been at times, that state would have an area of 163,347 square miles and a population of 20,527,000.

In some ways geographic features have influenced politics. The mountainous terrain has fostered a sense of localism which, in turn, has prevented the successful union of the Central American republics. It has also retarded construction of adequate roads and railroads. The general lack of mineral wealth explains why the early Spaniards turned their attention to Mexico in the north and Peru in the south. The pattern of settlement was thereby influenced at a very early date.

The effective parts of four of the five Central American countries (Nicaragua is the exception) are in the highlands—the intermontane valleys. Because of El Salvador's small area and its intensive agricultural exploitation, for practical purposes the whole country comprises effective El Salvador. In

TABLE 3-1 Politically Significant Statistics

	Area (sq. mi.)	Pop. in Thousands; 1970 Est.	Pop. of Capital in Thousands; Varying Dates	Pop. Density per Km.; Varying Dates	Percent Urban Pop., 1975	Annual Growth Rate 1965–1970	Percent White (W), Indian (I), Black (B), Mixed (M), Unspec. (U), Varying Dates	Adult Literacy Rate 1970
Guatemala	42,042	7,100	731	48	36	2.9	54(I), 46(U)	47
Honduras	43,277	3,595	302	24	37	3.4	1(W), 7(I), 2(B), 90(M)	62
El Salvador	8,260	4,813	337	170	42	3.4	5(W), 20(I), 75(M)	58
Nicaragua	50,193	2,733	398	14	51	3.0	17(W), 5(I), 10(B), 68(M)	57
Costa Rica	19,575	2,286	215	37	42	3.1	98(W), 2(B)	89
Totals	163,347	20,527						

Sources: *Statistical Abstract of Latin America, 1977,* and *Political Handbook of the World, 1977.*

Honduras, though the historic and current political centers of gravity are undoubtedly at Tegucigalpa, the north coast has developed an economic importance and centricity of its own, introducing a curious dichotomy into many aspects of Honduran life; the country seems to be almost two worlds in miniature.

Costa Rica presents a peculiar situation: The important part of the country is essentially the Meseta Central, a highly cultivated and heavily settled intermontane basin that measures only about eighty miles by forty miles. Costa Rica's four principal cities are located in the Meseta; in recent decades San José, with its prestige as a national capital, has outstripped the other three in importance and size. The Meseta as a whole is a well-integrated, coherent economic and political area, one of the most advanced small patches of all Latin America.

In Nicaragua the effective portion of the country is a narrow strip extending about one hundred fifty miles to the west and northwest of Lakes Nicaragua and Managua. This small part of Nicaragua includes not only the national capital but also the historically and politically important towns of Granada and León.

The present five Central American republics (plus the southernmost Mexican state of Chiapas) were united during the long colonial period in the captaincy general of Guatemala. In July 1823 a constituent assembly in Guatemala City proclaimed the formal independence of "The United Provinces of Central America." In late December of the same year a brief series of "constitutional bases" for an organization to be called the Federated States of the Center of America were issued. These bases were in actuality a constitution, though a sketchy one. Constitution writers of the day were, not surprisingly, imprecise: They wrote of *federation,* but what they really established was de facto *confederation.* The office of federal president was created, and each province was to have its own president. But it was politics, not constitutions, which determined the sorry course of Central American development. Conservatives opposed Liberals; province feuded with province.

The so-called Liberals managed to elect a president in 1829, but with largely fictitious authority, especially in the more distant states. Disintegration proceeded apace. The masses were ignorant, apathetic, and displayed a suspicion born of generations of bitter experience. To try to extend political participation to them would have been farcical.

The coup de grâce for the federation came primarily from Guatemala. Conservatives, who dominated the politics of that province, were addicted to the concept of centralism. They found even federalism, and much more confederation, distasteful. An illiterate and reactionary mestizo, Rafael Carrera, leading a fanatical band of Indians conquered Guatemala City in 1838. At the end of May 1838 the federal congress resolved that the provinces were free to govern themselves as independent units, and during the next few years provincial authorities implemented the action. The early effort to achieve Central American unification was a sad failure.

Even so peculiarly close political relationships among the five states continued. It was almost the middle of the century before the states officially began to refer to themselves as republics. The five states share what might be called a common political nervous system. A pinprick or a wound, such as an attempted revolution, experienced in one part is likely to create political tension in other parts of Central America. Political parties in the various republics, insubstantial though they were, frequently bore the same names, and Liberals or Conservatives in one country would often lend moral and sometimes material and military support to their similarly designated political compatriots elsewhere.

If the political climate in one state became too hot for dissidents, it was easy for them to step across the border into an adjoining republic and there, perhaps, plot their return to power in the country they had just left. The political annals of the five states, even in the 1950s and 1960s, often included invasions, rumored or attempted, from neighboring countries. Before an international political conscience had begun to develop in the hemisphere, as it now fortunately has, these invasions would stand or fall on the strength of the contending forces. Now they are often contained—even the open though undeclared Soccer War between El Salvador and Honduras in 1969—or forced to withdraw by the application of international pressures. In the 1930s the existence of dictatorships in all Central American states except Costa Rica made that country's capital, San José, the haven for exiled politicos from the other four states.

Because of their political background it was almost inevitable that the five republics would formally try to reestablish union, yet all attempts have failed when undertaken on an organic basis. A new and interesting approach to the problem of unification came at the end of the nineteenth century. The Central American Unionist Party (Partido Unionista Centroamericano) was formally established in 1904 with branches in each of the five states. Its guiding genius until his death in 1958 was a Nicaraguan, Salvador Mendieta. He made the party an educational and intellectual agency, but though Mendieta was a dedicated crusader, he was given little more than lip service in responsible and powerful political circles.

In 1951 another tack was tried with the establishment of an entity known as the Organization of Central American States, usually abbreviated ODECA, from the initials of its Spanish name. It was set up at San Salvador with the concurrence of the five incumbent Central American presidents. ODECA might be said to be aimed at functional rather than organic union among the isthmian states. Its record has certainly not been brilliant; still, its survival for three decades in the turbulent vortex of Central American politics is in itself no small accomplishment.

Economic integration of the five Central American nations was an idea born of a series of treaties beginning in 1958 and culminating with the General Treaty of Centroamericano Economic Integration in 1960. After enjoying nine highly successful years, the Central American Common Market (Mercado Común Centro Americano, or CACM) suffered a potentially fatal setback in the latter half of the 1960s and the early 1970s. The first major problem was the trade imbalance among the five member states. While Honduras and Nicaragua—the least developed of the common market members—were importing more from Guatemala and El Salvador than they were exporting to them, the latter were enjoying improved trade benefits. Another serious setback to CACM's two-decade history was the Soccer War between El Salvador and Honduras and the concomitant de facto withdrawal of Honduras from the common market in 1969 as a result of the war. Renewed hostilities between the two countries in 1976 as well as the Nicaraguan civil war in 1979 continued to stifle CACM's overall effectiveness. During the two months preceding Somoza's overthrow, the Pan American Highway—the main artery for common market goods—was virtually closed to all commercial traffic through Nicaragua. Costa Rica, at the end of the common market conduit, suffered with Nicaragua from this break in the pipeline.

Guatemala

POLITICAL CULTURE AND ENVIRONMENT

For many years Guatemala, the political center of the captaincy general, continued to overshadow the disunited Central America. For twenty-seven years after the disintegration of the union, Guatemala was dominated by Rafael Carrera, the illiterate Indian who caused the downfall of the confederation. Although he established internal peace, he contributed little to progress.

Next in the long succession of Guatemalan strongmen was Justo Rufino Barrios, who dominated the state's politics for fourteen years beginning in 1871, the last twelve years as president. Barrios was a Liberal who made anticlericalism the chief plank in his platform. A new constitution in 1879 (which was to survive for almost two-thirds of a century) established a strong presidency, a unicameral legislature, and elective judgeships; it completely separated church and state and included a relatively advanced bill of rights.

Manuel Estrada Cabrera succeeded to power in 1898 and doubtless represented the nadir of Guatemalan government. He conducted the pretense of elections in 1905, 1911, and 1917, never with any opposition to himself, but he was finally declared mentally incompetent and removed from office. The 1920s saw Guatemalan government at its best, or at least its most liberal and democratic, for some decades. But it was followed by yet another dictator.

General Jorge Ubico, who "reigned" from 1931 to 1944, was an intelligent, energetic, ruthless dictator. His habit of making unannounced visits to various parts of the country to check on the administrative integrity and diligence of even minor officials led to the occasional description of his regime as "government by motorcycle." His government was highly paternalistic, but the father image became increasingly oppressive. A general strike in neighboring El Salvador in May 1944, which brought the retirement of that country's dictator, triggered a student and military rising against Ubico the following month—an example of the Central American nervous system at work—which soon forced him out of office.

Four months later a new military action, this time engineered by young officers, brought Guatemala to the eve of its social revolution. A new constitution, which took effect in March 1945, included a detailed statement of individual and social guarantees obviously influenced by Mexico's basic law, but it had few structural innovations.

The first president elected under the new constitution was Juan José Arévalo, who described himself as a "spiritual socialist." Arévalo was a sincere reformer, but he was somewhat naive and unacquainted with the hard realities of Guatemalan politics. He tried to institute a democratic reform program, but the large dose of liberalism and freedom was more than Guatemala could easily digest. The freedom of labor, press, party, and legislature, unrestrained either by self-discipline or governmental action, tended to get out of hand. Communist activity began to increase significantly.

The 1950 presidential election gave the top position to Major Jacobo Arbenz Guzmán, one of the young army officers who had headed the October 1944 coup. Arbenz was both more radical and more realistic than Arévalo. The agrarian reform law of 1952 became the showcase of his administration. Its aim, the expropriation and distribution of large agricultural properties, brought him into direct conflict with the United Fruit Company. "La Frutera," on its part, had become the symbol of foreign "imperialistic" domination.

Arbenz's flirtation with and support from the Communist party continued to be a thorn in the side of the United States. Matters came to a head in May 1954 when the United States learned that Guatemala had received arms from Poland. In June the United States Central Intelligence Agency sent military supplies to Honduras to aid the Guatemalan invasion force led by Colonel Carlos Castillo Armas, a dissident Guatemalan who had been in exile for some three years. The invasion was successful, and Arbenz was forced from the country. Castillo Armas was soon in power as provisional president.

Castillo Armas was in power for three years, until his assassination in mid-1957. A confused political situation existing for some months after Castillo Armas's assassination was followed by election of General Miguel Ydígoras Fuentes to the presidency in 1958, but he was ousted in 1963.

A semblance of democratic process was restored in 1966. Presidential elections were held in March under a new (1965) constitution. Julio César

Méndez Montenegro, Revolutionary party candidate, won. It was the first time in the twentieth century that a Guatemalan regime had peacefully turned over power to its political opposition. Méndez's term was marred by violence that often reached the proportions of terrorism. At different times in 1968 both the United States military attaché and the United States ambassador were assassinated.

Principal candidates in the election of March 1, 1970, were Mario Fuentes Pieruccini of the government Revolutionary party and Colonel Carlos Arana Osorio, candidate of the Institutional Democratic party and the National Liberation Movement. The popular vote gave a plurality to Colonel Arana, and congress confirmed his election. President Arana immediately declared a state of siege, suspended most constitutional liberties, and began a vigorous antiterrorist campaign which claimed thousands of lives.

The 1974 presidential and legislative elections were laced with charges and countercharges of electoral fraud. The government declared that General Kjell Eugenio Laugerud García, the candidate of the ruling right-wing coalition, had obtained a plurality but not a majority of the votes cast. The congress, which was also controlled by the conservatives, was called upon to designate the winner, and it named General Laugerud. From its inception President Laugerud's term in office was fraught with turmoil.

An earthquake in 1976, which destroyed much of Guatemala City and claimed the lives of almost 23,000 people, injured 77,000, left 1,277,000 homeless, and caused an upsurge in left-wing terrorist activities. As a response to the terrorist activities of the leftist Guatemalan Army of the Poor (Ejército Guerrillero de los Pobres, or EGP), the government replaced the paramilitary organization, La Mano Blanca (White Hand) with two groups, the Escuadrón de la Muerte (Death Squad) and the Buitre Justiciero (Vulture of Justice). President Laugerud tried to move his administration away from the extreme right elements that had backed his candidacy, but the conflict between the legislature and the executive deepened, and the ruling party soon lost its legislative majority to the opposition Revolutionary party.

In 1978, just five weeks before President Laugerud was to turn the office of president over to his successor, disaster hit again. In a little peasant town northwest of Guatemala City, large landowners had begun to oust the peasants from land the peasants had worked and lived on for many years. The peasant had traditional rights but no legal title to the land. When peasants marched to protest to the local *alcalde,* they were met by a group of landowners accompanied by an army patrol, which opened fire. At least one hundred peasants were either shot or drowned while trying to escape.

Elections in 1978 retained the bitter taste of fraud prevalent in 1974 and added a dash of suspense: For over a week the outcome was in doubt. Three main candidates, all military men, ran for president. After days of confusion, General Romeo Lucas García emerged the victor by a narrow margin. He was not able to win a majority of the popular vote. The military favored his candidacy and did not hesitate to let the opposition-controlled congress know it. The prospect of a repressive National Liberation Movement (Movimiento de Liberacíon Nacional, or MLN) government seemed to persuade the leaders of the moderate left, including the illegal United Front of the Revolution (Frente Unido de la Revolución, or FUR), to align with the centrists and the moderate right. This alliance convinced the army to persuade President Lauge-rud that Lucas García should be selected by congress as the next president. He then won a narrow congressional majority.

After taking office in July, President Lucas García began an immediate crackdown on all popular opposition movements, which had been growing steadily since the 1960s. A protest against an increase in bus fares in October 1978 left thirty people dead. The new version of *La Mano Blanca,* the Secret Anti-Communist Army (Ejército Secreto Anticomunista, or ESA) began its draconian attacks on the opposition by going after its top leaders, including former Foreign Minister Alberto Fuentes Mohr and the political leader of the newly recognized FUR, Manuel Colom Argueta. Both men were considered prime candidates for the presidency in 1982. By mid-1979 the word *coup* was spreading through the barracks.

GOVERNMENTAL AND POLITICAL STRUCTURES

As is true virtually throughout Central America, for practical purposes the president of Guatemala is the government. According to the 1965 constitution, the president is popularly elected for a four-year term and is ineligible for reelection thereafter.

Guatemala has never had a bicameral legislature. The country's small size makes a one-chamber congress logical, even though the lack of ethnic and economic integration does not. Membership, which was set at fifty-five in the 1965 constitution, now stands at sixty-one legislators who serve four-year nonrenewable terms. Its powers are the traditional ones, though it is author-ized to choose a president from the top two contenders when no candidate has a clear majority of the popular vote.

The Supreme Court of Justice heads the judiciary, according to the 1965 constitution. Its members as well as those of the six courts of appeal are elected by the congress. Twenty-eight courts of first instance and a much larger number of municipal justices complete the judicial pyramid.

The major administrative subdivision in Guatemala is the department; there have been twenty-two departments in addition to the municipality of Guatemala City. The departments vary greatly in size and population; El Petén in the north encompasses about a third of Guatemala's area but has a population of less than 65,000. Each department has a governor who is appointed by the president and serves as his political lieutenant; before 1945 the governor was known as *jefe político,* a more logical title.

A semblance of local control does prevail at the basic level of the *municipio.* Guatemala is divided into more than three hundred *municipios* which, like the departments, vary greatly in area and population. *Municipios* elect their *alcaldes* and councils; however, given the large unassimilated Indian population, the voters often have little comprehension of the significance of the political process. Insufficient fiscal resources usually hold locally controlled services to a minimum; the national government can and does crack a financial whip over the localities.

The 1956 and 1965 constitutions made voting compulsory for all literates, both men and women, over the age of eighteen and optional for illiterates above the same age. Beginning in the 1950s Guatemala experimented with a system of proportional representation for selecting national deputies, but it resulted in much confusion and dissatisfaction. Proportional representation is of course an invitation to party fractionation.

Party Structures

In 1963 the military junta decided to dispense with party as well as legislative activity, thus deactivating the nine parties that participated in the 1959 elections. The groupings that have been most important in recent years were formed after 1955. The Revolutionary party (Partido Revolucionario, or PR) is a moderate leftist but non-Communist party advocating land reform, administrative change, and more rapid national development. The National Liberation Movement (MLN) dates back to the anti-Communist stance of Castillo Armas who deposed Arbenz in 1954. The MLN formed an alliance with the Institutional Democratic party to support the successful candidacies of Colonel Arana in 1970 and General Laugerud in 1974. The Christian Democratic party (Partido Demócrata Cristiano, or PDC), also known as the Democracia Cristiana Guatemalteca (DCG), is a pro-Church, conservative group which does not share the reformist orientation of Christian Democratic parties in several other Latin American countries. The Institutional Democratic party (Partido Institucional Demócrata, or PID), which represents the conservative-military business interests and military point of view, was founded in 1965 under the military junta which ruled from 1963 to 1966. The United Front of the Revolution (FUR) won recognition in March 1979; but the party's leader, Manuel Colom Argueta, was assassinated a few days later. The Guatemalan Labor party (PGT), a Communist group that has been outlawed since the overthrow of the Arbenz government in 1954, supports the strategies of the Armed Rebel Forces (Fuerzas Armadas Rebeldes, or FAR), a terrorist group. The Armed Rebel Forces was founded in 1963 by former "13th of November Movement" members; the Guerrilla Army of the Poor (EGP) began its terrorist activities in 1975 but stepped up its activity after the 1976 earthquake.

Several of these groups have gained only a precarious hold on life and all have been subject to regrouping at various times. Some have obvious ideological orientations, but most are thinly rooted and concerned primarily with parliamentary and electoral maneuvering.

DEVELOPMENTAL PROSPECTS

The Arévalo–Arbenz period introduced a degree of social and political ferment that the conservatism of even Castillo Armas and Ydígoras could not entirely wipe out. Agrarian reform, low-cost housing, social security, and other such innovations attracted considerable popular interest, but few solid and permanent accomplishments were realized. Organized labor, which, by the time Arbenz was ousted, claimed membership of 100,000 (an inflated figure), lost some five-sixths of that membership thereafter. The Catholic church had been essentially without political impact since the time of Justo Rufino Barrios. Other pressure groups were too weakly organized to have any real effect on public policy; politics remained the plaything of the politicos who in turn were at the mercy of the army.

The 1978 presidential elections continued to demonstrate the Guatemalan army's deep control over government. With his election as president, Lucas García became the third successive military man to hold the reins of government.

Violence marked the Lucas García administration. Civilian opposition continued to grow despite the government's attempt to wipe out all opponents. Dissension within the army continued to mount, public disputes among top ranking officials in the administration continued, and the thorny treaty dispute over Belize remained unsettled.

Honduras

POLITICAL CULTURE AND ENVIRONMENT

The political development of Honduras during the nineteenth and twentieth centuries has not, on the whole, been outstanding or inspiring. A state with a small population, it was frequently at the mercy of its neighbors. In 1907, by international action of the Central American states with the blessing of the United States and Mexico, Honduras was theoretically neutralized and immunized from the political turbulence of its neighbors; the agreement was a novelty which was more impressive on paper than in reality.

Presidents in the second half of the nineteenth century were for the most part undistinguished and often remained in office only by the sufferance of Carrera or Barrios or, later, by that of the Nicaraguan dictator Zelaya.

The same pattern of political confusion persisted into the twentieth century. Some improvement came in 1923 when the National party was formed. It emphasized the need for national unity and an end to administrative chaos. In 1933 General Tiburcio Carías Andino finally realized his ambition and assumed the presidency. Democracy was then shelved as a new dictator consolidated his position.

Carías was succeeded in 1949 by an able civilian, Juan Manuel Gálvez, representing the National party, but the opposition Liberals chafed. In 1954 Carías ran again on the National ticket, but a large segment of the party broke away and organized the Reformist party. The Liberal party regrouped and nominated Dr. Ramón Villeda Morales, who received slightly less than a clear majority of popular votes. Legislative obstruction prevented his confirmation. In December 1957 Villeda Morales was chosen president for a term to run until late 1963. A new constitution became effective when he was inaugurated.

The new president instituted a program of moderate reform embracing a liberal labor code, social security, and at least gestures towards land distribution. For a time it seemed that he would be able to surmount the succession of petty crises and complete his term, but in early October 1963, just ten days before new presidential elections were scheduled, a military coup forced him from office. The resulting all-too-familiar junta dissolved the congress and the civil guard, set up a partially civilian regime, and tried to reestablish Honduras in the good diplomatic graces of other states of the hemisphere.

The junta convened a constituent assembly dominated by the National party; after drafting a new basic law, it converted itself into a regular legislative body and proceeded to elect the junta head, General Osvaldo López Arellano, as president for a six-year term. This action gave a façade of constitutionality to what continued to be essentially a military dictatorship, though certainly not the hemisphere's worst. Nationalists exceeded Liberals in the sixty-four–member congress by thirty-seven to twenty-seven.

López Arellano laid the groundwork for a new civilian government in 1971 by setting up a Pact of National Unity. Among other things it decreed that the two major political parties share governmental posts, including representation in the congress, the cabinet, and the supreme court, an arrangement similar to the National Front in Colombia. On June 6, 1971, Dr. Ramón E. Cruz, the National party candidate, became the first popularly elected president in forty years. Just eighteen months after taking office, President Cruz was overthrown by the military, and General López again took office. Although the Soccer War between Honduras and El Salvador had taken place during the López regime, Cruz had taken a hard stand against any reconciliation with El Salvador until the border dispute involving thousands of Salvadoran settlers was resolved. Trouble also broke out between the Liberal and National parties, who were not accustomed to sharing governmental posts. On December 4, 1972, General López assumed power, brought the party pact to an end, and announced that he would serve the remainder of Cruz's five-year term.

López's regime was cut short, however, by news of a scandal involving the United Brands Company and a "high Honduran official." The U.S. Securities and Exchange Commission was investigating a United Brands Company agreement to pay a $2.5 million bribe to obtain a reduction in banana taxes. López refused to cooperate with investigators, and he was soon replaced by Colonel Juan Alberto Melgar Castro in a military coup.

On taking office President Melgar stated that the country would be returned to civilian rule by 1979, at the latest, but he subsequently changed it to 1980. Melgar enjoyed good relations with the United States but was not as fortunate at home. His new regime promised a land-reform program which would expropriate 1.5 million acres of uncultivated land and distribute it to 120,000 landless farm families. There have been numerous clashes between landowners and the National Front of Peasant Units, which claims a membership of 140,000. In 1975 thousands of peasants marched on the capital to urge a speedup in land reform. The ensuing gunfight left fifteen peasants dead. In 1976 another border clash with El Salvador brought renewed tensions to the country.

President Melgar's not-so-secret ambition to become a constitutionally elected president was quickly halted on August 8, 1978, when he was suddenly deposed in a bloodless military coup—the thirteenth in Honduras's 142 years as a republic. Melgar was replaced by a three-man army junta which pledged to abide by Melgar's promise to hold elections in 1980 and to continue discussions with El Salvador over its border dispute.

GOVERNMENTAL AND POLITICAL STRUCTURES

In Honduras the president, whether civilian or military, is clearly the central figure in the structure and operation of government. According to the constitution of 1965, the president is popularly elected for a six-year term and may not be reelected.

In practice the extraordinary position of the army, established by the 1957 and 1965 constitutions, partially straitjackets the president. True, in Carías, Honduras had a classic dictator, but in the 1950s and the 1960s the country had two moderate and constructive presidents, Juan Manuel Gálvez and Villeda Morales, who represented opposite parties. The Honduran president is subject to certain constitutional restraints, but a more subtle restraint may be the political climate of Honduras, which has seemed less suitable for the nurturing of strongmen than is true in certain other Central American states.

The sixty-four–member unicameral National congress is composed of deputies popularly elected for six-year terms on a population basis. Congress has little importance. Although not as unimportant as the Mexican congress, between the political power granted the executive and the army, little is left for the legislature.

Judicial machinery is headed by a nine-member supreme court of justice. Formerly elected by the congress for six-year terms, it is now designated by the president. Despite a quite specific grant of the power of judicial review to the supreme court, the effectiveness of the judiciary is limited by the relatively short term of supreme court judges and the coincidence of their term (as is also true of the legislators) with that of the president.

Honduras's eighteen territorial departments vary greatly in area and population. The constitution of 1965 dealt only briefly with the departmental system. Governors of the departments are appointed by the president but have little power or political personality.

Honduras's 281 *municipios* elect their own councils and show the rudiments of a democratic process; however, their financial resources are extremely inadequate. The national capital is a specially governed Central District.

Under the 1965 constitution the vote was given as an obligatory matter to everyone over eighteen. Compulsory voting is honored only in the breach. The basic law also recognized the existence of political parties.

Party Structures

When Honduran parties have functioned normally and freely, the country has in effect had a biparty system. Both the dictator Carías and the relatively democratic Gálvez who followed him represented the National party (Partido Nacional, or PN). It was a conservative grouping although, at least under Gálvez, not reactionary. Since the coup of 1963, the National party has been strongly allied with López and the military. As the natural heir of the Conservatives of the nineteenth century, it still tends to represent propertied interests.

The Liberal party (Partido Liberal de Honduras, or PLH), oriented toward an urban and labor following, is somewhat more democratic and reformist in its stance, but it also cannot be called an ideological group. The National Reformist Movement (MNR) traces its political ancestry to 1890. In

1954 it threatened to break down the traditional two-party division by seceding from the National party in favor of younger leadership, but it was later largely absorbed by other parties. A leftist student movement in the 1960s, the Frente de Juventud Democrática Hondureña, took a fidelista and pro-Soviet position.

Before the 1978 coup that deposed him, President Melgar formally recognized two new political groupings, the Unity Innovation party (Partido de Innovación Nacional y Unidad, or PINU) and the Christian Democratic party (Partido Demócrata Cristiano, or PDC). It was speculated that he had intended to use the Christian Democratic party as his vehicle to the presidency. As a result of the suspension of the Pact of National Unity set up by President López Arellano and of the three coups since 1971, the role of political parties in Honduras is uncertain.

DEVELOPMENTAL PROSPECTS

The Honduran political process, sparked by renewed party vigor, showed definite though erratic gains in the decade and a half since Carías withdrew in 1948. The organized institutional foundation for normal political expression is thin, however, and the country's financial underpinnings meager. The Church is ineffective. Organized labor is weak except on the north coast in the banana industry, and even there its numbers are not large. The country is reasonably well integrated ethnically. Transportation is poor, and thus the prosperous north coast is far removed in political psychology from effective Honduras, the area surrounding Tegucigalpa. But also the capital has grown slowly, which has reduced the political impact of a disgruntled urban proletariat. All in all, the situation has played into the hands of the army.

At times the Honduran army has shown considerable responsibility, but at others it has acted very undemocratically. The 1957 and 1965 constitutions gave the Honduran army a status almost unique among Latin American military machines, now or in the past. The constitution established the position of chief of the armed forces and granted the post considerable independence. One article provided that, whenever differences arose between the chief of the armed forces and the president, they must be submitted to the congress which, by a majority vote, would render a final decision. This was an unprecedented constitutional removal of the military from full presidential control. There was no occasion before the 1963 coup to see what would happen legally should such a showdown occur. Theoretically, the authority conferred on the congress to decide such differences between the civil and military authority would have meant a long step toward a parliamentary regime, but that was merely an academic possibility. Consequently, the army, even when there is not a military president, is now the arbiter of Honduran politics and government.

El Salvador

POLITICAL CULTURE AND ENVIRONMENT

The political evolution of El Salvador, like that of Honduras but unlike that of Guatemala, is not easily divisible into distinct periods. El Salvador never developed leaders who displayed the power and personality of Guatemalan leaders. This fact, plus the country's small population and its accessibility to its three immediate neighbors, led to its long and sordid involvement in the international politics of Central America.

El Salvador remained strongly committed to the ideal of union; hence, it did not formally assume the title of republic until 1856. Presidents (most of them petty *caudillos*) and constitutions were changed frequently during the early decades of independence. This dreary situation began to disappear in the late 1880s and the 1890s. A new constitution, effective in August 1886, lasted for more than half a century, and El Salvador became less of a political football than it had been in the nineteenth century. A coffee-planting aristocracy with a vested interest in peace and order became more influential in determining the political climate.

Assassination of the president in 1913 opened the office to Carlos Meléndez, first of a family dynasty which would hold the presidency for fourteen years. For a decade and a half Salvadoran politics was dominated by its "fourteen families," the political-socioeconomic oligarchy of the land. Unsettled conditions in 1931 and a coup late in the year brought General Maximiliano Hernández Martínez to the presidency. Hernández Martínez soon joined the contemporary fraternity of Central American dictators, even though his slight, unprepossessing figure and his mysticism and addiction to spiritualism made him an unlikely candidate for the role of a "man on horseback." The increasing repressiveness of the regime precipitated a general strike in San Salvador in May 1944, which quickly toppled the general from power.

The political and constitutional situation remained disturbed. Major Oscar Osorio was elected president in 1950; he instituted minor social and economic reforms but did not even make gestures toward effective democracy. In a rigged election in 1965 he was succeeded by a fellow officer, Col. José María Lemus. Politics remained unstable under military control for several years. In 1968 the Christian Democratic party surprised many by scoring impressive victories over candidates of the "government party" in most of the country's municipal elections.

The presidential election in February 1972 showed an increasing fractionation of the party structure. Four candidates ran for the office. With roughly two-thirds of the electorate abstaining, the candidate of the party of National Conciliation (Partido de Conciliación Nacional, or PCN, the government party), Colonel Arturo Armando Molina, received a slight plurality but not a majority over Napoleón Duarte, the coalition candidate of the Christian Democrats (PDC) and the Nationalist Opposition Union (Unión Nacional Opositora, or UNO). Despite charges of fraud, Molina's election was ratified by the PCN-controlled assembly. An abortive but bloody coup did not prevent his swearing in on July 1, 1972.

In the 1977 elections General Carlos Humberto Romero, candidate of the governing PCN, won by a two to one margin, although the opposition presidential candidate Colonel Ernesto Claramount charged fraud. President Romero's term, which began with the killing of almost one hundred people in a protest demonstration over his election and ended with his overthrow in October 1979, will be remembered for its Public Order Law and for the upsurge of opposition to military and oligarchy control.

GOVERNMENTAL AND POLITICAL STRUCTURES

The governmental and political organizations and functions in El Salvador are so conditioned by ethnic, social, and demographic factors that these should be considered first. Such elements probably have greater impact on politics in El Salvador than in any state in the isthmus.

As noted before, almost all of this small state's area constitutes effective El Salvador.[1] El Salvador has almost twice the percentage of agriculturally usable land as any other Central American state. Although Honduras is listed as having a higher percentage of mestizos, the people of El Salvador are probably more completely homogenized than those of any of the other Central American countries. Nationalism is well developed. Occasionally Salvadorans make a propagandist point of the fact that all other Central American countries have names ending in *a* or *as*; their national personalities are hence feminine. But *El* Salvador is masculine, virile! They tried to prove this point in the border war with Honduras in 1969.

Class differences are considerable and persistent, as evidenced by the long monopoly of political power by a small oligarchy. The middle class has not become especially significant, either numerically or politically. The Church has little impact on politics. The development of organized labor is belated; it has only a rudimentary industrial structure as a base. Agricultural associations, representing coffee growers and stock raisers, are reasonably important, but of course they reflect only the organized, land-owning oligarchy. Hence,

[1] In 1950 El Salvador suffered the irony of finding, as the result of a new and more accurate aerial survey, that its area was more than 13,000 square kilometers *less* than the commonly accepted figure, a reduction of slightly more than three-eighths in its presumed extent. It is almost exactly the size of Massachusetts.

by all odds, the best organized and most politically influential interest group in the country is the army.

The Salvadoran army's officer corps, like those of most Latin American countries, is drawn chiefly from the middle and lower-middle classes. It is the most professionally trained officer corps of any isthmian country. With a conscious responsibility for maintaining the honor and stability of the country, it is politically motivated and active, despite the constitutional prescription that it be nonpolitical. The officers' socioeconomic interests are, at least unconsciously, those of the middle class, but the concern with national stability dictates that they maintain a working alliance with the oligarchy.

The class-conscious oligarchy or aristocracy, the "fourteen families," is fearful of a fidelista-type revolution. It remembers Guatemala in the early 1950s and also the massacre by Hernández Martínez of several thousand Salvadoran "Communist" peons in the early 1930s. In oligarchic eyes moderate but controlled reform is obviously the better alternative. Reform falls far short of social revolution, but it is greater, and more controlled, than elsewhere in the isthmus, except of course in the Guatemala of Arévalo and Arbenz and possibly in recent Costa Rica.

It is in this context, then, that the governmental machinery of El Salvador functions. The president is almost inevitably an army officer, but military occupancy of the office is more reasonable—if not more democratic—than in other Central American states. The constitution of 1962 established a presidential term of five years. The constitutions of 1950 and 1962 made a gesture toward civilian control, but that stipulation is easily circumvented by a candidate's technical retirement from the military. The cabinet is often composed principally of civilians, but this has not diminished the military coloration of successive regimes.

The fifty-four members of the unicameral legislative assembly serve for two-year terms and may be reelected. The legislature is usually wholly subservient to the president. This is naturally true when all deputies are members of the president's party because opposition parties have boycotted the election; it is only relatively less true when a substantial contingent of minority-party members is elected, as happened in 1964.

The Salvadoran judiciary is headed by a ten-member supreme court of justice. The judiciary has developed no more independent strength than has the legislature.

Local government has few distinctive characteristics. The fourteen small departments into which the country is divided are grouped in three zones: western, central, and eastern. They are subdivided into 261 *municipios,* which in turn are subdivided into almost 3,300 *caseríos*—obviously minuscule units. The fourteen departments have presidentially appointed governors.

The political process is most viable at the *municipio* level. In an elementary way, a spirit of simple democracy prevails locally. As elsewhere in Latin

America, limited financial resources hamstring local government in El Salvador. All in all, the *municipio* has more political vitality than administrative authority or financial independence.

Party Structures

Political parties have been numerous, although several have been lightly rooted and short-lived, depending mostly on personal leadership. The specification in 1963 that proportional representation would be used in future elections appears likely to encourage even more parties. The modern pattern of parties dates from the campaign of 1950 and the organization at that time of the Revolutionary Party of Democratic Unification (Partido Revolucionario de Unificación Demócrata, or PRUD) and a second synthetic party, the Renovating Action party (Partido Acción Renovadora, or PAR). PRUD won the election and became much better established than any other political group. It was essentially metamorphosed into the National Conciliation party (PCN) in 1960. The PCN has the support of the military and the aristocracy, along with some peasant groups. Its candidate has won the last three elections.

The most recent opposition party is the Christian Democratic party (PDC). Although it has never been in power, the party did hold a small majority in the 1968–1970 national assembly.

The National Revolutionary Movement (Movimiento Nacional Revolucionario, or MNR) is a liberal party which entered into coalition with the Christian Democrats in 1972 and 1974 to form the Nationalist Opposition Union (Unión Nacional Opositora, or UNO). The UNO won eight legislative seats in 1972 and fourteen in 1974; it seemed destined to win a larger share in the 1976 municipal elections. But in 1975 the government passed an electoral reform law that increased the voter base of each deputy to 70,000 and also stipulated that coalitions must be declared fifteen days before election campaigns are announced.

Then in 1976, as the municipal election campaigns were getting underway, the electoral council rejected the UNO slate of deputies for the hotly disputed San Salvador district. One candidate was disqualified and, according to the electoral law, a new candidate could not be allowed to take his place; therefore, the entire list was annulled. The UNO boycotted the election entirely, and the PCN walked away with all fifty-four seats in the national assembly.

Within the last decade several guerrilla groups from both the Right and Left and several opposition groups have emerged. Leftist guerrilla groups include the People's Revolutionary Army (Ejército Revolucionario del Pueblo, or ERP), which emerged shortly after the election of Colonel Arturo Armando Molina in 1972. The killing of the ERP leader Dalton García by a faction within the ERP led to a split and the eventual formation of the Armed Forces of National Resistance (Fuerzas Armadas de Resistencia Nacional, or FARN) in 1975. Another left-wing guerrilla group, the Popular Liberation Forces (Fuerzas Populares de Liberación, or FPL), in existence since 1970, is considered the largest of the guerrilla groups operating in El Salvador.

A right-wing terrorist group that calls itself the Armed Forces of Anti-Communist Liberation of Wars of Elimination (Fuerzas Armadas Libertadoras Anticommunistas de Guerras de Eliminación, or FALANGE) has sentenced to death many clerics and labor organizers in the past few years. Another rightist group known as the White Warriors' Union, reportedly made up of retired army officers linked with government security forces, has assumed responsibility for the slaying of six priests since 1972. A paramilitary peasant group called the National Democratic Organization (Organización Democrática Nacional, or ORDEN) was founded by the government in 1968 to "combat Communism in the countryside" by spying on fellow peasant workers.

Mass opposition groups have grown as hostility to the military regime has increased. Among such groups, the United Popular Action Front (Frente de Acción Popular Unida, or FAPU), the Popular Revolutionary Bloc (Bloque Popular Revolucionario, or BPR), the Federation of Christian Peasants, and the Salvadoran Communal Union have shown impressive growth in membership since they were formed in the 1970s.

The Catholic church was divided in its support of the Romero regime. Four of the six Salvadoran bishops supported the regime, while Archbishop Oscar Arnulfo Romero (no relation to then President Carlos Humberto Romero) became the opposition voice of the masses until his assassination in March 1980. Many of the local priests in the countryside have supported the peasant movements in their struggle for higher wages, lower rents, the right to own land, and the right to organize.

DEVELOPMENTAL PROSPECTS

The crucial issues confronting the government in El Salvador include the uncontrolled violence and the need for sweeping socioeconomic reforms. In this Central American republic land ownership is concentrated in the hands of a few while landless peasants work long hours for thirty cents a day. In 1976 President Molina's program of Agrarian Transformation in two departments met with little success. The wealthy landowners, led by the National Association of Private Enterprise and the Agriculturalists and Cattle Raisers Front (FARO), campaigned bitterly against any type of agrarian reform, and the government was forced to abandon the program.

In an attempt to eliminate the violence begun in 1972, President Romero signed a Public Order Law in 1977 which gave the government sweeping powers to arrest "anyone holding public meetings, organizing trade unions or writing articles critical of the Government." The law did not eliminate the violence; instead the conflict has escalated into civil-warlike struggles between the right-wing, military-sponsored government supported by the fourteen families on one side and the country's several million peasants and workers on the other.

President Romero was overthrown in a bloodless coup by the military, and a five-man junta was placed in power in October 1979. The junta, consisting of two military leaders and three civilians, had little previous political experience, and few Salvadorans believed that the new government could do much to help curb political unrest.

Nicaragua

POLITICAL CULTURE AND ENVIRONMENT

Nicaragua provides an excellent illustration of the interplay of geographic, economic, demographic, and political factors in Latin America. Early Spanish explorers moving up from Panama found a tractable and rather densely settled Indian population on the west side of Lake Nicaragua. The Indians provided a good labor force and the vicinity was developed as small-scale plantation agriculture. This settlement became Granada.

Later another Spanish settlement, León, was established to the northwest. The type of land and the scarcity of labor at León resulted in a subsistence agriculture which kept León impoverished in comparison with Granada. The wealth and greater stratification of society at Granada turned that settlement almost inevitably into a conservative center; León, by reaction, became more liberal. The rivalry continues to this day. In time León and Granada became confirmed as, respectively, the liberal and conservative centers of the country, thus establishing a political watershed which has significantly affected Nicaraguan politics.

During the days of the confederation, the provincial capital at León provided a potential center of Nicaraguan nationalism. Hence the Granadinos reacted by quickly accepting the authority of the confederation government at Guatemala City. Power politics took over center stage for a time in the mid-1850s with the advent of the filibuster, William Walker, whose ambitions led to temporary abandonment of the chronic rivalry between parties and towns.

Following the liquidation of Walker, the Conservatives entrenched themselves in power and retained control for a third of a century. A revolution in 1893 ended the long Conservative control by placing a young Leónese Liberal, José Santos Zelaya, in the presidency. For sixteen years he remained there as Nicaragua's first real strongman—a ruthless but passably constructive dictator. A new constitution in 1893 introduced a unicameral legislature, the first time such a structure, common elsewhere in Central America, had been tried in Nicaragua.

After Zelaya's fall in 1909 Nicaraguan politics was highly confused for a time. The United States intervened and soon came to dominate the republic; from 1912 on the United States stationed a small marine unit as a "palace guard" in Managua. Nicaragua from 1909 to 1932 could with little error be called a United States protectorate. In the latter half of the 1920s the United States became deeply involved in the intricacies of Nicaraguan politics. An election in 1928, supervised by the United States, put the Liberal general José María Moncada in the presidency for a reasonably successful four-year term.

Neither Moncada nor the United States marine force was able to capture a guerrilla general named Augusto César Sandino. The near-legendary Sandino became a folk hero, but soon after he voluntarily ceased his resistance he was assassinated, probably with the collusion of the chief of the Nicaraguan National Guard. Thirty years later, in 1962, a motley group of left-wing rebels took Sandino's name and founded the Frente Sandinista de Liberación, or Sandinistas.

The Somoza Dynasty

The Liberal Juan B. Sacasa was elected president in 1932, but almost from the first he was overshadowed by his nephew-by-marriage, National Guard commandant General Anastasio Somoza. Though Somoza was constitutionally ineligible for the presidency on two counts, he declared in 1935 that he would "eliminate" all who barred his way to that office. In 1936 he won the presidency in a heavily rigged election. When he took office at the beginning of 1937, the last of a quartet of concurrent Central American dictators was in power. Somoza occupied or dominated the presidency until his assassination in 1956.

Somoza was not as heavy-handed as Ubico, as stodgy as Carías, or as sinister as Trujillo. Nonetheless, he was a thorough-going dictator. He established a family dynasty that, unlike Trujillo's, successfully carried on after him. Somoza was only a nominal Liberal, though he saw fit to reorganize the party as the Nationalist Liberal party.

His assassination in September 1956 rudely changed the course of politics. His elder son, Luis Somoza Debayle, at the time the First Designate (vice-president), succeeded him as president and, with an able assist from his brother, Anastasio *hijo* (Junior), commandant of the National Guard, consolidated and continued the family hold on power. The Nicaraguan opposition was disorganized and lacked the leadership to capitalize on their opportunity. The younger Somoza repeatedly promised that no family member would succeed him as president, and in the election held in February 1963 a Nationalist Liberal puppet, René Schick Gutiérrez, was named president with only token opposition; he died, however, in August 1966. Internal restiveness reached a climax in late January 1967 with a so-called twenty-four-hour revolt, easily suppressed by the government. The pathetic protest did not prevent the easy election in early February of another member of the dynasty, Anastasio Somoza *hijo,* longtime commandant of the National Guard.

Constitutionally, Somoza could not succeed himself in office when his term ended in 1972. So by political agreement, a three-man junta occupied the presidency, but Somoza actually continued to rule. The interim triumvirate (consisting of two Liberals and one Conservative) oversaw the drafting of a new constitution which would allow Somoza to be reelected. He was reelected on September 1, 1974, and inaugurated on December 1 for a six-year term.

The 1972 earthquake, which killed ten thousand people, not only destroyed central Managua but shook the very foundations of Nicaraguan politics. Political moderates and some friends of the government were shocked and angered by the way the Somozas used the disaster to build up their wealth. Corruption, always present, grew to such proportions that several foreign governments complained about the misuse of their aid.

In 1974 the Sandinistas launched a major but unsuccessful attempt to overthrow the government. The rebels had made little headway in their initial efforts to overthrow Somoza in the sixties, but in the ensuing years they had emerged from their role as terrorists to become a revolutionary group that gained the support of prominent businesspeople, lawyers, and clergy. The assassination of Pedro Joaquín Chamorro, a longtime opponent of President Somoza and leader of the opposition coalition, Democratic Liberation Union (Unión Democrática de Liberación, or UDEL), on January 10, 1978, set the stage for the revolution which followed. In August the Sandinistas took control of the National Palace and held fifteen hundred hostages, including ministers, members of congress, and Somoza's cousin and nephew, for forty-five hours until demands for money and the release of political prisoners were granted. The next ten months saw the fighting flare into an all-out civil war in which some forty thousand people were killed and six hundred thousand left homeless. In the last days, Somoza directed his National Guard against the Sandinistas from his bunker in Managua. Using C–47s, T–33 jets, and Cessnas equipped with rockets, the Guard bombed factories and homes alike in a last desperate effort to wipe out the rebel forces. But the dynasty was at an end, and on July 18, 1979, President Somoza resigned and flew to political exile in Miami and then Asunción, Paraguay. Two days later the five-member Sandinista-sponsored Junta of the Government of National Reconstruction rode triumphantly into Managua. The revolution, which marked the downfall of the forty-three-year Somoza dynasty, would surely go down in history as one of the most significant political events in Latin America.

GOVERNMENTAL AND POLITICAL STRUCTURES

Until the provisional government assumed power in 1979, Nicaragua had a bicameral legislature unique among the Central American states. Representatives in both houses were chosen by a system of proportional representation, and opposition parties were guaranteed a minimum of one-third of the membership of each chamber. Both senators and deputies served five-year terms. Despite the guarantee of opposition party membership, however, the congress was a rubber stamp for the Somoza regime. The 1974 constitution instituted by Somoza retained a presidential form of government with a six-year presidential term.

The supreme court of justice was made up of seven members; minority party representation was constitutionally guaranteed but meaningless.

The major administrative subdivision in Nicaragua was the department. There were sixteen departments, each with a presidentially appointed *jefe político.* The departments were subdivided into 125 *municipios,* each with its *alcalde* and other local officials, all appointive. Local government, consequently, lacked almost any viability.

Upon taking control from the Somoza dictatorship, the five-member junta announced its commitment to hold free elections within the next five years for a constituent assembly, municipalities, and president.

Party Structures

Before the ouster of Somoza in July 1979, political party structure consisted of a relatively simple division between Liberals and Conservatives. Within the Liberal camp was the "government party" of Somoza, the Nationalist Liberal party (Partido Liberal Nacionalista de Nicaragua, or PLN), renamed early in the Somoza dynasty but a descendent of the old Liberal party. Although the historic opposition conservative group was the Traditionalist Conservative party (Partido Conservador Tradicional, or PCT), another conservative faction known as the Nicaraguan Conservative party (Partido Conservador Nicaragüense, or PCN) lent a façade of opposition while continuing to enjoy patronage positions under the Somoza regime.

Other opposition groups included the Independent Liberal party (Partido Liberal Independiente, or PLI), reduced to impotency during the Somoza regime; the Social Christian party (Partido Social Cristiano, or PSC), which identified with other Christian Democratic parties in Latin America; the Liberal Constitutional Movement (Movimiento Liberal Constitucional, or MLC); and the National Salvation party (Partido de Salvación Nacional, or PSN). The Nicaraguan Social party (Partido Social Nicaragüense, or PSN) and the Republican Mobilization (Movilización Republicana, or MR) were both outlawed. The UDEL group, with the martyred Pedro Joaquín Chamorro as its candidate, was set to oppose the Somozas in elections which had been promised in 1981. Instead, Chamorro's assassination in January 1978 became the rallying cry for the revolution that ultimately toppled the Somoza regime.

DEVELOPMENTAL PROSPECTS

Nicaragua's future development will no doubt be influenced by the success or failure of the new provisional government. The five-member junta was made up of Sergio Ramírez Mercado, a writer who acted as liaison between the right- and left-wing members of the junta; Violeta de Chamorro, vice-president of the Inter-American Press Association's Freedom of the Press Committee and widow of Pedro Joaquín Chamorro; Alfonso Robelo Callejas, an industrialist and founder of the Nicaraguan Democratic Movement, one of the groups in the Broad Opposition Front; Moisés Hassan Morales, Dean of Arts and Letters of the University of Nicaragua, a guerrilla leader during the civil war, and member of the United People's Movement in the National Patriotic Front; and Daniel Ortega Saavedra, a member of the guerrilla movement for twenty years.

From its temporary base in Costa Rica before the resignation of President Somoza, the junta stated its basic policy of stimulating private business in what would be a "mixed economy." It promised to respect all private property except that belonging to the Somoza family. The junta discounted fears of a Cubanlike takeover by weighting the eighteen-member cabinet of the government with moderately inclined businessmen, managers, lawyers, and technical experts.

Upon assuming power on July 20, 1979, the junta's first official act was to efface the Somoza name from public buildings. It then abolished the 1974 constitution, disbanded the supreme court, and dissolved the legislature. The National Guard was disbanded, and the Sandinistas installed as the Nicaraguan military, the Sandinist Popular Army. The Army immediately began plans to institute a draft and to train a local militia. The rebel army's top three commanders, Luis Carrión Cruz, Humberto Ortega Saavedra, and Tomás Borge Martínez, were named a three-man directorate to head the new army. Although the junta had stipulated that members of the military would not be allowed to take an active part in politics other than to vote, Borge now holds the dual position of member of the army triumvirate and interior minister.

While those outside the country speculated on the country's ideological direction after the revolution, Nicaragua found itself faced with severe shortages of food, housing, money, jobs, and foreign exchange, a $1.5 billion foreign debt, and a 40 percent devaluation of the Nicaraguan córdoba. Although the provisional government had pledged to return the country to representative democracy, its most immediate task was to provide food and housing for the country and to begin the even more difficult task of rebuilding an economy that the Somozas had plundered for years.

But questions remain. Can those disparate groups within the Sandinistas which brought about the downfall of the Somoza regime continue to work together during the reconstruction period for Nicaragua's future? How effectively will the broad-based junta, three of whom had spent recent years outside the country, work with the Sandinistas, all of whom had been fighting the civil war inside the country? How long can the junta, pledged to rule by committee, continue without a clearly defined leader? As one analyst so aptly put it, "The military battle for democracy [has] ended . . . The political struggle for democracy has just begun."[2]

Costa Rica

POLITICAL CULTURE AND ENVIRONMENT

Costa Rica's Meseta Central had no large or tractable Indian population which the first Spanish settlers could exploit as a labor supply. Hence the few Spanish families that settled in Costa Rica in the sixteenth century had to farm their own land. A hacienda society and a landed aristocracy did not develop; Costa Rica became a democracy of small and poor farmers, each working his own *minifundio* (small land holding). This had a powerful though invisible effect on the political climate of the later republic. By the end of the eighteenth century the four towns of the Meseta had been established; it was a century later before San José began to outstrip the others. Educational progress, the high level of literacy, and the country's pride in such achievements helped direct the course of political evolution.

In the mid-1830s the country made the novel decision to rotate the national capital for a year at a time among the four towns of the Meseta, but San José soon won out as the permanent location. The dominant political figure in the small society of the time (Costa Rica only had eighty thousand inhabitants in 1844) was Braulio Carillo. New constitutions and presidents followed irregularly but fairly rapidly for a few years.

[2]See *New York Times,* July 22, 1979, Sec. IV, p. 1.

A coup in 1870 brought to the presidency Colonel Tomás Guardia, almost the only quasi strongman Costa Rica has had. For a dozen years he occupied or dominated the presidency. Guardia was a military dictator who very likely retarded democratic development; still, like Barrios in Guatemala, he considerably furthered material growth. An important trend of the Guardia regime was the deflation of the power of the Church (though it remains more influential in Costa Rica than elsewhere in Central America) and of the would-be aristocratic families. Guardia, to legitimize his regime, wrote a new constitution in 1871; with a two-year interruption, it lasted for three-quarters of a century.

What has been called the first comparatively free and popular election which the Republic had ever known was held in 1889. It resulted in a lasting increase of political consciousness. Presidential manipulation of politics and overshadowing of the legislature were not unknown thereafter, but they were less bald and blunt. Completion of presidential terms, unmarred by coups, revolutions, or assassinations, became the standard pattern.

The one exception occurred early in 1917 when the war minister, General Federico Tinoco, overthrew the incumbent president, Alfredo González, and installed himself as a dictator. But Costa Ricans do not suffer dictators gladly, and after two and a half years Tinoco was forced out. The period from 1919 to 1936 was one of transition and some ferment. An older generation of leaders was passing; new and younger faces were coming onto the political stage. Perhaps the most articulate of these was Manuel Mora, an able professional who in 1929 organized the Costa Rican Communist party. This was the first party in the country to have an ideological base; earlier and many later ones were personalistic parties, usually with flimsy organizations.

In 1936 the National Republican party succeeded in electing a president, and he was followed in 1940 by a party colleague, Dr. Rafael A. Calderón Guardia. Calderón Guardia stepped up the pace of reform which antagonized some of Costa Rica's wealthier individuals and families. Calderón Guardia then swung toward more cooperation with Mora and the Communists. In 1943, following the ostensible dissolution of the Comintern, the Communists had reorganized as the Vanguardia Popular and even received the scarcely veiled approval of San José Archbishop Víctor Sanabria.

The National Republican party elected Teodoro Picado president in 1944 and also won a majority of legislative seats; four Vanguardia members were elected to the legislature. Communist influence in the Picado administration resulted in the formation of two new parties, a simple matter in Costa Rica. They were the relatively conservative National Union party (Partido de Unión Nacional, or PUN) led by Otilio Ulate, a prominent San José newspaper publisher, and the more liberally oriented Social Democratic party, whose principal leader was José ("Pepe") Figueres, a prosperous coffee grower who advocated a broader socioeconomic program for the government and vigorously attacked Communist penetration.

The February 1948 elections provided the critical mass which triggered a political explosion. Calderón Guardia sought reelection as the National Republican candidate. The other parties united behind Ulate as the National Union candidate. Campaigning was far more bitter than Costa Rica had ever experienced. The electoral tribunal announced that Ulate had won, but two days later the Picado-dominated legislative assembly decided to annul the elections.

This action was the cue for Figueres to lead a small-scale popular uprising on behalf of Ulate. The movement quickly snowballed and after a few weeks forced Picado from power, sending him and Calderón Guardia into exile in Nicaragua. Figueres became president of a provisional junta which governed for eighteen months and undertook a number of reforms, including the drafting of a new constitution. In November 1949 Figueres voluntarily turned the presidency over to Ulate, who served a four-year term.

Figueres became increasingly dissatisfied with the moderate course of Ulate's administration. Between 1949 and 1953 he gathered around himself a group of young men, fired them with his own enthusiasm for social reform, and organized the National Liberation party (Partido de Liberación Nacional, or PLN) on the foundations of his earlier Social Democratic party. He ran as its presidential candidate in 1953 and was overwhelmingly elected. His comprehensive but well-designed reform program could not be fully realized, but he brought to Costa Rica more of a social revolution than it had yet experienced, as important, perhaps, for the changed political psychology of the country as for its specific legislative enactments.

A split among National Liberation party leaders resulted in the 1958 election by a narrow margin of Mario Echandi, the National Union candidate. His administration was moderate, less conservative than opponents had feared, just as Figueres had turned out to be less radical than his enemies had dolefully forecast. In 1962 Ulate was nominated as the National Union candidate for the following year's elections, and the now reunited National Liberation party named Francisco Orlich, a close collaborator of Figueres, as its nominee. Orlich was elected in February 1962, and the National Liberation party was again returned to power. But party control changed once more when, in February 1966, José Trejos, the PUN candidate, won the presidency over Daniel Oduber, nominee of the PLN.

In June 1968 Figueres announced his candidacy for the PLN presidential nomination in 1970, a declaration that led to Oduber's withdrawal as a potential candidate. Despite early doubts about the strength of its hold over Costa Rican youth, PLN seemed to have retained sufficient support from this group. In the elections on February 1, 1970, Figueres won a new term with a vote of 295,000 to 222,000 over former president Mario Echandi. The remaining votes were distributed among three minor candidates.

In the peaceful elections of 1974, the presidency passed to Figueres's political protegé, Daniel Oduber Quirós. It was the first time in history that the PLN had won a second consecutive presidential election.

The 1978 elections, which gave United Opposition (Unidad Opositora, or UO) candidate Rodrigo Carazo Odio 50 percent of the vote, cost over $11 million. Carazo's major campaign issue was the presence of the fugitive American financier Robert Vesco and Vesco's close links with prominent members of the PLN. Carazo promised Vesco would be expelled if he were elected, but his supporters did not gain a majority in the Assembly. Of the fifty-seven available seats, twenty-seven went to the United Opposition, twenty-five to the PLN, three to the People United (Pueblo Unido, or PU), and one each to the constituency of Cartago and the leader of the Popular Front (Frente Popular, or FP).

In recent years Costa Rica has demonstrated on several occasions its ability and willingness to abide by electoral results, even when they favored opposition candidates. Democracy seems as firmly planted in Costa Rica as it is precarious in other Central American republics.

GOVERNMENTAL AND POLITICAL STRUCTURES

The Costa Rican presidency is as different from that in the other Central American states as the country's ethnic composition is unlike that elsewhere in the isthmus. The president is elected for a four-year term and is almost always a civilian—not primarily because of constitutional prescription but because of political tradition. Indeed, the civilian tone of the government is one of its most basic characteristics; Costa Rica has not had a military presidency since 1917–1919 and even then it had become the exception rather than the rule. The president is assisted by two elected vice-presidents and a cabinet. The president, of course, names the cabinet, which currently includes fourteen portfolios.

As a result of the effort to manipulate the 1948 election, the new constitution went as far as any in Latin America to assure adequate restriction on the filling of the presidency and control of the office once filled. The new document specified that the Supreme Electoral Tribunal should have absolute control of the election. It provided that eight years must elapse after expiration of a term before a president could again run for reelection. The president's power of decree is severely limited, and the president may not suspend constitutional guarantees unless the legislature is in recess; since the legislature is in session most of the year, this is an important restriction. The comptroller general and certain other officials are appointed by the legislative assembly for eight-year terms, and they assume office in the middle of the president's term. Terms of the many fully or partly autonomous agencies are staggered; therefore, an executive's term is well along before appointees (who in many cases must be confirmed by the legislature) constitute a majority within an agency.

Restrictions on the executive are not merely constitutional; they are also political. The political climate is hostile to anyone even remotely resembling a poseur; the typical Latin American pomp, ceremony, and aloofness of the presidential office are entirely absent in Costa Rica. Even though the tenacious tradition of democracy quickly whittles any presidential delusions of grandeur down to size, it is still through political channels that presidents gain, if they can, governmental weight and influence. Recent executives like Ulate and Echandi and even Orlich have mostly been content to operate within the constitutional trammels of the office. If a president's party controls a majority of the legislature (and recently only Figueres and Orlich have) the president obviously has fewer difficulties. True, a more charismatic and dynamic president, such as Figueres, can exert greater leadership, but this is largely because of his influence on public opinion. In general, the dimensions of the presidential office in Costa Rica are the most modest to be found anywhere in Latin America.

In contrast the legislature enjoys an independence, even an irresponsible independence, not present elsewhere in Latin America. The fifty-seven members of the single-chamber legislative assembly are all elected for four-year terms concurrently with the president, but they are not eligible for reelection until after an intervening term. Thus, a reelected president will not have many of the same legislators in office during the second term. Proportional representation for the legislature, while not constitutionally imposed, is used in practice.

The legislature holds two regular annual sessions of three months each. This would normally leave the legislators free for half the year, but the long-standing practice of holding special sessions (allegedly in large part so that the members can collect the generous per diem pay) means that the legislative assembly actually operates for virtually the entire year. Daily sessions, though often short, are lively and even boisterous. The legislature can and does interpellate cabinet members; even the president may get a rough going-over at times.

The Costa Rican judiciary, too, exercises an unusual degree of independence. The seventeen members of the supreme court are elected for eight-year terms by the legislature, and unless a justice is turned down by the assembly by a two-thirds vote at the end of that period, the individual continues in office. The supreme court possesses—and occasionally uses—the power of judicial review.

Local government in Costa Rica differs in a number of ways from its other Central American counterparts. The major subdivision is the province rather than the department. The seven provinces have presidentially appointed governors but no legislative councils; they are, in fact, merely administrative units subject to the supervision of the minister of government. Roughly equivalent to the *municipio* in many Latin American states is the Costa Rican canton. Each of the sixty-eight cantons has a popularly elected council, but local budgets are scrutinized by a national official. The cantons are subdivided into 383 districts.

Perhaps what is most significant about local government in Costa Rica is that democracy is so lightly rooted. But democracy in Costa Rica is essentially a national trait, not a local one.

It is in the role of the individual in the national Costa Rican community that the most important contribution to the democratic viability of the nation is probably to be found. Almost a century of relatively uniformly democratic procedures, with serious challenges only in 1917 and 1948, have bred in Costa Ricans a sense of the value of their own participation in the governing process. They guard it jealously and exercise it vigorously, though not always responsibly.

The bill of rights is detailed and realistic. An extensive set of constitutional amendments in 1943 for the first time established social as well as individual rights. These were carried over substantially intact into the constitution of 1949. The vote is given to all citizens over the age of eighteen.

Party Structures

Political parties are less well matured in Costa Rica than the democratic state of the country would lead one to expect. The explanation may lie partly in the intimate, highly localized character of the political community. This logically adds to the difficulty of maintaining formal, tightly organized, well-disciplined, permanent, and ideologically based parties. Since the middle of the century, however, greater party longevity seems to have been attained, and the general pattern of party competition appears somewhat more stabilized.

At least one current party, aside from the opportunistically motivated Communist organization (later rechristened the Vanguardia Popular and now outlawed), has an ideological base. Parties are still not well disciplined; schisms can and do occur. A multiparty pattern, encouraged by a legislative (not a constitutional) prescription of proportional representation, seems reasonably well established. Personalism is still a major factor in the organization and continuance of individual parties, and these groups have yet a long way to go toward genuine institutionalization.

The largest, best organized, and most ideologically based of the contemporary groups is the National Liberation party (Partido de Liberación Nacional, or PLN). The creation of José Figueres in 1952, it continues to be dominated by him, although it has developed important secondary leaders. The PLN is semi-socialist but strongly anti-Communist and in general can be described as a national revolutionary party. The PLN became Costa Rica's most effective political group, possibly because it appealed to the imagination of the younger generation of the electorate.

Although the PLN candidate won the presidential elections in 1974, it won only twenty-six of the fifty-seven seats in the Assembly. The 1978 elections were lost to the Unidad Opositora coalition, partly because of the Robert Vesco scandal. Vesco's name was closely identified with the party and its leaders, former Presidents Figueres and Oduber.

The National Unification party (Partido de Unificación Nacional, or PUN) is an electoral group incorporating several conservative, traditional, and personalist parties; the PUN includes: the Republican party (Partido Republicano, or PR), the personal vehicle of former President Rafael Angel Calderón Guardia who died in 1970; the Revolutionary Civic Union (Partido Unión Cívica Revolucionaria, or UCR), led by Frank Marshall Jiménez; the National Union party (Partido Unión Nacional, or PUN), which was led by former president Otilio Ulate Blanco, who died in 1973; and the Authentic Republican Union party (Partido Unión Republicana Auténtica, or PURA), headed by former president Mario Echandi Jiménez. The National Unification party won sixteen legislative seats in the election of February 1974 and no seats in the 1978 elections. In 1976 the Calderonist Republicans withdrew from the National Unification party to form the Calderonist Republican party (Partido Republicano Calderonista, or PRC) under the leadership of the former president's son, Rafael Angel Calderón Fournier.

The Democratic Renovation party (Partido de Renovación Democrática, or PDR) was formed in 1969 by Rodrigo Carazo Odio when he left the PLN after losing the presidential nomination to José Figueres. The party captured only three seats in the Legislative Assembly in 1974 but went on to capture the presidency in 1978 (with help from four other parties). The Unidad Opositora coalition was formed by the alliance of the Renovación Democrática, the Partido Republicano Calderonista, the Christian Democrats, and the Unión Popular to support the successful candidacy of Carazo as president in 1978.

The National Independent party (Partido Nacional Independiente, or PNI) was organized to promote the 1974 presidential candidacy of a wealthy Costa Rican businessman, Jorge González Marten. The People United (Pueblo Unido or PU) is a Communist-Socialist coalition which won three legislative seats in the 1978 election.

Other groups or agencies that can exert pressure on Costa Rican politics are few and simple: Newspapers are vigorous and for the most part party-oriented, but they do not rank among the hemisphere's outstanding periodicals. The Catholic church is probably stronger spiritually, if not politically, than in any other isthmian country; its image is a curious mixture of conservatism and liberalism. Organized labor is predominantly affiliated with non-Communist international groups, though a small, liberal Costa Rican labor organization, *Rerum Novarum,* operates under the aegis of the Church.

DEVELOPMENTAL PROSPECTS

Costa Rica should be best remembered as the tiny Central American nation that has been able to maintain a democratic system without an army. The latter part of the statement deserves qualification. It is true—and not surprising in view of the circumstances of its writing—that the 1949 constitution proscribed the army "as a permanent institution." In its place, however, a National Guard of twelve hundred men has been established. It is well equipped and has had some practical experience in more than one small-scale invasion from Nicaragua, but it is essentially civilian-oriented. It is far from reflecting the minuscule militarism of the other Central American countries and would be highly vulnerable to a major offensive from the latter.

Costa Rica has excelled in democracy. In the past twenty-five years, seven peaceful presidential elections have been held. The seventh electoral contest witnessed the surprising defeat of the dominant National Liberation party's candidate by a political underdog, Rodrigo Carazo. This marked a break with the *continuismo*[3] pattern which has governed Costa Rican politics since 1948.

The whole political climate of Costa Rica is, indeed, civilian, democratic, egalitarian. Political behavior is not always as mature as it might be, but still, the political ethos is a refreshing contrast to that of the nation's isthmian neighbors.

ASSESSMENT OF THE CENTRAL AMERICAN FIVE

As noted in the introduction to this chapter, the five Central American states do vary—in population, literacy, area, and organization. They also share some things in common. Compared to the rest of Latin America, the area is economically and politically underdeveloped. During the early years of the Central American Common Market, the five nations advanced well beyond being simply "banana republics," but the advancement of those early years has been slowed or become almost nonexistent today. The poor in the region continue to get poorer; land and money remain in the hands of a few. Violence and terror are daily occurrences in much of the region. The continued bitterness between Honduras and El Salvador keeps the memory of the Soccer War alive.

[3] *Continuismo* refers to a quasi-legal practice of continuing oneself in office.

The Sandinista victory in Nicaragua has given the military governments of Guatemala, Honduras, and El Salvador cause to be concerned about the possible pinprick effect on the Central American nervous system. All three countries had supported Somoza's regime until just weeks before his downfall.

In Guatemala, where the landed elite and military continue to hold the reins of government, the Guerrilla Army of the Poor has been encouraged by the events in Nicaragua and has intensified its campaign against the government. Honduras, where the Army has effectively taken over the role of government, is experimenting with land reform programs whose possible spread effects are feared by the conservative regime in Guatemala. The military coup in El Salvador in October 1979 was staged to break the momentum of the well-organized opposition groups. The inexperienced junta which was placed in power is hard-pressed for solutions to cope with the increasing frustrations among dissident sectors in the country. Costa Rica, a political world apart from its military neighbors, had opposed the Somoza regime for years and had broken off diplomatic relations with Nicaragua in 1978. Three members of the Nicaraguan junta spent much of the last year in San José before returning to Nicaragua in July 1979.

As a result of the Nicaraguan situation, the Carter administration has impressed on the governments of Honduras, El Salvador, and Guatemala its concern about human and political rights' violations and has supported even the smallest land reform attempts and social programs in Guatemala and El Salvador. Realistically, however, the United States knows it may well be too late to begin policies that would turn the tide and prevent a Nicaraguan-type revolution in those countries. Cuba, for its part, is moving swiftly to unify dissident groups in those countries to prepare them for the revolutionary struggles ahead.

In other parts of Latin America, reactions to the concern that the overthrow of the Somoza dynasty could lead to another Cuba were mixed. While the military regimes in Chile, Argentina, Brazil, Uruguay, and Paraguay decided to take a more cautious "wait and see" attitude, the five countries in the Andean Bloc, as well as Mexico, Panama, and Costa Rica not only supported the revolution but have pledged to work with the provisional government in its objectives to bring about a freely elected government.

Although it will be years before the full impact of the Nicaraguan revolution is felt throughout Central America, the idea of other Latin countries coming to the aid of their neighbor to restore human dignity and liberty augurs well for the future of the region.

REFERENCES

ADAMS, RICHARD N. *Cultural Surveys of Panama, Nicaragua, Guatemala, El Salvador, Honduras.* Reprint of 1957 ed. Detroit: Blaine, Ethridge, 1976.

———."The Development of the Guatemalan Military." *Studies in Comparative International Development* 4:5 (1969), 91–110.

AMERINGER, CHARLES D. *Don Pepe: A Political Biography of José Figueres of Costa Rica.* Albuquerque: University of New Mexico, 1979.

ANDERSON, CHARLES W. "Central American Political Parties: A Functional Approach." *Western Political Quarterly* 15 (March 1960), 125–139.

———."Politics and Development Policy in Central America." *Midwest Journal of Political Science* 5 (November 1961), 332–350.

ANDERSON, THOMAS P. *Matanza* (El Salvador). Lincoln: University of Nebraska Press, 1971.

BALCÁREL, JOSÉ LUIS. "Crítica de la situación crítica de Guatemala." *Cuadernos Americanos* 174:1 (January–February 1971), 7–44.

BELL, BELDEN, ed. *Nicaragua: An Ally Under Siege.* Washington, D.C.: Council on American Affairs, 1978.

BROWNING, DAVID. "The Rise and Fall of the Central American Common Market." Review article in *Journal of Latin American Studies* 6:1 (May 1974), 161.

BUSEY, JAMES L. *Notas sobre la democracia Costanicense.* San José: Editorial Costa Rica, 1968.

———."Foundations of Political Contrasts: Costa Rica and Nicaragua." *Western Political Quarterly* 11 (September 1958), 627–659.

CHAMORRO CARDENAL, PEDRO J. *Estirpe Sangrienta: Los Somozas.* Buenos Aires, n.p., 1959.

COX, ISAAC J. *Nicaragua and the United States.* New York: Gordon Press, 1976.

DeNOGALES, RAFAEL. *The Looting of Nicaragua.* New York: Gordon Press, 1976.

DUNCAN, CHARLES F. *Patterns of Costa Rican Politics.* Boston: Allyn & Bacon, 1971.

ENGLISH, BURT H. *Liberación nacional in Costa Rica. The Development of a Political Party in a Transitional Society.* Gainesville: University of Florida Press, 1971.

GALEANO, EDUARDO. *Guatemala: Occupied Country.* New York: Monthly Review Press, 1969.

GEIGER, THEODORE. *Communism versus Progress in Guatemala.* Washington, D.C.: National Planning Association, 1953.

GILLIN, JOHN, and KALMAN H. SILVERT. "Ambiguities in Guatemala." *Foreign Affairs* 34 (April 1956), 469–482.

GOLDRICH, DANIEL. *Sons of the Establishment, Elite Youth in Panama and Costa Rica.* Skokie, Ill.: Rand McNally, 1966.

GOODSELL, JAMES N. "Guatemala: Edge of an Abyss?" *Current History* 62 (February 1972), 104–108.

HALSELL, GRACE. *Getting to Know Guatemala and the Two Honduras.* London: F. Muller, 1964.

JOHNSON, KENNETH F. "On the Guatemalan Political Violence." *Politics and Society* 4:1 (Fall 1973), 55–82.

KALJARVI, THORSTEN. *Central America: Land of Lords and Lizards.* New York: D. Van Nostrand, 1962.

KANTOR, HARRY. "Contemporary Government in Central America." Chapter 8 in *The Caribbean: The Central American Area,* ed. by A. Curtis Wilgus. Gainesville: University of Florida Press, 1971.

———. *The Costa Rican Election of 1953: A Case Study.* Gainesville: University of Florida Press, 1958.

McCAMANT, JOHN F. *Development Assistance in Central America.* New York: Holt, Rinehart & Winston, 1968.

MARTIN, PERCY F. *Salvador of the Twentieth Century.* New York: Gordon Press, 1977.

MARTZ, JOHN D. *Central America: The Crisis and the Challenge.* Chapel Hill: University of North Carolina Press, 1959.

————. "Costa Rican Electoral Trends, 1953–1966." *Western Political Quarterly* 20 (December 1967), 888–909.

MILLETT, RICHARD *Gardians Historia of the Dynasty.* Maryknoll, N. Y.: Orbis, 1977.

MONGE ALFARO, CARLOS. *Historia de Costa Rica.* San José: Imprenta Trejos Hermanos, 1966.

OSBORNE, LILLY DE J. *Four Keys to El Salvador.* New York: Funk, 1956.

PALMER, THOMAS W., JR. *Search for a Latin American Policy.* Gainesville: University of Florida Press, 1962.

PARKER, FRANKLIN D. *The Central American Republics.* London: Oxford University Press, 1964.

PERERA, VICTOR. "Guatemala: Always La Violencia." *New York Times Magazine,* June 13, 1971.

ROSENTHAL, MARIO. *Guatemala: The Story of an Emergent Latin American Democracy.* Boston: Twayne, 1962.

SCHNEIDER, RONALD. *Communism in Guatemala, 1944–1954.* New York: Holt, Rinehart & Winston, 1959.

STOKES, WILLIAM S. *Honduras: An Area Study in Government.* Madison: University of Wisconsin Press, 1950.

SZULC, TAD, ed. *The United States and the Caribbean.* Englewood Cliffs, N.J.: Prentice-Hall, 1971.

WALKER, THOMAS W. *The Christian Democratic Movement in Nicaragua.* Tucson: University of Arizona Press, 1970.

4

PANAMA

The Politics of Artificiality

POLITICAL CULTURE AND ENVIRONMENT

From the time that Balboa, "on a peak in Darién," looked out over the great South Sea, the unique geographic value of Panama has been obvious. Panama is strategically located between the Caribbean and the Pacific on the isthmus linking North and South America. Colombia is to the east and Costa Rica to the west. The eastern portion of the country consists of a rain forest, and both coasts consist of lowlands. The Canal Zone, extending five miles on each side of the waterway, cuts across the country from Colón to Balboa. Panama's population (1,751,275 exclusive of the Canal Zone) is the smallest of the Latin American countries, and it ranks comparatively high in per capita wealth mainly because of the economic stimulus of the Canal.

Approximately 70 percent of the population is a mixture of Caucasian, Indian, and black; approximately 9 percent is pure Caucasian and 14 percent pure black; the balance are of Indian and of other origins. Panama numbers among its resources rich farmland (about half the people are farmers), huge copper deposits, and the Canal. Bananas are the most important export crop, followed by sugar and coffee.

Effective Panama is only that part immediately surrounding Panama City at the Pacific end of the Canal, with perhaps a satellite enclave in the area around Colón at the Atlantic end of the waterway. The rest of the republic just does not carry much weight politically or economically; the section from a few miles east of Panama City to the Colombian border is practically terra incognita.

Under Spanish rule in the 1500s and 1600s Panama served as the shipping route for Inca treasure to Spain. The Spanish were overthrown in 1821, and Panama became a province of Colombia in that country's various political and administrative transmutations. Panama City catered only to the traffic across the isthmus. It was no more than a transient settlement, long treated as a stepchild by Colombia; secession was more than once discussed in Panama.

On November 3, 1903, Panama declared its independence from Colombia, assisted by President Teddy Roosevelt and the U.S. Marines, who protected the fledgling government. Panama, of course, was indebted to the United States for its assistance. In fact, it was so grateful that on November 18 of that year the United States and Panama signed the Hay-Bunau-Varilla Treaty, generously giving the United States the delimited zone "as if it were the sovereign" for a payment of $10 million plus $250,000 a year. The phrase in quotes would later cause Panama great political and diplomatic anguish.

Intensive measures to rid the country of the mosquitoes that caused yellow fever and malaria were begun in 1904, and construction of the canal was started in 1907. On August 14, 1914, the first ship went from the Atlantic to the Pacific through the Canal.

Panama, however, was ill prepared for a fully independent life. Its only nucleus was the city of Panama, which was simply superimposed on the country, not truly a part of it. Even within Panama City eight or ten families who frequently intermarried—Alfaro, Amador, Arias, Arosemena, Boyd, Chiari, Obaldía, and a few others—dominated the local society and the economic and political life of the entire country.

After 1914, when the Canal was opened, Panamanian life revolved almost wholly around "the Ditch." A large part of public and private income, at least in effective Panama, derived directly or indirectly from the Canal. The cities of Panama and Colón became cosmopolitan marketplaces for the world's consumer merchandise and took on a certain tawdriness. Politics was flimsy, government unstable.

A new Canal treaty negotiated in 1936 increased the size of United States annuity payments to compensate for the recently devalued dollar and also abandoned the United States guarantee of Panamanian independence. The abandoned guarantee, if it had any effect on Panamanian domestic politics, probably encouraged even more instability.

Arnulfo Arias, who appeared to admire Nazism, was elected president in 1940 but was ousted in October 1941; he came close to winning reelection in 1948. The following year, with the help of José Antonio Remón, chief of the 3,300-man police force, Arias was reelected. Six months later he was again ousted when Remón found him uncooperative. It soon became clear that Remón was the strongman in Panamanian politics as he made and unmade four presidents in five years. In 1952, after Remón had himself legally elected

The basic provisions of the two treaties deserve brief mention. The Panama Canal Treaty approved on April 18 supersedes and terminates previous treaties concerning the Canal. It also defines how the Canal is to be operated and defended until the year 2000. According to the treaty, Panama will assume "full responsibility for the management, operation, and maintenance of the Canal" when the treaty ends on December 31, 1999. In the meantime, however, the Panama Canal Commission, a new United States agency of five Americans and four Panamanians, will be responsible for operating the Canal. When the treaty took effect on October 1, 1979, Panama assumed jurisdiction of the Canal Zone, which is scheduled to be integrated into Panama during a thirty-month transition period. Until 1999 the United States will assume the major responsibility for the Canal's defense and for organizing a combined board of officers for consultation and cooperation on defense affairs. Both countries are sworn by the treaty to negotiate only with each other for a sea-level canal across Central America.

Panama further agreed not to become involved in any such undertaking except with the United States. Several reservations concerning the Panama Canal Treaty were adopted by the United States Senate. One called for the United States to use force unilaterally if required; another specified conditions under which intervention was permissible (for example, to keep the Canal open) and not permissible (to interfere in Panama's domestic affairs). Still another dealt with nullifying the mutually exclusive commitment clause on a sea-level canal. After the signing and ratification of the treaties by the U.S. Senate in 1978, the U.S. House of Representatives next had to approve legislation to implement the treaties. Approval came on June 21, 1979, by a vote of 224 to 202—but only after a complete rehash of the entire Canal debate and charges by the treaty's opponents that Panama was aiding and abetting the revolution in Nicaragua by giving arms and asylum to the Sandinista guerrillas.

On the political front Torrijos has shown his desire to return the country to political normality by naming a high-level commission to study ways of changing the constitution and reinstating political parties. Elections in August 1978 for the 505 seats in the new national assembly gave Torrijos a majority, enabling him to put into the presidential office anyone of his choosing, which many expected would be himself. Instead he nominated Aristides Royo, Minister of Education, as his choice for president. His abrupt passing of the reins to a civilian and dropping out of the Panamanian political limelight led to speculation that Torrijos preferred to leave the presidential office to Royo while he continued to head the National Guard during its return to the barracks and presumably out of politics.

A more probable hypothesis would be that General Torrijos will use his time to build a broader political base for his presidential candidacy in 1984, a base including political sectors other than the nationalist Panamanian party (Partido Panameñista, or PP) which has been his chief political support for many years.

GOVERNMENTAL AND POLITICAL STRUCTURES

The governmental structure in Panama is almost incidental alongside its tortured politics. The 1972 constitution established the office of Supreme Leader —the chief of government—of the Panamanian Revolution and the ceremonial offices of president and vice-president. A 505-member People's Assembly granted actual executive authority to General Torrijos. The president and vice-president were elected by the assembly for six-year terms. Historically, the presidency has almost always been limited to members of the oligarchy, and almost without exception the president has been a civilian.

Cabinet positions, at present numbering eleven, are filled by the chief of government. The National Assembly of Community Representatives was elected in 1972 for a six-year term. Each community is allowed one representative, regardless of the size of the electorate. Its primary function has been to legitimize the executive actions of the legislative council, composed of General Torrijos, the president, vice-president, the cabinet, and nine members of the assembly, including the assembly president.

The nine appointed members of the supreme court serve eighteen-year terms, and one justice is appointed every two years. Two superior courts, several circuit courts, and a larger number of local courts complete the judicial structure.

Panama is divided into nine territorial provinces and one territory, each with presidentially appointed governors. The provinces are subdivded into sixty-three municipalities, which have elected mayors and councils. Sentiment for local control of local affairs, while still not strong, is increasing.

Party Systems

Before the 1968 coup, which brought General Torrijos to power and ended political party activity, political parties proliferated with abandon. Because of their general transience, it is logical to look for political tendencies or groupings within the Panamanian party panorama. In the 1968 election, for example, the government candidate, David Samudio, was backed by the coalition of the People's Alliance (Alianza del Pueblo), which included the Agrarian Labor, the National Liberal, and the Progressive National parties as well as the Movement of National Liberation; the victorious Arnulfo Arias was supported by the other coalition, the National Union of Opposition (Unión

Nacional de Oposición), which included his own Panameñista party, the Democratic Action party, the National Patriotic Coalition, the Third Nationalist party, the Republican party, and two groupings called the United Front and the Independent Liberals. The Christian Democratic party ran its own candidates.

For more than a quarter of a century Arnulfo Arias has exploited nationalism, chiefly in the guise of xenophobia. He has built this into a Panameñista movement which, given the socioeconomic distortion and lack of integration that are normal in Panama, has had wide appeal. Nationalism has been demagogically presented as an answer to the chronic frustrations confronting many Panamanians. This nationalism has at times been badly manipulated, but it is a brand of nationalism that is difficult to control. Various student groups in the national university and the principal secondary school, the National Institute, also invoke nationalism but with more ideological overtones than are generated by the arnulfistas (followers of Arnulfo Arias).

The Christian Democratic party, generally similar to such movements in other Latin American countries, is a relative newcomer to the Panamanian political arena. Nevertheless it has been highly vocal. When Torrijos announced on March 8, 1978, that political parties would not be allowed to interfere in the August 1978 national assembly elections, eyebrows were raised in party circles. The Christian Democratic party threatened to abstain from the 1978 electoral contest unless given certain minimal guarantees, such as impartiality at the polls and political noninvolvement of the Guardia Nacional.

Reacting to General Torrijos's hard line on parties, political leaders such as David Samudio of the Liberal party emphasized that if the regular channels for popular participation remained closed, Panama might well experience the same kind of anomic activity that has plagued other Central American countries, notably El Salvador, Guatemala, and Nicaragua.

At the end of his constitutional term as head of government in October 1978, Torrijos lifted the ban on party activity. Political parties were allowed to gain legal status by submitting the signatures of thirty thousand supporters to the government by June 1979. A new left-of-center populist party, the Democratic Revolutionary Party (Partido Revolucionario Democrático, or PRD) founded by former Vice-President Gerardo González and González Revilla as the official government party, was the first to gain legal recognition. David Samudio's National Liberal Party (Partido Liberal Nacional, or PLN) was the second party to meet the quota of thirty thousand signatures and was officially recognized in June 1979. Other political parties still seeking the necessary signatures to qualify for legal status are the communist People's Party of Panama (Partido del Pueblo de Panamá, or PPP); the Popular Front (Frente Amplio Popular, or Frampo), considered to be slightly left of the PRD on the political spectrum; and the conservative Agrarian Labor Party (Partido

Laborista Agrario). Two opposition parties, the Panameñistas and the Christian Democrats, refused to register.

DEVELOPMENTAL PROSPECTS

Underlying the pulling and hauling of these disparate elements is the economic and social picture—the great economic underdevelopment of the country; the labor unrest stemming from the continued inflation and rising unemployment; the enormous imbalance between imports and exports; the lack of ethnic, social, economic, and political assimilation of the West Indian blacks; and, above all, the continued presence of the canal with its alien and sometimes aloof personnel arrogating to itself a superiority galling to many Panamanians.

At this juncture, all that can be said for the new Canal treaties is that they do represent a major effort by both the United States and Panama to reduce friction and create the necessary cooperative environment needed to help heal a political sore which has been festering since 1903.

An atmosphere of cautious optimism about the importance of the accord seems to prevail in official Panamanian circles. Torrijos, as well as other Panamanians, realized that the signing of the accord merely concluded a thirteen-year negotiating process.

After the Canal negotiators reached an agreement on principles for a new Canal treaty in August 1977, General Torrijos was quoted as saying, "The Treaty is like a little pebble which we shall be able to carry for 23 years, and that is better than the stake we have had to carry in our heart."[2]

What this all suggests is that the last chapter on the Panamanian Canal undoubtedly has not yet been written.

REFERENCES

Arosemena Arias, Carlos. "Emerging Panama: Politics and Problems." Chapter 9 in *The Caribbean: The Central American Area,* ed. by A. Curtis Wilgus, Gainesville: University of Florida Press, 1961.

Biesanz, John B., and Mavis Biesanz. *The People of Panama.* Reprint of 1955 edition. Westport, Conn.: Greenwood, 1977.

Biesanz, John B., Mavis Biesanz, and Luke M. Smith. "Panamanian Politics." *Journal of Politics* 14 (August 1952), 386–402.

Burns, E. Bradford. "Panama: A Search for Independence." *Current History* 72 (February 1977), 65–67.

Busey, James L. *Political Aspects of the Panama Canal.* Tucson: University of Arizona Press, 1974.

Commission on U.S.–Latin American Relations. *The United States and Latin America: Next Steps.* New York: Center for InterAmerican Studies, December 20, 1976.

[2] *Time* 110:8 (August 22, 1977), 10.

Cox, Robert G. "Choices for Partnership or Bloodshed in Panama." Pp. 132–184 in *The Americas in a Changing World*, Commission on U.S.–Latin American Relations. New York: Quadrangle/New York Times, 1975.

Department of State, Bureau of Public Affairs, Office of Media Services. *Documents Associated with the Panama Canal Treaties.* Washington, D.C.: U.S. Department of State, 1977.

Goldrich, Daniel. *Sons of the Establishment; Elite Youth in Panama and Costa Rica.* Skokie, Ill.: Rand McNally, 1966.

Goldrich, Daniel, and Edward W. Scott. "Developing Political Orientations of Panamanian Students." *Journal of Politics* 23 (February 1961), 84–107.

Gravel, Mike. *The Panama Canal, A Re-examination; A Report to the Committee on Environment and Public Works,* U.S. Senate, Washington, D.C.: U.S. Government Printing Office, July 1977.

Gudeman, Stephan. *The Demise of a Rural Economy: From Subsistence to Capitalism in a Latin American Village.* London and Boston: Routledge & Kegan Paul, 1978.

LeFeber, Walter. *The Panama Canal: The Crisis in Historical Perspective.* New York: Oxford University Press, 1978.

Lindsay, F. *Panama.* 2 vols. New York: Gordon Press, 1976.

Liss, Sheldon B. *The Canal: Aspects of U.S.-Panamanian Relations.* Notre Dame, Ind.: University of Notre Dame Press, 1967.

McCullough, David. *The Path Between the Seas.* New York: Simon & Schuster, 1977.

Martínez, Orlando. *Panama Canal.* London and New York: Gordon and Cremonesi, 1978.

Pippin, Larry L. *The Remón Era.* Stanford, Calif.: Stanford University Press, 1964.

Poppino, Rollie. *International Communism in Latin America.* New York: Free Press, 1964.

Ryan, Paul B. *The Panama Canal Controversy: U.S. Diplomacy and Defense Interests.* Stanford, Calif.: Hoover Institution Press, 1977.

Smith, Norman M. "Our Changing Role in Panama: An Overview." *Parameters: Journal of the U.S. Army War College* 8:3 (September 1978), 10–16.

U.S. House of Representitives, Committee on International Relations. *A New Panama Canal Treaty: A Latin American Imperative.* Washington, D.C.: U.S. Government Printing Office, 1976.

U.S. Senate, Committee on Foreign Relations. *Senate Debate on the Panama Canal Treaties; A Compendium of Major Statements, Documents, Record Votes and Relevant Events.* Washington, D.C.: U.S. Government Printing Office, 1979.

Part Three

THE CARIBBEAN

5

CUBA

The Politics
of Revolutionary
Development

POLITICAL CULTURE AND ENVIRONMENT

Cuba, Preston James maintains, is closer to the United States than any other republic of Latin America, even Mexico (though perhaps a question might be raised about Panama), in population nuclei, the orientation of political and economic interests, and such. Of course, he was writing B. C.—before Castro! Mexican politics has been conditioned by the country's closeness to the United States; Cuban politics has been far more affected, for better or worse, by the same factor.

During the last generation of the colonial era propinquity to the United States had a significant effect on Cuba. Now Cuba has become the dark and fateful ground of current revolutionary experimentation in Latin America, again in large measure conditioned by the closeness and impact of the United States.

Most of Cuba's slightly more than 44,000 square miles is usable for agriculture; only three other countries of Latin America (Uruguay, El Salvador, and Argentina, in that order) have more usable farmland. Of its more than 9,600,000 people (1978 estimate), approximately 40 percent of those economically active were engaged in agriculture. Cuba's agriculture economy is distinctive; for years it has been one of Latin America's prime examples of a monocultural economy. Sugar, the island's bitter sweet, still accounts for at least 80 percent of the value of all exports.

In the late 1930s the composition of Spanish migration to Cuba began to change significantly as numerous refugees from the Spanish Civil War found asylum there. The new immigrants included many urbanites with industrial or technical training and radical political orientation. The Castro regime later used some of them as political organizers and operators of nationalized industries.

In recent years Cuba's approximately 35,000 Chinese have been in an ideological tug of war between Nationalist and Communist China. Cuba's English-speaking population (sometimes called the ABCs—Americans, British, and Canadians) has decreased since Castro came to power.

Cuba is a highly urbanized country. The 1970 census indicated that 46 percent of the population were city dwellers, a percentage exceeded only in Argentina and Chile. Like many Latin American countries, it has its megalopolis—Havana, with approximately one-third of the island's population. Hence the economic, political, and social centers are in the capital city. Havana's prominence has significantly affected the political psychology of the fidelista movement. The movement was originally geared, at least ostensibly, to the plight of the underprivileged rural population, but Castro quickly discovered that the more dynamic and malleable elements of the population were in Havana, especially among university students.

Cuban Independence

Cuba's emergence as an independent state came about of course as a product of the Spanish-American War and the subsequent United States occupation of the island for three and a half years. As a condition of independence the United States required Cuba to accept the Platt Amendment, a series of leading strings which formally established the basis of continuing relations between the two countries. The Cuban constituent assembly was forced to add the Platt Amendment as an appendix to the new Cuban constitution.

The Platt Amendment, even though abrogated willingly by the United States in 1934, is still a matter of controversy in Cuba and has been made an important whipping boy by the Castro regime. The feelings of inferiority and futility which it implanted in the minds of many politically articulate Cubans persisted for many years. For years *plattismo* was seen as a "yoke of foreign imperialism."

When Cuba gained independence in May 1902, it was at first under the leadership of Tomás Estrada Palma, a man of high rectitude but long a resident in the United States and indeed almost a stranger in his own land. Under his influence the island's constitution was—perhaps quite naturally—patterned after that of the United States, except, of course, that a federal system was not adopted. But it was political facts, not constitutional or even legal ones, which were to govern the course of Cuban public development in the coming years —as has, indeed, been true of most Latin American countries.

Estrada Palma was duly reelected in 1906, but Liberal party opponents soon revolted. The situation quickly reached a stalemate and reluctantly, the United States again intervened. The second intervention, under civilian rather than military administration, lasted for more than two years. During this time the United States governor sought to revise the electoral laws, reorganize the parties, and in other ways prepare Cubans to resume control of their island.

The new period of self-government began early in 1909 under José Miguel Gómez, Liberal party leader, who had been elected in the closing months of the United States administration. Gómez was perhaps Cuba's most typical president—genial, easy-going, popular, complaisant toward his friends, and not vindictive towards opponents. The presidency shifted from Liberals to Conservatives in 1912 with the election of Mario García Menocal[1] but it made no essential difference in administration: Corruption and cynicism continued. Menocal's second term in office differed only in degree from his first. Cuba's compliant entrance into World War I, only one day after that of the United States, permitted Menocal to govern more arbitrarily, but in general politics continued apart from the people; the more cultured elements in the Cuban community preferred not to be involved.

Alfredo Zayas, long a leader of the Liberal party, deserted that group in 1920 and formed the Popular party, an action indicative of the looseness of Cuban party lines and the ease of redrawing them. Allegedly with the blessing of Menocal, considerable Conservative support went to Zayas—enough, at least, to elect him president. Once in office he took Cuba still farther and faster along the road of political corruption and graft.

The Liberal party candidate lost to General Gerardo Machado y Morales in 1924. Machado started out with a considerable reservoir of popular confidence. As the 1928 elections approached he managed by bribery, patronage, and other means to dominate all three major parties—Liberal, Conservative, and Popular. He then easily induced a constituent assembly to amend the constitution to enable him to continue in the presidency for six years. The constituent assembly also performed a constitutional appendectomy by removing the Platt Amendment from the 1901 basic law.

Machado quickly became Cuba's first dictator. He closed the university because of hostile demonstrations, organized a Cuban gestapo which established a virtual reign of terror, jailed many opponents, exiled others, tortured some. The climax came on August 12, 1933. An army ultimatum forced the resignation and departure of Machado. Thus ended, with one or two minor exceptions, the domination of Cuban politics by the "men of '95," the group of political figures, most of them military men, who had used the resistance

[1]Menocal illustrates an irregularity occasionally found in the use of Latin American names. Under common usage he would have been known as García Menocal, but, as an exception— perhaps because he was educated in the United States, perhaps because his maternal ancestry was more prominent than his paternal—he chose to use his mother's surname.

movement against the Spanish as their springboard for entering politics and staying there for a long generation. Carlos Manuel de Céspedes became provisional president but was supplanted three weeks later by the sergeants' revolt.

Batista

The "sergeants' revolt" was masterminded by an army stenographer whose military responsibilities and innate canniness had given him an excellent working knowledge of army politics and the generally turbulent condition of Cuban affairs. Fulgencio Batista y Zaldívar proved to be a Cuban Warwick, a president-maker of pronounced success with a career longer than that of Sumner Welles. His coup was followed by a government junta of five, which soon gave way to the provisional presidency of Dr. Ramón Grau San Martín, a popular but previously nonpolitical medical professor. For seven years Batista pulled the strings from behind the scenes before he decided to enjoy the title as well as the substance of power.

Grau was political amateur. He was a naive reformer, and, had he been free of pressures from Batista, the United States, and the worldwide depression, he might have led a social revolution of sorts for Cuba. His proposals were generally popular, but the irregular manner of his accession almost automatically put him in disfavor with the U.S. State Department. Batista soon realized that, realistically, support from the United States was more important than support for Grau. Hence he jettisoned Grau and began his career of making and unmaking presidents. Grau's followers more or less spontaneously set up the Partido Revolucionario Cubano (Auténtico), soon familiarly shortened to the Auténticos. This proved to be a poorly disciplined and naive reform party with students as its chief strength; though initially idealistic, it later became cynical and corrupt.

In 1940 Batista made constitutional revision a prelude to his self-elevation to the presidency. The new constitution was extremely detailed and inclusive. Its chief structural innovation was a provision for a modified form of parliamentary government with a prime minister. A coalition of parties, none of them important alone, put Batista formally into the presidency in 1940, defeating Grau, the candidate of the Auténticos. Batista's victory was a personal rather than a party triumph. His term, from 1940 to 1944, was relatively uneventful and reasonably constructive, perhaps partially because insular prosperity permitted the heavy hand to relax somewhat.

In 1944 Batista imposed Carlos Saladrigas, his prime minister, on the conservative Democratic party as its presidential candidate. His principal opponent was Grau, candidate of the Auténticos. Surprisingly, Grau was elected. Batista retired to Florida to enjoy the several million dollars of wealth acquired since his sergeancy. In the years following his short first presidency,

Grau had learned much about politics. Although he perhaps remained personally honest during his second term, 1944–1948, his Auténtico colleagues certainly had no qualms about feeding heavily and noisily at the public trough. Irresponsibility, extravagance, and administrative looseness reached new heights despite Grau's gestures toward reform.

So considerable was the dissatisfaction with the Auténtico slide from rectitude that Eduardo ("Eddy") Chibás, long a staunch Auténtico, broke with Grau and formed the schismatic Cuban People's party, or Ortodoxos. The colorful Chibás was probably honest and certainly popular. He failed to be elected in 1948. He might have been elected in 1952 had he not, at the end of an impassioned radio broadcast on August 5, 1951, dramatically shot himself, ironically only moments after he had been cut off the air; he died eleven days later. Chibás was the most charismatic figure Cuban politics had yet produced; only Castro would later surpass him. The Grau-imposed Auténtico candidate in 1948, the affable and loyal Prime Minister Carlos Prío Socarrás, was easily elected. Corruption steadily increased, and governmental services progressively deteriorated.

Batista, who had prudently remained out of Cuba for some years, returned as an elected senator in 1948 and organized his own party. In the 1952 campaign he was again a candidate for the presidency. But when his early assessment seemed to indicate that he would have little chance in a free election, Batista decided to take a hand in molding history. On March 10, 1952, he consummated his second coup; in a tightly organized plot he smoothly took over control of the government, suspended the constitution and the congress (though continuing to pay its members), dissolved all political parties, exiled Prío, and put himself back in business as a dictator. Batista's actions did not initially arouse overt resistance, but neither did they attract enthusiasm. He subsequently described his rule as "mild, suave, and sweet," but this revealed either complete cynicism or an ironic sense of humor.

On July 26, 1953—a date destined to become politically famous—a young Cuban lawyer with a band of fewer than two hundred supporters undertook a preposterously futile attack on the Moncada barracks in Santiago. The young man was Fidel Castro. He became "responsible for the spreading of more printer's ink across more acres of newsprint over the world than any other Latin American in history."[2] More than a quarter century later he must still be painted in vivid and clashing colors in huge strokes on a gigantic canvas. Castro has been charismatic and controversial, confusing and confused.

Opposition to Batista grew and with it his despotism. The situation began to deteriorate badly in 1956, and the closing three years of Batista's rule were

[2]Russell H. Fitzgibbon, "The Revolution Next Door: Cuba." *Annals of the American Academy* 334 (Latin America's Nationalistic Revolutions) (March 1961), 114.

a repetition of the Machado tyranny. On December 2, 1956, Castro landed on the south coast of Oriente province at the head of a small invasion group trained in Mexico. All but a dozen were killed or captured; the rest escaped to the nearby Sierra Maestra mountains. Castro began a fantastic guerrilla resistance to the Batista regime, a resistance which reached a climax on January 1, 1959, with Batista's flight from the island. The "26th of July Movement" (M26 in the symbolic language of painted wall slogans) had triumphed, and Castro ruled Cuba.

The Castro Success

Until shortly before his final victory, Castro had no more than a few hundred men under his command. But Castro's was a dedicated and well-disciplined group; the regular army was largely apathetic, if not shot through with disaffection. The attempted general strike undertaken at Castro's order in Havana in April 1958, though a dismal failure, proved to be a blessing in disguise for Castro. Batista thereafter resorted to a much more repressive policy, which quickly and completely alienated any remaining middle-class support or sympathy.

More basically Castro's triumph may largely be credited to the general anomie which characterized Cuban society and public life. The Church had not provided any important elements of polarization or unification; its clergy was heavily weighted with Spanish priests and largely urban-oriented. The army, though large, had not developed an esprit de corps; it lacked any deep sense of national responsibility or patriotism. In addition, many of its higher officers had succumbed to graft and politicization. The press was perhaps as venal as any in Latin America. The business community was largely oriented toward the United States and consequently its patriotism was dubious. Political parties were artificial and fluid; their appeal was usually frenetic, frothy, and futile. Despite Cuba's potential for great prosperity and progress, it reflected, perhaps better than any other Latin American country, a glitter that certainly was not gold.

The end came quickly on January 1, 1959—so quickly that Castro was not prepared for it. But 26th of July units in Havana very efficiently moved to restore order and prevent looting and unauthorized reprisals. Manuel Urrutia, the president-designate handpicked by Castro, arrived in Havana and tried to take the first hectic steps of a responsible public official. The *líder máximo* (supreme leader) in the meantime was making a triumphal procession across Cuba, arriving in the capital on January 8.

Castro's role had suddenly shifted. Before he had been a dramatic oppositionist; now he became the head of a government, if not formally the chief of a state. This perhaps explains his curious position via-à-vis government and the political and administrative processes. The norms of formal political expression—constitutions, elections, representative legislatures, a hallowed judiciary, respected administrative machinery—not only did not interest Castro, but he often showed impatience with them in his compulsion to get on with the business of the Revolution.

Friction quickly developed between the rebel army and the predominantly civilian cabinet. The regular army—that is, Batista's force—was soon liquidated. Many of its officers were executed, along with scores of other *batistianos,* real or alleged, in the blood bath of revolutionary trials during the first half of 1959. Units of the rebel army, closely associated with the 26th of July Movement, supplanted the former forces; they in turn largely gave way to the militia organized by the new regime. The revolutionary militia was built up to a strength of 250,000 men and women, well supplied with arms imported from Soviet-bloc countries, thoroughly drilled and indoctrinated. But even by 1964 evidence that the militia was no longer fully trusted by the regime was multiplying. Later, the militia was partially supplanted by a conscript army.

The civil service underwent a thorough housecleaning, a reform which the lax and bloated Cuban bureaucracy long had needed; large numbers of employees were replaced or dropped. New standards of administrative honesty were applied, partly by administrative fiat from above, partly through the enthusiasm which naturally accompanied the reform program. *Botellas,* or sinecures, were eliminated by the thousands.

The regime nominally issued legislation through the Council of Ministers. Ways of arriving at a consensus, insofar as departure from Castro's own views was tolerated at all, were casual or careless. Castro in television addresses often announced government policies and programs of which cabinet members collectively or individually had no prior knowledge. When he announced the highly important Agrarian Reform Law in the spring of 1959, five cabinet members resigned because they had not been previously consulted. On a later occasion still more cabinet members, some of them fidelistas, resigned because they refused to join in ministerial condemnation of Major Hubert Matos, a current scapegoat, in October 1959.

Late in 1960 President Osvaldo Dorticós revealed to a *New York Times* correspondent something of the *modus operandi* of the government. Its real business, he said, was undertaken by a small group of Cuban leaders—Castro, his brother Raúl, "Che" Guevara, Antonio Núñez Jiménez, director of the National Institute of Agrarian Reform (Instituto Nacional de Reforma Agraria, or INRA), Finance Minister Rolando Díaz Aztaraín, and a few others—who met weekly as a central planning council to seek economic coordination and formulate policy. The Council of Ministers, according to Dorticós, met chiefly to ratify decisions in the form of law. Little or no formal line was drawn between economic and political matters.

Such Communist deviants as Tito and Mao departed from the parent ideology, practice, and leadership only after they had long been associated with it. Castro, on the other hand, came into the Moscow-led community from the stance of a nationalistic revolution which was solely his own creation. It was obvious almost from the start that Moscow and much less Peking were not as free to discipline the stormy petrel as they might sometimes wish. But Castro changed, too, from a maverick of the 1960s to a leader whose policies hardly differ from those of his Soviet benefactor in the 1970s.

In the 1970s Cuba's foreign policy expanded to recognize Moscow's leadership and its complete ideological and political alliance with the Soviet bloc. Cuba initiated a campaign for closer ties with the Third World and made efforts to bring nonaligned nations within the Soviet Union's sphere of influence. Cuba returned to membership in the Latin American club and continued to support Communist parties in Latin America. Cuba has also indicated an apparent willingness to reestablish friendly relations with the United States.

As a member of COMECON (Council for Mutual Economic Assistance), Cuba now enjoys the fruits of this vast integrated economic organization.

GOVERNMENTAL AND POLITICAL STRUCTURES

No other revolution in Latin America has been so much the embodiment of a single individual. The nature of Cuban government, as well as the course of Cuban politics, has in large measure been a product of Castro's own mind, and neither the outside world nor perhaps he himself has known how to predict it from one month to another.

At first he advocated a return to respectful observance of the constitution of 1940. That was later forgotten. On various occasions before and after coming into power he solemnly promised popular elections; that, too, was forgotten—the people in their mass rallies were deliriously giving him a mandate better than any election. The congress was eliminated; legislation was wholly by decree. Courts were treated cavalierly or contemptuously. Ministries and other agencies were made and unmade with casual lack of concern for administrative stability and logical or historical relationships.

New ministries, such as the Ministry for the Recovery of Misappropriated Property, the Ministry for the Study of Revolutionary Laws, and Ministries of Industry, Economy, and Social Welfare, were created to reflect more closely the emphasis of the new regime. Occupants of the various ministries were occasionally changed, progressively deepening the fidelista coloration and making the orientation toward communism more pronounced.

Governmental Reorganization

On February 15, 1975, Cuba's first nationwide election since the revolution gave 97.7 percent approval to a new constitution recognizing the Communist party as "the highest leading force of the society and state."

The new constitution provides for a pyramid of governing institutions. At the base are 10,743 popularly elected members of municipal assemblies and 455 delegates to the National Assembly of People's Power. The municipal assemblies have responsibility for such enterprises as hospitals, schools, public utilities, restaurants, and local transportation systems. They also choose judges to preside over the People's courts.

Provincial assemblies control intercity transportation, provincial commerce, and the selection of judges for provincial tribunals. The national assembly regulates all basic industries, controls curricula in the schools, and names supreme court judges. As the national legislature, it selects a thirty-one–member Council of State with its president as the head of government. The head of government proposes the names of the Council of Ministers; they are approved by the national assembly and have the major responsibility for administration.

The 6 old provinces have been replaced by 14 new ones, the original 407 municipalities have been decreased to 169, and the 58 regions created in 1963 have been abolished.

Castro's new governmental system described in the 1976 constitution is seen as a major step toward curbing the excesses of centralized power structures that emerged after the Revolution. It is difficult to say, however, how responsive the parliamentary system has been to the needs of the Cuban people. Some feel that "the institutionalization of the Revolution," as the parliamentary process and regional change are called, will be generally successful; others argue that the overall effectiveness of the scheme will be short-circuited by the watchdog role of the Cuban Communist party. Several elections have nevertheless been held under the 1976 charter; the most recent were the municipal elections in April 1979, which reportedly had a massive turnout.

Political Support Structures

In the early months the chief support of the Cuban Revolution came from the middle classes, but by the time Castro took over at the beginning of 1959 his backing in Cuba was virtually unanimous. Support and leadership of the resistance movement during the twenty-five months it opposed Batista before his downfall had, indeed, been largely middle-class and hence urban. Theodore Draper has explored and exploded the myth that the movement, before and after January 1959, was a peasant movement. One element backing Castro was the old parties that had opposed Batista, principally the Auténticos and the Ortodoxos. Despite the fact that Castro had been a congressional candidate on the Ortodoxo ticket in 1952 and that Roberto Agramonte, its chief, had been temporarily in Castro's first cabinet, Fidel had little use for the old-time parties—including the Communists—and made few gestures of conciliation toward them. The parties were later prohibited from activity of any kind, even though the rationale of Castro's repeated postponements of popular elections was that he wanted to wait until an effective party opposition had been established.

Various student groups, organized labor, and professional and business associations were early participants in public life after the takeover. These, especially the student and labor groups, had long been politically conscious and had often served as effective pressure groups. Students and faculty of the University of Havana had over the years been as much immersed in politics as perhaps any university community in Latin America. The University reaction early in 1959 was in general fanatically loyal to the reforms that it assumed Castro would immediately bring. The student body was later badly torn between pro- and anti-Communist factions. After the university was purged of its dissenting elements, it was wholly brought in line with the new Communist orientation. The veteran Communist Juan Marinello became its rector.

Labor unions had earlier been successfully manipulated by Batista. By early 1959 the major labor organization, the Cuban Workers' Confederation (Confederacíon de Trabajadores de Cuba, or CTC) had been brought under fidelista domination. Castro dramatically intervened in a CTC convention in November 1959 to insist on the election of a "unity slate" giving Communists more power. Soon they had all the power; the non-Communist leader was removed and, when caught trying to escape from Cuba late in 1960, was thrown into prison.

Institutional devices beyond traditional Cuban ones had to be found. One of the most comprehensive and important within the governmental organization chart was the gigantic INRA. It was created under the Agrarian Reform Law of May–June 1959, the first important legislative indication of where the Revolution was headed. No counterpart to such organizational mushrooming as INRA represented can be found in other Latin American governmental experience, even in Perón's Argentina. Agricultural lands and other properties began to be expropriated and turned over to INRA at a wholesale rate. INRA quickly became an exceedingly powerful entity, assuming a variety of miscellaneous economic planning and administrative functions. In early 1961, however, new ministries absorbed some of the departments previously included within INRA and the government seemed to be consciously downgrading it.

Popular Socialist Party (PSP).   A more important institution than INRA, one of a quite different and more fluid sort, was the Popular Socialist party (Partido Socialista Popular, or PSP), the vehicle by which Communism took over the Revolution. The Communists quickly realized that Castro could provide them with an immense popular appeal and a movement such as Latin America had never before seen. They could ride to initial success in Cuba and perhaps from there to far more exciting conquests elsewhere in Latin America.

Meanwhile, Castro soon saw that the mechanism of Cuban communism, the Popular Socialist party, could furnish him a disciplined cadre of intelligent, determined supporters which even his fanatically loyal 26th of July Movement could not provide; it had organizational ability and skills which he badly needed.

Communism in Cuba goes back to the mid-1920s. With its penetration of the labor movement in the early 1930s and its contribution to the overthrow of Machado, it gained in prestige and political influence. Blas Roca (his real name is Francisco Calderío) became its secretary general in 1934 and from then on remained one of the top Cuban Communists. The Communist party tried to sabotage the first Grau administration and remained a reasonably consistent opponent of the Auténticos thereafter. By backing Batista in the late 1930s the Communists won legal standing. Juan Marinello and Carlos Rafael Rodríguez served as ministers without portfolio during Batista's presidency. Later Carlos Rafael Rodríguez became one of the few PSP leaders to obtain several important positions in the Castro administration because of his loyalty to Fidel. Grau and Prío began to attack Communists more actively in the late 1940s and gradually won control of the CTC for the Auténticos. Batista, after returning to power in 1952, moved away from the Communists and declared the party illegal in October 1953. The party, however, maintained a highly disciplined sub rosa activity.

There is some evidence to suggest that the Communists regarded Castro's movement as simply a romantic, badly organized, and poorly led activity which had no chance of succeeding and with which they consequently did not want to be associated. It was not until well into 1958 that the first important Communist contacts with Castro were made. Prior to that time Castro had on occasion been critical of the Communists, especially for their failure to support the Havana general strike in April 1958. (These were words which Castro would later retract.)

In the exciting and disorganized days of January 1959, the Revolution was essentially without a dialectic. In his famous "History Will Absolve Me" speech in October 1953, Castro had advocated general reforms within the framework of the 1940 constitution. By the beginning of 1959 he was talking about a vague problem of "humanism"—probably inspired in large part by ideas of the great nineteenth-century Cuban hero, José Martí.

During his April 1959 visit to Washington, Castro met with then Vice-President Richard Nixon but did not gain any concrete support for his regime. His nationalistic language irked many in Washington's high places. Castro thus eventually opted for the Moscow connection to protect the viability of the Revolution. The Communists were fully prepared to provide him with an ideology, subtly refurbished to make him think it was his own. The fact that he had long admired what the Communists worked for, as he later admitted, notably in his famous speech of December 2, 1961, doubtless made it easier for him to incline toward them at an early date. Such an inclination was very probably reinforced by the even more obvious sympathies of his two closest colleagues, his brother Raúl and "Che" Guevara.

Of course, it was not possible for Castro to admit any sympathy for communism as early as January 1959. To have done so would have alienated a large part of the Cuban support which was being given to him so uncritically and wholeheartedly. Many of his own 26th of July followers were strongly anti-Communist. Support by the PSP in the early months of 1959 made it easier for Castro to place more and more reliance on them, just as Arbenz had come to do six to eight years earlier in Guatemala. By as early as April 1959 Castro was identifying anti-Communism with counterrevolution. The nationalization of almost four hundred Cuban-owned businesses in October 1960 moved the regime a long step toward socialism. In his May Day speech in 1961, just after the collapse of the Bay of Pigs invasion, Castro alluded vaguely to socialism and implied that a new socialist constitution would be drafted to replace the law of 1940. At the same time Guevara was referring to the Cuban movement as "the first socialist revolution of Latin America."

The PSP had been permitted to reorganize, a function periodically felt necessary by Cuban parties, though even the 26th of July Movement was not allowed to regroup itself as a political party; indeed, Castro let it wither on the vine almost from the time of coming into power. Simone de Beauvoir, a sympathetic French writer, was given the impression in 1960 that the movement was felt to be characterized by a petty bourgeois mentality and motivation which could not sufficiently or rapidly readjust to the stepped-up pace of the revolution.

After trial balloons the regime announced in June 1961 that a new, all-embracing revolutionary group would be set up in two stages: first, a transitional entity to be known as the Integrated Revolutionary Organizations (Organizaciones Revolucionarias Integradas, or ORI); then a United Party of the Socialist Revolution (the Partido Unido de la Revolución Socialista, or PURS). No timetable was set nor were the leadership and program of ORI announced at once. It soon became obvious that ORI was simply a larger vehicle for the further triumphal procession of the PSP and that the latter's leaders would play similar roles in ORI. In early March 1962 the ORI leadership announced formation of a directorate and two weeks later Castro stated that he himself would be first secretary, his brother, Raúl, would be second secretary, and Guevara, Dorticós, and Blas Roca would be among the members of the secretariat.

The final step was taken on October 3, 1965, when PURS was supplanted by the Cuban Communist party. Fidel and Raúl continued as its first and second secretaries. Of the 104-member central committee only fifteen were old-line Communists. Actual direction of the party was in the hands of the eight-man politburo (headed by Castro) and the six-man secretariat.

In the meantime many of those who saw or sensed the drift towards communism became disturbed to the point of protest or defection. The most dramatic case was that of President Manuel Urrutia who, as early as June 1959, expressed his concern with the growing Communist influence in the regime. He was forced out of the presidency in humiliating fashion by Castro and supplanted by the more amenable and inflammatory Osvaldo Dorticós Torrado. Dorticós entirely lacked the qualms of Urrutia about the further penetration by communism.

On a number of occasions in 1961, in speeches or interviews, Castro suggested cautiously and gradually his shift towards communism. In many ways he was almost apologetic about his earlier ignorance of the merits of the Communist position, although it was doubtless not temperamentally possible for him to subject himself to complete abasement. Communist formula phrases appeared more and more in Castro's addresses. The climax came in Castro's much publicized speech of December 1-2, 1961. In it he again ate humble pie, confessed to Communist exposure during his university days, and came out with the ringing declaration that "I am a Marxist-Leninist, and I will be one till the last day of my life."

Nonetheless, Castro did not want to surrender completely—or at least there were times when he did not want to surrender. In March 1962 he lashed out bitterly at Aníbal Escalante and other (unnamed) old-line Communists, whom he accused of interfering and of packing the ORI with Communists. Escalante was again in trouble in 1968 and in February was sentenced to 15 years in prison for pro-Soviet acts against the Cuban regime. It seemed likely at various times that Castro wanted to serve notice that he himself would not be displaced as the central figure of the regime and the chief architect of the Communist dialectic, Cuban version.

DEVELOPMENTAL PROSPECTS

In its torrential pace the Cuban Revolution has moved toward the remaking of the island's society and economy. As its goals became better known, it progressively sacrificed support from the upper, then the professional and middle, and then certain segments of the lower classes. Those elements of a pluralistic society simply had no function or future in revolutionary Cuba. Some 80 percent of Cuba's economically active population came to be employed, directly or indirectly, by the government. Ninety percent or more of Cuban industrial activity was nationalized. This trend put a premium on managerial experience just when many of Cuba's most skilled administrators and entrepreneurs were fleeing the island.

Social, economic, and political mobility almost entirely ceased or at least was channeled into purely arbitrary and artificial lines dictated by compliance with the Revolution and the regime. Earlier pluralistic loyalties and energies were all forced to give way to a single-minded devotion to Castro himself. The symbol of the egocentric *jefe máximo* reflected Latin America's greatest development of *personalismo* and exceeded even the emphasis placed on the Revolution. Never before—neither in the cult of Rosas, the professional glorification of Guzmán Blanco, the synthetic exaltation of Trujillo, nor in any other such manifestation—had a Latin American nation's political expression and destiny so revolved around one man.

Revolutionary Cuba offers a number of significant points of comparison and a few of contrast with totalitarian regimes that the world has elsewhere experienced in recent decades. First, Castro's regime must be recognized as far more totalitarian than any ever before found in Latin America. In that respect it resembles Russia under Stalin and Khrushchev, Germany under Hitler, China under Mao, possibly Italy under Mussolini. In the degree and effectiveness of his exploitation of charisma, Castro can probably be compared only to Hitler. The evolution of a general scheme of government has resembled that found in various Communist-bloc states, with occasional ministries of the same names set up and reliance on committees and institutes which often surpass more formal agencies in power and prestige. In the relationship between government and party, Cuba moves toward the Communist pattern, though it has not as yet reached the point of theoretical subordination of all else to the party. The erratic and contradictory nature of Castro's own personality will probably delay or prevent such a consummation as long as he remains in the picture. Nor has there been in Cuba the formal, organized association of party and government which took place in Fascist Italy and Nazi Germany.

Perhaps the most basic thing that can be said about Cuban politics since Castro came into power is that it demonstrates the fragile nature of the institutional development of pre-Castro Cuba. The military, the Church, the private economy, organized labor, political parties, and all the lesser groups and agencies of a pluralistic society have been subordinated to or remade by a determined revolutionary oligarchy which would brook no opposition and virtually no criticism.

Just as it is impossible to separate internal governmental considerations from political considerations in Castro's Cuba, so is it futile to try to isolate developments in domestic politics from those in international politics; they are inextricably intertwined. Castro's pursuit of revolutionary objectives at all times embodied his attacks on the United States. And the United States instituted policies and actions to try to contain Castro. The interaction was almost constant; highlights during the first decade of Castro's rule were the Bay of Pigs invasion in April 1961 and the missile crisis of October 1962. The complete failure of the incredibly miscalculated invasion enormously strengthened Castro's hand in Cuba. It provided him with the necessity and the occasion for acknowledging more specifically the new orientation toward communism. It induced almost total despair among his domestic opponents and produced a correspondingly great psychological setback for the United States and for Cuban exile groups in the United States.

The missile crisis in the fall of 1962 was quite different and had other consequences. Castro's internal hold was not weakened, for the potential opposition was by that time too nearly reduced to impotence to be able to take advantage of the loss of face which Castro suffered.

Cuba in the 1970s continued its foreign policy of hostility toward the United States, although late in the decade a cooling-off period began when the two countries established "interest sections" in friendly embassies at each other's capitals. The release in 1978 of approximately one thousand political prisoners was seen as another step toward normalization of relations with the United States, but Cuba's involvement in Angola and Ethiopia that same year put the brakes on the return to normal ties between the two countries.

Cuban military personnel in Africa is estimated at forty thousand (though around three thousand were reported withdrawn from Ethiopia in August 1979, allegedly to play down Castro's military involvement in Africa for the September 1979 Conference of Non-Aligned Countries in Havana), ready to support left-wing revolutionary movements and governments on the African continent.

Many observers feel that the African missions are an attempt to keep the Revolution alive. The Cuban Revolution is a mere twenty years old. Over 45 percent of today's 9.7 million Cubans were born after their *jefe máximo* came down from the Sierra Maestra and marched triumphantly into Havana. These young revolutionaries are too young to remember the missile crisis or the Bay of Pigs. The African campaigns are perhaps one way to give them a taste of what their predecessors fought against during the days of Batista and the "Yankee invaders." The Revolution has, with the help of the Soviet Union, withstood its economic problems and Cuba will no doubt be a full-fledged member of the international economic community in the near future. Economically, politically, and ideologically, the Cuban Revolution has in only two decades matured and extended its influence beyond the Latin American sphere into other third-world countries. At the 1978 Belgrade Conference of Non-Aligned Countries, Cuba was selected as the 1979 Conference site.

The 1979 Conference, meeting for the first time in Latin America, succeeded in deemphasizing the nonaligned character of the Movement and obtaining continued support for the economic concerns of the nations of the Third World. While the final resolution of the Conference tended to be ambiguous in its position toward the United States and the Soviet Union, Fidel Castro, as the president of the Conference for the next three years, received an additional boost to his already growing international prestige.

REFERENCES

BATISTA, FULGENCIO. *The Growth and Decline of the Cuban Republic.* New York: Devin-Adair Co., 1964.

BENDER, LYNN D. *The Politics of Hostility; Castro's Revolution and U. S. Policy.* Hato Rey, Puerto Rico: Inter-American University Press, 1975.

BONACHEA, RAMON L., and MARTA SAN MARTIN. *The Cuban Insurrection: 1952–1959.* New Brunswick, N.J.: Transaction Books, 1974.

BONACHEA, RAMON L. and NELSON VALDES, eds. *Cuba in Revolution.* New York: Doubleday Anchor Books, 1972.

BONSAL, PHILIP W. *Cuba, Castro, and the United States.* Pittsburgh: University of Pittsburgh Press, 1971.

BOUGHTON, GEORGE J. "Soviet-Cuban Relations, 1956–1960." *Journal of Inter-American Studies and World Affairs* 16:4 (November 1974), 436–453.

CALDERÍO, FRANCISCO (pseud. Blas Roca). "New Stage in the Cuban Revolution." *World Marxist Review* 4:10 (October 1961), 3–10.

CASTRO, FIDEL. *Diez años de la revolución cubana.* n.p.: Pueblos Unidos, n.d.

———. *El proceso revolucionario.* n.p.: Tres Americas, 1973.

———. *La revolución cubana.* Mexico City: Era, n.d.

———. *Pensamiento Político, Económico, y Social de Fidel Castro.* Havana: n.p., 1959.

CHAYES, ABRAM. *The Cuban Missile Crisis.* New York: Oxford, 1974.

DEBRAY, RÉGIS. *Revolution in the Revolution.* New York: Grove Press, 1967.

DIVINE, ROBERT. *The Cuban Missile Crisis.* Chicago: Quadrangle Books, 1971.

DOMINGUEZ, JORGE I. "Cuban Foreign Policy." *Foreign Affairs* 57:1 (Fall 1978) 83–108.

———. *Governing Cuba: Political Order, Change and Revolution in the Twentieth Century.* Cambridge, Mass.: Harvard University Press, 1978.

DRAPER, THEODORE. *Castro's Revolution: Myths and Realities.* Holt, Rinehart & Winston, 1962.

———. *Castroism: Theory and Practice.* New York: Holt, Rinehart & Winston 1965.

DUMONT, RENÉ. *Is Cuba Socialist?* trans. by Stanley Hockman. New York: Viking, 1974.

FAGEN, RICHARD R. "Charismatic Authority and the Leadership of Fidel Castro." *Western Political Quarterly* 18 (June 1965), 275–284.

———. *The Transformation of Political Culture in Cuba.* Stanford, Calif.: Stanford University Press, 1969.

FAGG, JOHN E. *Cuba, Haiti, and the Dominican Republic.* Englewood Cliffs, N. J.: Prentice-Hall, 1965.

FITZGERALD, FRANK T. "A Critique of the 'Sovietization of Cuba' Thesis." *Science and Society* 42:1 (Spring 1978), 1–32.

FITZGIBBON, RUSSELL H. "The Revolution Next Door: Cuba." *Annals of the American Academy* 334 (March 1961), 113–122.

———. *Cuba and the United States, 1900–1935.* New York: Russell and Russell, 1964.

GOLDENBERG, BORIS. *The Cuban Revolution and Latin America.* New York: Holt, Rinehart & Winston, 1965.

GONZALEZ, EDWARD. *Cuba Under Castro: The Limits of Charisma.* Boston: Houghton Mifflin, 1974.

GOODSELL, JAMES N., ed. *Fidel Castro's Personal Revolution in Cuba: 1959–1973.* New York: Knopf, 1975.

GUEVARA, ERNESTO "CHE." *Che Guevara on Guerrilla Warfare.* New York: Random House, 1968.

————. *Reminiscences of the Cuban Revolutionary War*. New York: Grove Press, 1968.

HALPERIN, MAURICE. *The Rise and Decline of Fidel Castro*. Berkeley: University of California Press, 1972.

HENNESSY, C. A. M. "The Roots of Cuban Nationalism." *International Affairs* (London) 39 (July 1963), 345–359.

HOROWITZ, IRVING L. *Cuban Communism*. New Brunswick, N.Y.: Transaction Books, 1972.

JOHNSON, CECIL E. "Cuba: The Domestic Policies of the Castro Regime." *Arnold Foundation Monographs* 9 (1961), 3–16.

KAROL, K. S. *Guerrillas in Power: The Course of the Cuban Revolution*. New York: Hill and Wang, 1970.

LEWIS, OSCAR, RUTH M. LEWIS, and SUSAN M. RIGDON. *Living the Revolution: An Oral History of Contemporary Cuba*. Urbana: University of Illinois Press, 1977.

LOCKWOOD, LEE. *Castro's Cuba, Cuba's Fidel*. New York: Random House Vintage, 1969.

LLERENA, MARIO. *The Unsuspected Revolution: The Birth and Rise of Castroism*. Ithaca, N.Y.: Cornell University Press, 1978.

MACGAFFEY, WYATT, and CLIFFORD R. BARNETT. *Cuba: Its People, Its Society, Its Culture*. Reprint of 1962 edition. Westport, Conn.: Greenwood, 1974.

————. *Twentieth Century Cuba*. New York: Doubleday, 1965.

MATTHEWS, HERBERT L. *The Cuban Story*. New York: G. Brazilier, 1961.

————. *Revolution in Cuba: An Essay in Understanding*. New York: Scribner's, 1975.

MESA-LAGO, CARMELO. *Cuba in the '70's*. rev. ed. Albuquerque: University of New Mexico Press, 1978.

————. *Revolutionary Change in Cuba*. Pittsburgh: University of Pittsburgh Press, 1971.

MIGNONE, A. FREDERICK. "Whither Cuba?" *South Atlantic Quarterly* 51 (April 1952), 199–210.

O'CONNOR, JAMES. *The Origins of Socialism in Cuba*. Ithaca, N.Y.: Cornell University Press, 1970.

PEREZ, LOUIS A., JR. *Army Politics in Cuba, 1898–1958*. Pittsburgh: University of Pittsburgh Press, 1976.

PHILLIPS, RUBY HART. *Cuba: Island of Paradox*. New York: McDowell, Obolensky, 1959.

RATLIFF, WILLIAM E. *Castroism and Communism in Latin America, 1959–1976: The Varieties of Marxist-Leninist Experience*. Washington, D.C.: American Enterprise Institute, 1976.

RITTER, ARCHIBALD, R.M. "The Cuban Revolution: A New Orientation." *Current History* 74:434 (February 1978) 53–56.

RUIZ, RAMON EDUARDO. *Cuba: The Making of a Revolution*. Amherst: University of Massachusetts Press, 1968.

SEERS, DUDLEY, ed. *Cuba: The Economic and Social Revolution*. Chapel Hill: University of North Carolina Press, 1964.

SILVERMAN, BERTRAM. *Man and Socialism in Cuba*. New York: Atheneum, 1973.

SMITH, ROBERT F. *Background to Revolution; The Development of Modern Cuba*. New York: Knopf, 1966.

STOKES, WILLIAM S. *Latin American Politics*, Chapters 15, 18. New York: Harper & Row, 1959.

SUAREZ, ANDRES. *Cuba: Castroism and Communism, 1959–1966*. Cambridge, Mass.: MIT Press, 1967.

SUCHLICKI, JAIME. *Cuba, Castro, and Communism*. Coral Gables, Fla.: University of Miami Press, 1972.

————. *University Students and Revolutions in Cuba, 1920–1968*. Coral Gables, Fla.: University of Miami Press, 1968.

TANNENBAUM, FRANK. "Castro and Social Change." *Political Science Quarterly* 77 (June 1962), 178–204.

————. *Ten Keys to Latin America,* Chapter 10. New York: Knopf, 1962.

THOMAS, HUGH. *Cuba.* New York: Harper & Row, 1971.

WARD, FRED. *Inside Cuba Today.* New York: Crown, 1978.

WILKERSON, LOREE A. R. *Fidel Castro's Political Programs.* Gainesville, Fla.: University of Florida Press, 1965.

ZEITLIN, MAURICE. *Revolutionary Politics and the Cuban Working Class.* New York: Harper Torchbooks, 1970.

tures to presidential opponents; it was a worthy addition to the unsavory *mazorca* (the secret police force used by Juan Manuel de Rosas of Argentina) and *porra* (the secret police force used by President Gerardo Machado of Cuba) of earlier days and other lands. Other thugs were known as the *capoulards* (secret terroristic and punitive force used by Duvalier).

The president's term legally ended on May 15, 1963, and opponents both in and out of Haiti vowed that he would not be permitted to remain in office after that date. But force dictated events; he stayed in office. Duvalier's egomaniacal course climaxed on April 1, 1964, when he decreed himself president for life. This was "ratified" by a national referendum on June 14, and ten days later he was installed for his ostensible lifetime term.

Although at any given moment it seemed impossible that the situation could worsen, the political and economic picture became progressively darker. A pathetically ineffective bombing attack was made on Port-au-Prince in May 1968, and thirteen months later it was repeated, accompanied by an equally ineffectual invasion attempt. In the meantime it was reported that the army was grooming three officers to form a junta in the event that Duvalier, who was recurrently reported to be seriously ill, should die.

By 1970 "Papa Doc" had made his choice for a successor: his nineteen-year old son, Jean-Claude. To make this possible, Duvalier's legislature amended the constitution, lowering the minimum presidential age from forty to twenty. The people were permitted to vote in February 1971 on this proposition: "Citizen Dr. François Duvalier . . . has chosen Citizen Jean-Claude Duvalier to succeed him to the President for Life of the Republic. Does this choice answer your aspirations and your desires? Do you ratify it?"[1] The affirmative vote was 2,391,916; no dissenting votes were noted. Then on April 21, 1971, Dr. Duvalier died and Jean-Claude assumed the presidency. "Papa Doc" left as a legacy the most durable dictatorship in the country (twenty-three of the thirty-six presidents before him had been either murdered or overthrown).

Many observers either feared or hoped that "Baby Doc" would not be able to hold the reins of government and felt that a long and bloody power struggle was inevitable. But "Baby Doc" managed to survive the "ups and downs" of his presidential reign, including a family feud over who should be the president—Jean-Claude or his sister. Ambitious cabinet ministers tried in vain at various times to gain control of the island's political life. Meanwhile the real power behind the throne in the past seven years seemed to be Madame Simone Duvalier, the president's mother and widow of "Papa Doc."

The United States government began to aid Haitian agricultural and industrial projects in 1972. The Inter-American Development Bank (IDB) also began a loan program to the country. These decisions no doubt encouraged

[1] *New York Times*, April 23, 1971. Sec. C, p. 44.

the American private sector to resume investing in the country. Elections were held on February 11, 1973, after a lapse of nearly twelve years, to elect fifty-eight representatives to the legislative chamber. Since opposition parties are not permitted in Haiti, all three-hundred candidates were from the official party of President Duvalier, the Party of National Unity (Parti de l'Unité Nationale).

In the 1979 parliamentary elections, however, Jean-Claude allowed a tiny (one) voice of opposition in the fifty-eight-seat parliament. Alexandre Lerouge, a former local government official, ran as an independent candidate in the city of Cap-Haïtien—and won about 90 percent of the votes.

GOVERNMENTAL AND PARTY STRUCTURES

Considering the chaotic nature of Haitian politics, especially in recent years, it becomes futile to put much reliance on the institutions and agencies of government as such. "After all," Duvalier might seem to say, "what's the constitution among friends?" Or enemies either, for that matter. It is more realistic to examine political forces.

With constitutional limitations upon the executive office having become a travesty, it stands to reason that the cabinet would be in an especially vulnerable and humiliating position. Almost without exception cabinets are definitely subordinate to presidents in Latin America, but in Haiti cabinet members are no more than contemptuously treated pawns on a political chessboard. Indeed at times they have had to keep a weather eye cocked on a precarious political situation in order to desert a failing administration in time to escape being charged too strongly with "guilt by association." Most of the time in recent years the cabinet has included either eleven or twelve portfolios.

In 1961 the former national assembly became a unicameral body composed of fifty-eight members elected by universal suffrage for six-year terms. The legislature is completely subservient to the president. In more than one election a single slate of candidates—progovernment, of course—has been listed on the ballot.

Although the judiciary appears to be established on a slightly more dignified basis, this is illusory. It is headed by the court of cassation: nine justices appointed by the president for ten-year terms. In almost all respects it functions as an appellate court. Lower levels of the judiciary include courts of appeal, civil courts, and local justices of the peace. All officials in the judicial branch are appointed by the president. Theoretically, they can be removed only by impeachment, but so honored in the breach is that provision that, as an insurance policy, the court of cassation frequently discusses important cases with the president before officially passing on them. Constitutionally, the president can be impeached by a high court of justice, but this provision is the deadest of dead letters.

Local government reflects French organization but largely in matters of nomenclature. The country is divided into nine territorial departments, these into *arrondissements,* and these in turn into communes. The departments are headed by prefects named by the national executive. The communes elect their mayors, but this is only of nominal importance. Mayors have extremely limited powers, and all taxes collected by the communes are paid directly into the national treasury.

Party and Interest Structures

The first presidents after the United States ended its occupation in 1934 represented the mulatto elite. Most notable in upholding its point of view was Daniel Fignolé, founder of the Peasant Worker's Movement (Mouvement Ouvrier Paysan, or MOP) in 1946. The MOP perhaps had the potential for social revolution, but it was never able to get off the ground. Duvalier quickly ended mulatto hegemony and introduced a new racism punctuated by the elimination of about three thousand followers of Fignolé in the MOP. It is significant that, with Duvalier aiming his political appeal to the masses and allegedly making use of Vodun as a channel of influence, the qualifications for voting should not include literacy. Otherwise the electorate would have been limited largely to the urban, mulatto elite.

So repressive was the recent attitude of Duvalier that organized party activity that was not entirely sycophantic had be to carried on outside Haiti. Thus, the Revolutionary Haitian Movement (Mouvement Révolutionnaire Haïtien, or MRH) began functioning in Colombia in 1961. The following year the National Democratic Union (Union Démocratique Nationale, or UDN) was organized in Puerto Rico. Neither group was effective. Since 1960 a number of exiled groups have surfaced in the United States. The official government party during the Duvalier years has been the Party of National Unity. As mentioned earlier the three hundred candidates running in the 1973 legislative elections were Duvalier supporters.

No systematic or adequate means of political education exist in Haiti. With literacy so low, television and radio facilities so limited, and the press so controlled, political propagandizing or campaigning is abnormally limited. The difficulty is partly remedied by the *télédiole,* an institutionalized but informal communication network in which information is widely transmitted by word of mouth.

The army is the most obvious force in the anarchic picture of Haitian political society. It is modestly equipped but reasonably well disciplined, and its leading officers are almost necessarily politically minded. For years the Garde d'Haïti operated as a praetorian force and could make or break presidents almost at will. Duvalier cleverly managed to neutralize it in large measure by his reliance on the *tonton macoutes* and other irregular bully boys. It is also significant that some of the artillery was stored in the basement of the presidential palace, which had been transformed into a virtual fortress.

The Port-au-Prince elite, far more tightly knit and class conscious than the oligarchy in most Hispanic American countries, is customarily on the defensive, especially in the face of so racist a president as Duvalier. Inflation and decreased incomes have forced a downward mobility upon a reluctant fraction of the traditional elite.

The middle class lacks organization and unity; hence it does not pose an immediate threat to the government. Some elite families have been forced into it, as just noted, and occasional peasants who find an opportunity to gain an education almost automatically become members of the middle class. Occupational outlets for the middle class are very limited; the civil service, entirely operated according to a spoils-system psychology, is no answer. The middle class, such as it is, is almost inevitably a frustrated group.

The great mass of peasants is politically inarticulate. Numerically the blacks so overwhelm the elite that, were they to become aroused by demagogic appeals, they could subject Haiti to a blood bath reminiscent of the 1790s. Their man is in the presidential palace for life, however, and they have nothing to worry about—except the consequences of a $200 per capita annual income, Latin America's worst soil erosion problem, blighting health conditions, subsistence or starvation diets, no education, and similarly baneful problems, to all of which they are accustomed.

The Catholic church is in many respects on the defensive. Haiti has a concordat with the Vatican, and the constitution of 1950 stated that the Catholic church, as a consequence, enjoyed a special position. But Catholicism has to fight the invisible menace of Vodun, and it does so largely with a clergy that includes many foreigners. They are thereby targets for chauvinistic attacks which Duvalier has not hesitated to levy against them, even to the expulsion of a number of priests and bishops.

Organized labor is weak—there are probably not more than ten thousand union members—and is under the close and constant scrutiny of the government. It is not a political force.

DEVELOPMENTAL PROSPECTS

Jean-Claude Duvalier has found himself engaged in a precarious balancing act between two factions: the "old-guard" hardliners, headed by his mother, Simone; and the Jean-Claudists, whose rhetoric includes a desire to modernize Haiti and establish a more "liberal" political process. Parliamentary elections in February 1979 were seen as a victory for Madame Duvalier, who continues to be the power behind the dictatorship.

Although still the poorest nation in the Western Hemisphere, per capita income had risen from $60 to $75 a year in 1971 to almost $200 a year in 1976. A drought in 1977 brought about widespread starvation and wiped out any slight advancement the economy had begun to make. Another fundamental defect in the political system is the alienation of the mass of the people from the government. The rank and file of Haitians neither exercise a sense of popular possessiveness over their government nor benefit from services rendered by it. Finally the lack of institutionalization of politics must be mentioned. Government is by whim. The constitution and the laws are quite possibly more lightly regarded than in any other country of Latin America. Political parties have no viability; pressure groups are all but nonexistent. The political process has no reflection other than raw force. It is not a pretty picture.

Jean-Claude made some improvements in the political environment and reestablished friendly relations with many foreign countries. Yet, in early 1980, hundreds of Haitians were arriving in Miami eight hundred miles away in overloaded boats without food, water, or shelter for much of the journey, to seek political and economic asylum.

A simple conclusion can be drawn from the turbulent record of recent Haitian politics: The country has not yet passed the stage of *caudillismo.* But explaining the reasons behind the situation is more difficult than describing it. In considerable part it stems from the fact that Haiti is an incredibly poor country.

The Dominican Republic

POLITICAL CULTURE AND ENVIRONMENT

The Dominican Republic is most clearly distinguished from Haiti demographically by its considerably lower population density. It has 5,125,000 inhabitants (1978 estimate), giving it an overall density of 270 per square mile, slightly more than half the density of Haiti. The Dominican Republic is more urbanized than Haiti; three out of every ten Dominicans live in towns or cities. The capital, Santo Domingo (named Ciudad Trujillo from 1935 to late 1961), has an eighth of the whole republic's population.

The ethnic composition of the Dominican population differs significantly from that of Haiti. The 1970 census indicated some 15 percent were black, 15 percent white, and 70 percent mixed. Various socioeconomic indices show a generally more favorable basic situation than that in Haiti, though still less favorable than in many other Latin American countries.

Fate left "the land that Columbus loved" in a backwater until well into the nineteenth century. Not only did the French and Spanish fight over the colony before its independence, but Haitians and Dominicans struggled for control after the Europeans were nominally gone. In the early decades of independence, Haiti, with its stronger *caudillos,* bigger armies, and larger population, succeeded in overrunning the Dominican end of the island from 1822 to 1844.

Late in 1844 a new constitution was drafted, setting up a form of government that in some respects resembled that of the United States. For several years thereafter Dominican government operations were extremely precarious. The country made a number of unsuccessful attempts to place itself under the protection of a foreign power (Britain, France, the United States), then succeeded in becoming a colony of Spain from 1861 to 1865. After restoration of a still tenuous self-rule, politics continued to be the plaything of successive *caudillos.* Constitution writing was still easy, involving both temporary restoration of earlier laws and the drafting of new documents. Exercises of the latter kind were undertaken in 1866, 1872, 1874, 1875, 1877, 1878, 1879, 1880, 1881, 1887, 1896, 1907, and 1908. Many of the new constitutions obviously had to be based in large part on earlier models.

In a sordid seventeen-year dictatorship at the end of the century (1882–1899), General Ulises Heureaux, vain, arrogant, and ignorant, reached the nadir of Latin American rule. The following seventeen years, up to 1916, brought repeated threats of foreign intervention because of the country's near bankruptcy. In 1904 the United States pressured a tottering Dominican regime into accepting a large degree of fiscal control by the United States. A succession of weak, corrupt, and politically short-lived presidents solved nothing.

Events culminated in the landing of United States forces in 1916, beginning an eight-year occupation by the United States and adding another Caribbean protectorate to the one which had been established in neighboring Haiti the year before. In contrast to the administration of Haiti, which was conducted behind the façade of puppet presidents, that in the Dominican Republic had no veneer of national control up to withdrawal in 1924. The occupation regime was a military government under military law, administered by naval officers. It was efficient but unpopular—and for good reason. Administering officers were in many cases not *simpático;* considerable brutality occurred; and a marine-trained Dominican constabulary pointed to a nascent militarism. In 1924, at the time of United States withdrawal, Horacio Vásquez was installed in the presidency. Vásquez was not a strongman. He sought to practice a Dominican version of *continuismo* at the end of his term in 1930 but was forced to give way—although he would later enjoy a short provisional presidency—to one who decidedly was a strongman, Rafael Leonidas Trujillo Molina.

Trujillo was virtually sui generis among Latin American presidents. His thirty-one year reign was not the longest in the history of *caudillismo,* but in airtight and cold-blooded efficiency Trujillo stood alone, at least among twentieth-century dictators. The more than three decades are very properly labeled —as Jesús de Galíndez, a biographer and murder victim of the dictator, titled his book—the *Era of Trujillo*. The Dominican population was not politically articulate; civic education or participation had been almost wholly ignored; effective parties had never existed; and top-level leadership was unimpressive.

The new iron man had an early opportunity to demonstrate his talents. A hurricane very nearly leveled Santo Domingo, the capital city, and Trujillo energetically and efficiently acted to restore order and services, rebuild the city along more modern lines, and, perhaps incidentally and prophetically, take a generous personal cut from relief funds under his control. The new ruler was obviously going to take considerable interest in public works; accomplishments in this area easily provided means for self-glorification, and, more subtly, they demonstrated his interest in things rather than ideas. The regime would not be burdened with any attempt at dialectic or rationale. No body of political thought such as *justicialismo*—Perón's social justice creed in Argentina—or a modified Comptian positivism cluttered the simplistic, heavy-handed materialism which formed the core of Trujillo's rule.

The main characteristic of the regime was force—force in a physical-military sense. But it also involved the employment of a fine Italian hand— Trujillo was Latin America's Machiavelli par excellence. He built up the army and treated it generously. Officers were given many perquisites and opportunities for graft and political entree normally denied civilians. The only price for such favored treatment was unquestioned allegiance to Trujillo.

Another major characteristic of the Trujillo years was the economic "acquisitiveness" of the inner circle—a euphemism, perhaps, for wholesale graft and stealing. It was, however, orderly graft and controlled theft. Trujillo monopolized the tobacco and salt industries; he controlled practically all sugar refining; he demanded and received a cut on all cattle transactions. He, his family, and his retainers acquired unbelievably extensive holdings in urban property and especially in rural estates.

Trujillo succeeded in paying off almost the entire debt of the government, both internal and foreign. The government, which a quarter century before he came into power had been on the edge of public bankruptcy, established a remarkably good credit rating. But along with such fiscal rectitude went incredible swilling at the public trough. The whole take of Trujillo, his family, and his friends will probably never be known, but it has been conservatively estimated that their enrichment at Dominican expense reached at least a half billion dollars. After Trujillo's assassination it was estimated that 35 percent of the economically active Dominican population had been government employees and that an additional 45 percent had been directly employed in enterprises controlled by the dictator or his relatives or friends.

A third characteristic of the dictatorship was its pandering to Trujillo's vanity, which reached unparalleled heights and was served by institutionalized techniques never before or since achieved in Latin America. Not Rosas, Fran-cisco Solano López, Guzmán Blanco, Duvalier, nor even Castro could match Trujillo in the cloying adulation he demanded and received at every turn.[2] Pervasive nepotism also characterized his rule. It was a government of, by, and for the Trujillos.

A final characteristic may be mentioned: Trujillo systematically rotated officials, both civil and military, to prevent them from developing power roots or devoted followings that could potentially threaten his political dominance. It became standard practice for Trujillo to require officials, including members of congress and judges, to file their signed but undated resignations with him when they assumed office. These he would, at will, date and publish. The official thus dismissed might receive another post, perhaps distant or unrelated to what he had been doing, or he might be cast into political oblivion.

Soon after his accession to power, Trujillo abolished the existing political parties and substituted a new organization, the Dominican party (Partido Dominicano), designed to be mass-based. Membership was compulsory for all government employees (they were subjected to a 10 percent salary deduction to fill the party treasury) and was highly expedient for professionals and businesspeople.

Trujillo at times had an almost contemptuous attitude toward the Dominican party; it was a toy rather than an institution. As a preliminary to the presidential campaign of 1942, he saw fit to organize the Trujillo party (Partido Trujillista). This was not a competing party but rather a distillation of the Dominican party. Membership was reserved for the elite of the regime, a cordon bleu of loyalty. In December 1940 the dictator was officially named the "only Chief of the Trujillist party." This inner-sanctum organization was so patently synthetic and purposeless that it was soon allowed to die on the vine.

In 1947, in preparation for another presidential campaign, Trujillo or-dered two "opposition" parties formed. They created, for the incredibly naive, the illusion of a democratically contested election. Trujillo may have derived cynical amusement from the supineness with which the country accepted his hypocrisy. It would be difficult to find in the whole landscape of Latin Ameri-can political parties as debased and humiliating a scene as was found in the Dominican Republic during his dictatorship.

Trujillo's poise was shaken in 1960 when his attempted assassination of

[2]For example, Santo Domingo, the oldest Spanish city in the New World, was renamed Ciudad Trujillo (the name has since been changed back); new provinces were named or old ones renamed for him. At one time or another he received such titles as Benefactor of the Fatherland, Generalissimo, Restorer of Financial Independence, the Protector of Organized Workers, the Greatest Worker in the Republic, the Father of the New Fatherland—the list could be continued *ad nauseam*. For further examples, see Jesús de Galíndez, *La Era de Trujillo: Un Estudio Casuístico de Dictadura Hispanoamericana.* 4th ed. (Buenos Aires: Marymer, 1962).

President Rómulo Betancourt in Venezuela failed and backfired. Internal disaffection in the Dominican Republic reached new levels, and the dictator felt it necessary to undertake a much more extensive armament program, which hurt the economy and led to new indebtedness. Catholic bishops had two successive critical pastoral letters read in all churches, respectfully but strongly pressing for more humane treatment of political prisoners.

On the night of May 30, 1961, the dictator was shot to death in an ambush on a highway several miles west of Ciudad Trujillo.

President Balaguer and Trujillo's sons — especially Ramfis—and brothers, Héctor and Arismendi, now represented the regime. Balaguer was made of far less stern stuff than Trujillo, and he made early gestures toward democratizing the system, not only to placate the dazed but crystallizing forces of the internal opposition but also to assuage the criticism of the inter-American community. Disorder in the capital city and elsewhere was relatively light, considering the potentially tremendous repercussions of the assassination. It was as if the political feelings of the country had been so anesthetized that time was required for sensation to return to the body politic.

The Trujillo family did not succeed in closing ranks as well as Somoza's sons had in Nicaragua a few years earlier. The uncles in particular tried to maintain the ancien régime, but they and Ramfis were permanently forced out before the end of 1961. The departure of the political members of the family allowed conditions to settle down in large degree. Army officers were becoming more politically active. When the prohibition on party activity was lifted in 1961, new groups sprang up like weeds after a spring shower; in all, more than twenty became active. Most were lightly rooted. They represented almost the whole spectrum, from right-of-center to far left. The Dominican party carried on, if only for a time, by sheer momentum.

The ground under Balaguer began to erode rapidly toward the end of 1961. He tried, with only temporary success, to make himself president of a council of state. Much of the council's energies during 1962 were devoted to preparations for presidential elections. In mid-September 1962 the council approved a revised version of the constitution of 1955. A commission chosen by the Organization of American States did yeoman work in suggesting revisions to the electoral laws.

Politics during most of 1962 focused on the forthcoming presidential election. The council of state firmly insisted on a free and orderly political process. The electoral tribunal undertook a remarkable campaign of civic education. As the party scene gradually crystallized, seven parties finally presented candidates for the presidency. The chief parties were the Dominican Revolutionary party (Partido Revolucionario Dominicano, or PRD), a non-Communist liberal group led by the long-exiled Juan Bosch, and the National Civic Union (Unión Cívica Nacional, or UCN), a moderately conservative party whose candidate was a previously nonpolitical physician, Dr. Viriato

Fiallo. The election, on December 20, 1962, was orderly and popular. Bosch won, receiving a somewhat surprising three-fifths of the total votes (628,000 of 1,055,000) cast for all presidential candidates who continued in the race.

Bosch was inaugurated late in February 1963. His hold on the reins of government was weak, and he failed to consolidate his position with certain power elements in the country, notably the army and the Church. The army was increasingly worried by the allegedly Communist overtones of the administration. In September 1963 a coup, led by Minister of the Armed Forces Viñas Román and the politically ambitious General Wessin y Wessin, overthrew Bosch and vested power in a civilian-military junta. The junta received the open or tacit support of most of the republic's political parties, except of course the PRD and the more conservative power elements such as the landowners, the business interests, and the Church.

Pro-Bosch elements staged their own coup late in April 1965, immediately forcing the junta out of office. The United States added to the confusion by intervening unilaterally almost immediately with large contingents of troops, ostensibly to protect and evacuate the several thousand United States and other foreign nationals but actually to forestall the alleged threat of a Communist takeover. The United States soon made a virtue out of near necessity by turning over at least nominal responsibility for the intervention and the continuing occupation to the Organization of American States, which grudgingly agreed to provide a joint military force to maintain order in and around Santo Domingo.

After prolonged and precarious negotiation among the various factions, the impasse was uneasily resolved by an agreement to install Héctor García Godoy, a previously nonpolitical businessman, as provisional president. Crisis became almost continuous. The reduced numbers of foreign troops were frequently called upon in the late months of 1965 and 1966 to maintain order.

The provisional regime attempted to make plans for new, supervised elections in mid-1966. Bosch returned to the Dominican Republic and, despite his petulant behavior, remained an influential political figure with considerable popular support. After much uncertainty, the election was held on June 1, 1966. Bosch's vacillation and his apparent lack of courage in campaigning cost him support; Balaguer succeeded in gaining strength by purging his image of earlier association with Trujillo while retaining, among the lower classes, some credit for distribution of largesse under Trujillo's auspices. Balaguer and his newly organized Reform party (Partido Reformista, or PR) won easily—he polled 745,409 votes to Bosch's 517,784 and Rafael Bonnelly's 45,079. Balaguer was inaugurated July 1, 1966. The country wrote a new constitution in November 1966.

Balaguer's path was rocky. He was only partially successful in reducing the political importance of the army by exiling some of its restive leaders to diplomatic posts abroad. Bosch went into voluntary exile in Europe, and the PRD underwent a partial split, to the consequent advantage of the Reformistas. In the early weeks of 1970, political tensions and strife were heightened markedly. The prevailing belief that President Balaguer would manipulate himself into another term in office led all opposing candidates to threaten a boycott of the election unless Balaguer resigned his office before the balloting. On April 16 he compromised by taking a leave of absence. Juan Bosch and his Dominican Revolutionary party persisted in their boycott of the election, and Bosch made vague threats of an uprising that would establish a "popular dictatorship." Violence marked the closing of the campaign: In the three weeks before the balloting, twenty-nine people were killed and forty-seven wounded in political disorders.

In the voting on May 16, Balaguer won the expected victory, with 607,707 votes of a total of 1,111,853. The combinations of apathy and violence, abstentions and frustrations did not augur well for the near future of Dominican politics.

Balaguer successfully dealt with an attempted coup in 1971. In the 1974 election campaign the coalition of several opposition parties advanced the candidacy of Antonio Silvestre Guzmán Fernández against Balaguer. Extreme violence marked the campaign, and at the last minute Guzmán withdrew, charging election fraud. With virtually all of his opposition abstaining, Balaguer received 80 percent of the vote. Guzmán demanded annulment of the election results but later agreed not to press his demand after Balaguer assured him that he would not stand for reelection in 1978.

But, despite his promise, Balaguer did run for a fourth successive term. By late 1977 a number of party favorites, including Juan Bosch of the Dominican Liberation party (Partido de Liberación Dominicana, or PLD) and General Wessin y Wessin of the Quisqueyan Democratic party (Partido Quisqueyano Democrático, or PQD) had announced their candidacies. The PRD had earlier in the year opened the selection of its presidential candidate to the members of the party through local primaries. In a close convention runoff Antonio Guzmán won the nomination. The democratic convention was a far cry from the autocratic style of its founder, former President Juan Bosch, and greatly strengthened the party for the upcoming campaign.

The campaign itself was rather smooth and mild compared to the election and its aftermath. Many Dominicans felt that Balaguer could not lose an election; even many from Guzmán's own party felt that the best they could hope for would be such a good showing that Balaguer would be forced to resort to fraud to stay in power. This would, they felt, bring heavy consequences to him both from within and outside the country.

The Abduction of Democracy

As the voting returns started trickling in the day after the election on May 16, President Balaguer was, to everyone's surprise, losing his battle to win a fourth term. But before all the ballots could be counted, a strange set of events occurred. Soldiers burst into the electoral board office and ordered all vote counting stopped. All television and radio broadcasting throughout the country ceased. Two days of silence passed before President Balaguer broadcast to the nation that he would respect the election results whoever proved to be the winner and declared that the counting should continue.

What happened in those two days of silence is pure speculation. It is known, however, that the United States State Department and the ambassador to the Dominican Republic as well as the presidents of Venezuela, Colombia, Panama, and Costa Rica made their views known. The Dominicans themselves demonstrated their disgust and outrage over such a crude and blatant effort to prevent the opposition from winning. It has been speculated that, although Balaguer did not authorize the coup, he did nothing to stop it until forced to by pressure from the United States and Venezuela and from within the Dominican Republic itself.

By the end of May, President Balaguer conceded defeat and sent his congratulations to Guzmán. It was not until July 7, however, that the electoral board officially announced Antonio Guzmán's election. Once inaugurated he swiftly replaced five military officers involved in the attempted May coup. Guzmán's inauguration marked the first time in the country's history that a freely elected president succeeded another to the presidency.

GOVERNMENTAL AND POLITICAL STRUCTURES

Since the 1966 constitution and the governmental structure authorized by it have not yet been fully tested, comment on the mechanics of governmental composition and operation will be brief. According to the most recent formal provision, the president serves for a four-year term, is elected by direct popular vote, and is eligible for immediate reelection. The size of the cabinet has varied from time to time, but under Guzmán it included thirteen ministers, all serving, of course, at the pleasure of the president. The bicameral congress includes a senate of twenty-seven members (one per province and one for the Federal District) popularly elected for four-year terms and a chamber of deputies based on population (currently with ninety-one members), also popularly elected for four-year terms. Universal suffrage for men and women over eighteen years of age prevails.

The judiciary includes the supreme court with a minimum of nine justices, a constitutional minimum of five courts of appeal, courts of first instance, local civil courts, and a number of special courts. Judges of the higher courts are elected by the senate.

Local government includes a hierarchy of units: the provinces (most recently set at 26, though the number has changed several times), which have presidentially appointed governors; 76 municipalities, roughly equivalent to counties; and 1,606 *secciones,* which could be likened to townships in some respects. The capital city is organized as a National District, governed by an elected council.

Party Systems

At the beginning of the 1970s, the political party system in the Dominican Republic was far from stable. At the time of the 1962 election the National Civic Union (UCN), chiefly backed by the business and professional community, seemed a possible challenger to the PRD, but in the next few years it evaporated almost completely. The young Reformist party (PR), on which Balaguer rode to victory in 1966, 1970, and 1974, drew heavily on peasant and middle-class support. In a monstrous "sleight of hand" ruling in the 1978 election, the election committee gave the PR candidate thousands of uncast ballots in the senate races. This gave the PR a majority of sixteen to eleven in the senate. It was a matter of speculation whether the party would survive once Balaguer left the scene.

The Revolutionary Social Christian party (Partido Revolucionario Social Cristiano, or PRSC) is patterned after other Christian Democratic parties of Latin America. The PRSC was part of the coalition which advanced the candidacy of Guzmán in the 1974 elections and later participated in the boycott of that election. The conservative Quisqueyan Democratic party (PQD) appeared in 1967 as the political vehicle of General Wessin y Wessin following his exile in the United States. General Wessin was the PQD's candidate in 1970 but supported the 1974 boycott. He was the PQD's candidate again in 1978.

The Dominican Revolutionary party (PRD) was founded by former President Juan Bosch Gaviño in 1939. In the early post-Trujillo period the PRD enjoyed the reputation as the country's leading political group. After the mercurial Bosch left the country following his defeat in 1966, the party suffered from factionalism and declined in strength. It boycotted both the 1970 and 1974 elections, charging "colossal fraud." In the May 1978 presidential election of Antonio Silvestre Guzmán, the PRD regained its stature as an opposition party to be reckoned with by scoring an unexpected victory over the PR candidate, Joaquín Balaguer. The PRD has lost much of its nationalist and semirevolutionary trappings of the '60s, which is, of course, the main reason for the United States's assurance of continued friendly relations with the Dominican Republic during the Guzmán administration.

The Dominican Liberation party (PLD) was formed by Juan Bosch as a split from the PRD in 1974 to put forward his candidacy for president. He ran again in the 1978 election on the same ticket.

Another party called the Movement of National Conciliation (Movimiento de Conciliación Nacional, or MCN) was organized in 1968 to sponsor the presidential candidacy of Héctor García Godoy. The MCN also boycotted the 1974 elections.

DEVELOPMENTAL PROSPECTS

As in other Latin American states with a prevailing cult of personalism, neither the Dominican constitution nor the laws dictate the form and functioning of public life. Rather politics calls the turns, even without Trujillo. By February 1963, when Juan Bosch was installed as president, the results seemed almost too good to be true. A liberal president was put in office after a campaign and election that were truly heartening in their demonstration of a revived democratic political process. But democracy proved to be only lightly rooted. Militarism, even without the banner of Trujillo, had not yet lived out its day. The idealistic and inexperienced Bosch proved unequal to the task of restoring a viable democratic system in the republic.

President Balaguer tried to succeed where Bosch failed. A longtime protégé of Trujilo, Balaguer was able to keep the country at peace during his three consecutive terms, a great boon to the $90 million tourist industry. But Balaguer was not able to control the 20 percent unemployment rate in 1978 nor to alleviate the economic slump caused by a sharp drop in sugar prices. Although perhaps himself an honest man, Balaguer's regime was blamed for allowing corruption to flourish, especially within the ranks of the military. Balaguer was by no means unaware of what was going on. He was a master at keeping the powerful generals divided among themselves yet supporting him, and he never retained one general in a post long enough to amass any real power.

President Guzmán pledged full support for the military and their traditions. He promised the armed forces improved living conditions and continued professionalization. According to Guzmán, the military would never regret their decision to accept the 1978 electoral verdict. He won the tacit endorsement of the United States government as the winner of the 1978 elections. His victory over Balaguer was proof enough for the PRD that the masses wanted a change—not a drastic change, but at least a change.

Many problems awaited President Guzmán in the presidential office, including economic stagnation and such related problems as unemployment, malnutrition, a need for a housing development program, and a shortage of capital, not to mention petty party rivalry within the ruling PRD. The wealthy cattle rancher and coffee planter will have to use all his political and economic skills to hold the ship of government afloat in the murky waters of Dominican militarism.

REFERENCES

ATKINS, G. POPE, and LARMAN C. WILSON. *The United States and the Trujillo Regime.* New Brunswick, N. J.: Rutgers University Press, 1972.

BOSCH, JUAN. *Crisis de la Democracia de América en la República Dominicana.* Mexico: Costa-Amic, 1965.

———. *The Unfinished Experiment.* New York: Holt, Rinehart & Winston, 1965.

BROOKE, EDWARD W. *Review of Factors Affecting United States Diplomatic and Assistance Relations with Haiti.* Washington, D.C.: U.S. Government Printing Office, 1977.

COURLANDER, HAROLD, and RÉMY BASTIEN. *Religion and Politics in Haiti.* Washington, D.C.: Institute for Cross-Cultural Research, 1966.

CRASSWELLER, ROBERT D. *Trujillo: The Life and Times of a Caribbean Dictator.* New York: Macmillan, 1966.

DE ONIS, JUAN. "The Hispanic Caribbean." In *The United States and the Caribbean,* ed. by Tad Szulc. Englewood Cliffs, N. J.: Prentice-Hall, 1971.

DEYOUNG, MAURICE. *Man and Land in the Haitian Economy.* Gainesville: University of Florida Press, 1958.

DIEDERICH, BERNARD, and AL BURT. *Papa Doc: The Truth about Haiti Today.* New York: McGraw-Hill, 1969.

FAGG, JOHN E. *Cuba, Haiti and The Dominican Republic.* Englewood Cliffs, N. J.: Prentice-Hall, 1965.

GALÍNDEZ, JESÚS DE. *La Era de Trujillo: Un Estudio Casuístico de Dictadura Hispanoamericana* 4th ed. Buenos Aires: Marymer, 1962.

GLEIJESES, PIERO. *The Dominican Crisis: The 1965 Constitutionalist Revolt and American Intervention,* trans. by Lawrence Lipson. Baltimore: John Hopkins University Press, 1978.

GOLD, HERBERT. "Haiti: Hatred without Hope." *Saturday Evening Post* 238:8 (April 24, 1965), 74–80.

GORDON, RAOUL, ed. *Image of the Dominican Republic; The Dominican Miracle.* New York: Gordon Press, 1978.

GUTÍERREZ, CARLOS MARÍA. *The Dominican Republic: Rebellion and Repression.* New York: Monthly Review Press, 1972.

KURZMAN, DAN. *Santo Domingo: Revolt of the Damned.* New York: Putman, 1965.

LOGAN, RAYFORD W. *Haiti and the Dominican Republic.* London and New York: Oxford University Press, 1968.

LOWENTHAL, ABRAHAM F. *The Dominican Intervention.* Cambridge, Mass.: Harvard University Press, 1972.

MARTIN, JOHN B. *Overtaken by Events.* New York: Doubleday, 1966.

ORNES, GERMÁN E. *Trujillo: Little Caesar of the Caribbean.* New York: Nelson, 1958.

PAYNE, JAMES L. *Incentive Theory & Political Process: Motivation and Leadership in the Dominican Republic.* College Station, Texas: Lytton Publishing, 1976.

RICE, BERKELEY. "Haiti: Last Act of A Tragicomedy." *Harper's Magazine* 226:1356 (May 1963), 65–75.

RODMAN, SELDEN. *Haiti: The Story of the Black Republic.* rev. ed. Old Greenwich, Conn.: Devin-Adair, 1974.

ROTBURG, ROBERT I. *Haiti; the Politics of Squalor.* Boston: Houghton Mifflin, 1971.

SZULC, TAD. *Dominican Diary.* New York: Delacorte Press, 1965.

WIARDA, HOWARD J. *The Dominican Republic: Nation in Transition.* New York: Holt, Rinehart & Winston, 1969.

———. "Politics of Civil-Military Relations in the Dominican Republic." *Journal of Inter-American Studies* 7 (October 1965), 465–484.

WINGFIELD, ROLAND, and VERNON J. PARENTOLIN. "Class Structure and Class Conflict in Haitian Society." *Social Forces* 43:3 (1965), 338–347.

Part Four

THE ANDEAN SECTOR

7

VENEZUELA

Petro Politics
in a Democracy

POLITICAL CULTURE AND ENVIRONMENT

Venezuela is a land of great and often violent contrasts in geography, history, culture, and politics. In politics the farsighted dictator Bolívar can be contrasted with the repressive dictator Gómez. Over long periods the state was virtually a private fief; it has had protracted dictatorships and more years of military presidencies in a recent six-decade interval than in almost any other Latin American state. In late years this has given way to constructive and imaginative democratic progress, significant development of political parties, and interparty accommodation. In geography, economy, and culture the emptiness and backwardness of the *llanos,* or plains, contrasts vividly with the modernity and even sophistication of Caracas.

The most important section of Venezuela is the highlands, the spur of the Andes running across northern Venezuela. That region contains the bulk of the population and most of the major cities. It has played a central role in the history, culture, and politics of the country. The Maracaibo basin, the extensive lowland area surrounding the curious ocean-connected "Lake" Maracaibo, is economically important for its fabulous petroleum deposits and consequently has had direct and considerable influence on politics. Other regions of Venezuela have less political importance.

Venezuela's 352,051-square-mile area makes it seventh in size among the Latin American countries; its 14,134,000 inhabitants (1980 estimate) make it sixth in population, only slightly below Peru. More than half of Venezuela's area is not productive, either actually or potentially; the only large country with a higher proportion of unproductive land is Chile with its extensive northern deserts. The lack of geographical integration, vividly illustrated by the sorry state of transportation, encourages regional separatism, facilitates dictatorial movements and revolutions, and in still other ways retards the growth of democracy.

Venezuela is primarily a mestizo country—according to recent estimates 70 percent of its population is mestizo, 20 percent white, 8 percent black, and only 2 percent Indian. Although the ethnic distribution almost mirrors that of neighboring Colombia, the European-descended fraction in Venezuela makes a much smaller psychological imprint on politics than its counterpart in Colombia. This discrepancy may be partially explained by the considerably higher literacy rate in Colombia.

As is usual in Latin American countries, the capital city is far larger than any other; in 1972 metropolitan Caracas had an estimated population of 1,035,500—more than a tenth of the whole population of Venezuela. The population of Caracas has grown rapidly in recent years, at times reaching the fantastic rate of 7 percent annually. Such growth has inevitably caused serious problems of economic and social absorption and created a situation of at least potential political explosiveness.

The imbalance in the population pattern is fully matched in the psychological and cultural profile of the country. The *llaneros* of the plains and other cattle-raising areas, cultural cousins of the nineteenth-century gauchos of the Argentine pampas, still lead a rugged existence innocent of all amenities. They are contemptuous—perhaps partly in self-defense—of the sophistication of the cities. On the other hand Caracas and a few of the other cities reflect an architectural, economic, and cultural veneer which is essentially alien to the rest of Venezuela. The symbols and manifestations of wealth, intentionally designed to impress and attract tourists, are less a reflection of the real Venezuela than of the great gulf between conflicting cultures and economies. Only a strong hand could hold such diversity together—which helps account for the prevalence of dictators in Venezuela.

Economic disparity is probably as great in Venezuela as in any other Latin American country. Although the per capita share of the GNP in 1974 was almost $1,000 a year (second only to Argentina in Latin America), this figure is misleading, since it reflects the vast income from the oil industry, which goes to a relatively few people. Moreover the high wages paid petroleum workers drain off labor from the other parts of the country and from other economic activities and add to inflation.

Political Development

Stresses and distortions in politics have equalled those in geography and demography. Bolívar, born in Venezuela but most influential outside of it, yielded in that country at the end of the 1820s to *llanero* José Antonio Páez, the first of a long series of *caudillos.* At the same time that Gran Colombia disintegrated, an independent Venezuela emerged and in September 1830 took its first step as a nation by writing a separate constitution. Despite (or perhaps because of) the largely personal character of the government, this constitution proved to be Venezuela's most long-lived—it was not supplanted until 1857. Dictators of lesser stature followed after the downfall of Páez in 1846, but political stability or genuine issues were almost entirely absent. After a short-lived experiment with unitarism in Venezuela, a new constitution in 1864 recognized the vigorous and deep-rooted regionalism by returning to a federal form of government which has since been maintained through numerous succeeding constitutions.

Another major *caudillo* emerged at the beginning of the 1870s. Antonio Guzmán Blanco became president in 1870 and completely dominated the country for almost two decades thereafter. Despite his egocentricity governmental efficiency and material conditions improved, but no substantial gain in democracy or the political process can be credited to his rule.

A more mercurial though less important dictator, Cipriano Castro, ruled despotically from 1899 to 1908. When he went to Europe late in 1908 for medical treatment, he left his fief in the hands of a trusted political lieutenant, the Venezuelan vice-president, Juan Vicente Gómez. A few weeks later Gómez took over and continued as one of Latin America's most absolute dictators for more than a quarter of a century. Despite his ruthless methods, order prevailed, agricultural production increased, and road building and other public works were stimulated. Many of these public improvements were merely showpieces, however, and basic transportation and living conditions were little improved.

The development of petroleum drilling, especially in the Maracaibo basin, fundamentally altered the Venezuelan economy. By about 1930 Venezuela had become the second or third largest oil producer in the world, a rank the country usually maintained thereafter. Gómez saw to it that good returns were assured from the United States and foreign investing companies to the enrichment of Venezuela—and himself. The foreign debt was paid off and elaborate new public works were built, but the country's economy became badly unbalanced, and the cost of living increased tremendously.

The iron control imposed by Gómez did not preclude continued exercises in constitution writing. Seven basic laws were drafted during Gómez's years in power.

The death of the dictator—peacefully in bed—unleashed a brief whirlwind of riot and reprisal by the residents of Caracas who for so long had been severely repressed, but the army quickly closed ranks behind Gómez's war minister (and son-in-law), General Eleazar López Contreras, as provisional president. The following quarter of a century was a time of much political fluctuation, with democratic experiment alternating with dictatorial repression. It is surprising that, considering how long and how tightly the lid had been held down by Gómez, Venezuela did not immediately turn toward violent, uncontrolled, and extreme social and economic revolution, as Mexico did after the downfall of Díaz or Cuba after the ouster of Batista.

Was it more than happenstance? Perhaps Venezuela's relative tranquility at Gómez's death in 1935 can be explained partly by the complete absence of any political parties or other institutions for channeling and focusing political opinion. Under superficially similar circumstances such instrumentalities existed in both Mexico and Cuba, even if sometimes in rudimentary and inchoate form. Because Gómez had suppressed all such activity, the agencies to express political opinion had to be created completely from scratch, and that obviously could not be done overnight.

López Contreras headed what could be called a pseudodemocratic government; although the army was naturally the major element, owners of businesses and *latifundia* also exercised a significant role. The congress, even though composed largely of gomezistas, had little practical choice but to elect López Contreras as constitutional president in April 1936. He sponsored some reform legislation, but it fell short of a social revolution. His term of office was noteworthy for laying the groundwork for the birth of Venezuela's first real political party, Democratic Action (Acción Democrática, popularly known as AD).

Plans for the congressional election of a successor to López Contreras crystallized in 1940, and the young AD supported Rómulo Gallegos, one of Latin America's most distinguished novelists. But as prearranged by the president, General Isaías Medina Angarita, like López Contreras a former minister of war, was overwhelmingly elected president in late 1940.

Medina's regime was even more moderate and potentially liberal than that of López Contreras, but with party activity now beginning to rear its eager head—or heads—he was riding a restless team of unmatched chargers down an unsurveyed political racecourse. To the political right of Medina were the lopezistas and the discredited but still somewhat influential remnants of the Gómez regime. To the left were Acción Democrática, a small and unorganized group of middle-rank military officers, and miscellaneous elements. Medina's seeming inclination toward the civilian sectors, and especially toward organized labor, began to make him suspect with the army.

A complex political scene in 1945 resulted in a successful coup in mid-October led by AD and disgruntled army officers. Government was provisionally put in the hands of a seven-man junta; only two of its members were army officers. The army elements in the center of political activity at the time professed sympathy with civilian, democratic, and constitutional control.

The principal member of the junta, the man who became provisional president, was Rómulo Betancourt, perhaps the best known leader, other than Gallegos, of Acción Democrática. Betancourt had been a political exile under Gómez. He had briefly belonged to the Communist party and had later become a severe critic of it. He had strongly supported a Venezuelan labor movement.

A new constitution was promulgated in July 1947; although it contained much unnecessary and statutory detail, it was by far the most democratic Venezuela had ever had.

Army restiveness, Communist agitation, and oil workers' demands compounded the difficulties of the junta during 1947, but it proceeded with plans for presidential elections late in the year. Acción Democrática, clearly the best organized party, had again nominated Rómulo Gallegos. A more conservative party was the Social Christian party (Comité Organizador Pro Elecciones Independientes) which is usually abbreviated to its initials and, like the better known Apra of Peru, has been taken into political parlance as a single, synthetic word, Copei. Copei was composed primarily of businesspeople and the wealthier upper classes and was generally oriented toward the Catholic church. The Democratic Republican Union (Unión Republicana Democrática, or URD) was a small group whose views were essentially similar to those of AD but which, partially for personalist reasons, followed a separate path. Communists also nominated a candidate. The new constitution provided for a popular election and, as was expected, Gallegos won by a large majority, carrying with him major support in both houses of the congress.

Soon after his inauguration in mid-February 1948, certain of Gallegos's actions increasingly began to alienate the army. The growing crisis culminated with an army coup in late November 1948, which ousted Gallegos and installed a military junta. Gallegos, Betancourt, and many others went into exile. The coup in Venezuela followed by only a few weeks a somewhat similar one in Peru; the two, together with the contemporarily deteriorating political situations in Colombia, Argentina, and elsewhere, seemed to betoken a widespread and serious reversal for civilian governments. The Venezuelan upset can probably best be explained by the wish of Acción Democrática to make an impressive record in a short time, its undue bypassing of the army, and Gallegos's political ineptness.

The junta adopted increasingly undemocratic and repressive measures, including the outlawing of both Acción Democrática and the Communists. After the junta president was assassinated late in 1950, the harshness of the regime immediately and sharply increased. A civilian was named to fill the junta presidency, but the clearly dominant figure in the junta was Colonel Marcos Pérez Jiménez, obviously a potential "iron man." The junta promised elections for late 1952, though with AD and the Communists still banned, the public had little confidence in junta sincerity. With Acción Democrática out of the way, the principal opposition was provided by the Democratic Republican Union.

The first published results of the election indicated that URD candidates ran far ahead of all others. The junta then suspended the vote counting, declared a state of siege, temporarily prohibited all publication of newspapers or broadcasting of radio programs, and, after a few days' delay, announced "official" final figures which gave its own synthetic Independent Electoral Front an overwhelming victory. Pérez Jiménez was declared the provisional president of Venezuela. Early the following year he was named constitutional president for a five-year term by a new constituent assembly. The actions of late 1952 were as bold an imposition of a presidential candidate as Latin America had experienced in a long time.

Pérez Jiménez was now free to begin an excessively harsh period of dictatorship. It was not as crude as the regime of Gómez, but the army as an institution was enthroned in even greater degree. The regime proclaimed a new constitution in April 1953 to provide itself with a semblance of legal foundation, but its control remained based on raw force. Pérez Jiménez (or "P.J.") did not even attempt a façade of reform such as his contemporary, Rojas Pinilla, initially undertook in neighboring Colombia.

In mid-December 1957 Pérez Jiménez, after another rigged election, was declared president for a second term. This maneuver precipitated an insurrection that began on the last day of the year. The dictator temporarily recovered control but was forced to leave Venezuela on January 23. A junta headed by Admiral Wolfgang Larrazábal Ugueto took control. The junta began, apparently in good faith, to prepare the country for free and democratic elections late in the year.

The Democratic Transition

Acción Democrática was again legalized and immediately assumed a lead in the electoral campaign. In the presidential balloting on December 7, 1958, its candidate, Rómulo Betancourt, was elected. Prior to his inauguration on February 13, 1959, he succeeded in arranging a coalition among AD, the Social Christians (Copei), and the Democratic Republican Union (URD).

Betancourt's five-year term was a succession of crises. He was a controversial and tough-minded president, staunchly democratic in his philosophy (though he frequently was compelled to impose press censorship), and fearlessly adamant toward political opposition, whether domestic or international. Although his resoluteness enabled him to surmount the various crises, these crises seriously interfered with the reform program he hoped to implement. In June 1960 there was a sensational attempt to assassinate the president, an attempt that evidence linked unquestionably to the Dominican government and probably to Trujillo himself.

The party coalition began to disintegrate by late summer of 1960, and the following year it was reorganized as an alliance between only AD and Copei. Betancourt, originally an admirer of Fidel Castro, quickly became disenchanted with the excesses and the Communist rapprochement of the Cuban dictator and, as a result, increasingly became the target of Cuban propaganda. By 1963 the Cuban effort to export its revolution to Venezuela was facilitated by the sustained terrorism of the Armed Forces of National Liberation (Fuerzas Armadas de Liberación Nacional, or FALN), a sub rosa Venezuelan group with at least a high nuisance value.

Betancourt began resolutely preparing for elections in December 1963. Seven candidates competed for the presidency, chief of whom were Raúl Leoni (AD), Jóvito Villalba (URD), and Rafael Caldera (Copei). AD was badly fractured. The FALN pulled out all stops in an effort to disrupt the election; nonetheless, an unusually high 90 percent of the eligible voters went to the polls. Leoni won, and his term, 1964–1969, represented a continuation of the policies and program of Betancourt. His administration was relatively stable despite continued guerrilla activity.

Political parties underwent important modification. Acción Democrática appeared to be losing some of its appeal to Venezuelan youth. For the election of December 1, 1968, AD nominated Gonzalo Barrios; the Social Christians (Copei) renamed their perennial candidate, Rafael Caldera. A close race between Caldera and Barrios was assured. The officially announced returns showed the Christian Democrat the winner. It was the first time in Venezuelan history that an administration in power turned over the reins of government to an opposition party which had won in a peaceful, orderly election. Caldera was inaugurated on March 11, 1969.

Caldera was the first Christian Democratic president in Venezuela and the second in Latin America, following Eduardo Frei of Chile. Caldera sought to "normalize" Venezuelan political life and will be remembered for his pacification program, aimed at reducing terrorism in Venezuela. He gave legal recognition to the Communist party, providing the terrorists with a viable alternative.

Caldera was also successful on the economic front. Late in 1970, Congress passed legislation which put the Venezuelan monetary control firmly into the hands of domestically controlled banks. Banks with more than 20 percent foreign ownership were not allowed to accept savings deposits, issue negotiable certificates of deposit, or sell foreign exchange purchased from the Central Bank. The oil reversion law passed by congress in 1971 gave the government power to take over within three years unexploited oil concessions held by foreign oil companies.

Despite his domestic successes, his most impressive achievements were in foreign relations. Caldera rejected his predecessors' philosophy of not recognizing those regimes within Latin America that had gained power by nondemocratic means. He exchanged ambassadors with the Soviet Union and other Eastern-bloc nations. In 1973 Venezuela took another giant step under his regime with its entry into economic integration with the Andean group of Bolivia, Chile, Peru, Ecuador, and Colombia. He established cordial relations with such governments as Russia and Cuba, and he continued to maintain friendly relations with Western countries, including the United States.

The 1973 election, the fourth since the overthrow of Pérez Jiménez, climaxed almost three years of party campaigning. Both AD and Copei candidates had hired foreign campaign specialists to project their "public image." The Venezuelan government provided free media time to fourteen candidates representing twenty-two political parties. The chief candidates were Jóvito Villalba, perennial candidate of the URD, Lorenzo Fernández of Copei, and Carlos Andrés Pérez of the AD. Fernández and Pérez were the two strong contenders. Despite their lack of color, both candidates were well qualified. Fernández, thought by many to be the stronge. of the two candidates because of his close ties with President Caldera, pledged to follow Caldera's policies of ideological pluralism and to continue his progress in such areas as road building, agriculture, and public health.[1]

Pérez, meanwhile, who had close ties with former President Betancourt, pledged to continue the fight against poverty and advocated a less conciliatory attitude toward Cuba. He also called for greater efforts in achieving land reform. But it was perhaps an event that took place outside Venezuela which gave the advantage to Pérez and the AD.

The Copei party leaders were identified with the Christian Democrats of Chile, who had given at least conditional support to the junta that overthrew Salvador Allende. This position, unpopular among many Venezuelan Christian Democrats, might have cost Fernández and Copei the election. Nevertheless, the election results were fairly close, as Table 7-1 shows.

TABLE 7-1   1973 Election Results

Candidate	Popular Vote	Percent
Pérez (AD)	2,006,214	48.61
Fernández (Copei)	1,518,385	36.79
Galárraga (MEP)	210,513	5.10
Rangel (MAS)	174,954	4.21
Villalba (URD)	126,401	3.06

The steep climb in oil prices which began in 1973 proved a tremendous stimulus to the Venezuelan economy. Critics of the Pérez regime were quick to point out, however, that bureaucratic inefficiency and government overspending squandered the oil wealth. Agricultural production did decline in the last year of the Pérez regime, and after three years, the government was still behind in carrying out land reform. In the industrial sector, rising costs and labor problems contributed to an overall decline in growth.

[1]George W. Grayson, "Venezuela's Presidential Politics," *Current History,* 66:389 (January 1974), 24.

Still, Venezuela continued to prosper during the Pérez regime. Inflation was running at about 8 percent in 1978, down from the 1975 figure of 10.2 percent. Venezuela's efforts to assist other Latin American countries were a major victory for the Pérez regime; Venezuelan aid programs are now the largest in Latin America. The Dominican Republic, Peru, Jamaica, Bolivia, Costa Rica, Honduras, Nicaragua, and Cuba have all been recipients of this aid.

The December 1978 election was dubbed a "contest of personalities without any personalities."[2] Although Luis Piñerúa of Acción Democrática was considered the man to beat, Luis Herrera Campins of Copei continued to maintain a close race with Piñerúa during the campaigning and by October was leading in the opinion polls. The two rather colorless candidates were aided in their election campaigns, as were their predecessors, by United States advisers brought in to brighten their political images. In May, just as the campaign was beginning to look like a rather dull horse race, Diego Arria, the former information minister under President Pérez, announced that he would also be campaigning for the office. Since Diego Arria was a member of AD, his entry into the race came as a surprise even to his party's official candidate, Luis Piñerúa. By the end of the campaign there were ten presidential candidates. Spending by all candidates, and especially the two major party candidates, was well over $100 million. When the voting was over on December 5, 1978, Luis Herrera Campins emerged the victor with 47 percent of the vote.

Venezuela maintained its record as a democracy with one of the highest levels of voter participation; approximately 88 percent of the electorate cast their ballots in the election.

GOVERNMENTAL AND POLITICAL STRUCTURES

The turbulent course of Venezuelan politics is complicated by the country's federal organization. Federalism has been the nominal basis of constitutional structuring since 1864. Of course during the various Venezuelan dictatorships, federalism was a complete fiction. How federalism fared during the democratic interludes was chiefly determined by politics. Although the constitution of 1961 flatly characterizes Venezuela as a federal state, that same constitution labels the country as "the Republic of Venezuela," whereas earlier basic laws had referred to it as "the United States of Venezuela."

In formal structural terms the states—there are now twenty—are described as "autonomous and equal as political entities." They are given constitutional authority to change state names, to organize local governments, and to perform a number of other functions which make their positions nominally

[2] *Latin America Venezuela Special Report,* Supplement to *Latin America Economic Report* (January 1978), p. 2.

rather impressive. But their importance is illusory. The several states of Venezuela have less historical basis for participation in a federal system than the Brazilian states or the Argentine provinces; comparison of the Venezuelan states with those of Mexico is difficult because widely differing circumstances affect the politics of the two countries; however, in both republics the financial dependence of the subdivisions, to mention only one pragmatic reason, renders genuine federalism almost impossible.

The Executive Structure

Venezuela's sorry experience with dictatorship has made the country wary of provisions or situations that might lead to renewed dictatorship. The constitution places specific limitations on who may run for the presidency and further states that a retiring president, if he has served more than half a term, may not again become chief executive until two terms, or ten years, have lapsed. Although election of the president has at times been vested in the congress or handled in yet other ways, the present constitution specifies that the office goes to the candidate receiving a plurality (the constitutional phrase is "relative majority") of the popular vote. A vice-presidency, which has at times been included in the Venezuelan structure of government, is not provided currently.

Nevertheless the constitution gives the president very extensive powers. Given the political history of the country, to do otherwise would be highly unrealistic, despite the very real possibility of renewed dictatorship. The president is given several "blank checks," although some are nominally limited by the need for approval by other agencies: authority to fix the size of the armed forces, complete control over foreign relations, and relative freedom to negotiate national loans and to decree credits outside the budget. It is pointless to differentiate between those powers which the president may exercise on his own initiative and those which the council of ministers must approve, since the president has a completely free constitutional hand to appoint and remove all ministers.

As is almost universally true in Latin America, political rather than constitutional considerations mark the real limits of presidential authority. The major factor contributing to recent changes in the presidency in Venezuela is the growth of political parties. Venezuelan parties have not become as much a part of the political life of the country as, at least in "normal" times, have those in Uruguay, Chile, Colombia, or Mexico, but they play a role in politics which would have been inconceivable three or four decades ago. They consequently impose subtle limitations on the president's freedom of action. Even a strong executive such as Betancourt has had to take into account the actual or potential weight of opposition parties in the congress and the country at large.

"acciondemocratistas" in exile in Mexico in 1957. In its overall appearance the program, like that of most aprista-type parties, reflects a somewhat theoretical and idealistic view of national problems. Nonetheless, Acción Democrática, probably more than any other similar party, has had an opportunity to translate its program into law and measure the success of its actions against the promises of its program.

The theoretical and practical relations of Acción Democrática with two long-established Venezuelan institutions, the army and the Church, inevitably posed problems. AD's first fall from power in 1948 was caused primarily by its inability to establish a satisfactory working relationship with the military. When it returned to power a decade later, it had learned the lesson. Betancourt was now more politically aware of the army's potency and of the need for treating it with consideration, not to say tenderness. The government has acceded to the army's wish to maintain a high status and has also granted it material perquisites and favors.

The relationship of AD and its governments with the Catholic church is complicated by the fact that another of the new political parties, Copei (or the Social Christian party), is much more definitely oriented toward the Church than AD ever was or presumably will be. The AD party position toward the Church, established in the 1950s, was more specific than were the clerical provisions included in the 1961 constitution, which went little beyond providing for freedom of religion.

Copei.   The bright star in the current Venezuelan political firmament is Copei, the Christian Democratic party. (The name Partido Social Cristiano, or Social Christian party, is also used.) Copei dates back to the 1946 post-Gómez period and was largely the creation of Rafael Caldera. He and Betancourt had been contemporaries and rivals during their university days, and an element of personalism entered into the establishment of the competing parties. Nonetheless Copei also had an ideological foundation—it was considerably influenced by the papal encyclicals *Rerum Novarum* (1891) and *Quadragesimo Anno* (1931). Its greatest strength was traditionally located in the conservative Andean states, especially Táchira.

Copei had functioned in a sometimes uneasy coalition with AD under Betancourt, but his successor, President Leoni, found it impossible to continue this alliance with Copei during the early months of his term. Rafael Caldera, Copei's candidate in the presidential election of 1963, came in second, with just over a fifth of the popular vote and five years later won the presidency by a narrow vote. Copei's candidate in the 1978 presidential election, Luis Herrera Campins, won by a comfortable margin over AD's candidate, Luis Piñerúa Ordaz. Copei's landslide victory in municipal elections in 1979 (50 percent of the total compared to 30 percent for AD) has earned it first place over the Acción Democrática.

Other Parties. The Democratic Republican Union (URD), whose principal founder was Jóvito Villalba, was not organized until after the 1945 revolution. It inclined toward a reform program but was often at odds with AD, chiefly on personalist grounds. Nevertheless, URD joined the Betancourt coalition in 1958. It was a tenuous alliance, however, and a cabinet reorganization in November 1960 which omitted the URD from representation caused that party to join the opposition. Jóvito Villalba continued to be the presidential candidate of the party.

The Communist Party of Venezuela (Partido Comunista Venezolano, or PCV) was formally established by student opponents of Gómez in March 1931. It was admitted to membership in the Communist International in 1935 and in general faithfully followed the Moscow line. Communists had great influence in the ranks of organized labor for some years, but they were largely supplanted in that role by AD after 1944. For several years beginning in 1945 Venezuelan Communists were split into two groups, the "Reds" and the "Blacks" (from the color of the ballots their candidates used in elections), though some doubt has been cast on the sincerity of the friction between the two groups. The Communist party later strongly supported Castro in Cuba and moved in almost identical channels with the FALN in its program of terrorism in Venezuela. The party would have had more influence and appeal had it not been for the existence of a vigorous non-Communist party of the democratic Left, as was AD. Héctor Mújica was the PCV presidential candidate in 1978.

The People's Electoral Movement (Movimiento Electoral del Pueblo, or MEP) was founded in 1967 as an offshoot of the AD in a schism over the party's choice of the presidential candidate in the 1968 election.

The party of former president Marcos Pérez Jiménez, the Nationalist Civic Crusade (Cruzada Cívica Nacionalista, or CCN) is a right-wing party with very little popular support.

The Movement to Socialism (Movimiento al Socialismo, or MAS) was started as a schism from the PCV in 1971. Recently the MAS had tended toward a policy of favoring the West European Communist parties. José Vicente Rangel continued as its presidential candidate in the 1978 election.

The Movement of the Revolutionary Left (Movimiento de Izquierda Revolucionaria, or MIR) was founded in the 1960s as a radical student movement engaged in urban terrorism. The Caldera administration legalized the MIR in 1973.

The three major political parties—AD, Copei, and URD—all advocate reform programs in varying degrees and hence are not diametrically separated on an ideological basis. At times, however, they have bitterly opposed each other in practical politics, chiefly because of leadership rivalries and inability to agree on division of spoils when operating in coalition. But Venezuela's experience with free party politics over a quarter of a century, admittedly with serious interruptions, has probably moved that state permanently into the group of Latin American countries in which party organization and activity will play a significant part in the political process.

DEVELOPMENTAL PROSPECTS

During the last two decades Venezuela has known an unprecedented period of stability and growth, both politically and economically. The country's oil wealth is surpassed only by its reservoir of political stability since the overthrow of Pérez Jiménez in 1958. Since that time Venezuela has matured from a country with a reputation of having more military presidencies in one six-decade period than practically any other Latin American state into a country which has seen four successive free and honest elections in which the reins of government were turned over to an opposition party.

Although the Venezuelan economy has hit snags in its efforts toward industrialization, in the last twenty years the country has made significant strides in laying the groundwork for a more diversified economy. Oil continues to be the most important resource; the oil industry accounted for 95 percent of the country's exports and 70 percent of its ordinary revenues in 1976. The growing increases in the price of oil in the last few years have given the country reason for optimism in its projected improvements in agriculture, education, and the infrastructure. How well Venezuela is able to meet its projected goals may well depend largely on its ability to educate and train a corps of technical and managerial personnel.

With the country's wealth has come power, both within and outside Latin America. Former President Pérez viewed OPEC countries in general and Venezuela specifically as having a responsibility to the third-world countries in their fight against inflation, rising prices, and the lowered value of the dollar. This stand, along with Venezuela's aid to other Latin American countries, has gained it many friends in the Third World. Venezuela has used its vast oil resources as a tool in its foreign relations policy. The most vivid example was the implicit threat given to then President Balaguer of the Dominican Republic during the vote counting in the 1978 presidential elections that a coup at that time could precipitate an oil embargo.

Venezuela has all this and stability too. The armed forces seem satisfied to let the politicians run the country. They have continuously pledged complete neutrality, and one general was recently overheard to say that "coups d'etat were as out of date in Venezuela as the charleston."[3]

The 1978 preelection debates centered on the national economy and society. Despite the extraordinary abundance of financial resources and stabil-

[3]*Latin America Political Report,* 12:13 (April 7, 1978), 103.

ity, no solution has been found for the plight of the "have-nots," the unskilled workers and landless peasants in Venezuela who have not yet benefitted from the *petrobolívares* (oil dollars).

Upon taking office in March 1979 President Herrera stated that he had inherited "a mortgaged country." Clearly, Herrera faces a challenge in living up to his inaugural promises of reducing the balance of payments debt of some 80 billion bolívares, curbing public spending, slowing down the country's rush toward industrialization, and still giving priority to education, agriculture, and the country's poor and middle classes.

REFERENCES

ALEXANDER, ROBERT J. "Democratic Revolution in Venezuela." *Annals of the American Academy* 358 (March 1965), 150–158.

———. *The Venezuelan Democratic Revolution: A Profile of the Regime of Rómulo Betancourt.* New Brunswick, N.J.: Rutgers University Press, 1964.

BERNSTEIN, HARRY. *Venezuela and Colombia.* Englewood Cliffs, N.J.: Prentice-Hall, 1964.

BETANCOURT, RÓMULO. *Venezuela, Politics and Oil,* trans. by Everett Bauman. Boston: Houghton Mifflin, 1978.

BLANK, DAVID EUGENE. *Politics in Venezuela.* Boston: Little, Brown, 1973.

BONILLA, FRANK, and JOSÉ SILVA MICHELENA, eds. *The Politics of Change in Venezuela,* Vol. 1. Cambridge, Mass.: MIT Press, 1967.

FARLEY, RAWLE. "The Economics of Realism: A Case Study of Economic Change in Venezuela." Pp. 279–303 in *The Economics of Latin America,* ed. by Rawle Farley. New York: Harper & Row, 1972.

FREIDMANN, JOHN. *Venezuela: From Doctrine to Dialogue.* Syracuse, N.Y.: Syracuse University Press, 1965.

GILMORE, ROBERT L. *Caudillism and Militarism in Venezuela, 1810–1910.* Athens: Ohio University Press, 1964.

GRAYSON, GEORGE W. "Venezuela's Presidential Politics." *Current History* 66:389 (January 1974), 23–40.

HARDING, TIMOTHY F., and SAUL LANDAU. "Terrorism, Guerrilla Warfare and the Democratic Left in Venezuela." *Studies on the Left* 4:4 (Fall 1964), 118–128.

KANTOR, HARRY. "The Development of Acción Democrática in Venezuela." *Journal of Inter-American Studies* 1 (April 1959), 237–255.

KOLB, GLEN L. *Democracy and Dictatorship in Venezuela, 1945–1958.* New London: Connecticut College, 1974.

LEVINE, DANIEL H. *Conflict and Political Change in Venezuela.* Princeton, N.J.: Princeton University Press, 1973.

LIEUWEN, EDWIN. *Venezuela.* 2nd ed. London: Oxford University Press, 1963.

LOTT, LEO B. "The Executive Power in Venezuela." *American Political Science Review* 50 (June 1956), 422–441.

MAMALAKIS, MARKOS. "The New International Economic Order: Centerpiece Venezuela." *Journal of Inter-American Studies and World Affairs* 20:3 (August 1978), 265–295.

MARTZ, JOHN D. *Acción Democrática: Evolution of a Modern Party in Venezuela.* Princeton, N.J.: Princeton University Press, 1966.

————. "Dilemmas in the Study of Latin American Political Parties." *Journal of Politics* 26:3 (August 1964), 509–531.

————. "Policy-Making and the Quest for Consensus. Nationalizing Venezuelan Petroleum." *Journal of Inter-American Studies and World Affairs* 19:3 (August 1977), 483–508.

MARTZ, JOHN D., and DAVID MYERS, eds. *Venezuela: The Democratic Experience.* New York: Holt, Rinehart & Winston, 1977.

MICHELENA, JOSÉ A. *The Illusion of Democracy in Dependent Nations.* Cambridge, Mass.: MIT Press, 1971.

PETRAS, JAMES, MORRIS MORLEY, and STEVEN SMITH. *The Nationalization of Venezuelan Oil.* New York: Holt, Rinehart & Winston, 1977.

POWELL, JOHN D. *Political Mobilization of the Venezuelan Peasant.* Cambridge, Mass.: Harvard University Press, 1971.

SALAZAR-CARRELLO, JORGE. *Oil in the Economic Development of Venezuela.* New York: Holt, Rinehart & Winston, 1976,

SERXNER, STANLEY J. *Acción Democrática of Venezuela: Its Origin and Development.* Gainesville: University of Florida Press, 1959.

SMITH, T. LYNN, ed. *Agrarian Reform in Latin America.* New York: Knopf, 1965.

TUGWELL, FRANKLIN. *The Politics of Oil in Venezuela.* Stanford, Calif.: Stanford University Press, 1975.

VERNON, RAYMOND. *Sovereignty at Bay.* New York: Basic Books, 1971.

8

COLOMBIA

The Instability of Parity

POLITICAL CULTURE AND ENVIRONMENT

Colombia has been called "the gateway to South America." Geographically, the claim is valid, but when the economic and cultural implications of the statement are considered, qualifications are necessary.

About two-thirds of the republic's territory lies outside what may be called effective Colombia. The most important section of the country is the highland and intermontane areas and the Caribbean coast. The geography of this region and its pattern of historic evolution have produced some fourteen traditional population clusters that display an almost inevitable diversity of political reaction and affiliation. Nonetheless Colombia has developed a re-markable cultural maturity and a political significance.

Colombia's total area of 439,513 square miles makes it the fifth largest Latin American country. The rugged terrain and the concentration of the population in the mountainous portion of the country obviously create very difficult transportation problems. Medellín, Colombia's third largest city, was almost entirely isolated from the rest of the country by the Magdalena River until the last century. The coming of the airplane helped lessen the physical provincialism of the country, but it obviously cannot solve all of Colombia's transportation problems. Lack of adequate transportation contributed greatly to a political tradition in which federalism should have developed as a logical form of government. Even now the existence of a number of widely removed centers of political tradition and psychology prevents the capital, Bogotá, from dominating the political life of the country as Montevideo does in Uruguay, La Paz in Bolivia, or Santiago in Chile. Although Bogotá continues to be the political hub of Colombia, other cities—at least Medellín and Cali—are in a position to challenge the capital in other respects and lessen the degree of single-city dominance.

Colombia's population, estimated at 30,215,000 in 1980, places it third among Latin American countries. The population is increasing very rapidly, which tends to lessen the historic impact of the various widely removed population clusters. Statistics of ethnic composition (often notoriously unreliable for any country) indicate that Colombia's population is almost 75 percent mestizo, about 20 percent white, and approximately 4 percent black.

Political Development

As the diversity in Colombia would suggest, its political development has been checkered. Bogotá, though far inland, isolated, and hard to reach, served as a viceregal capital in the late generations of the colonial period, but it was naturally much less important than Lima and Mexico City. Bolívar's larger Republic of Colombia (it was only later that historians began labeling it Gran or Great Colombia) did not continue as a unit; it was perhaps inevitable that it should soon separate into the major units which made it up: Ecuador, Colombia (proper), and Venezuela. The split came in 1830. As later phrasemakers have put it, in apt if oversimplified form, Ecuador was a monastery, Colombia a university, and Venezuela a barracks. Even within what is now Colombia, deep internal divisions occurred in the 1820s.

Bogotanos and other Colombians did not like Bolívar's lapse into dictatorship. Hence they were the more willing to follow the lead of a less important rival, General Francisco de Paula Santander, whose near unique political behavior was illustrated by the epithet he won: *"el hombre de las leyes"* ("a man of law"). Apparently, he genuinely wanted to observe constitutional forms and restrictions. Colombia proper, continuing after 1830 as the Republic of New Granada, faced two major political issues: how centralized political power should be and what the political position and influence of the Catholic church should be. The Church had played a long and influential role in colonial Colombia, and its hierarchy naturally wished to continue that role in the independent period.

The early years of independence saw the rise of two political groups: one favored centralization and an intimate and cordial Church-government relationship; the other advocated secularization and decentralization. These were, respectively, the Conservative and Liberal parties.

The republic of New Granada adopted constitutions in 1831 and 1832. The 1832 document established a unitary government, a good prima facie indication that the centralists or Conservative party was in control at the time. Nonetheless regional loyalties and interregional jealousies prevailed throughout most of the nineteenth century and even precipitated civil wars. Toward the middle of the century, the Liberal party came into ascendancy and in 1853 wrote its own new basic law, which introduced a considerable degree of decentralization and paved the way for the early establishment of a federal state. When the Conservatives returned to power, they established the 1858 constitution, which in effect created a federal government.

A more definitive constitution, retaining the United States of Colombia, was later adopted in 1863. This law continued the federal system in Colombia; if anything, the pendulum swung further in the direction of confederalism— extreme localism seemed firmly established. Political confusion and civil war were perhaps inevitable.

The long regime of Tomás Cipriano de Mosquera, a Conservative turned Liberal, gave way in the 1870s to that of Rafael Núñez. Núñez, says Hubert Herring, "began as an eager Liberal and ended as an intense Conservative." A new basic law, Colombia's longest lived constitution, was adopted in 1886 and included many concessions and compromises. Unitary government was restored, and states were reduced to the level of departments. The Church gained greatly in power; its new position was enhanced and confirmed by the negotiation of a concordat in 1887 making numerous concessions to the Church. Despite the establishment of a unitary government, the departments received important concessions, in line with the oft-quoted Colombian formula of "political centralization and administrative decentralization."

In 1899 Liberals began the "Thousand Days' War," the most serious civil conflict Colombia had yet experienced. A few months later, in November 1903, Panama seceded, and with at least moral support from the United States, it was established as an independent state and promptly concluded a Canal treaty with the North American power. These two disasters seemed to refine the metal of Colombian politics; a more mature and even sophisticated period began. Conservatives continued in control, often with little effective Liberal competition, until 1930.

A Conservative party split in the election of 1930 resulted in the victory of a moderate Liberal, Enrique Olaya Herrera; his peaceful accession to office, representing a change of party control, was unusual in Latin American politics. Olaya yielded in 1934 to a "New Deal" Liberal, Alfonso López, and he in turn to a relatively moderate Liberal, Eduardo Santos, in 1938. López was elected for a second term in 1942. Friction between the two Liberal wings was growing in intensity; López and Santos, though both wealthy members of the elite, were far from seeing eye to eye politically. A Liberal split in the election of 1946, a reversal of the situation of 1930, permitted a moderate Conservative, Mariano Ospina Pérez, to be elected president. Party strife became more bitter, fanned on one side by the intractable and reactionary Conservative leader Laureano Gómez and on the other by the charismatic, rabble-rousing, and opportunistic Liberal, Jorge Gaitán.

La Violencia

The dramatic assassination of Gaitán on April 9, 1948, during the meeting of the Ninth International Conference of American States at Bogotá set off an explosion which rocked Colombia to its depths. The martyred Gaitán would undoubtedly have been the Liberal candidate for the presidency in 1950, but under the highly strained circumstances of the time the Liberals boycotted the election—moved up to 1949—and Gómez was chosen without opposition at the polls. The inauguration of Gómez in 1950 intensified the bitterness, and by 1952 virtual civil war prevailed.

The disorder soon was given the generic name of *la violencia.* At first it was almost wholly a party war, intensified by the arrogant intransigence of Gómez after 1950. It later began to lose its political overtones and became a way of life for many notorious hinterland bands who often killed inoffensive villagers seemingly only to indulge a blood lust. The impact of the *violencia* not only on Colombian politics but also on the psychology and general life of the country was tremendous. Its cost in human lives probably reached two hundred thousand!

The dictatorship of Gómez was brought to a sudden end by an army coup in June 1953. Its leader, General Gustavo Rojas Pinilla, assumed the provisional presidency. He restored a considerable degree of order after the blood bath and virtual civil war of the previous five years. His accession to power was greeted with general enthusiasm, relief, and optimism that democratic government would quickly be restored. But Rojas's regime was inept—after all, Colombia had had almost no experience with military control. As time went on Rojas seemed to lean more toward commitment to certain aspects of a corporative state and a broad long-range program of social reform. When it became clear in the early months of 1957 that Rojas planned to remain in office beyond the end of his term in 1958, opposition rapidly crystallized, and Bogotá experienced a brief reign of terror. The army, not accustomed to occupying the center of the political stage, turned against General Rojas and in May 1957 forced him from office and into exile.

The military junta which then took power initiated a sincere plan to return control to civilian hands. The two major parties—the Conservatives, led by the wily, doughty Laureano Gómez, and the Liberals, led by the astute young Alberto Lleras Camargo, who had been provisional president for a year in 1945–1946—undertook a long and complicated series of negotiations culminating in a pact which was later frozen into constitutional prescription. The agreement, called the National Front, provided for a sixteen-year period of *alternación* (alternation) in the presidency, with the first president to be a Conservative, and *paridad* (parity), which equally divided cabinet positions, congressional seats, departmental governorships, and other executive and legislative posts between the two parties.

Almost from the beginning of the pact both major parties experienced internal divisions, sometimes serious ones that split them into supporters and opposers of the National Front. Lleras, president from 1958 to 1962, was wondering publicly by 1960 if the two-party agreement could last its intended life of sixteen years; foreign observers had been pessimistically speculating about its survival since its inception.

For the 1962 election, the majority (National Front) wing of the Conservative party chose Guillermo León Valencia, a political moderate, as its presidential candidate. Although he was elected, the National Front's majority in congress was reduced. Valencia lacked Lleras Camargo's political ability, and his relations with congress progressively deteriorated. He approached the end of his term of office, however, without an overt governmental crisis and was able to announce in July 1966 that the *violencia* had been ended.

Carlos Lleras Restrepo, a cousin of Lleras Camargo, was elected on May 1, 1966, over José Jaramillo Giraldo, candidate of the intransigent wing of the Conservatives. Only some 40 percent of the qualified electorate cast ballots. Lleras was inaugurated on August 7.

De facto alliance between leftist Liberals, led by López Michelsen, and rightist Conservatives, led by Rojas Pinilla, seemed more threatening than ever. Under normal circumstances these two would have made the strangest of political bedfellows, but expediency can be a powerful force in Latin American politics. Though it certainly seemed unlikely that Liberals and Conservatives would ever amalgamate, the meaningful alignments in congress appeared to be those between the two National Front wings (Liberal and Conservative) and between the anti-Front extreme Left and Right.

As the last four years of the National Front experiment approached, the political tempo inevitably picked up. In December 1969 the Conservative party convention gave half of its votes to Misael Pastrana Borrero, ambassador to the United States, but the other half remained unpledged. Pastrana was opposed by three other Conservatives; the best known was the former dictator Rojas Pinilla, nominee of the rightist National Popular Alliance (Acción Nacionalista Popular, or Anapo).

The campaign developed into a tight race between Pastrana and the demagogic Rojas Pinilla. Because of dark threats of force by followers of Rojas, the election on April 19 was accompanied by considerable tension and two days later was followed by declaration of a state of siege (martial law). On April 23 the first of four successive official tallies of the vote was announced; Pastrana was declared the winner and was inaugurated, on schedule, on August 7, 1970.

During its four years in office the government of Pastrana was unable to solve the country's economic and social problems. Violence and inflation were both on the rise during these years of the seventies. Pastrana did little to solve unemployment, which affected one-fifth of the labor force; his economic programs were ineffectual in halting the growing disparities in the distribution of wealth—40 percent of the population had 9.42 percent of the wealth although 6.67 percent of the people controlled 37.58 percent of the wealth. The agrarian reform program proved to be of little value.

In the 1974 elections, the first since the National Front pact had ended, five presidential candidates and more than ten thousand legislative candidates campaigned hotly over the issues. The Conservative party candidate, Alvaro Gómez Hurtado, a son of Don Laureano, campaigned on a platform of law and order and economic development; the Liberal party candidate stressed moderate social, economic, and political reform to solve Colombia's problems. Other candidates included María Eugenia Rojas de Moreno Díaz, daughter of former dictator General Gustavo Rojas Pinilla, who ran as the candidate of the National Popular Alliance (Anapo) and campaigned on a platform advocating socialism, Colombian-style. Two other opposition parties also ran candidates.

On April 21, 1974, López Michelsen won by more than 1 million votes over his nearest competitor—an astounding 55 percent of all the votes cast. Between them the two major parties polled 87.3 percent of all votes cast.

López Michelsen inherited a deplorable economic situation. One military officer was heard to comment that inflation "had become so serious that if the new government did not produce some solutions there could be 'a popular explosion.' "[1] López's regime developed radical economic measures which cut the rate of inflation from 30 percent at his inauguration to 20 percent in the first 13 months. His restructured tax system increased revenues by 55 percent in the first half of 1975, and he gradually eliminated subsidies on many products, helping to stimulate production and foster competitive prices. His credit policies generated an upturn in exports and brought some relief to the 12 percent unemployment rate. But in some areas López did not rate high marks. The unequal distribution of income did not improve to any considerable degree, and the nutritional and health deficiencies of millions of Colombians continued. His gradual reformist approach did not set well with the radical sector of society, and a strong current of violence began to take shape.

The rise in the popularity of cocaine in the United States gave the government of López Michelson its biggest problem. Although Colombian dealers pocket less than a third of the eventual profits from the sale of the cocaine, their annual trade is reportedly valued at more than $2 billion—twice the value of Colombia's coffee earnings. Together with the illegal exports of beef, coffee, and cement, these illegal pesos fanned the flame of inflation, which

[1] *New York Times,* April 23, 1974, Sec IV, p. 2.

by 1978 was back at 30 percent—the level when López assumed the presidency.

By 1978 López was forced to agree with the military that stricter measures would be necessary to cope with the violence and kidnappings that were taking place. In January he signed a decree that absolved the police and security forces of blame for death or injury caused in operations against kidnappers and drug smugglers. This controversial decree did little to stop the violence, and the closing months of his term saw the government plagued by corruption, ministerial reshuffling, and firings. The government resorted to martial law to control the social discontent, including antigovernment guerrilla insurgency. López's most serious defeat came in 1977 when factions in congress who opposed his bill for a fifty-member constituent assembly took their case to the supreme court, alleging procedural irregularities, whereupon the court rejected the entire proposal.

In the February 1978 primary elections Julio César Turbay Ayala received the nomination of the Liberal party and Belisario Betancur the nomination of the Conservatives. Although both factions of the Conservative party backed their party's candidate, two Liberal candidates, Turbay and Carlos Lleras Restrepo, vigorously opposed each other. This division, coupled with the apathy of the Colombian electorate, almost cost the Liberals the election in June. Betancur's attractive personality and vigorous campaign helped capture votes for the Conservatives; Turbay's lack of charisma was a definite liability to his campaign.

Unlike the elections of 1974, those in June 1978 were so close that both candidates were claiming victory until the last votes were counted. Although Turbay managed to squeak by Betancur, his margin was so small and the vote so light that many observers openly questioned his ability to mend divisions within the Liberal party, let alone heal the discontent of the majority of Colombian voters.

GOVERNMENTAL AND POLITICAL STRUCTURES

The Executive Organization

The president, while clearly the central figure in Colombian government, almost always operates within certain well-defined limits. He cannot play God, as is possible and indeed customary in some of the more traditionally dictator-ridden countries of Latin America. Perhaps the most important restraint on the president is exercised by that significant segment of the population with an advanced degree of political consciousness, which it jealously guards. Colombians are not normally inclined to allow their chief executive to act arbitrarily and irresponsibly. Then too, Colombia has established a tradition of civilian presidencies. Since 1927 only the approximately four years under General Rojas Pinilla and a year under the military junta in the 1950s marred a long record of civilian dominance. Even the military junta which succeeded Rojas Pinilla was scrupulously correct in recognizing the principle of civilian control. A third restraint on the president is the extraordinarily strong role which parties have developed in Colombian politics.

The requirement that all positions in the bureaucracy would be divided equally between Liberals and Conservatives, in force from 1958 to 1974, was extremely frustrating to presidents. An agreement between the two parties in 1973 continued parity in the executive branches on the national, departmental, and local levels until 1978. However, President Turbay continued the practice in his cabinet appointments, giving five cabinet seats to Conservatives and seven to Liberals.

A formal description of the presidency offers little that is unusual except for some provisions of the novel constitutional changes voted in 1957. The president is chosen by direct, popular vote for a four-year term. Even before the amendments of 1957, the incumbent was ineligible to succeed himself immediately. The congress elects a *designado* (a presidential substitute) for a two-year term should the presidential office become vacant. Because the rotation scheme introduced in 1958 made possible an awkward division of party affiliation between president and *designado,* an amendment in 1959 provided that the *designado* must be of the same political affiliation as the president.

The constitution describes presidential powers in considerable detail. Four articles systematically define what the executive may do in legislative, judicial, and administrative matters and what actions he may take in the event of foreign war or domestic strife. The provision governing civil disturbances became tragically relevant, of course, with the long continuance of the bloody *violencia.*

The Legislative Structure

Colombia has traditionally had a bicameral congress. Members of the senate and chamber of representatives are both elected on a population basis for a four-year term. The senate is composed of two senators for each department, plus an additional senator for each two hundred thousand people (or fraction thereof). The lower house has two representatives for each department, plus one representative for each one hundred thousand people (or fraction thereof). In the two congressional elections since the end of the National Front in 1974, Liberals have held a majority in both houses. Elections in 1978 gave the Liberals 62 seats in the senate to the Conservatives' 49 and one to the National Opposition Union (Unión Nacional de Oposición, or UNO). The Chamber consisted of 109 Liberals, 86 Conservatives, and four UNOs.

The Colombian legislature is certainly not a rubber-stamp congress. It provides a forum for airing party views and rivalries, and it is often critical of executive actions and policies. The major issue of the 1977 legislature was a proposal for a fifty-member constituent assembly to be elected simultaneously with the president in 1978. This measure, which President López believed would put Colombia "into the twentieth century," was seen by others as a means of keeping the National Front alive under another name. The bill was railroaded through a plenary session of congress but only after a massive walkout by the opposition. The case was taken to the supreme court, which subsequently rejected it as unconstitutional.

The Judicial Structure

The supreme court of justice includes twenty members, a number determined by law and not by the constitution. The court is, by law, divided into four *salas* dealing respectively with civil appeals, criminal matters, labor, and general litigation. Justices and alternates are elected, half by the lower chamber and half by the senate, from panels presented by the president of the republic. Members of the court serve during good behavior until the compulsory retirement age.

Article 90 of the constitution confers on the supreme court the power of judicial review in those cases in which the president objects to a bill on grounds of unconstitutionality. This power of judicial review does not operate in as broad a context as in the United States, but it does give the supreme court a potentially significant weapon. Judicial review has been used moderately; the supreme court has invalidated a number of congressional acts and executive decrees.

The supreme court's 1977 ruling that the electoral reform law passed by congress was unconstitutional and its rejection in 1978 of the proposed constituent assembly project were severe blows to the López regime.

Colombia also has a relatively complete system of administrative courts, patterned, at least in principle, after French practice. Each department is given an administrative tribunal, whose chief function is to hear complaints brought by individuals against the government or public officials. At the head of the hierarchy of administrative tribunals stands the council of state, which, according to the plebiscitary changes of 1957, is held to be equal in rank with the supreme court. In general the council is less important in actual practice than it appears on paper. Closely affiliated with the judiciary proper is the public ministry, headed by the attorney general. He is elected by the chamber of representatives from a presidentially nominated panel, serves a four-year term, and has the broad "power and duty to defend the interests of the Nation." He also exercises general supervision over lower levels of the public ministry, which include prosecuting attorneys of superior and circuit courts.

Local Structures

The principal administrative subdivision in Colombia is the territorial department. Colombia now has twenty-two departments, which vary widely in area and population. The administrative head of each department is a presidentially appointed governor; these officials have often been chosen from the military. The nature of the department head's political and administrative responsibilities aligns the governor more closely with the president of the republic than with the department.

In addition each department has a popularly elected assembly. Its role is not especially impressive, either legislatively or administratively. Service in a departmental assembly is a recognized rung on the ladder of political advancement.

In general the role of the Colombian department is intermediate between that of the Brazilian, Mexican, or Venezuelan states and the Argentine provinces and that of the chief subdivisions in the other unitary republics. In normal times both the Argentine provinces and the Brazilian states are governmentally and politically more important than the Colombian departments. But in a number of instances the Colombian departments can lay claim to historic and political importance. They probably have more weight and potential than the major administrative subdivisions in any other Latin American centralized state.

Comparable to the departments in area but not in population are two lesser categories of administrative units, the intendancy (*intendencia*) and the commissary (*comisaría*). There are now three intendancies and five commissaries. Their small populations, minor economic importance, and generally remote locations result in simple patterns of administrative machinery.

The lowest unit of local government is the *municipio*. It is created or abolished by the departmental assembly. Each municipality has an *alcalde* who is administratively tied to the department governor. Each also has an elected municipal council with very limited functions and authority. Some in Colombia feel that municipal government in general should be strengthened. Except in certain of the larger and more historically rooted cities, however, the political process at the local level has little viability. Since 1945 Bogotá has been organized as a special district, not subject to the regular municipal system.

Party Structures

It is the political party picture that is unique in contemporary Colombian government and politics. Perhaps only in Uruguay, Chile (both in normal times), and Mexico—and, of course, Cuba in an exceptional way—does the party structure have as great an impact on the political process and life of the country as in Colombia.

Neither of the two major parties has real grass roots, though each has an effective and extensive organization throughout Colombia. Both are essentially elitist parties: They draw almost all of their leadership and much of their inspiration from the upper and upper-middle classes. Ideological differences that had been valid in, say, the second quarter of the nineteenth century have lost their sharpness. Liberals tend to favor popular suffrage, religious toleration, and at least elementary social reform. Conservatives usually advocate a close rapprochement with the Church—Laureano Gómez was often described as *mas católico que el papa* (more Catholic than the pope)—and sometimes show intolerance toward non-Catholics; at least in theory they support class privilege and domination of politics by the elite, a restricted suffrage, and a strongly centralized government. In both parties, though especially in the Liberal, these positions are maintained chiefly because they are traditional. Actual differences between the two major parties are often more personal, political, and pragmatic than ideological.

Internally the parties are similarly organized, though the Conservatives have a more effective hierarchical structure at the lower levels. At least the main wings of both parties have normally been able to exercise considerable control over their members in congress. Functioning of the Conservative party has been rather more tight and undemocratic than that of the Liberals; Laureano Gómez tried to play the autocrat and would not willingly brook internal party opposition or dissent.

Both of the traditional parties have suffered recent schisms. So pronounced has the fractionation become that at times Colombia almost gives the appearance of having four or more major parties instead of two.

Conservative intraparty difficulties flowed from the long competition between two main party wings, led by the redoubtable Laureano Gómez and the more moderate newcomer, Mariano Ospina Pérez. Throughout the 1950s Conservative effectiveness was handicapped by feuding between laureanistas and ospinistas; the personalistic contrasted with the relatively antipersonalistic character of the leadership of the two wings—the one took its unofficial designation from the given name and the other from the surname of the respective leaders. After Don Laureano's death, his son Alvaro fell heir to the wing leadership and that faction became known as the alvaristas. The split between the alvaristas and the ospina-pastranistas continued into the 1970s.

Although the two factions of the Conservative party held separate national conventions in 1978, both endorsed Belisario Betancur as the presidential candidate. This momentary unity of the Conservatives almost won them the elections. Although Conservatives are not divided ideologically, a deep historic jealousy and resentment exists between the two factions.

The Liberal party is also divided into two factions. The most important split resulted in the organization of the Liberal Revolutionary Movement (Movimiento Revolucionario Liberal, or MRL) in 1958 by Alfonso López

Michelsen, whose father had twice been president. Alfonso *hijo,* who as a young lawyer during his father's presidencies had often been derisively referred to as Alfonsito, made his first bid for the presidency in 1962 and received 24 percent of the popular vote. In 1967 López made peace with the orthodox faction of the Liberal party; he became the party's candidate in the 1974 elections and won 55 percent of the votes.

In the 1978 elections the party split between the lleristas of former President Carlos Lleras Restrepo and the turbayistas of President Turbay. The split from the party in 1979 by the lleristas to form the Popular Liberal Union (Unión Liberal Popular) was the result of the party machine's agreement with the Conservative party to continue the "parity" pact between the two parties.

Differing factions from the two parties have often worked together. For example during the heated debate in the 1977 legislature, the alliance of the llerista Liberals and the ospina-pastranista Conservatives walked out of the congress as a gesture of their opposition to the constituent assembly bill.

Other Political Parties.   A more radical version of the MRL of the 1960s is the Firmes movement which grew out of the pre-1978 election campaign to channel popular discontent into a unified left-wing party. The movement won some support from former Anapo members and had the support of some left-wing intellectuals. It is also the legal spokesman for the "19th of May Movement," or M–19. Firmes could benefit from the internal strife among the Liberal party in the form of support for its idea of a unified left-wing movement.

The Alianza Nacional Popular (Anapo) was founded as a split from the Conservative party by Gilberto Alzate Avendaño. Ex-dictator Gustavo Rojas Pinilla attempted to use the Anapo as a party vehicle, but following his ouster the party greatly declined. When Rojas was allowed to return from exile and even to resume political activities, the Anapo recovered strength. It operated within the framework of the Conservative party, which gave it a share in the Conservative half of national legislators. After the 1964 elections its strength in congress was approximately equal to that of the MRL. Although Rojas made a strong showing in the 1970 elections, in 1974 his daughter, Senator María Eugenia Rojas de Moreno Díaz, polled a poor 9 percent of the vote. Rojas died in 1975, but the party remained under the leadership of his daughter. The party lost all its congressional seats in the March 1978 elections and its members split into many factions in the presidential elections of June 1978.

The left side of the party spectrum has not gone unrepresented in Colombia. Although a Socialist party was organized in 1920, it remained doctrinaire, academic, and ineffective; for many years the Socialists operated on the periphery of Colombian politics. The party had some influence in university and intellectual circles, almost none among organized labor. Communists, a more important element in the Colombian Left, first entered the party picture in the mid-1920s. They had a potential for considerable impact. Because of the monopoly of political power by the elitist traditional parties, the working classes were more susceptible to Communist appeals. The Communists reached a peak of electoral strength in 1944. Communists long used that name but later reorganized as the Social Democratic party (Partido Social Democrático, or PSD). In the mid-1960s the Communists split into pro-Moscow and pro-Peking wings.

Jorge Gaitán at an early stage in his career organized the National Leftist Revolutionary Union (Unión Nacional Izquierdista Revolucionaria, or UNIR), but he later returned to the Liberal party, which offered a more likely road to political success. Liberal feuding in 1944–1945 largely destroyed the effectiveness of the elder López, and Gaitán exploited the situation by posing as the new champion of the slowly stirring masses, which incidentally weakened potential Communist appeal. Gaitán might have become a Colombian Perón or even Castro; his assassination left a serious void in the play of party power politics. After his death Gaitán's daughter Gloria and her husband Luis Emiro Valencia, an economist, organized the National Popular Movement (Movimiento Nacional Popular, or MNP) to try to continue the momentum generated by Gaitán's charisma. The MNP became definitely pro-Castro in orientation. In March 1962 it and a number of other leftist groups founded the United Front of Revolutionary Action (Frente Unido de Acción Revolucionaria, or FUAR), a common front similar to, but much weaker than, the Popular Action Front (FRAP) in Chile in the 1960s.

A recent addition to the left side of the political spectrum is the National Opposition Union (UNO), a grouping of Communists, Maoists, and Anapo dissidents organized prior to the 1974 election. The UNO acquired two seats in the senate and five seats in the chamber in the 1974 election, but in 1978 the UNO won only one seat in the senate and four seats in the chamber. Initially the party had announced that it would dissolve before the 1978 elections and that its members would support former President Lleras Restrepo. It reversed its decision, however, and endorsed the candidacy of Julio César Pernía.

Assessment of the Party Scene

The National Front accord between the Liberal and Conservative parties has had unfortunate consequences for Colombian parties and politics. As an expedient solution to an unprecedented critical political and governmental dilemma in 1957, the National Front was perhaps justified. Although the pact was to have formally ended in 1974, in 1973 the two parties agreed to continue parity at the national, departmental, and local levels, and President Turbay continued the practice at the cabinet level in 1978. The new electoral reform law passed in congress in May 1979 has institutionalized the National Front pact.

Under the new law, the electoral court will have four representatives each from the two major parties and one from the third largest party, which at this point would be the conservative Anapo party, thereby giving the Conservatives control over the electoral court.

The National Front is basically undemocratic for at least three reasons: (1) It completely excludes all minor parties from any share in the governing process by restricting all elective and appointive offices to Conservatives and Liberals; (2) regardless of the size of the Liberal and Conservative vote, the division of offices is equal and thus does not reflect real party strength or popular preferences between even those parties; (3) it encourages a resurgence of *personalismo* within the major parties. Greater relative weight had previously been placed on issues and principles rather than on men; charisma, the *caudillo,* the flaming personality, and perhaps by the same token the common forms of venality and graft had not normally been prominent in Colombian politics.

The National Front concept has no counterpart elsewhere in Latin America. It is true that the Uruguayan *colegiado* (collegiate executive) involved a fixed party division in executive bodies at national and lower levels, but it imposed no artificial party parity. It is also true that Venezuela under Betancourt experimented with a party coalition in cabinet support of the president, but this was a matter of political implementation and not constitutional imperative, and it was neither rigid nor permanent.

Other Political Structures

Certain pressure groups are becoming more effective in Colombian politics, but such elements still lack the impact they normally have in Mexico or Argentina. This is primarily because the traditional parties have attained so great an influence that the customary pressure groups have had little opportunity for political impact. Both organized employers in industry, commerce, banking, and agriculture and organized labor are beginning to assume political roles.

The national labor organizations dramatized their frustrations for the first time in twenty years with a national strike in September 1977 to protest inflation, which had doubled food prices. The unions demanded a 60 percent, across-the-board wage increase, but the government would only agree to a 20 percent increase in the $59 a month minimum salary. By 1978 both the Confederation of Colombian Workers (Confederación de Trabajadores de Colombia, or CTC) and the Union of Colombian Workers (Unión de Trabajadores de Colombia, or UTC) were ruled by antigovernment factions. In 1978 employees of oil producing centers, transportation workers, teachers, and public employees called strikes.

The political position of the army is complex and somewhat indeterminate. Generals were active in politics as both Liberals and Conservatives during much of the nineteenth century; a few brief periods could be called military dictatorships. Soon after the turn of the century, however, civilian control rapidly gained headway. The drift to de facto civil war after the assassination of Gaitán tended to draw the military back into politics. Gómez, as Professor Edwin Lieuwen aptly puts it, converted the army "into an instrument of right-wing Conservative rule."[2] Complexities in the political picture led the army to oust Don Laureano. His successor, the far from subtle Rojas, made over Colombia in the image of a military dictatorship. He more than once referred to his regime as "government of the armed forces."

Nevertheless, the army was not wholly comfortable in the role that circumstance, molded by Gómez and Rojas in turn, had thrust upon it. It turned on Rojas in 1957, as it had on Gómez four years earlier, and the military junta that followed scrupulously avoided partisan politics. The army duly returned the country to civilian control and voluntarily retired to the background. It will not necessarily remain there, but as long as civilian regimes do not restrict its size and perquisites too stringently, it will probably be willing to let civilians make the mistakes and reap the headaches of governmental control.

The Church is still powerful, almost more so than the army. Its position has come more from its traditionally strong position and widespread allegiance than from the privileges the concordat confers upon it. But Colombia, like virtually all of Latin America, has become an increasingly pluralistic society, and this necessarily weakens the old hold of the Church over its members; they probably do not follow the political lead of the clergy and the hierarchy quite so unquestioningly as they once did. Indeed, the Church has even known apostasy within its own ranks, as witnessed by the defection and unfrocking of Father Camilo Torres, who became a leader of fidelista-type reformers until his death in combat in February 1966. It is noteworthy that in 1968, Medellín, Colombia, was the site of the Second Latin American Bishops' Conference where progressive bishops formulated a "liberation theology" document which put the Church on the side of social justice.

DEVELOPMENTAL PROSPECTS

Along with Venezuela, Colombia has long been praised as an example of democracy in South America, but strong currents of unrest in the country are beginning to be felt. Strikes by poorly paid workers and riots by frustrated young students in the recent past have caused much concern to the Colombian government. The assassination of a former interior minister in September 1978

[2]Edwin Lieuwen. *Arms and Politics in Latin America.* (New York: Holt, Rinehart & Winston, 1965), p. 880.

gave impetus to President Turbay's all-out antisubversive security statute. The seinelike statute swept up the legitimate protesters along with the criminals and terrorists. Many foreigners were detained and harassed during the military's zealous hunt for subversives. The expanding drug trade has given rise to a fear that the industrial class may be displaced by an emerging class of wealthy drug dealers. Violence showed a marked upswing in early 1980 with the holding of diplomats from seventeen foreign countries in the Dominican Embassy by the M-19 guerrilla group.

Another cause for concern is the growing indifference of the Colombian electorate. One can only speculate about the reason for this apathy at the polls. Some argue that the Colombian masses are not yet fully politicized; others contend that the National Front arrangement of the political parties contributed to the indifference of the Colombian electorate. (Table 8–1 would seem to substantiate that claim. The election of 1957 was the plebiscite on the National Front; those of 1958, May 1962, 1966, 1970, 1974, and 1978 were for the presidency; the others were for congress.) Whatever the reason, the alienation and frustration of the masses does seem to be growing and will no doubt be harnessed by one group or another.

TABLE 8–1   Recent Voting Statistics

	Eligible Voters	Ballots Cast	Percentage Voting
1957	6,080,342	4,397,090	72.3
1958	5,365,191	3,108,567	57.9
1960	4,397,541	2,542,651	57.8
March 1962	5,338,868	3,090,203	57.9
May 1962	5,404,765	2,634,840	48.8
1964	6,135,628	2,261,190	36.9
1966	6,611,352	2,649,258	40.1
1968	6,696,723	2,496,455	37.3
1970	7,129,000*	3,930,940*	55.1*
1974	9,000,000†	4,500,000†	50.0
February 1978	12,300,000	3,690,000	30.0

*Estimated
† Approximate

REFERENCES

Bailey, Norman A. "Colombian Black Hand: A Case Study of Neo-Liberalism in Latin America." *Review of Politics* 27 (October 1965), 445–464.

Bernstein, Harry. *Venezuela and Colombia.* Englewood Cliffs, N.J.: Prentice-Hall, 1964.

Berry, Albert. "A Positive Interpretation of the Expansion of Urban Services in Latin America, with Some Colombian Evidence." *Journal of Developing Studies* 14:2 (January 1978), 210–231.

BERRY, ALBERT, and RONALD G. HELLMAN, eds. *Coalition Government in Colombia.* New York: Cyrco Press, 1976.

CAMPOS, JUDITH TALBOT, and JOHN F. McCAMANT. *Cleavage Shift in Colombia: Analysis of Elections.* Beverly Hills, Calif.: Sage Publications, 1972.

CORR, EDWIN G. *The Political Process in Colombia.* Denver: University of Denver, Graduate School of International Studies, 1971–1972.

DIX, ROBERT H. *Colombia: The Political Dimensions of Change.* New Haven, Conn.: Yale University Press, 1967.

————. "The Varieties of Populism: The Case of Colombia." *Western Political Quarterly* 31:3 (September 1978) 334–351.

FALS-BORDA, ORLANDO. *Peasant Society in the Colombian Andes.* Gainesville: University of Florida Press, 1957.

————. *Subversion and Social Change in Colombia.* New York: Columbia University Press, 1969.

FITZGIBBON, RUSSELL H. "Colombia as a Laboratory for Change." *Civilisations* 11:2 (1961), 130–142.

FLUHARTY, VERNON L. *Dance of the Millions: Military Rule and the Social Revolution in Colombia, 1930–1956.* Pittsburgh: University of Pittsburgh Press, 1957.

GIL, FEDERICO G. "Colombia's Bipartisan Experiment." Chap. 6 in *The Caribbean: Contemporary Colombia,* ed. by Curtis A. Wilgus. Gainesville: University of Florida Press, 1962.

GROVES, RODERICK T. "The Colombian National Front and Administrative Reform." *Administration and Society* 6:2 (August 1974), 316–336.

GUZMÁN, GERMÁN, ORLANDO FALS BORDA, and EDUARDO UMAÑA LUBA. *La Violencia en Colombia.* Bogotá: Tercer Mundo, 1963.

HELGUERA, J. LEÓN. "The Changing Role of the Military in Colombia." *Journal of Inter-American Studies* 3 (July 1961), 351–358.

HOBSBAWN, ERIC J. "The Revolutionary Situation in Colombia." *World Today* 19 (June 1963), 248–258.

HOLT, PAT M. *Colombia Today and Tomorrow.* New York: Holt, Rinehart & Winston, 1964.

HOSKIN, GARY, and GERALD SWANSON. "Political Party Leadership in Colombia: A Spatial Analysis." *Comparative Politics* 6:3 (April 1974), 395–424.

HUNTER, JOHN. *Emerging Colombia.* Washington, D. C.: Public Affairs Press, 1962.

JOHNSON, KENNETH F. "Political Radicalism in Colombia; Electoral Dynamics of 1962 and 1964." *Journal of Inter-American Studies* 7 (January 1965), 15–26.

McGREEVEY, WILLIAM P. "Urban Growth in Colombia." *Journal of Inter-American Studies and World Affairs* 16:4 (November 1974), 387–408.

MARTZ, JOHN. *Colombia: A Contemporary Political Survey.* Reprint of 1962 edition. Westport, Conn.: Greenwood, 1975.

————. "Political Parties in Colombia and Venezuela: Contrasts in Substance and Style." *Western Political Quarterly* 18: (June 1965), 318–333.

MAULIN, RICHARD. *Soldiers, Guerrillas, and Politics in Colombia.* Westport, Conn.: Greenwood, 1973.

RANDALL, STEPHEN J. *The Diplomacy of Modernization: Colombian-American Relations, 1920–1940.* Toronto: University of Toronto Press, 1977.

URRUTIA MONTOYA, MIGUEL. *The Development of the Colombian Labor Movement.* New Haven, Conn.: Yale University Press, 1967.

WILLIAMSON, ROBERT C. "Toward a Theory of Political Violence: The Case of Rural Colombia." *Western Political Quarterly* 18 (March 1965), 35–44.

9

ECUADOR

The Politics
of National Revolution

POLITICAL CULTURE AND ENVIRONMENT

Ecuador has been described as a land of "constitutions and *caudillos,*" as a "country of contrasts," and most accurately as a "tale of two cities." Ecuador has truly had more than its share of constitutions and *caudillos;* it does have many contrasts; and Ecuadorian life—economic, social, and cultural, as well as political—partially reflects the old and continuing rivalries and contrasts between Quito and Guayaquil, the capitals of Ecuador's two most important regions.

About the size of Colorado, Ecuador with 109,482 square miles is the third smallest South American country. The country's 1980 estimated population ranks it ninth in Latin America, between Cuba and Guatemala.

Ecuador is easily broken into geographical subdivisions, and these regions have been prominent politically, economically, and psychologically. The Oriente region, the area east of the Andes, is hard to reach, little developed, and sparsely populated, almost entirely by Indians. Ecuadorians have long nurtured roseate dreams, largely based on ignorance of realities, about the wealth of the Oriente and the advantages of incorporating it effectively with the rest of the nation.

The two more important regions are the sierra and the costa, or coastal region. The costa, chiefly agricultural, comprises slightly more than a fourth of the country's area. For many generations the coast in some ways was even more isolated than the remote sierra. Before the opening of the Panama Canal, Guayaquil was merely an unimportant west-coast port, far removed from any major ocean traffic routes; today it is the country's chief port and largest city. The opening of the canal enormously improved the city's economic position, giving it and the coastal area it dominates far better opportunity to challenge the political supremacy of the sierra.

Despite the coastal region's rapid gains in recent decades, many still consider the sierra Ecuador's most important region. Geographically it is a high valley between two cordilleras of the Andes. The whole mountain and valley complex is about one hundred miles wide and includes about one-fourth of the country's area. Most of the sierra's people are Quechua-speaking Indians, direct descendants of the old Inca empire.

Subsistence crops and cattle raising form the backbone of the sierran economy. As a consequence the region is more economically isolated from the outside world than is the coast. This isolation has its social and political reflections. The social structure of the sierra is a rigid class system, approaching castes. It includes those of European ancestry, the mestizos, who in the sierra are called *cholos* (in the coastal region they are termed *montuvios*), and the Indians.

Class differentiations in the sierra were put under premium from the beginning by the Spanish need for a large supply of cheap and docile labor. The religiosity of the Indians—their deep devotion to the Catholic church—has been instrumental in their continued submissiveness. The Indians' profound love of their land, which becomes almost an emotional mystique, adds to their traditional immobility. The whites have retained almost complete economic, cultural, and political control and consciously dominate the sierra. Their social mores are rigidly and conservatively maintained, dress is sober and colorless, manners are formal, the concept of "family" in a narrow social sense is emphasized.

Between the Spanish-descended dominant class and the Indians are the numerically expanding and psychologically maturing *cholos,* who may in time provide a social bridge more effectively uniting top and bottom. But it will be a slower process in the sierra than on the coast.

Political Development

During the colonial period Ecuador was little more than an appendage. As a presidency (a unit administered by a *presidente*), it was first attached to the viceroyalty of Peru, then after 1717 to the new viceroyalty of New Granada; Quito was politically subordinate, first to Lima and then to Bogotá. After independence Ecuador was precariously united with her northern neighbors in the Republic of Colombia for eleven years.

Ecuador seceded from the union on May 13, 1830, a date that some Ecuadorians have called "the last day of despotism and the first day of the same thing." Ecuador was ill prepared for independence. In the early days of independence the *pensadores* and the *caudillos* competed for political power; but the *pensadores* were poorly equipped to give political battle, and center stage was for years left to the *caudillos.*

Following 1845 came fifteen years of near anarchy: Ecuador had seven presidents (four of whom were generals) and four provisional juntas; it drafted three new constitutions. Nationalism continued and was transformed into xenophobia—even Colombians and Venezuelans were referred to as foreigners.

Beginning in 1859 the remarkable Gabriel García Moreno dominated the political scene, first as the head of a provisional regime and later as president, and until 1875 the history of Ecuador was virtually García Moreno's biography. The new dictator was a man of intense Catholic faith and a conservative. García Moreno turned Ecuador into a theocratic state; the Church was purged of unworthy priests, Jesuits were brought into the country and given positions of influence, citizenship was limited to practicing Catholics, the congress was persuaded to vote money to the Vatican, and as a climax in 1873 Ecuador was solemnly dedicated to "the Sacred Heart of Jesus."

García Moreno was responsible for two new constitutions (in 1861 and 1869), an efficient treasury and a uniform currency, better roads and agricultural methods, and a growing trade. Liberal opposition to him grew, though most of it perforce had to be directed from outside the country. Soon after being reelected in 1875 for a second successive six-year term, García Moreno was assassinated. An exiled opposition leader and pamphleteer exclaimed exultantly in Colombia, "My pen killed him!"

The two decades following were characterized by great instability and petty dictatorships. Two new constitutions were written in 1878 and 1884. The Church rather than the army continued to be the major institutional force in Ecuadorian affairs. This interim period was ended by the Radical Liberal revolution of 1895, which brought to the forefront another remarkable though less sharply delineated figure, General Eloy Alfaro. The era of the Radical Liberals lasted for half a century, until 1944. Alfaro himself, president from 1895 to 1901 and again from 1906 to 1911, was primarily a Liberal party leader rather than a constructive president; he is remembered chiefly for orienting Ecuadorian politics toward anticlericalism and government control of education.

Three new constitutions were drafted in the half century from 1895 to 1944. Even the first of them was essentially liberal—the voting age was lowered to eighteen and, although Roman Catholicism was the only religion permitted, no religious qualifications for exercise of civil or political rights were established.

The Radical Liberal half century was marked by political instability, especially during the 1930s. Fifteen presidents held office in the ten-year period from 1931 to 1940. Among them was José María Velasco Ibarra, who served his first tenure of about a year in 1934–1935. Electoral honesty deteriorated, but much of the political instability could be traced indirectly to the bludgeoning effects of the depression, which decreased the demand for the products of Ecuador's colonial economy. The period of Radical Liberal control was brought to an end in 1944.

Political disorder and uncertainty got worse before it got better. A revolt, sparked by the exiled Velasco from just across the Colombian border, forced the incumbent from office in May 1944, and Velasco took power, remaining in office a little more than three years. Two new constitutions were written during his term. Another revolt forced out Velasco in late August 1947. Four successive presidents held office in the month from August 20 to September 20; the last managed to survive politically for almost a year.

Reasonably honest elections in 1948 placed in office Galo Plaza Lasso, the candidate of an independent moderate and centrist group. Somewhat to the surprise of persons both in and out of Ecuador who had come to assume that instability was permanent, Plaza served out his four-year term (the first such instance in two decades) and presided over an honest election in 1952. Plaza later served as Secretary General of the OAS from 1968 to 1975. The charismatic Velasco followed the more predictable Plaza and acceded to his third term in office, which he completed uneventfully. Three major candidates and one minor aspirant took part in the 1956 elections. The close vote between the top two candidates, plus the fact that the three non-Conservative nominees polled 70 percent of the vote, seemed a bad omen, but President Camilo Ponce Enríquez completed his term of moderate administration.

Four candidates also ran in the 1960 presidential election: the Conservatives, the Concentration of Popular Forces (Concentración de Fuerzas Populares, or CFP), the National Democratic Front (Frente Democrático Nacional, or FDN), and a new group, the Velasco National Federation (Federación Nacional Velasquista, or FNV), a personal vehicle for Velasco Ibarra. Considerable tension and many minor disturbances marked the campaign. Results of the polling surprised many foreigners but few Ecuadorians, who were directly exposed to the magic of Velasco. He won by a wide margin.

The 1960 election was the fourth in succession carried out on schedule under comparatively orderly conditions. September 1, 1960, marked the end of the third uninterrupted presidential term. The 1945 constitution had remained in effect for more than a decade and a half, a longevity unsurpassed except by the constitution of 1906. Many persons, both in Ecuador and abroad, assumed that the country had outgrown its period of political turbulence and had reached civic maturity. This judgment unfortunately proved to be premature.

Velasco, who had completed only one presidential term in four tries, soon fell out with his vice-president and tried to remove him. But Velasco's own flimsy support was crumbling, and he himself was ousted by a coup in 1961. The vice-president succeeded to the presidency, but his political support also proved fragile; in July 1963, he was ousted by a military coup, provoked largely by his overfondness for alcohol.

The military junta, headed by a naval captain, moved energetically, if not democratically. It outlawed the Communist party, closed Ecuadorian universities, postponed the 1964 elections, and announced plans for a new constitution. The junta might well have undertaken a program of social reform in 1964, but hardening public sentiment, probably provoked by fears that an out-and-out dictatorship would develop, caused it to move cautiously. A trial balloon sent up to test public reaction to the proposed new constitution found that most Ecuadorians believed a president, as in Mexico, should not be allowed to serve more than one term. Such a provision, if adopted, would eliminate not only the hard-to-down Velasco Ibarra but also two others who allegedly still had political ambitions, Plaza Lasso and Ponce Enríquez.

On March 29, 1966, following a week of rioting and demonstration against the military regime, the chiefs of the armed forces suddenly ousted the military junta and replaced it with a civilian executive who on April 2 cancelled the elections scheduled for the following July and announced that balloting would be held in September for a constituent assembly. This assembly met in early November 1966, to draft a new constitution to supplant that of 1946 and also to name a new provisional president. In the meantime, two former presidents returned to Ecuador and again became active in politics—Camilo Ponce and José María Velasco Ibarra. In elections held June 2, 1968, Velasco was returned to office by a substantial vote for an unprecedented fifth term.

In June 1970, with the army's blessing, Velasco seized dictatorial powers to keep public order. He suspended the 1967 constitution and closed congress and the supreme court. When he scheduled elections for June 1972, the army retaliated. On February 16, 1972, just four months before the scheduled elections, the army ousted Velasco for the fourth time. The army feared the prospect of the populist candidate, Assad Bucaram, as Ecuador's next president. It also did not like the idea of the leftist leader gaining control of the newly discovered oil in the Oriente.

The junta, headed by General Guillermo Rodríguez Lara, immediately annulled the upcoming elections, flew the seventy-eight-year-old Velasco to exile in Panama, imposed a state of siege, and returned the country to the 1945 constitution. Velasco lived in voluntary exile in Argentina for the next seven years, returning to Ecuador on February 15, 1979. The eighty-five-year-old *caudillo* died of a heart attack the following month.

President Rodríguez immediately focused his attention on the oil boom which he hoped would provide the necessary revenues to carry out the military government's policy of "economic nationalism," similar to the military populism of Peru in 1972. On September 1, 1975, a single army unit headed by Armed Forces Chief of Staff General Raúl González Alvear attempted to overthrow the Rodríguez government in a coup which was crushed later the same day by government troops. The unsuccessful rebels accused the government of political and economic mismanagement of the country's new-found oil wealth.

Although President Rodríguez did announce that he would resign to make way for a return to civilian rule, he was displaced in a successful coup on January 11, 1976, brought on by a government crisis during which his entire cabinet resigned. The right-wing junta headed by Vice Admiral Alfredo Poveda Burbano promised to hand over power to civilians at the end of 1977 and stated that the 1972 reform program of the armed forces would be honored. Then in mid-1977 the military regime announced that the junta would remain in control through September 1978.

Campaigning began in November 1977, as political parties jockeyed for candidates who would be acceptable to the military. In February 1978, the military ruled out the popular Concentración de Fuerzas Populares (CFP) candidate, Assad Bucaram, from the elections. According to the military, the new electoral law specified that presidential candidates must have Ecuadorian parents since under the new constitution the president becomes commander-in-chief of the armed forces. This provision naturally ruled out the favorite Bucaram, whose family was Lebanese. The new electoral law also eliminated two other contenders, Carlos Julio Arosemena Monroy and José María Velasco Ibarra, by specifying that ex-presidents may not run again.

This move on the part of the military could have been the rallying force needed to unify the left-of-center parties. The CFP nominated Jaime Roldós Aguilera, a relative by marriage to Bucaram. As the first of the two-tiered elections drew near, many observers were wondering what new obstacle would be placed in the path of the left-wing groups. The candidates were: Jaime Roldós of the CFP; Sixto Durán Ballén of the National Constitutional Front (Frente Nacional Constitucional, or FNC), Raúl Clemente Huerta of the Liberal party; Rodrigo Borja of the Democratic Left party (Partido Izquierda Demócrata, or ID); and the Left Broad Front candidate, René Mauge Mosquera.

Jaime Roldós confounded the military and even many of his own supporters by winning the first round of balloting with about 32 percent of the votes; Sixto Durán Ballén trailed with about 23 percent. The second half of the presidential election was first scheduled for September 1978 but was later postponed to April 29, 1979. Although the official reason for the delayed timetable was the administrative work entailed in the simultaneous congressional and presidential elections, most observers suspected that the real motive was to find a new and exotic way to keep the populist candidate, Roldós, from the presidency. Roldós, the underdog in the first round balloting nine months before but the electoral favorite in the April 29 elections, selected Osvaldo

Guayas provinces (containing Quito and Guayaquil, respectively) are much more important politically than any others.

The provinces are divided into cantons. Each is headed by a "political chief," appointed by the president on recommendation of the respective governor. The cantons are subdivided into parishes, classified by law as either urban or rural. Each parish is administered by a political lieutenant, also appointed by the president on the advice of the intermediate officials. The urban parish is essentially a voting unit.

The cantons are municipalities, but it must be remembered that the Latin American municipality *(municipio)* includes rural as well as urban territory. Each municipality has a cantonal or municipal council chosen by popular election. Some feeling exists, especially in the large cities, that a greater degree of municipal autonomy should prevail. This necessarily conflicts with the tradition of presidentially imposed controls from above. It is usually the latter that wins out.

Party Structures

In the early years of independence there were no political parties, even in the early Ecuadorian nineteenth-century Latin American sense of the term. There were only political points of view which quite naturally divided into liberal and conservative. In this sense, Rocafuerte was a Liberal, Flores a Conservative. Their respective followings, even then centering in the Guayaquil and Quito areas, were personal followings with no real attributes of party organization. Gabriel García Moreno was a far more authentic Conservative than any who had preceded him, and he rallied around himself a well-knit group of like-minded followers, but again, they were simply followers and not a party.

The Conservative party as such began to develop slowly after García Moreno's assassination. Because García Moreno had so deeply entrenched the Catholic program in Ecuador, the Conservatives had time to perfect a reasonably good party organization before they encountered organized competition. The party suffered a half-century hiatus from the mid-1890s to the mid-1940s, but thereafter it again began gaining strength. Its presidential candidates in 1948 and 1952 made very respectable showings; its vice-presidential candidate won in 1948, and in 1956 its candidate was elected.

Conservative strength is still centered in the sierra, the party is still oriented toward the Church, and its leadership is still largely drawn from the wealthy, aristocratic, landed class. Age, experience, and family position play a considerable part in determining Conservative leadership. Although its quasi-philosophical orientation toward the Church and the aristocracy may be less sharply defined now than previously, the Ecuadorian Conservatives still represent a more definite ideological position than is usual among Latin American political parties. Tactically, the Conservatives have gained when women were granted suffrage in 1929 since women are normally more influenced by the Church than men in their voting. It also redounds to Conservative benefit that priests and nuns are permitted to vote, but soldiers are not. However, the increasing tempo of Ecuadorian economic life, the relatively greater prominence of the coast in national affairs, and the added articulateness of new and younger political groups have all chipped away much of the former prominence of the Conservatives.

The Conservative candidate, Camilo Ponce Enríquez, narrowly won the presidential election of 1956. In 1976 a party split between right- and left-wing factions resulted in an alliance joined by ten other center-right parties, the National Constitutional Front (Frente Nacional Constitucional, or FNC). The Front's second-place winner in the 1978 first-round balloting, Sixto Durán Ballén, was soundly defeated by Jaime Roldós in the final election of April 1979.

The other of Ecuador's historic parties is the Radical Liberal, often called simply the Liberal party. It was founded in 1878 but did not win power until its demigod, General Eloy Alfaro, led a successful revolt in 1895. The Radical Liberals enjoyed power for forty-nine years before being ousted by Velasco Ibarra, essentially a nonparty man.

The Radical Liberal party platform favored agrarian reform, separation of Church and state, and popular education. Their liberal program looked wonderful on paper but received almost no implementation. In fact the programs of the Radical Liberals and the Conservatives resembled each other in many ways, but one had a liberal and the other a conservative tinge.

The ouster of Arroyo del Río in 1944 precipitated a rapid and serious deterioration in the Radical Liberal party. An Independent Radical Liberal party was formed, composed of opponents of Arroyo del Río and claiming to be the heir apparent of the old party; few politically articulate Ecuadorians accepted this claim.

The Radical Liberal party's initial candidate in the 1978 elections, Francisco Huerta Montalvo, was replaced by Raúl Clemente Huerta Rendón when the former was disqualified by the supreme electoral tribunal. The latter placed a close third in the 1978 first-round ballot.

The long-dominant coastal political leader, Carlos Guevara Moreno, used the Radical Liberal party as a vehicle at times. But by 1954 he had decided that the better political course was to organize a new group, the Concentración de Fuerzas Populares (CFP), which absorbed some of the Radical Liberal strength. Historically, the CFP favored broad-based socioeconomic changes. Carlos Guevara Moreno was the party's candidate in the 1956 elections. The party played a major role in past elections and its popular leader, Assad Bucaram, was conceded to be the leading candidate in the aborted elections of 1972. His popularity among civilians did not extend to the right-wing military junta, however, and was one of the reasons for the coup and subsequent annulment of elections in 1972. His nomination in 1978 by the CFP as their presidential candidate precipitated a new electoral law which disqualified him because of his parentage. Bucaram then effected the candidacy of his nephew-in-law, Jaime Roldós, with the theme "Roldós in the presidency, Bucaram in power." Roldós's surprising first-place victory over the other three candidates in the first round of balloting in July 1978 gave him the courage to assert his independence from the party leader. Bucaram, for his part, resented the success that Roldós was enjoying while his own popularity was declining. Despite the internal strife in the group, the CFP and its supporters, the ID, won a solid majority of the sixty-nine–member chamber in the 1979 elections.

The Socialist party, formed in 1925, falls between a major and a minor party; it has had as many as a sixth of the congressional seats but has never, even in coalition, controlled power. The party is composed largely of middle-class professionals and intellectuals and has had a doctrinaire and orthodox Socialist position. The Socialist party has been the only Ecuadorian party to pay even lip service to the problems of the Indians. Socialists have had some influence but never any real control, over the organized workers in the coastal area. The party has at times been subject to the seemingly endemic Socialist weakness of schism. In 1956 Radical Liberal dissidents joined with a group of Socialists to organize the Frente Democrático Nacional to support the presidential candidacy of Raúl Clemente Huerta.

The Communist party originated as an offshoot from the Socialists in 1928. Its program has been orthodox, but its membership has usually been small and its support weak. During periods when *"imperialismo yanqui"* could be inflated into a rousing issue, the Ecuadorian Communists have profited correspondingly. Castro's rising star in 1959 and afterward bolstered the Ecuadorian Communists. They suffered tactically and psychologically, however, by government success in crushing small revolutionary guerrilla bands in the Andes. In 1963 the military junta outlawed the party.

The most obvious phenomenon of the recent party scene in Ecuador has been the development of what Blanksten calls *"ad hoc* parties," fluid and often transitory groups set up to meet short-range objectives, groups which easily moved from one position or bloc to another. Some such groups represent distinctive ideological positions; others are only organizations of expediency. Perhaps the first major group of this type was the National Democratic Civic Movement (Movimiento Cívico Democrático Nacional, or MCDN), which was technically responsible for the election of Plaza in 1948. It was formed in 1947 primarily as a vehicle to oppose the Conservatives and was thus composed of such disparate elements that it contained within it the seeds of its own disintegration. Its situation was similar to that of the Whig party in the United

States, also a poor actuarial risk, whose components were initially united only by the one bond of opposing Andrew Jackson. The MCDN did disintegrate in the early 1950s.

The Federación Nacional Velasquista (FNV) was organized in 1952 to include the personal following of the maverick Velasco Ibarra. The Partido de Izquierda Democrática (ID), a moderate social democratic group, supported the candidacy of Rodrigo Borja Cevallos in the first round of voting in 1978 but threw its support to Jaime Roldós in the 1979 presidential elections, which was a major factor in his decisive victory.

The party picture in Ecuador reflects an uncertainty and flux which marks the country's political parties as highly immature and even rudimentary. In part, the situation reflects the small degree of participation in the broad political process that has been delegated to the masses of the people. Although parties are still far from being mass-based and mass-appealing organizations, the Roldós victory in 1978 showed that populism had become attractive to the middle class as well as to the lower class.

Other Political Structures

Ecuador's pressure groups are even more immature than its political parties. Though the country's economy is primarily agricultural, it is not the sort of agriculture that lends itself well to organization and exercise of political pressure, either by landowners or by workers. Mining is almost nonexistent— surprising for an Andean country; hence, miners' unions, usually a potent source of political pressure, do not enter into Ecuadorian politics. Manufacturing is not well developed, and industrialists are correspondingly weak as an interest group. By the same token, organized labor is not an especially effective pressure force. However, two long-established institutions, the military and the Church, are sources of political pressure.

The Military. The army has been thoroughly involved in Ecuadorian politics since the time of independence. About a third of the country's presidents have been from the military. "The last step in a military career," runs an oft quoted Ecuadorian maxim, "is the presidency of the republic." The army has often been top-heavy with officers, almost a built-in invitation to military politicking.[1] Most of the Ecuadorian officer class is drawn from the sierra, a fact that adds to the regional rivalry between coast and sierra. As in other Latin American countries, considerable competition exists between army and police, a rivalry usually more successfully exploited by the army.

In certain states at given times—for example, the Aramburu regime in Argentina, the post-Rojas junta in Colombia, the military government in

---

[1]John J. Johnson notes the startling fact that in 1910 officers numbered 3,500 of a 6,000 man army. *The Military and Society in Latin America* (Stanford: Stanford University Press, 1964), p. 72.

Venezuela following Pérez Jiménez—the army in politics has been able to place itself above the political battle, as it were, and to convince the country of its integrity and its wish to return the government to civilian hands. Ecuador's military has not been so fortunate. Following the 1963 coup, civilians grew increasingly impatient with military rule and showed a growing distrust toward what was essentially an anachronistic control; such attitudes contributed to the later return to constitutional government. The military returned in 1970 to rule the government during the great petroleum era but kept its promise in 1979 to return the country to civilian control. Nevertheless, the military and militarism will continue as forces to be reckoned with in Ecuador.

The Church.   The Catholic church has always been a powerful political force in Ecuador. Probably only in Colombia is a Latin American ecclesiastical establishment more influential. It is natural that an entente should usually have existed between the Church and the Conservative party. But not even the Radical Liberal party during its half century in power attempted to destroy the Church; Church privilege and influence were reduced during that period, but a good deal of the ground then lost has been regained since 1944, when the last Radical Liberal president went out of power.

As might be expected, the influence of the Church is measurably greater in the more socially conservative sierra than in the coastal region. The Church has capitalized on the traditionalism that is deeply rooted in the Ecuadorian political character. As society becomes more pluralistic in Ecuador as elsewhere, however, there is some doubt where the trend will leave the Ecuadorian Church hierarchy politically.

Presumably Ecuador will never again experience the abnormally excessive degree of Church influence that prevailed during the tenure of García Moreno, but the Church, like the army, is still a force of real political consequence.

DEVELOPMENTAL PROSPECTS

Ecuador presents a confused and confusing picture. For several successive administrations, regularity, order, and relative stability appeared to have come to the country's politics and government. Then the erratic Velasco Ibarra returned to power, failing as usual to complete his term. Velasco was reelected in 1968 and was overthrown for yet a fourth time in 1970, just six months before the oil boom. The military junta which seized power experimented with a Peruvian style of popular nationalism. This experiment was short-lived, and with the ouster of General Rodríguez Lara in 1972, the right-wing faction which took over conceded that although the new oil wealth had helped the middle- and upper-income classes, it had actually accentuated the poverty of the poor. With the commitment to change a thing of the past, the military promised to return the country to civilian rule and in January 1978 the electorate voted on a new constitutional draft that would put the machinery in motion for elections later that year.

The first round in the *ballotage* system of elections held in July 1978 was won by the eleventh-hour candidate of the CFP, Jaime Roldós, who again swept the ballot box in the final race in April 1979.

It is perhaps well to remember that the army did not want a populist president, and many observers speculated that the August inauguration would not take place. The army used every tactic imaginable to keep the popular Bucaram from the presidency only to have his stand-in elected by a 34 percent margin over his conservative opponent. On August 10, 1979, the military stepped down and a civilian assumed the presidency—significant in itself since it is one of the few times that a governing military junta in Latin America has kept its promise and returned a country to civilian rule. President Roldós, sounding more like a president than a surrogate for the controversial *caudillo,* Bucaram, has said, "I am not going to overlook a single citizen, but I am going to put the principal emphasis on those who need the most."[2]

While it is too early to pin any great hopes on the CFP as a populist movement with any solid footing in the Ecuadorian political scene, many of the poor saw the inauguration of the young, energetic Roldós as a ray of sunshine at the end of a very dark tunnel.

REFERENCES

AVILES, J. J. *Ecuador.* New York: Gordon Press, 1977.

BLANKSTEN, GEORGE I. *Ecuador: Constitutions and Caudillos.* New York: Russell & Russell, 1964.

CUEVA, AGUSTÍN. *El Proceso de Dominación Política en el Ecuador.* 2nd ed. Quito: Ediciones Crítica, 1973.

"Ecuador." *Atlantic Monthly* 216:5 (November 1965), 12–22.

FITCH, JOHN S. *The Military Coup d'etat as a Political Process: Ecuador, 1948–1966.* Baltimore: Johns Hopkins University Press, 1977.

LINKE, LILO. *Ecuador: Country of Contrasts.* New York: Gordon Press, 1976.

———. "Ecuador's Politics: President Velasco's Fourth Exit." *World Today* 18 (February 1962), 57–69.

MARTZ, JOHN D. *Ecuador: Conflicting Political Culture and the Quest for Progress.* Boston: Allyn & Bacon, 1972.

PIKE, FREDERICK B. *The U.S. and the Andean Republics of Peru, Bolivia and Ecuador.* Cambridge, Mass.: Harvard University Press, 1977.

PLAZA LASSO, GALO. *Problems of Democracy in Latin America,* Chap. 2. Chapel Hill, N.C.: University of North Carolina Press, 1955.

WRIGHT, FREEMAN J. "The 1968 Ecuadorian Presidential Campaign." *Inter-American Economic Affairs* 23 (Spring 1970), 81–94.

[2]*New York Times,* May 1, 1979, Sec. IV, p. 9.

10

PERU

Dynamics of Military
Social Revolution

POLITICAL CULTURE AND ENVIRONMENT

Peru is sometimes said to comprise three worlds, a greatly oversimplified and hence partially unsatisfactory description that can apply either geographically or historically. Geographically Peru consists of three quite diverse regions: the coastal area; the cordillera, or sierra; and the densely forested eastern slopes of the mountains, or the *montaña*. Historically Peru has included such varied cultures as the civilization of the Incas (and their predecessors), the Spanish conquest under Pizarro, and the partial fusion of the two in modern times.

Nowhere else in Latin America, except possibly in Panama, are the capital and power center so alien to the rest of the country. Apart from its *barriadas,* or slums, Lima presents surface glamour and glitter (partly an inheritance from colonial days) that still justify its epithet, the City of Kings. But the rest of Peru does not share that scintillation. Its problems are hard and immediate. They have usually been ignored by power elements that were in, but neither of nor for, Peru.

Lack of integration is the outstanding characteristic of Peru. Although true unification was achieved during the remarkable era of the Incas, whose empire covered an area much larger than contemporary Peru, the abrupt and ruthless substitution of new economic, social, and psychological values by the Spanish *conquistadores* brought a disruption to the life of the country which has still not been overcome.

The city of Cuzco[1] dominated the Inca realm, which has seldom, if ever, been surpassed for sheer genius of adaptation to the environment. Inca government was a paternalistic socialism with a fantastically minute regulation of all aspects of life and consequent stifling of individual imagination, initiative, and ambition.

The Spanish introduced a surplus-for-profit economy, drained Peru of its accumulated wealth in precious metals, oriented the economic and political life of the area toward Spain, and even altered the pattern of transportation. The Spanish opened roads from coastal ports to the mines in the hinterland. Inca roads, along with the advanced irrigation systems, were allowed to deteriorate. Under the Spaniards, Lima—the City of Kings—replaced Cuzco as the center of activity. The establishment of the viceregal capital on the coast, an area previously neglected and scarcely even occupied, permitted a degree of Spanish entrenchment, both civil and ecclesiastical, that might successfully have defied the independence movement if revolution had not been imported from the south and north by San Martín and Bolívar. By the same token, it also meant that most of the political, economic, and social development of both colonial and independent Peru had very little identification with the great mass of the population, which continued to live in the cordillera.

Peru's present area, 496,228 square miles, makes it the fourth largest country of Latin America. The area east of the Andes has not formed a part of effective Peru, which is limited to the coast and the sierra. Agricultural land constitutes only one-ninth of the country's area. The great decline of the food supply after the Spanish conquest, combined with the importation of diseases against which the Indians had no natural immunity, decimated the population. Some authorities estimate that the Inca empire included twice or more the population that the same area now contains.

A 1974 estimate put Peru's population at 15,383,000. Of this total an estimated 2,863,000—more than 16 percent—live in metropolitan Lima, making it larger than all other Peruvian cities combined. Lima's mushrooming slums, a social cancer, account for the rapid growth of the capital. Approximately 45 percent of the population is Indian, a significant number of whom do not even speak Spanish. Those of European ancestry—less than one-twentieth of the population—are traditionally dominant politically, economically, and socially. They constitute a Lima-based segment of the population that in general has little knowledge of or contact with the majority of the people.

Political Development

Even the casual student of Peruvian political development must be impressed with its general sterility until recent decades. Because of the unchallenged dominance of the Church, inherited from colonial times, there was no

---

[1]The name is the Quechuan word for navel; it is explained either by the configuration of the valley in which the city lies or the fact that it was the center of the far-flung empire.

clerical issue. Nor was there a centralist-federalist conflict; Lima, the superimposed capital, had uncontested superiority and inflicted its will on the amorphous and normally passive country. The cultured but self-contained and self-satisfied Lima society provided little support for contending political groups based on genuine or fictitious rivalry. About the only ground for potentially developing any significant political division or issue would have been the memory—sometimes the desperately invoked memory (as in the abortive rebellion of 1780)—of the glories of the ancient Inca realm. But after the savage suppression of the followers of Túpac Amarú, any Indianist aspiration for a position or program in Peruvian politics had to wait for more than a century. Túpac Amarú's dream of reestablishing an Indian empire remained just that—a dream.

The early independent period saw a considerable, but not always felicitous, interposition by Bolívar. Although Peru had dictators during the following years, they all fell short of a Rosas, a Portales, or a Santa Anna. Constitutional experimentation, usually at the hands of the *pensadores,* flourished during the years when the *caudillos* were playing with power politics. A new but short-lived constitution written in 1856 was a product of the revolutionary spirit of 1848. A new basic law adopted in 1860, in large part modeled after that of the United States, survived for six decades (though twice briefly supplanted) and remains by far the longest-lived constitution Peru has yet had.

By about the middle of the nineteenth century Peru began to realize—and exploit—its great potential wealth in the enormous deposits of guano on the Chincha Islands. Wholesale shipments to Europe brought large returns to the government, providing an irresistible temptation to political corruption. Exploitation of the guano resources developed a new plutocracy of Lima-based entrepreneurs. The growth of this economic elite tended to shift the social center of gravity away from the older landowning aristocracy. Political control became even more firmly concentrated in the hands of limeños. Middle-class energies and ambitions turned to careers in the bureaucracy instead of to development of Peru's hinterland. Prosperity would have been further increased by profits from Peruvian-owned nitrate areas in the south, but Peru lagged far behind Chile in exploiting them.

Two wars within two decades badly injured Peru's economy, political stability, and pride. The first, a war with Spain in the early 1860s over control of the Chincha Islands, was not especially serious. The second, the War of the Pacific with Chile from 1879 to 1883, resulted in major loss of life and territory, destruction of property, decline in governmental revenues, and disruption of political morale. Recovery was slow. A strong leader did not emerge until Augusto Leguía came onto the Peruvian stage in the twentieth century. Leguía, a civilian, served as president from 1908 to 1912 and as dictator from 1919 to 1930, inevitably becoming a highly controversial figure. He exiled or imprisoned his political opponents, suppressed civil liberties, and stifled political expression. The outstanding political development during the years of Leguía's dictatorship was the formation of Peru's first important political party, the Popular American Revolutionary Alliance (Alianza Popular Revolucionaria Americana, or Apra[2]), which became one of the most interesting and significant political organizations of all Latin America.

Even in the early days of Peruvian independence, groups of one sort or another had been called parties. Such factions were unstable personalist groups, usually formed at the suggestion of a strong leader. An exception was the Civilista party, organized in the early 1870s as a civilian-sponsored reaction to the near chaos caused by a dreary succession of military governments. It succeeded in electing Peru's first civilian president in 1872. Among numerous late nineteenth-century groups, the National Union party, dominated intellectually by Manuel González Prada, became the party godfather of Apra, the vastly more important ideological party of the 1920s.

The principal student leader in the early 1920s was Víctor Raúl Haya de la Torre. Late in 1923 he was exiled from Peru, after serving a prison sentence, and spent most of the rest of the decade in Mexico, the United States, Russia, and Western Europe.

In Mexico City on May 7, 1924, Haya proposed the creation of a reform group for all of Latin America—Apra. Its five-point program included opposition to "Yankee imperialism," advocacy of the political unity of Latin America (Haya preferred to call it Indo-America), nationalization of land and industry, internationalization of the Panama Canal, and a proclamation of solidarity with all peoples and all oppressed classes. Haya hoped to make the new movement solidly intra–Latin American, but its main impact, activity, and membership were consistently found in Peru.

Both the program and the leadership of Apra gave it considerable appeal in dictator-ridden Peru. Intellectuals, middle-class liberals, the more articulate labor leaders, opponents of Leguía of whatever stripe—all found a common cause in the ranks of Apra. Opposition to Apra came from the large landowners, representatives of foreign capital, the Church, and of course, Leguía.

The overthrow of Leguía in 1930 led to the accession of another *caudillo,* Colonel Luis Sánchez Cerro. In 1931 Sánchez Cerro ordered the holding of presidential elections. Haya was the Apra candidate for the presidency and, as the apristas claimed and most foreign observers conceded, probably won the election. The government counted the votes, however, and Sánchez Cerro remained in power. He was assassinated in April 1933. General Oscar Benavides succeeded as president. Benavides allowed the apristas a few months of relative freedom but, by late 1934, Apra had been driven underground. It was

---

[2]From this synthetic root word are derived *aprismo,* the movement; and *aprista,* as a noun —an individual belonging to the party; as an adjective—of, relating to, or possessing a quality or property of the party.

prohibited from nominating a presidential candidate in 1936, but demonstrated aprista power led the government to cancel the elections and extend Benavides's term for three years.

Election of the unopposed Manuel Prado in 1939 inaugurated a more conciliatory regime. Apra became almost openly active. The political situation, already deteriorating by 1947, collapsed in 1948; the president named almost all military men to his cabinet and increasingly began to turn against Apra. Apristas were blamed for a naval revolt in early October 1948, the party was outlawed, and many members were jailed. In spite of the president's inclination to rely increasingly on the army, he was deposed and exiled by the military in late October. As a result of this coup an army-controlled provisional regime was immediately established under the leadership of General Manuel Odría. For more than five years (1949–1954), Haya took political asylum in the Colombian embassy in Lima.

The question may well be asked why, when once the apristas had so nearly attained power, they bungled their opportunity so soon. A part of the answer may be that, once in positions of influence, they overplayed their hand, unduly and too quickly antagonized the army, and failed to consolidate a popular base that was both strong and emotionally powerful enough to make the army consider carefully the cavalier action it proposed. A Latin American group whose primary role has long been opposition and which has spent much time underground is not always psychologically prepared to assume responsibility requiring constructive but moderate action. This is even more true if the party has long emphasized a theoretical and perhaps even doctrinaire approach to politics.

General Odría served as provisional president until 1950, when he was elected constitutional president for a six-year term. His actions were basically constructive but he had a heavy hand, especially in the persecution of apristas, and his regime generally continued to be labeled a dictatorship. Its termination was novel in two respects: Odría voluntarily gave up power at the end of his term in 1956, and the favored, or government, candidate in the election of that year ran a poor third. The campaign of 1956 marked the entry onto the political stage of Fernando Belaúnde Terry, a young architect and the leader of the recently organized Popular Action party (Partido de Acción Popular, or PAP). Former President Prado defeated Belaúnde by about 110,000 votes.

It was apparent that the 1962 elections would provide an impressive test of party and personal strength. The more prominent candidates were Haya, who had been the Apra candidate three decades earlier; Belaúnde Terry, again running as the PAP nominee; and former President Odría, the candidate of the newly formed National Odriist Union (Unión Nacional Odriísta, or UNO). Despite persistent preelection efforts to make deals, all candidates, major and minor, remained in the race until the end. Distribution of votes among the leading candidates was so close that no candidate received a third of the popular vote. Haya de la Torre led the group with 32.97 percent, but Belaúnde was close behind with 32.13 percent, and Odría on his heels with 28.45 percent.

Before congress had a chance to decide the election, the army, which found even the possibility of Haya's election unbearable, took matters into its own hands. A coup on July 18, 1962 nullified both presidential and congressional elections and established a military junta. The junta announced that new elections would be held in June 1963. The 1963 election was again a close race among Haya, Belaúnde, and Odría. This time Belaúnde led the three major candidates with 39.05 percent of the votes to Haya's 34.36 percent and Odría's 25.52 percent. Thus, Belaúnde's total vote and percentage increased substantially in a year, Haya's increased just slightly, and Odría's declined.

Belaúnde began his administration vigorously, but his reform program was endangered by a precarious alliance among his own followers, the possibility of his opponents' putting together a majority combination to defeat specific proposals, and continued skepticism by the oligarchy toward any reform. Apra and the UNO moved ahead in 1964 to perfect an entente which was obviously purely opportunistic in view of their earlier mutual hostility.

Belaúnde's later years in the presidency were marked by a deteriorating political situation in both domestic and foreign affairs, especially in relations with the United States. Substantial defeat of two PAP candidates in congressional by-elections in November 1967 led to the withdrawal of the Christian Democrats from the progovernment coalition. The climax came in a military coup on October 3, 1968, which ousted and exiled Belaúnde. He was succeeded by General Juan Velasco Alvarado as head of a military junta.

The Velasco regime was, as Goodsell put it, "confounding." It defied categorization. It was not democratic, but neither was it totalitarian. His leftist regime nationalized most of the larger foreign-owned companies, beginning with Standard Oil's International Petroleum Company (IPC), and major public utilities including the electric and communication utilities. The "Inca Plan" of the Velasco regime called for the state to be the exclusive owner of "basic industry." His regime also instituted broad agrarian reform measures and overhauled the antiquated Peruvian educational system. His administration's decision to extend Peru's fishing rights to two hundred miles of sea embittered the United States.

By 1974 the regime had lost much of its popularity in both civilian and military circles. Many observers had spoken of the division of the military into conservative and radical sectors, but it was not until the expropriation of the press in May 1974 that the severity of the division was known.

Velasco had used the military split adeptly as he replaced one military man in his cabinet with another. In February 1975 he replaced Prime Minister Mercado Jarrín with Francisco Morales Bermúdez, who also became the army chief of staff and defense minister. Velasco's health was failing, and before long rumors were flying that Morales Bermúdez actually ruled the country while

Velasco became a mere figurehead. Meanwhile Velasco tried to hold on to the reins of government until Morales passed retirement age, but Morales moved quickly and skillfully to secure his position within the army. At the same time he increased his control over government operations by forcing the retirement of several radical officers. On August 29, 1975, with over one hundred representatives of the Conference of Non-Aligned Countries looking on, the military turned the presidency over to General Morales Bermúdez.

The Morales Bermúdez government launched what was called "Phase II" of the Inca Plan, or the Plan Túpac Amarú, in January 1976. The plan was considered too radical by right-wing elements in the military, and a revised Plan Túpac Amarú was announced on February 6, 1977. The plan called for constitutional reform, a return of elections, and the return of private enterprise. In trying to direct a social and political revolution, the military regime found it had lead Peru into an economic quagmire. Since coming to power the military had spent and borrowed more money for expensive arms purchases, public works projects, nationalization, and subsidies than the country could finance.

A general strike by all the major labor organizations in 1977 brought to light the clear distinction between the present military regime of Morales Bermúdez and the populist regime of former president Velasco. Velasco had led a socialist-type military revolution; Morales, who leaned more to the right, had tried to keep the rhetoric of the revolution while backtracking in the area of nationalization and labor reforms.

Despite heated objections among the military, Morales did keep his promise to hold an election of a hundred-seat constituent assembly in June 1978, preparing for a return to civilian rule. Rumors of coups during the 1978 election year were as numerous as there were generals to lead them.

Meanwhile the International Monetary Fund had absolutely refused Peru standby credit to pay its external debt of U.S. $8 billion unless severe austerity measures were taken. The government bit the bullet and substantially increased food, public transportation, and petroleum prices while keeping wages frozen. This brought on the third general strike in less than a year. With violence running high Morales agreed to postpone elections for two weeks while the government tried to find a scapegoat for the country's major ills; the Socialists were chosen. Days before the assembly elections, almost thirty of the left-wing group's leading candidates were deported or jailed for strike violations.

The resulting election tally was a predictable majority in the assembly for Apra and the Popular Christian party (Partido Popular Cristiano, or PPC). What did come as a surprise was the winning of almost a third of the seats by the combined left-wing forces. The distribution of seats is shown in Table 10–1 (see p. 198).

The constituent assembly, with the Apra-PPC coalition making up the

TABLE 10-1 Distribution of Seats, June 1978 Election

Party	Number of Seats
Apra	37
Partido Popular Cristiano (PPC)	25
Frente Nacional de Trabajadores	4
Movimiento Democrático Peruano	2
Unión Nacional Odriísta (UNO)	2
Frente Obrero, Campesino, Estudiantil y Popular (FOCEP)	12
Partido Socialista Revolucionario (PSR)	6
Communist	6
Unidad Demócratico Popular (UDP)	4
Partido Demócrata Cristiano (PDC)	2

majority, began work on July 28. After a year of conflicts among and between Apra and PPC, left and right factions, administration and the assembly, and military and the administration (to name just a few), the new constitution was completed and signed by assembly president Víctor Raúl Haya de la Torre on July 12, 1979. Meanwhile, speculation continued to run rampant on whether the assembly's work would come to fruition in the form of election of a civilian government or whether it would become a futile exercise as factions within the military continually tried to force President Morales to hold the reins of government. With inflation running at 80 percent a year, continued general strikes, and no real solution to the economic crisis in sight, the military government seemed determined to keep to its timetable to return the country to civilian rule in 1980.

GOVERNMENTAL AND POLITICAL STRUCTURES

The Executive

It is simply stating the obvious to say that the Peruvian presidency is the focus of governmental organization and operation. Indeed it is surprising that party impact on the dimensions of the office can be as great as it is in times of civilian control.

Historically the president has come from the ranks of the military or from the oligarchy. As provided in a 1939 constitutional amendment, he serves a six-year term. He is ineligible for immediate reelection and, since the Benavides days, *continuismo* has not been attempted. The 1979 constitution states that if the 1980 candidate does not receive at least 36 percent of the vote, Congress will decide between the top two candidates. In future elections, if a presidential candidate does not get an absolute majority (50 percent plus one), a second round, or a *ballotage*-like runoff, between the two leading candidates will be held to elect the president.

The normal path to the presidency is through army politics or party activity. Apra and PAP have been so closely attached to Haya and Belaúnde, respectively, that for either party to have nominated another candidate without full approval of the leader would have been unthinkable. Even in 1979 the Apra machine put forth the name of Haya for the 1980 elections knowing the eighty-four-year-old leader was dying of lung cancer.

The president, as described by the constitution, not only serves as the head of the state but also "personifies the nation." This latter description is perhaps not just rhetoric; the highly unintegrated nature of the Peruvian society and polity makes it all the more important that a central symbolic figure represent the unity of the state, and only the president could play such a role.

In general the president's formal powers are conventional, though somewhat restricted by constitutional amendments in 1936. He may not personally command the armed forces without congressional approval. His appointing power is relatively broad. He also has nominally important authority in relation to the Catholic church on matters of patronage, approval of publication of papal encyclicals and such. A provision in Article 155 of the constitution bestows on the president ex officio membership in the senate for one term after his presidential period.

The cabinet, officially termed the council of ministers, currently includes eighteen portfolios plus the cabinet presidency. The president of the council is often unofficially called the premier or prime minister, although his position falls far short of that of similarly named officials in full-fledged parliamentary governments. In reality cabinet members are under the control of the president of the republic, even though his appointments and removals of ministers other than the president of the council must nominally be approved by the council head.

The president of the republic will not ordinarily appoint a premier with sufficient power and prestige to constitute a possible political challenge or threat lest he then use his position to undermine the president's own authority and influence. Velasco's appointment of Morales Bermúdez was a highly unusual exception.

The attempt to get "the best of two worlds" by combining parliamentary and presidential governments has not worked successfully. Although certain congressional controls were instituted after 1945, they have been ineffective, and the president (in civilian regimes, of course) still has a free hand and normally exerts considerable control over congress. Such a Peruvian authority as Pareja Paz-Soldán has been critical of the semiparliamentary system, calling it "false parliamentarism."

The Legislative and Judicial Structures

Congressional organization, prestige, and power fall short of what the constitution purports to establish. The 1933 constitution prescribed that the upper chamber of the legislature should be a "functional Senate," but no action to implement the provision has ever been undertaken. Peru, unlike Ecuador, has not experimented in the selection of its upper house. The chamber of deputies is chosen in a conventional manner on a population basis. Proportional representation is used to select members of both houses, so that a spread of party representation is almost automatically guaranteed. Both senators and deputies are elected for six-year terms which run concurrently with that of the president.

The chief function of the Peruvian congress has become that of a sounding board, and it is only partially effective even in this respect. The serious lack of integration in the country is reflected in the inadequacies of the legislature. The country needs a national symbol, but congress cannot fill the need.

The constitution provides broad outlines for the judiciary, and congress has elaborated on them. The five-level system is headed by the customary supreme court of justice. Its members are elected by congress from panels nominated by the president and serve a life tenure. Needless to say the president actually controls the selections. The court is divided into two chambers, which deal with civil and criminal matters. The supreme court has no power or tradition of exercising judicial review.

The second judicial level consists of superior courts, one in each district of the country. Provincial capitals are provided with courts of first instance, or *juzgados,* whose judges are appointed by the president from nominations made by the respective superior courts. Below the provincial tribunals are courts served by legally trained justices of the peace; still lower courts in all towns are served by justices of the peace who need not be legally trained.

Administrative Machinery

Administrative control below the national level is in general highly centralized; some imitation of French models is evident, though not as much as in Chile. The demographic and social structure of the country suggests that federalism might be the most logical system of organization, but it has never been given a good trial.

The major unit is the territorial department. Peru has twenty-four, which inevitably vary greatly in population and importance. The departments are governed by presidentially appointed prefects. Departments are further divided into provinces, four or five to a department. The provinces are subdivided into districts. Executives of the provinces and districts are, respectively, the presidentially appointed subprefect and governor. If the district is divided into subdistricts, as sometimes happens, it is administered by a lieutenant governor. All levels are tightly controlled, and the central government is not anxious to encourage any wish for local autonomy that might threaten its own patronage and power.

In many instances municipalities are equated with districts. The constitution provides for elective municipal councils in provincial and district capitals, but they are viable only in the provincial capitals.

Grass-roots control of local government is deplorably underdeveloped, in large part because of the extreme lack of political integration in Peru, which places governmental control in a national capital far removed from and essentially alien to the heart of the country. The result is civic apathy on the part of the hinterland's potential electorate and chronic neglect of the hinterland's interests by the national government. There have been times in the past when the total government expenditure for local services in Lima and Callao, Lima's nearby port, have been almost as great as for all the rest of the country.

The Party Scene

With the political consciousness of the average Peruvian so limited, it is surprising that parties have made as much impact as they have in the last generation. Voting is compulsory for literate men and women from the age of twenty-one (eighteen if married) to sixty and optional thereafter. The electoral *libreta,* or identification card, is required for a variety of other services or privileges and has perhaps increased participation in voting. Illiteracy still disfranchises vast numbers of Peruvians. Voting and party activity are essentially urban phenomena; more than a third of all ballots are normally cast in Lima and Callao, perhaps another quarter in six or eight other cities. Although women have been allowed to vote since 1955, they have not avidly exercised the privilege.

Parties have been numerous—more than a dozen have registered for some elections. Most are small and transitory: There are not more than five significant and effective parties.

APRA.   Apra is still probably the most significant Peruvian party, though not necessarily the most effective or promising. Its importance is due partly to its traditions and its great impact on the political scene. Its intellectual inspiration came in part from the nineteenth century and can be traced especially to the writings of Manuel González Prada (1846–1918). He became a severe critic of the established social and political order, attacking the Church for its orthodoxy and conservatism and fighting to give the Indians and the working class a better status. He approved of revolution as an acceptable means of gaining solutions for social problems. González Prada influenced José Carlos Mariátegui (1895–1930), a tubercular cripple from a humble Lima environment, who became a confirmed Marxist during a trip to Europe just after World War I. Mariátegui had considerable influence on the young Apra but later broke away and founded the Peruvian Socialist party, affiliated with the Third International. Subsequently both apristas and Communists claimed to be Mariátegui's political heirs.

The immediate antecedents of Apra were the groups organized during the ferment in university student circles in Latin America at the end of the first World War. Student activity at the ancient University of San Marcos in Lima came to a climax in May 1923 in opposition to an effort by Leguía to dedicate Peru to the "Sacred Heart of Jesus."

Despite Apra's failure to become popular in many other Latin American countries, its advocacy of a far-reaching reform program for Latin America made it a model and a political lodestone of considerable influence in other countries. Apra's political philosophy was a sort of indigenous socialism, though it rejected Marxism as a vehicle and later became bitterly opposed to communism. It received the compliment of imitation in the form of apristalike parties in Venezuela, Paraguay, Cuba, Bolivia, Guatemala, Costa Rica, and elsewhere.

While Apra never captured the presidency, it has functioned as a symbol and a harbinger of the growing demand for social and economic reform through political action. Although the military regime has fought the party openly for more than forty years, Apra's cooperativist influences can be seen in many of the regime's plans of the past ten years.

The Apristas took a more conservative stance in the elections of 1978. While this temperance made the party more palatable to the growing middle class, much of the moderate element, even the reformist moderates, were still wary of Apra's past positions. The Aprista entente, or *convivencia,* first with Prado, then Odría, and more recently with the PPC, convinced many Peruvians that Apra was purely opportunistic and entirely willing to use its strength for bargaining purposes. This theory may have some weight in the light of events in late 1978 – early 1979, in which Apra began to vacillate in its ideological position first with its ally, the PPC, and next with the military junta.

Differences between Apra and PPC during the constitutional assembly in 1978–1979 were due mainly to the power struggle between left- and right-wing factions within Apra. During recent years the Apra leadership has tended to gear its policy toward a more favorable relationship with the military government to avoid endangering the timetable for elections on which Apra rested its hopes.

Over the years Haya de la Torre became a legend. The octogenarian presided over the conservative-oriented constituent assembly when it was formed in 1978 while continuing to lead the aprista movement in a plan to restructure the party with a more "modern image." The struggle for party leadership between left- and right-wing factions resurfaced in 1979 with the death of the charismatic Haya.

Popular Action Party.   The Popular Action party (PAP or AP) entered the Peruvian political scene in 1958 as the supporting vehicle for Belaúnde's first presidential campaign. It was closely attached to Belaúnde and might in some respects be considered personalistic, but it also deserves characterization as a major and even a quasi-ideological party. Popular Action appeals especially to young, middle-class reformers who favor such issues as land distribution, better communications, and nationalization of petroleum production. Its position precludes any support from the conservative oligarchy. It has never been professionally anticlerical, as Apra was at one stage; in the confusion of Peruvian politics, it attracted Communist support in 1963.

The party had not fully coalesced or matured its ideological position; as Professor Frederick Pike aptly wrote, it sometimes "presents the appearance of wanting to gallop off in all directions at once."[3] In some degree, it still seems self-conscious; in 1962 Belaúnde said he preferred a military takeover to an electoral victory by either of his major opponents; ironically, he soon got his preference. While Belaúnde's decision to boycott the 1978 constituent assembly elections cost him a chance for valuable exposure in general elections in 1980, he was not idle. He made numerous personal appearances and had several conversations with military leaders, adding fuel to rumors that the military would not oppose returning the presidency to the man they overthrew in 1968. The party announced in October 1978 that it would "go it alone" in the 1980 elections.

Christian Democratic Party.   Allied with Popular Action after 1963 was the Christian Democratic party (Partido Demócrata-Cristiano, or PDC), a small but viable member of the world Christian Democratic family whose electoral strength is centered in Arequipa and Lima. In 1963 support by PDC, coupled with a PDC vice-presidential running-mate for Belaúnde, was sufficient to give the PAP candidate his margin of victory, though Apra's vote was greater than that of PAP by itself. The Peruvian Catholic church has only tardily and perhaps reluctantly begun to listen to pleas for social reform; hence, the PDC has not enjoyed even an unofficial blessing from the hierarchy. Its popular appeal must be aimed at much the same element that Apra and PAP try to attract.

The PDC suffered a schism in the latter 1960s with the defection of a right-wing faction led by Luis Bedoya Reyes, which established the Partido Popular Cristiano (PPC). The PPC gained substantial prestige by winning a quarter of the 100 seats in the constituent assembly in the 1978 elections.

[3]Frederick B. Pike, "The Old and the New APRA in Peru: Myth and Reality," *Inter-American Economic Affairs,* 18 (Autumn 1964), p. 42.

Odriístas. The National Odriíst Union (UNO) is a conservative and personalist party. Despite his dictatorship, Odría won a certain following during his years in office, as did Rojas Pinilla in Colombia, Trujillo in the Dominican Republic, and Perón in Argentina. A few supporting deputies and senators during the 1956–1962 term maintained a semblance of Odriísta organization, and the general made a geographically limited but vigorous campaign for the presidency in both 1962 and 1963. His and UNO's strength was largely in Lima. He attracted both conservative oligarchy support, because it had nowhere else to go, and the backing of large numbers of Lima's desperately poor, because he had taken measures to alleviate their lot during his presidency. UNO is not ideologically based and Odría, unlike Perón, is not a charismatic figure. The party seems unlikely to survive Odría.

Other Parties. The Peruvian Democratic Movement (Movimiento Democrático Peruano, or MDP) dates back to 1956 and was the personal vehicle of former President Prado. It was organized during the 1956 campaign to put Prado into the presidency. Its position was right-of-center, even conservative, but it was not an ideological party. Its entente with Apra in 1956 stamped it as essentially opportunistic.

Peruvian communism began in 1928 with the organization of the Socialist party of Peru (Partido Socialista del Peru, or PSP) whose founding genius was José Mariátegui. From that time on, the Peruvian Communist party, as it soon came to be called, led a checkered career, primarily because of the far greater popularity of Apra and the aprista hold on organized labor. Hence, communists frequently collaborated with a succession of Peruvian dictators. The Communist party was made illegal at the beginning of 1961, but a year later this action was reversed to substantiate the claim that freedom of political expression was allowed in the 1962 elections.

Early in the 1960s dissatisfaction with the Apra party led one faction to defect. This group wanted to maintain the party's pristine revolutionary purity. Fidelista in orientation, it was known as Apra Rebelde, and later took the name Movement of the Revolutionary Left (Movimiento de Izquierda Revolucionaria, or MIR).

Communists became the dominant element in the National Liberation Front (Frente de Liberación Nacional, or FLN), founded late in 1961. The FLN was established to provide a political home for all extreme leftist groups, but it was only partially successful. It was particularly appealing to students, especially in the venerable and highly politicized University of San Marcos at Lima, and was loosely associated with Apra Rebelde and its successor, MIR. All of these groups were fidelista-oriented, and all attempted to proselyte among the Indians of the sierra.

The year-long constituent assembly gave political party leaders a stage to air their philosophies and to vie for alliances to strengthen their position before the 1980 elections. Within the center-right group, the PPC and Apra continued to debate who would assume leadership after Haya de la Torre. Although the left and center-left group boycotted much of the constituent assembly debate, its weight was felt. Many speculated that a united effort behind one candidate in 1980 by such parties as Christian Democratic (Partido Demócrata Cristiano, or PDC), Socialist Revolutionary party (Partido Socialista Revolucionario, or PSR), and Popular Democratic Unity (Unidad Democrático Popular, or UDP, which includes MIR, the Vanguardistas, and the Partido Revolucionario Comunista, PCR) would be difficult to beat.

Other Political Structures

The Church and the army are old and politically powerful institutions in Peru. The 1933 constitution devoted a separate, short title to religion and, while establishing freedom of worship, recognized the Roman Catholic church as the official church of Peru. The Church established itself solidly during the colonial period and has never been subject to serious threat as it has in Mexico and a few other Latin American countries. Apra in its earlier and more militant days was strongly anticlerical, but Popular Action is sympathetic to the Church and has been allied with the even more Catholic-oriented Christian Democratic party. Consequently a clerical issue has not crystallized as it once threatened to do.

Concordat relationships between government and Vatican date back to 1874. Since 1959 the Church has been partly subsidized by the government. The Peruvian hierarchy has traditionally been conservative and members of the clergy, at both low and high levels, have not hesitated to exercise political suasion with the faithful. Peruvian Catholicism has been little touched by the sort of liberal political leaven that has strongly affected the hierarchy, or at least parts of it, in such countries as Chile and Costa Rica.

The army has an equally long record of political influence. As noted earlier no civilian government ruled until 1872. Even since that time army regimes have been numerous. The army, navy, and air force are separately organized in Peru, and each has its own traditions, though the navy and air force are inclined to boast, at least privately, of more aristocratic organization and tone. The traditional and seemingly instinctive alliance between military and oligarchy, so characteristic of a number of Latin American countries, is less evident in Peru, where the military forms almost a distinct caste and has by no means always sided with the oligarchy.

Apra was traditionally antimilitary as well as anticlerical. Its hostility toward the military persisted even longer than its hostility toward the Church. This probably explains in large part the army's refusal to allow Haya, the plurality winner of the 1962 balloting, to take the presidency.

In Peruvian politics, labor has emerged as a major interest structure willing to politicize the economic crisis through the power of the strike. In 1978 labor unrest and violence reached its peak. The various labor unions struck frequently for higher wages and redress of other pressing demands. When the Union of Peruvian Education Workers (Sindicato Unico de Trabajadores Peruanos de la Educación, or SUTEP) called a general strike, the Morales administration declared the strike illegal and dissolved the powerful National Agrarian Confederation (Confederación Nacional Agraria, or CNA), with whom the political left was identified.[4] The CNA leadership was charged with divisionism among the six million Peruvian peasants and with subversive activity.

In September 1978 the military government was forced to negotiate with the powerful miners' union (Federación de Trabajadores Mineros y Metalúrgicos) to end a long strike involving close to 45,000 workers who had almost paralyzed the mining sector of the country. During the 1978 labor upheavals, labor organizations of different political tendencies joined ranks to achieve their common goals.

The Morales Bermúdez regime tried to establish an entente with the labor sector by promising amnesty and respect for ideological differences if labor would agree not to disrupt the economy. The military government finally guaranteed freedom with no reprisals for those arrested in connection with the strikes.

Other interest structures include the sixty Chambers of Commerce (Cámaras de Comercio), composed of thirty thousand enterprises. In 1978 the Federación de Cámaras de Comercio (FEDECAM) pledged support to President Morales's government in its efforts to resolve the financial economic crisis.

DEVELOPMENTAL PROSPECTS

The Peruvian oligarchy has eroded over the years, but it has certainly not lost all its political weight. It has, almost without exception, opposed major social reform, and as long as it held the power, no such reform could be expected. Apra provided the first challenge; the domestic planks of its platform touched on many of Peru's basic problems. Odría, like Rojas Pinilla in Colombia, was responsible for a modest reform program, but it definitely was not of sufficient magnitude to be called social change. Belaúnde's administration, too, moved to accelerate social change. Belaúnde argued that sierra communities need a variety of basic social services—such as schools, water supply, housing, and roads—which the government cannot finance on the vast scale needed and

---

[4]The CNA was created during the government of former President Juan Velasco Alvarado as the representative arm of the peasants; it would provide support for the government after enactment of the 1969 agrarian reform decree.

which consequently must be tackled locally, with government assistance in tools and technical aid.

The Velasco regime stepped in to replace the old oligarchy and launched what many Peruvians believed was the revolution that would transform Peruvian society. Some progress was made in the area of communications, schooling, and agrarian reform, but it did not begin to reach the lower levels of society. President Morales Bermúdez spoke of a new "revolution," but this time in more intellectual or philosophical terms. After Velasco's valiant attempt to bring social revolution to Peru, the new military regime found itself face to face with inflation that soared to an all-time high of 80 percent by the end of 1978. The economic crisis was eased somewhat in 1979 by $70 million in aid from the United States and by rescheduled loan payments from international money lenders. But the continued crippling strikes and labor violence accentuated the country's opposition to the military government's price increases, mass arrests of labor leaders, censorship of the press, and other belt-tightening measures which worked their greatest hardship on those who could least afford them.

What the political future holds for Peru has become a subject of considerable speculation. With the death of Haya de la Torre in 1979, the military's choice for president in the 1980 elections was thwarted; some within the military ranks oppose the entire idea of returning the government to civilian rule. President Bermúdez seemed committed to his decision to restore constitutional government with elections in July 1980. But, as he indicated on numerous occasions, the general elections in 1980 would simply effect "a transfer of government, not of power."

REFERENCES

ALISKY, MARVIN. *Peruvian Political Perspective.* Tempe: Arizona State University Center for Latin American Studies, 1972.

ASTIZ, CARLOS. *Pressure Groups and Power Elites in Peruvian Politics.* Ithaca, N.Y.: Cornell University Press, 1969.

ASTIZ, CARLOS, and JOSÉ Z. GARCÍA. "The Peruvian Military: Achievement, Orientation, Training, and Political Tendencies." *Western Political Quarterly* 25 (December 1972), 667–685.

BAINES, JOHN M. *Revolution in Peru: Mariátegui and the Myth.* University: University of Alabama Press, 1972.

BOURRICAUD, FRANÇOIS. *Power and Society in Contemporary Peru.* New York: Holt, Rinehart & Winston, 1970.

———. "Structure and Function of the Peruvian Oligarchy." *Studies in Comparative International Development* 2:2 (1966), 17–31.

BRUSH, STEPHEN B. *Mountain, Field, and Family: The Economy and Human Ecology of an Andean Valley.* Philadelphia: University of Pennsylvania Press, 1977.

CHAPLIN, DAVID, ed. *Peruvian Nationalism; A Corporatist Revolution.* New Brunswick, N.J.: Transaction Books, 1976.

CLINTON, RICHARD LEE. "The Modernizing Military: The Case of Peru." *Inter-American Economic Affairs* 24 (Spring 1971), 43–66.

DEW, EDWARD. *Politics of the Altiplano: The Dynamics of Change in Rural Peru.* Austin: University of Texas Press, 1976.

DOBYNS, HENRY F., and PAUL L. DOUGHTY. *Peru: A Cultural History.* New York: Oxford University Press, 1976.

EINAUDI, LUIGI. *Peruvian Military Relations with the United States.* Santa Monica, Calif.: Rand Corporation, 1970.

———. *Revolution from Within? Military Rule in Peru Since 1968.* Santa Monica, Calif.: Rand Corporation, 1971.

FITZGERALD, E. V. K. *The State and Economic Development: Peru Since 1968.* Cambridge: Cambridge University Press, 1976.

GOMEZ, RUDOLPH. *The Peruvian Administrative System.* Boulder: Bureau of Governmental Research and Service of the University of Colorado, 1969.

GOODSELL, CHARLES T. *American Corporations and Peruvian Politics.* Cambridge, Mass.: Harvard University Press, 1974.

———. "That Confounding Revolution in Peru." *Current History* 69:401 (January 1975), 20–23.

GORMAN, STEPHEN M. "Peru Before the Election for the Constituent Assembly: Ten Years of Military Rule and the Quest for Social Justice." *Government and Opposition* 13:3 (Summer 1978), 288–306.

HANDELMAN, HOWARD. *Struggle in the Andes: Peasant Political Mobilization in Peru.* Austin: University of Texas Press, 1974.

HAYA DE LA TORRE, VÍCTOR R. *Treinta Años de Aprismo.* Mexico: n.p., 1963.

HERNÁNDEZ URBINA, ALFREDO. "Los partidos políticos en el Perú." *Cuadernos Americanos* 186:1 (January–February 1973), 39–58.

HILLIKER, GRANT. *The Politics of Reform in Peru; the Aprista and Other Mass Parties of Latin America.* Baltimore: Johns Hopkins University Press, 1971.

JAQUETTE, JANE S. "Revolution by Fiat: The Context of Policy-Making in Peru." *Western Political Quarterly* 25 (December 1972), 648–666.

KANTOR, HARRY. "Aprismo: Peru's Indigenous Political Theory." *South Atlantic Quarterly* 53 (January 1954), 1–9.

———. "The Aprista Search for a Program." *Western Political Quarterly* 5 (December 1952), 578–584.

———. *The Ideology and Program of the Peruvian Aprista Movement.* New York: Octagon Books, 1966.

KUCZYNSKI, P. *Peruvian Democracy Under Economic Stress. An Account of the Belaúnde Administration, 1963–1968.* Princeton, N.J.: Princeton University Press, 1977.

LANDSBERGER, HENRY A. "The Labor Elite: Is It Revolutionary?" Pp. 256–300 in *Elites in Latin America,* ed. by Seymour Martin Lipset and Aldo Solari. New York: Oxford University Press, 1966.

MCNICOLL, ROBERT E. *Peru's Institutional Revolution.* Latin American Studies, Interdisciplinary Occasional Papers. Pensacola: University of West Florida Press, 1973.

MIDDLEBROOK, KEVIN J., and D. S. PALMER. *Military Government and Political Development: Lesson from Peru.* Beverly Hills, Calif.: Sage Publications, 1975.

MIRÓ QUESADA LAOS, CARLOS. *Autopsia de los Partidos Políticos.* Lima: Emecé, 1961.

NEEDLER, MARTIN C. "Cabinet Responsibility in a Presidential System: The Case of Peru." *Parliamentary Affairs* 18 (Spring 1965), 156–161.

OWENS, R. J. *Peru.* London: Oxford University Press, 1963.

PATCH, RICHARD W. "A Note on Bolivia and Peru." *American Universities Field Staff Reports* (West Coast South America) 9 (April 1962), 1–42.

————. "A Note on Peru and Bolivia." *American Universities Field Staff Reports* (West Coast South America) 6 (July 1959), 1–28.

————. "The Peruvian Elections of 1962 and their Annulment." *American Universities Field Staff Reports* (West Coast South America) 9:6 (September 1962), 1–17.

————. "The Peruvian Elections of 1963." *American Universities Field Staff Reports* (West Coast South America) 10 (July 1963), 1–14.

PAYNE, JAMES L. *Labor and Politics in Peru.* New Haven, Conn.: Yale University Press, 1965.

————. "Peru: The Politics of Structured Violence." *Journal of Politics* 27 (May 1965), 362–374.

PHILLIP, G. D. *The Rise and Fall of the Peruvian Military Radicals, 1968–1976.* Atlantic Highlands, N.J.: Humanities Press, 1978.

————. "The Peruvian Tightrope." *World Today* 33:12 (December 1977), 464–471.

PIKE, FREDERICK B. *The Modern History of Peru.* New York: Holt, Rinehart & Winston, 1967.

————. "The Old and the New APRA in Peru." *Inter-American Economic Affairs* 18:2 (Autumn 1964), 3–46.

PINELO, ADALBERTO. *The Multinational Corporation as a Force in Latin American Politics: A Case Study of the International Petroleum Company in Peru.* New York: Holt, Rinehart & Winston, 1973.

RAVINES, EUDOCIO. *The Yenan Way.* New York: Scribner's, 1951.

ROZMAN, STEPHEN L. "The Evolution of the Political Role of the Peruvian Military." *Journal of Inter-American Studies and International Affairs* 12 (October 1970), 534–464.

STUART, GRAHAM H. *The Governmental System of Peru.* Washington, D.C.: Carnegie Institution of Washington, 1925.

WERLICH, DAVID P. "The Peruvian Revolution in Crisis." *Current History* 72 (February 1977), 61–64, 81.

————. *Peru: A Short History.* Carbondale, Ill.: Southern Illinois University Press, 1978.

WHYTE, WILLIAM F., and GIORGIO ALBERTI. *Power, Politics, and Progress: Social Change in Rural Peru.* New York: Elsevier North-Holland, 1976.

11

BOLIVIA

The Politics
of a Frustrated Revolution

POLITICAL CULTURE AND ENVIRONMENT

Bolivia now has an area of 424,163 square miles, making it the sixth largest country of Latin America. Yet at the time of independence it claimed an area of slightly more than 900,000 square miles. Large pieces of its territory were annexed at different times and by various methods to each of Bolivia's five neighbors. The smallest cession, 46,333 square miles to Chile, was the most important because it included all of Bolivia's nitrate-producing Pacific littoral and thus left the country (along with Paraguay) in the resented position of being landlocked.

Effective Bolivia is the roughly one-third of its area which is composed of the Andes system. In the intermontane valleys and plateaus of that portion lives by far the largest part of the population, most of it in thin ribbons of settlement along the irrigated river valleys. Three of the most important cities, including the capital, La Paz, are at an altitude of more than 12,000 feet. Physical, climatic, and economic conditions in the Yungas, the heavily forested and rainy northeastern slope of the eastern portion of the cordillera, preclude it from effective development. The southeastern portion of Bolivia is also, at least at present, outside the effective area of the country. It is geographically a part of the Gran Chaco, shared with Paraguay, Argentina, and Brazil.

Bolivia's population, estimated in 1980 to be about 6,162,000, is more heavily Indian than that of any other Latin American country. Some 62 percent of the entire population is Indian, mostly of the Aymará and Quechua families. Another 25 percent is mestizo or *cholo* and less than 13 percent is white. Here, as elsewhere in the Andean region, social and psychological stratification is of greater importance than ethnic divisions. The Indian has been very difficult to move in significant numbers from the mountains and plateaus to other, and especially lower, parts of the country. The difficulty is perhaps more psychological than physiological.

It remains undoubtedly true that the occidental political process is an overlay which is only recently beginning to touch the large majority of Bolivians. The lack of ethnic integration is seriously, almost desperately, reflected in political and economic mirrors. And yet the transformation made since the beginning of the Bolivian Revolution in 1952 has been remarkable. That movement was one of the few true social revolutions yet to occur in Latin America, and its effects in Bolivia have been deep and widespread.

Political Development

The political and constitutional development of independent Bolivia has been about as troubled and erratic as that of any Latin American state. It is asserted that in its 155 years of independence, Bolivia has had more than 180 governments. In May 1826 the newly independent state's first constitution, written and instituted by Simón Bolívar, provided for a president elected for life (in effect, an uncrowned monarch) and other conservative and in some instances impractical features. The complex and unpopular system survived only five years.

Of a long series of early *caudillos* the most important was Andrés Santa Cruz, a mestizo who claimed descent from the Inca emperors. Most of the rest of the nineteenth century was a dreary story of dictators (most of them *caudillos*), anarchy, revolutions, and general misrule. The nadir of governance probably came during the reign of General Mariano Melgarejo (1864–1871), a fearless, cruel, stupid, vain, and debauched dictator.[1]

The greatest crisis Bolivia had yet experienced was the War of the Pacific. Knocked out almost immediately by the far better integrated and developed Chile, Bolivia retired to lick its wounds. The war resulted in the immediate and (presumably) permanent loss of all Bolivia's littoral, a loss which was more damaging psychologically than economically. Politically, the war seemed to have a chastening effect. A new constitution, the twelfth, was adopted in 1880; it proved Bolivia's longest lived to date (lasting just over half a century) and in general reflected a more democratic trend than the country had yet known.

The early years of the twentieth century brought little political stability.

---

[1]Melgarejo, ignorant and illiterate, has become almost the archetype of *caudillos* in the political depths.

In the 1920s, in particular, Bolivia was largely at the mercy of internal political exploiters and external financial profiteers. Depression at the end of the decade resulted in an evaporation of Bolivia's tin markets and brought quick economic and then political collapse. The election of the honest Daniel Salamanca as president in January 1931 seemed to augur a better day for Bolivia, but the following year the long-smoldering war with Paraguay over the Chaco Boreal broke out in all its fury. This conflict lasted three years, morally and financially exhausting Bolivia. Some nine-tenths of Bolivia's claims in the Chaco were lost by the peace settlement in 1938.

The national losses and humiliation of the Chaco War demanded scapegoats. The obvious ones were the "imperialistic" United States, the old-line domestic *caudillos,* and the "tin kings." Indians and *cholos,* conscripted for the army during the war, had now become acquainted with alien lands, and their horizons were more than merely geographically broadened. In particular they were angered by their shabby treatment at the hands of the government. Labor leaders and university students quickly became more politically articulate and demanding.

Colonel David Toro, made president in 1936, attempted to introduce a confused and fragmentary socialistic program, but he was displaced in 1937 by Colonel Germán Busch, who continued the revolutionary gesture. Busch died suddenly in 1939—either by suicide or assassination—and in 1940 a conservative and pro-Allied general, Enrique Peñaranda, was placed in power by the army. In December 1942, government troops massacred striking tin miners at the Patiño-owned Catavi mine, a prelude to later blood baths which would stain Bolivian politics. A year later, on December 20, 1943, another revolution ushered into power Bolivia's most significant contemporary political party, the Nationalist Revolutionary Movement (Movimiento Nacionalista Revolucionario, or MNR).

The army coup which ousted General Peñaranda in December 1943 was supported by a military officers' lodge in expedient alliance with the MNR. Major Gualberto Villarroel was installed as president. The party of the Revolutionary Left (Partido de la Izquierda Revolucionaria, or PIR) hoped for a share in the new government. When that was denied, it was forced into opposition, which made it the ostensible supporter of the great tin-mine owners and put it in a tactically indefensible political position. Villarroel, not much more than a figurehead, was in power for two and a half years, at a time of increasing political tension and repression. The principal political leaders during Villarroel's presidency were the intellectual Paz Estenssoro and Juan Lechín, a radical leader of the miners' union, politically inexperienced but adept and with a forceful personality. Lechín, who from that period on was a central figure in Bolivian politics, leaned heavily on the Revolutionary Workers' party (Partido Obrera Revolucionaria, or POR), which had established a strong position among the miners.

Mounting political pressures came to a head on July 21, 1946, with mass demonstrations against the government by huge crowds in an ugly mood. The mob lynched Villarroel and strung his body from a lamppost (which later served as a national shrine!). For sheer, bloody drama, the action had no real counterpart in twentieth-century Latin American politics except perhaps for the 1915 lynching of President Guillaume Sam at Port-au-Prince. During the next few years the regimes in power were generally ineffectual in the face of turbulent internal conditions. MNR leaders were of course personae non gratae and a number of them were in exile.

New presidential elections were scheduled for May 1951. The MNR, which had maintained considerable support within Bolivia despite official disfavor, nominated the exiled Paz Estenssoro, who won an announced 41 percent of the vote but claimed some four-fifths of the ballots. The army intervened, however, to forestall an MNR triumph and set up a military junta which promptly annulled the election. In April 1952, after months of plotting, the MNR, supported by segments of the military police, began a revolt. After two days of severe fighting, it ousted and exiled the junta. The leaders of the bloody revolt in La Paz were Juan Lechín and Hernán Siles Zuazo, the MNR vice-presidential candidate in 1951 and son of a former president. Paz quickly returned from exile and was promptly sworn in as president.

Since 1952 the Bolivian political scene has often been dominated by the MNR, which was not without internal dissension and schisms. High priority had to be given to the status of the large tin interests. Expropriation was proclaimed at the end of October 1952, but the operation of the big tin mines as a nationalized enterprise was not reassuring, though the regime had hoped to make them a symbolic showcase of its program. The MNR government soon began a large-scale program of agrarian reform designed to put the land into the hands of the Indians, who now tended to refer to themselves more frequently as *campesinos.*

Paz, for the whole of his first term in office, governed by decree, without a legislature. In June 1967 an MNR-dominated congress was chosen and Paz's vice-president, Hernán Siles Zuazo, became president.

As early as 1953 a split began to develop between right and left wings of the MNR. Former President Paz ran as the MNR candidate for the presidency in 1960 and was elected despite the defection of right-wing leader Walter Guevara Arze to form the Authentic Nationalist Revolutionary Movement (Movimiento Nacionalista Revolucionario Auténtico, or MNRA). Paz's second term was no less troubled than other recent administrations. The MNR managed to retain a tenuous hold in the legislative branch. Juan Lechín, Paz's vice-president, had ambitions of succeeding Paz in the Presidency if he could continue to keep the miners' protests in check. When Paz engineered modification of the constitution to permit immediate reelection of the president and then announced he would run again in 1964, Lechín withdrew from the MNR and organized the miners against the government. With Guevara Arze and Lechín no longer in the party, the way was clear for Paz's renomination for the presidency by the MNR. The military, which Paz had strengthened to quell any dissent over his amendment to the constitution, used their newly gained power to put forward Air Force General René Barrientos Ortuño as vice-presidential candidate on the MNR ballot. With other groups boycotting the election, some 69 percent of the electorate voted for the unopposed MNR.

El Gobierno de Turno

One crisis followed on the heels of another in the opening months of Paz's new term. In September 1964 the government announced discovery of a plot to overthrow it and exiled many political leaders. Antigovernment rioting by students and others broke out late in October, and on November 5, 1964, General Barrientos led a coup against the regime; Paz was ousted from the presidency and exiled from Bolivia. Barrientos headed a military junta which supplanted the 1961 constitution with that of 1945 as modified in 1947 and proclaimed that new elections would be held in late September 1965.

Barrientos's term in office was no smoother than that of Paz had been. In April 1965 Barrientos withdrew as a presidential candidate, Lechín was exiled by the junta to Paraguay, and the scheduled elections were cancelled. In late May General Alfredo Ovando Candía became "co-president" of the country. Political fireworks during 1965 included an attempt on Barrientos's life, paralyzing strikes by miners and others, and charges that parties sought to divide the solidarity of politically oriented army officers.

After General Barrientos returned to the presidency, he moved toward winning a constitutional term by resigning in January 1966 to campaign for the presidency in elections set for July. As the candidate of the Bolivian Revolutionary Front (Frente Revolucionario Boliviano, or FRB), he was successful, winning about 60 percent of the vote and leading five other party nominees.

A new constitution became effective February 5, 1967. But all else in that year was overshadowed by the sensational guerrilla activity of the elusive "Che" Guevara in the remote backlands. Why the Argentine chose the rugged Santa Cruz province as the site for his Castro-backed offensive is not clear. He received little support from the peasants since many owned their own land; he could not speak the Guaraní language; and he did not have the support of the Communist party. The most logical explanation would seem to be that, if successful in Bolivia, his centralized location would be ideal for commanding guerrilla operations in Argentina, Brazil, Chile, Paraguay, and Peru—all bordering Bolivia. Of course, this is mere speculation; Che's capture and assassination in October 1967 by a Bolivian army trained in counterinsurgency quickly put an end to the insurgency.

been correspondingly at the mercy of those elements in Bolivian power politics with the will and the means to paint the president into a corner. Chief of those has been the Bolivian army, dissolved after the 1952 Revolution but subsequently reorganized on a supposedly tractable basis. Other groups capable of exerting considerable pressure are the organized miners and the organized Indians, now usually called *campesinos.* Certainly the president, when a civilian, has not been master in his own house. The civil service would like to act as a pressure group, but it is inadequately staffed, ineffectively organized, and parsimoniously supported.

Legislative and Judicial Structures

The bicameral congress, when it is allowed to function, includes a senate of 27 members and a chamber of deputies of 117. Three senators are chosen from each of the nine territorial departments. The 1967 constitution made the novel provision that two of each department's three senators should represent the strongest party and the third the second strongest party. Senators serve six-year terms and deputies four-year terms. The two chambers have the traditional separate powers, but they are largely hollow.

Legislative sessions normally run for three months but may be supplemented by special sessions. The legislature's powers are conventional, its weight slight. Despite constitutional provisions Bolivia's legislature is normally without adequate defenses against either the executive or the army.

The Bolivian judiciary is likewise at the mercy of the more political branches of the government. It is headed by a supreme court, whose members are elected by the chamber of deputies. They serve for ten-year terms and are not eligible for immediate reelection. The supreme court traditionally sits not at La Paz but at Sucre, often described as the legal capital of the country. Theoretically, this should remove the judiciary from the buffeting of politics centered at La Paz, the national capital, but in practice it offers no such protection. Lower levels of the judiciary include the district courts, sectional judges (*jueces de partido*), and investigating judges (*instructores*). In addition to the regular hierarchy, there are a separate national labor court and an agrarian court.

Local Structures

Local administration is highly centralized. The major unit is the territorial department. Bolivia has nine, which vary enormously in population. The department is administered by a presidentially appointed prefect who has wide powers of political, military, and financial control. The prefect's legal and political chain of command points him toward the president, and in many cases he has little sense of identification with the department he rules. Departments are divided into provinces, administered by subprefects. Provinces in turn are subdivided into cantons, which are governed by *corregidores.* The canton consists essentially of a village and its surrounding territory. The more prominent towns and cities have elected councils, but mayors are appointed by the president from among the council members.

The politicization of large numbers of Indians, who were political ciphers before 1952, is one of the remarkable accomplishments of Latin American politics in recent decades. The acquisition of political consciousness is such a subtle matter that no census could be taken of those who possess it. And yet, despite the astonishing gains in this area, the great mass of the population still remains apart from the working political community.

The Revolution of 1952 brought about the removal of literacy and income qualifications for voting and established, without limitations, women's suffrage. There are now no general suffrage restrictions for Bolivians over the age of eighteen.

Party Structures

Political expression is, on the most basic level, channeled through political parties, which are recognized as having juridical personality. But political attitudes are also significantly articulated by the labor unions, particularly among miners, and by *campesino* syndicates.

Bolivian parties in the first decades of independence were as unrealistic as any in Latin America. Politics was so personalistic that parties in any genuine sense had no place in the field of public affairs. The turbulence of Bolivian political life virtually required the ostensibly strong hand of a military *caudillo,* and most officers of those decades had neither understanding nor tolerance of political parties.

The so-called Liberal party (it later became quite conservative) was formed in 1880 and was nominally in power from 1898 to 1920. Liberal party dissidents in 1914 formed the Republican party, which captured power in a political upset in 1920. In the meantime the National Union party (also called the Nationalist party) had been organized.

The Movimiento Nacionalista Revolucionario (MNR) was founded in 1941 by a group of intellectuals, most notably Víctor Paz Estenssoro, a distinguished economist. The MNR was highly nationalistic and oriented toward a social-reform program. Shortly after its founding the MNR was charged with fascism or pro-Nazism, perhaps because some of its early pronouncements had a definitely anti-Semitic tone. The handful of MNR deputies derived a good deal of political ammunition from the Catavi massacre in 1942; consequently, the MNR was later influential with the powerfully organized miners' unions.

From its founding the MNR espoused a reasonably consistent reform program. It advocated agrarian and educational reform, supported economic diversification and stimulation of agricultural production, and proposed incorporation of the Indians into the political and economic life of the country. Its program tended to give it a socialistic tinge.

From 1946 to 1951, the MNR extended its hold on the miners and began to gain influence with the peasant syndicates. With its rise to power in 1952, the MNR found itself confronted by repeated schismatic threats. The first secession occurred in 1960, when the conservative leader, Walter Guevara Arze, abandoned the party's ranks to form the Partido Revolucionario Auténtico (PRA) after he failed to win the MNR presidential nomination. He was followed not long afterward by Ñuflo Chávez, a left-wing leader and former cabinet member and vice-president, who organized a pro-Castro National Liberation Front (Frente de Liberación Nacional, or FLN). Lechín, prominent leftist leader, broke away in late 1963, when it became apparent that he would not receive the MNR presidential nomination for 1964; in January 1964 he formed the Partido Revolucionario de Izquierda Nacionalista (PRIN), which promptly named him as its presidential candidate.

The defections of Guevara, Chávez, and Lechín from the MNR were followed by that of former President Siles Zuazo, previously a responsible moderate within the party, who formed the Nationalist Revolutionary Movement of the Left (MNRI). Siles Zuazo heads the popular Unión Democrática Popular (UDP). This coalition of the MNRI, BCP, MIR, ALIN, and the Tupaj Katari stands as the prominent opposition party in Bolivian politics.

The Chaco war of 1937 prompted Bolivian exiles in Chile to organize the right-wing Falange Socialista Boliviana (FSB), a frank imitation of the Spanish Falange. It did not become immediately important, although it moved toward the center of party activity after the revolution of 1952.

The Falange was not associated with the regimes in power between 1946 and 1952 and hence did not fall heir to the popular ill will that haunted those political groups which had backed the government during that period. The FSB was thus in a strategic position to assume leadership of Bolivia's conservative elements during the ascendancy of the MNR following 1952. It emphasized order and discipline while endeavoring to disavow the fascist ideology it had earlier admired. The FSB won significant urban support in the 1956 election, although it enjoyed almost no backing in rural areas.

Four years later the FSB suffered competition from Guevara Arze's schismatic PRA, but in 1962 the two groups formed an entente. The FSB's own split came the following year, in June 1963, when a splinter group of militant Falangists formed the Unión Cívica Nacional.

Although never officially assuming the Christian title, the FSB has advertised itself as a Christian Democratic party. The party recognized by the Organización Democrática Cristiana de América (ODCA) as the official

Christian Democratic party is the Partido Demócrata Cristiano (PDC), previously called the Social Democratic party (PSD). The retired General René Bernal was the party's candidate in 1978.

A congress of leftist groups in 1940 organized the Partido de la Izquierda Revolucionaria (PIR), a Marxist-oriented aggregation led by distinguished intellectuals and supported in considerable measure by the embryonic ranks of organized labor. By 1947 it had become the largest single party in Bolivia. In the elections of that year the PIR, on the extreme left, formed a curious coalition with the Liberals, the most conservative of Bolivian parties. The PIR dissolved in 1952; its heir was the Bolivian Communist party.

A second party formed in 1940 was the Revolutionary Workers' party (POR). It was distinctly Trotskyist in orientation and soon affiliated with the Fourth International.

In the 1940s the PIR exercised great influence among organized labor, but the party lost both face and ground after the MNR coup in 1952. Rival orthodox Communist parties existed for a short time in 1952–1953 but soon merged. In 1952 the POR achieved a temporary importance because of its earlier friendship with the MNR, but the two parties later became alienated and the POR suffered internal splits. Over the whole post-Chaco period, however, the POR constituted the strongest and most active Trotskyist Communist party in any Latin American country. POR supported the candidacy of Casiano Amurrio in the 1978 elections.

Juan Lechín's Nacional Revolutionary Party of the Left (PRIN) capitalized on its leader's political prominence and following and immediately after its organization in 1964 moved into a commanding position on the left side of the party spectrum. The 1964 elections gave it the second strongest position in each congressional chamber, but the exile of Lechín in May 1965 threw PRIN into a state of confusion. It remained outlawed until the 1978 elections. The PRIN threw its support to the Frente de Izquierda candidate in these elections.

In general, the panorama of Bolivian parties since the Chaco War has shown a more pronounced ideological orientation than that of most Latin American countries. That is not to say that the parties have been stable or well grounded; indeed, the reverse has more generally been true. Pulls from the Right and Left have been normal, and any consideration of the vagaries of a normal party picture in Bolivia must be highly speculative.

Other Political Structures

Peasants. The parties are only one of a number of entities which provide political articulation for Bolivians. Another of these—possibly the most significant—is the peasants. Among Latin American states it is probably safe to say that only Mexican rural workers are as well organized and politically effective as those in Bolivia. The two situations differ significantly, particularly in that the Mexican rural element, represented by the National Peasants' Confederation (Confederación Nacional de Campesinos, or CNC), is fully subordinated to the government party, the PRI, whereas in Bolivia the peasants form an independent political sector and are not controlled by any single party or political group.

Like most major developments on the contemporary Bolivian political landscape, the politicization of the peasants is a product of the Chaco War. As soon as the conflict was over, peasants in a province in the department of Cochabamba formed an agrarian syndicate to enable them to present a united front to landlords who were trying to maintain a feudal hold over them.

Friction was bitter and bloody for the next few years, and by the late 1940s the economic warfare had spilled over into politics. Both the PIR and the MNR began making bids for *campesino* leadership, with the PIR enjoying an inside track, at least at first, because it advanced more radical objectives. With its rise to power in 1952 the MNR was in a position to develop a program of agrarian reform, though, for political reasons, first priority had to be given to nationalization of the big tin holdings. By that time the *campesinos* were well organized and thoroughly loyal to their own leadership, especially to the able young José Rojas, who for years had displayed single-minded devotion to their organization.

In late 1952 direct action tactics against landlords by the *campesinos* finally convinced the MNR that it must move its agrarian reform program into higher gear. Serious plans were formally launched at the beginning of August 1953. The core of the program involved the breakup of all of Bolivia's *latifundia*. Within a short time, Paz asserted, albeit exaggeratedly, that all of Bolivia's *campesinos* had already become landowners and that that aspect of the Revolution had been successfully completed.

Substitution of the *minifundio* for the large landholdings was psychologically gratifying to the previously landless Indians and provided considerable political mileage for the government. It was not economically sound, however; agricultural production declined seriously and added substantially to Bolivia's already deteriorating economic situation.

The government also proposed to elevate the dignity of the Indians as a class and to give them social mobility. By 1956 Bolivia's Indians had become semantically transformed into *campesinos;* indeed, to continue to refer to them as "Indians" was not only unfashionable but sometimes physically risky. The *campesino* gained greatly in political power but did not become a sophisticate. The average rural worker tended to retain the psychological attitude of approaching a *patrón* for favors, even though he substituted a political leader— Paz or Siles or Chávez—for his former landlord. Nonetheless, the Bolivian political clock cannot be turned back to reflect a time when the Indians were apolitical, any more than Argentina can erase Perón's accomplishment in bestowing political consciousness on the *descamisados.*

Miners.   Miners' unions constituted a second important channel for political expression by the underprivileged classes. As a factor in politics, the miners had certain advantages over the *campesinos:* Their unions antedated any peasant organization; the physical circumstances of their labor made it easier for them to organize and express themselves; and the vital role of metals in the Bolivian economy gave the miners leverage that the *campesinos* could not possess. Bolivia depends overwhelmingly on mining. Tin is the expensive but unreliable backbone of the industry, but lead, copper, tungsten, zinc, antimony, silver, and sulfur are also mined. In only one year from 1950 to 1958 did metals fail to constitute at least 90 percent of all Bolivian exports, and during that period they attained a high of 96.9 percent.

Organized labor, whose strength centered in La Paz and the sites of big mining operations, provided the bulk of the fighters who overthrew the military regime in April 1952. During the first several years of the revolutionary regime, an unofficial agreement enabled the Central Obrera Boliviana (COB) to propose four members of successive cabinets. Following the nationalization of the big mines, the government set up the Bolivian Mining Corporation (Corporación Minera de Bolivia, or Comibol) to operate them. Juan Lechín had his power base in the miners' unions and exploited it fully, though both Presidents Siles and Paz succeeded in cutting ground from under him at various times.

Despite the question marks presented by the intimate interrelationships between the nationalized tin industry and Bolivian politics, miners and their leaders continue to have a significant impact on the political scene. Following the 1978 coup, plans were made to convene the fifth congress of the COB to coordinate the goals of disparate labor groups within the country. The miners have continued as the most important group in labor. In 1978 they spearheaded the struggle for salary increases from the de facto government of General Pereda Asbún and are expected to continue to play a major role in future governmental decision making.

The Military.   Although the army cannot be called a channel for popular political expression, it certainly must be regarded as a political instrument of real and often decisive power. Bolivia's rough political path in the nineteenth century virtually assured the frequent dominance of military *caudillos* and the role of the army as the final arbiter of politics. The situation improved nominally in the twentieth century, but the shaky position of post-Chaco War governments made it inevitable that the army would be in the wings, if not at center stage.

During the period from 1943 to 1946, the MNR formed a somewhat uncomfortable alliance with an army officers' lodge named the Reason of the Fatherland (Razón de Patria, or Radepa). The MNR's coup against a military junta in 1952 meant that the army would be in the bad graces of the new regime. As a consequence, the army was dissolved. The *carabineros* (military police), who had aided the MNR in gaining power, were reduced in numbers. For armed backing, the regime preferred to rely on labor and *campesinos,* who received guns as well as status.

In July 1953, however, the government saw fit to reconstitute the army, presumably along new lines and, it was hoped, subject to the civilian arm of the regime. The army did not become Frankenstein's monster until November 1964. The officers who had been reinstated and elevated had presumably been those who had shown loyalty to the MNR, but even in the case of General Barrientos, the party's vice-presidential candidate in 1964, that loyalty turned out to be only shallow. It appears unlikely that the MNR's reform of the army was more than superficial or that the military mentality in Bolivia showed any genuine change.

Since the death of Barrientos, six generals have been in the presidency: Alfredo Ovando Candía, Juan José Torres, Hugo Banzer, Juan Pereda Asbún, and David Pidilla Arancibia. One may assume that the military have grown accustomed to the presidential limelight and will continue to influence Bolivian politics.

Other interest groups fall far short of the *campesinos,* the miners, and the military in effectiveness. The Catholic church is officially recognized by the constitution, as it had been earlier, but the Church has little impact on politics.

University students exercise little political influence. Bolivian universities lack the prestige of those in various other Latin American countries, and students are less influential than they have been, chiefly because the politicization of *campesinos* and miners has so broadened the base of political activity that students have become relatively less numerous and weighty.

Bolivia's economic interests, other than the "big three" of its tin world, were so small, weak, and inarticulate that they played, and continued to play, almost no role in politics. Their natural reaction has been to shy away from associations with reformist tendencies, but aside from their protests against government concessions to labor, they have remained in the background.

DEVELOPMENTAL PROSPECTS

Bolivia shares with Mexico and Cuba the accomplishment of a social revolution (1952) more complete than that anywhere else in Latin America. The social revolutions in all three countries were aimed at a forced readjustment of the relationships among social and economic segments of the population and toward a lowering of the political center of gravity. But the Bolivian Revolution, unlike the others, was almost immediately successful in its conquest of power. The fighting phase in Mexico lasted for a long and bloody decade before final resolution of the anarchic contest for power. In Cuba, Castro required a military buildup of more than two years before Batista abdicated. But in Bolivia not even ten days, let alone ten years, were needed to put the MNR in power. There it remained until the coup of late 1964.

Both the Bolivian and Mexican Revolutions were indigenous; that is, they were not characterized by any abdication of their powers or responsibilities to a foreign government or ideology. The Cuban Revolution was mortgaged to communism, at first furtively and then openly.

The Bolivian Revolution more nearly resembled the Cuban than the Mexican in being channeled through one party or party pattern in its early phases. No dominant party emerged in Mexico for almost two decades after the Revolution began. On the other hand, a single party has come to dominate the changes in Mexico and Cuba to a more monopolistic degree than in Bolivia. The military was massively downgraded in Mexico; after 1969 the military again dominated politics in Bolivia.

The inauguration of Walter Guevara Arze on August 8, 1979, ended the fifteen-year military regime but did not put an end to the numerous problems confronting Bolivia. In less than one hundred days, two new administrations were ushered into the Palacio Quemado (presidential palace), increasing the number of coups to 201 in Bolivia's 175-year history.

On November 16, 1979, President Gueiler assumed the precarious position of president of a country with a $2 billion foreign debt and annual payments of $300 million. The per capita annual income of the Bolivian worker in 1979 was only $350, and the prospects of continued austerity would put an additional burden on the low-income majority in the country.

While opposing factions of the military and organized labor threatened the tenuous existence of the Gueiler administration, the president attempted to restore some semblance of order to the economy. Until a strong economic base and consensus can be attained among political parties, military, organized labor, businesspeople, and intellectuals, the prospects for a viable democracy in Bolivia will continue to be very slight. It would be foolhardy to attempt to predict what the next decade will bring.

REFERENCES

ALEXANDER, ROBERT J. *The Bolivian National Revolution.* New Brunswick, N.J.: Rutgers University Press, 1958.

ARNADE, CHARLES W. "Communism in Bolivia." *South Atlantic Quarterly* 53 (October 1964), 454–463.

BAPTISTA GUMUCIO, MARIANO. *Páginas para la Revolución.* La Paz: Editorial Centro de Estudios Latinoamericanos, 1970.

BERGSTEN, C. FRED. "Social Mobility and Economic Development: The Vital Parameters of the Bolivian Revolution." *Journal of Inter-American Studies* 6 (July 1964), 367–375.

COHEN, SANFORD. "Little Bit of a Revolution: Bolivia." *South Atlantic Quarterly* 65 (Winter 1966), 12–20.

CORBETT, CHARLES D. "Military Institutional Development and Sociopolitical Change: The Bolivian Case." *Journal of Inter-American Studies and International Affairs* 14 (November 1972), 399–435.

————. *The Latin American Military As a Socio-political Force: Case Studies of Bolivia and Argentina.* Washington, D.C.: Center for Advanced International Studies Institute, 1972.

GREENE, DAVID G. "Revolution and the Rationalization of Reform in Bolivia." *Inter-American Economic Affairs* 19:3 (Winter 1965), 3–25.

HEATH, DWIGHT B., CHARLES J. ERASMUS, and HANS C. BUECHLER. *Land Reform and Social Revolution in Bolivia.* New York: Holt, Rinehart & Winston, 1969.

HENNESSY, C. A. M. "Shifting Forces in the Bolivian Revolution." *World Today* 20 (May 1964), 197–207.

KLEIN, HERBERT. *Parties and Political Change in Bolivia, 1880–1952.* New York: Cambridge University Press, 1969.

MALLOY, JAMES M., ed. *Beyond the Revolution: Bolivia Since 1952.* Pittsburgh: University of Pittsburgh Press, 1971.

————. *Bolivia: The Uncompleted Revolution.* Pittsburgh: University of Pittsburgh Press, 1970.

MAYORGA, RENÉ ANTONIO. "National-Popular State, State Capitalism and Military Dictatorship in Bolivia: 1952–1975." *Latin American Perspectives* 5:2 (Spring 1978), 89.

MITCHELL, CHRISTOPHER. *The Legacy of Populism in Bolivia: From the MNR to Military Rule.* New York: Holt, Rinehart & Winston, 1978.

OSBORNE, HAROLD. *Bolivia, a Land Divided.* New York: Gordon Press, 1976.

PATCH, RICHARD W. "Bolivia: Decision or Debacle." *American Universities Field Staff Reports* (West Coast South America) 6 (April 18, 1959), 1–18.

————. "Bolivian Background." *American Universities Field Staff Reports* (West Coast South America) 5 (October 10, 1958), 1–24.

————. "The Bolivian Falange." *American Universities Field Staff Reports* (West Coast South America) 6 (May 14, 1959), 1–10.

————. "Bolivia: The Restrained Revolution." *Annals of the American Academy* 334 (March 1961), 123–132.

————. "Bolivia Today: An Assessment Nine Years After the Revolution." *American Universities Field Staff Reports* (West Coast South America) 8:4 (March 17, 1961), 1–19.

PIKE, FREDERICK B. *The United States and the Andean Republics of Peru, Bolivia and Ecuador.* Cambridge, Mass.: Harvard University Press, 1977.

RAND, CHRISTOPHER. "Letter From La Paz." *New Yorker* 92 (December 31, 1966), 35–56.

ROLÓN ANAYA, MARIO. *Política y Partidos en Bolivia.* La Paz: n.p., 1966.

SPAIN, AUGUST O. "Bolivia: Case Study of Welfare State Politics." *Arnold Foundation Monographs* 9 (1961), 17–40.

12

CHILE

The Political Enigma

POLITICAL CULTURE AND DEVELOPMENT

In certain respects Chile appears to be a country which has overreached itself, which has achieved a prominence not indicated—perhaps even unjustified—by its geographic, economic, and demographic base.

Chile has traditionally been considered one of the leading three countries of South America, the alphabetically convenient ABC group—Argentina, Brazil, and Chile. And yet, the comembers of that unofficial trio far outstrip Chile when measured by most yardsticks. Chile's area, 286,396 square miles, is less than one-third of Argentina's and less than one-eleventh of Brazil's vast extent. Its population, estimated in 1977 to be 10,814,000, is only two-fifths that of Argentina and less than one-tenth that of Brazil.

Chile has perhaps the most unusual geographical features of any country in Latin America. Its length exceeds 2,600 miles, but its width is nowhere greater than 250 miles. The country can be divided roughly into thirds. The northern third, one of the world's driest regions, contains the Atacama Desert where nitrate, copper, and other mineral deposits are found. The southern third is a heavily forested, rainy and stormy archipelago. A hilly central valley makes up the last, and by far the most important, third of Chile. About 600 miles long and 45 miles wide, the central valley is the location of Chile's agriculture and industry and the home of approximately 90 percent of its population. Chile's island possessions include Easter Island, the Juan Fernández Islands, and other smaller Pacific Islands.

During Chile's colonial period, the native Araucanians either blended in with the conquering Spaniards, retreated south into remote areas to try to escape extermination, or slipped into Argentina to survive military campaigns directed against them by the Spaniards in reprisal for Indian uprisings.

Germans began to emigrate to Chile in the 1850s along with people from the Middle East, Italy, Switzerland, and other foreign countries. Many of these immigrant families achieved the highest leadership positions in almost every area of Chilean life. This mixture of races and nationalities resulted in a beautiful combination of ethnically European and mestizo (mixed Spanish and Indian).

Central Chile almost inevitably developed a tightly knit social structure, isolated and self-contained, hierarchically organized and well integrated.

Postindependence Chilean Development

Chile's progress toward independence was erratic and inevitably centered around Santiago. A revolutionary junta decreed the dissolution of the royal *audiencia.* [1] Even at this early time social stratification among the politically articulate was clearly reflected. As peninsular influence had been in the *audiencia,* creole elements were dominant in the junta. Even within the soon triumphant creole group a split between conservative and liberal wings quickly developed. Such political schisms would characterize virtually all periods of Chilean development.

The transition from colony to nation was marked by much political confusion. During this time Bernardo O'Higgins, son of a former viceroy of Peru, entered the Chilean political scene. He assisted José de San Martín in defeating the Spanish forces, which definitely established Chilean independence. For almost a decade and a half Chile experienced the greatest political turbulence in its history. There was little promise of stability in Chile.

Despite the generally personalistic rule that prevailed during these early years of Chilean independence, there were some experiments with constitutionalism. Several of the early attempts at constitutional government were premature, unrealistic, or both. In 1826 a constitutent congress with a strongly federalist composition constructed Chile's first and only federal form of government. In effect for two years, the experiment was a dismal failure—Chile was not yet ready to do without a firm hand at the national helm.

During this political turbulence, the major characteristic of Chilean political life for the following three-quarters of a century crystallized—the division of political expression between liberals and conservatives. This polarization, even if implanted by rudimentary party organizational machinery,

[1]The *audiencia* is a high-level, multimember Spanish colonial judicial and administrative body; it is also the territory over which it had authority.

developed earlier and more completely in Chile than in almost any other country of Latin America.

The coalescence of the Conservative and Liberal groups brought the high clergy, military leaders, and big landholders into the Conservative camp and the social ancestors of the Chilean middle class—a poorly defined group at best —into the Liberal fold. Conservatives had the advantage ideologically since they wanted to maintain the political and social organization of the colonial epoch under a strong centralized government. The Liberals, fuzzily influenced by French thought, advocated glamorous but often unrealistic political and social reforms. A tangible and important distinction was that Conservatives had the more capable leadership.

The contest resulted in civil war and total defeat of the Liberals. Conservatives then succeeded to power, and by 1830 Chile's era of political turbulence was for the time being over. For almost a century thereafter, Chilean political life was characterized by a comfortable periodicity: thirty years, beginning in 1831, of the "Conservative (sometimes called the autocratic) republic," thirty years of the "Liberal republic," and approximately thirty years of the "Parliamentary (or Democratic) republic."

The Conservative Stage of Development

By 1831 Conservatives were firmly in control and promptly moved to write a new constitution. They were favored by their social and geographic compactness. The Liberals were discredited not only by decisive military defeat but also by association with the unfortunate federal experiment of a few years earlier. It took many years for them to recover political face and even longer to gain political fortune.

The constitution of 1833, wholly a Conservative document, remained in effect for more than ninety years, becoming one of the longest-lived constitutions in Latin American political history. The bones of governmental structure provided by the new constitution resembled those of the 1828 document— somewhat surprising since the two laws were sponsored by different parties. The flesh that covered the bones more clearly revealed the temper of the new political organization: Roman Catholicism was solidly established as the state faith; suffrage was severely limited and based both on literacy and income or property-ownership requirements; elective offices were reduced to a minimum; the president was given vast control over election machinery; and primogeniture was preserved. In short the constitution was simply a recognition and formalization of the contemporary development and interaction of economic and social forces. The regime it established was essentially conservative, as it was designed to be. Political stability was gained by preserving the colonial organization of society at the expense of social evolution. Under the 1833 law presidential powers were very extensive; the legislative branch was comparatively weak.

The political landscape gradually became more varied. The functional social center, which had appeared to be permanently established in the *hacienda,* began almost invisibly to shift to the city. A new aristocracy based on business and learning slowly came into its own. Liberals received a degree of ideological stimulus from the European, especially the French, revolutions of 1848 and became politically more aggressive. The decade of the fifties saw the beginnings of party fractionation. An unusual alliance developed when the extremists of both parties, Conservatives and Liberals, joined to form the Nationalist party. Another group of Liberals, emphasizing constitutional reform, seceded to form the Radical party.

The Liberal Stage of Development

When the Liberals took office in 1861, a basic if not too well defined tenet of Liberal party policy was that presidential powers should be curbed. The most obvious step in this direction was a constitutional amendment in 1868 which forbade immediate presidential reelection. In following years proportional representation was established, thus encouraging minority parties and party fragmentation.

All of these changes might seem to point toward a sharp intralegislative division over issues, with consequent strong legislative support, at least from minority parties, for successive presidents. Such was not the case. A long-established elitist basis for the election and operation of the Chilean congress resulted in an aristocratic linkage among practically all members of the congress, regardless of party differences. The social structure resembled that of eighteenth-century England, and for a long time the socially dominant elements—that is, the great landed families—controlled economic activity and, to an even greater extent, political life. The social and political intimacy prevalent in upper Chilean circles in the latter half of the nineteenth century made the congress close ranks on many occasions in the face of any threat of executive aggression or independence. Party discipline was almost nonexistent. This was an automatic invitation to intraparty feuds and splits, so that politics, which was almost limited in scope to the congress, became increasingly atomized. Thus, the stage was quietly being set for the parliamentary republic to follow.

The Parliamentary Stage of Development

The election of José Manuel Balmaceda to the presidency in 1886 was the unwitting beginning of the end for the Liberal republic. Even his own Liberal party became increasingly dissatisfied with his interference in elections. In 1891 the friction hardened into civil war. Congressional forces were generally successful, and the president soon had to take refuge in the Argentine legation. Thus ended the three decades of the Liberal republic.

Only superficially did the transition from Liberal to Parliamentary republic appear abrupt. True, the change from executive dominance—or attempted executive dominance—to legislative control was as complete as occurred in England in 1689, but in Chile, even more than in England, the preparations for it had long been visible. Party discipline had almost disappeared; considerable numbers of both Liberals and Radicals had broken away from any semblance of party allegiance and operated simply as unattached senators or deputies. The Liberal party was moving toward a more conservative position, although it was still importantly divided from the Conservatives on clerical issues. All of the parties and their splinter factions operated without the grass-roots support which would have made them more meaningful and vital.

The triumphant parliamentary element quickly consolidated its control. Balmaceda's handpicked successsor was of course sidetracked in favor of a congressionally selected president. Ministers became entirely dependent on the congress. Although these changes were accomplished without constitutional amendment, they marked a complete alteration of the Chilean political climate and pattern of intragovernmental relationships. For the next three decades Chilean presidents would be as politically impotent as contemporary British monarchs or French presidents.

The new parliamentary system created chaos among the parties. Majorities in the congress depended on circumstance or even whimsy; groups who differed in principle often formed wholly expedient alliances. The cabinets reflected the instability of political parties; ministerial instability became entirely normal, more common in fact than in the French Third or Fourth Republic. Cabinets would sometimes last for only a week, in rare cases for not more than a day.

Conservatives and Radicals tended to represent the extremes in what little ideological basis could be claimed for party operation. The Conservatives distrusted mass education and wished to see the educational function administered by the Church, an institution which Conservatives felt the state should amply protect. Radicals, on the other hand, advocated the separation of Church and state; they felt that education should be a monopoly of the state and that freedom of worship should be maintained. Traditionally the Liberals were philosophically inclined to lean toward the Radicals, but socially and economically they veered toward the Conservatives. Party groups and subgroups were primarily personal followings.

That Chile could survive two or three decades of this semiorganized political confusion was due to three factors: the prosperous state of public finance after the War of the Pacific, which gave Chile a world monopoly of natural nitrates; the high educational and cultural achievements of the ruling classes; and the essentially apolitical role of the masses of the population.

But economic changes were inexorably moving toward development of political awareness in the working classes. The oligarchy, who were against social emancipation and advancement, tried to stop the clock. After all, it reasoned, Chile had prospered and advanced under the pattern that had prevailed for years and decades—why change? This attitude curiously foreshadowed that which prevailed in far more obvious and widespread fashion among the Latin American aristocracy half a century later.

The rising cost of living led to serious strikes as early as 1905. The advent of World War I, seemingly remote from Chile, greatly increased the demand for the country's nitrates and copper, but it also added to the rapidly spiraling inflation. The result was further hardship for the already distressed lower classes. "The public treasury is rich and the localities are poor," said one public figure in describing the problem. Politics could not indefinitely operate on an earlier status quo in the face of such economic and social pressures.

Through the port of Valparaiso, in the war-born commerce, Chile exported raw materials but imported radical ideologies—anarcho-syndicalism, various kinds of socialism, and a little later, communism. Incipient labor organization gained motivation, leadership, and a strong political orientation. At least a mild political revolution was likely as Chile approached the end of the parliamentary period which, between 1896 and 1920, saw over a hundred cabinets, with more than 500 ministers, in successive and precarious operation. Again, as in the 1850s and late 1880s, a time of crises and tension preceded a major shift in the organization and direction of Chilean politics and administration.

The beginning of the end of the parliamentary regime came in 1920. A tenuous "Coalition" party nominated as its presidential candidate a distinguished aristocrat, Luis Barros Borgoño; the more liberal "Alliance" named Arturo Alessandri, the middle-class son of an Italian immigrant. Alessandri campaigned on a platform of social and constitutional reform. He was elected by a dramatically close margin: he received 177 electoral college votes to Borgoño's 176.

The significance of the 1920 Chilean election lay in its demonstration that the political center of gravity was shifting—to a lower social stratum and a bit to the left in the political spectrum. The election cannot be interpreted as the beginning of a social revolution. Despite such national illustrations as Mexico and Russia, revolution on a worldwide scale was simply not in the air in 1920 and certainly not in the political environment of Chile. Alessandri was not a Chilean forerunner of Castro; at most he was an evolutionist, not a revolutionist, and he faced internal forces which would yield only grudgingly.

Parliamentary rule died hard in Chile. Alessandri, the "Lion of Tarapacá," commanded strong support in the chamber of deputies, though the political alliance which elected him did not long survive the balloting. In the more slowly changing senate, however, Conservatives were uncompromisingly in control. By the end of 1923 sentiment began to crystallize in favor of modifying the constitutional system to remove the senate's power to upset ministries and impede legislation.

The Postparliamentary Stage of Development

Alessandri, confronting what he regarded as an intolerable situation, resigned the presidency in 1924 only to resume it in March 1925. A constituent assembly that year drafted an entirely new basic law which definitely ended the parliamentary system. The new constitution, Chile's first in ninety-two years, established a strong executive and removed the irresponsible congressional controls over ministries. It also provided for separation of Church and state.

Chile's abandonment of parliamentary government brought to an end Latin America's most extreme experimentation with legislative control over the executive. It had been almost an unalloyed failure. No Chilean "out" party had ever developed an attitude even remotely resembling that of "His Majesty's loyal opposition" in Britain. No strong sense of party discipline or cohesiveness had developed. The basic reasons for the failure were the multiparty system, political venality, and lack both of political vocality on the part of the mass of the people and of party responsibility to the electorate. Latin America, even one of its most advanced countries, was simply not yet prepared to provide an adequate or successful substitute for the centuries-old power pattern of executive dominance.

Although he had a new constitution more to his liking, Alessandri encountered further stormy seas. The next few years were one of Chile's most politically disturbed periods. Colonel Carlos Ibáñez del Campo, elected president in 1927, ruled as a thinly disguised dictator. The killing of two students during a demonstration in 1931 raised a popular outcry which quickly forced Ibáñez's resignation and exile. The next year and a half was as chaotic a period as Chilean political life had experienced since the 1820s.

Elections late in 1932 overwhelmingly returned to the presidency Arturo Alessandri, who was nostalgically remembered as the champion of social reform. He succeeded in restoring order, ministerial and general executive stability, and presidential government. In the years that had elapsed since his first presidency, Alessandri had become more conservative.

In 1936 political opposition to the heavy-handed Alessandri crystallized into Latin America's first popular-front organization of parties, a bloc modeled somewhat after the similar grouping in France. The Popular Front included the majority of the Radicals (who had supported Alessandri in 1932), the Socialists, Communists, a portion of the Democrats, and the Chilean Federation of Labor. The political buildup for the 1938 presidential election was complicated by the return of Ibáñez to active politics, though he did not then become a presidential candidate. Pedro Aguirre Cerda, a moderate Radical leader nominated by the Popular Front, was elected in a close race.

The election of 1938 seemed to confirm the trend of the past two decades toward crystallization of Chilean parties and political factions into three broad positions—right, center, and left. Conservatives and Liberals formed the core of the right wing; the Radical party (partially schizophrenic though it was), the nucleus of the center; and Communists and various Socialist groups, the heart of the left wing.

Election of Aguirre reflected the more democratic political course Chile was by now pursuing; more people were becoming politically conscious and articulate. Political tension continued, however. With the formal secession of the Socialists early in 1941, the Popular Front collapsed.

The death of President Aguirre Cerda late in 1942 necessitated new presidential elections (for a full six-year term). Juan Antonio Ríos, the Radical nominee, easily won over the hardy perennial Carlos Ibáñez, who ran as the candidate of the Conservative party with added Liberal support.

The presence of large and well-disciplined German colonies in southern Chile added to the country's political nervousness. When the Soviet Union entered into World War II, the Chilean Communists suddenly gained greater political respectability and an increased voice. Partially successful attempts were made as early as 1942 to revive the Popular Front.

The 1952 presidential elections represented a novelty in recent Chilean politics: the election of a candidate—Ibáñez—who was essentially a personalist rather than a strong party man. Ibáñez, now seventy-five years old, had out-lived much of the disenchantment which many Chileans had earlier felt for him. He made appealing, though irresponsible, promises to correct the serious contemporary economic problems. He did not now pose as a military figure, but nonetheless he retained enough of the aura of a strongman to convince many Chileans that he could solve the country's economic woes.

He managed to surmount one crisis after another and to complete his six-year term, but the old warrior had lost much of his earlier fire. His second term in the presidency was another demonstration that repeat performances by Latin America's strong personalities, no matter how charismatic they may once have been, are frequently a disappointment; Ibáñez simply followed in the footsteps of Irigoyen of Argentina, Vargas of Brazil, and Velasco Ibarra of Ecuador and paralleled Batista of Cuba.

Before the 1957 congressional elections, Socialist groups and the Communist party organized the Popular Action Front (Frente de Acción Popular, or FRAP). In a sense, FRAP represented a revival of the old Popular Front, which had disintegrated in 1941. By early 1958 four major groups had emerged—FRAP, the Radicals, the Christian Democrats, and the Conservative-Liberal alliance.

As the campaign developed, Jorge Alessandri, a son of the earlier president, who was running as the Conservative-Liberal alliance candidate, campaigned on an independent platform, which some of his Conservative and Liberal supporters assumed was a mere pose. The election proved to be a close race between Alessandri and Salvador Allende, the FRAP candidate. As no candidate received a popular majority, the congress made the final choice and elected Alessandri.

By early 1962 lines were beginning to be drawn for the presidential elections of 1964. The principal candidates were, not unexpectedly, Allende for FRAP and Eduardo Frei for the Christian Democrats. The election was expected to be a close race between FRAP and the Christian Democrats, but the country's fear of a possible leftist national victory produced a surprising result: With about 90 percent of the eligible voters casting ballots, Frei won a clear majority.

The Frei Influence

It was the first time in years that a presidential candidate had ever won so resounding a victory. The immediate general interpretation was that the Communists had been soundly defeated and that Frei and the Christian Democrats, a new and more glamorous liberal leader and party, had a clear mandate to try to open the way to "Democratic socialism" as his campaign slogan declared. But the six years of the Frei "Revolution in Liberty" were fraught with factionalism within the Christian Democratic party. A moderate group called the *oficialistas* remained loyal to Frei, but the *rebeldes,* or rebels, who stood on the left criticized Frei for not carrying his reforms either far or fast enough and demanded a more "noncapitalist" answer to Chile's ills. Meanwhile, the *terceristas,* or third wing within the party, were calling for a more rapid pace in reform activities.

Against heavy odds, Frei was able to push for liberalization of labor laws and the purchase of at least one copper mining operation, the Anaconda, in 1969. He also led the way toward modernizing the universities in the mid-60s—but by so doing, opened a virtual "can of worms" of political and social ferment. The left wing group called the Revolutionary Movement of the Left (Movimiento de Izquierda Revolucionaria, or MIR) was formed at the University of Concepción as a call, first for student power in universities, and later to student activity in more basic issues of labor and peasant rights. MIR moved off the campuses during the late 1960s and into the *poblaciones* (shantytowns) surrounding Santiago. Later the movement spread into the rural areas of southern and central Chile. During his last year in office, two attempted coups were aborted. This was the climate in which election year 1970 began.

Elected Marxist Government

The political environment seemed to tighten as political parties jockeyed for position and searched for possible coalitions for what would obviously be a highly significant election for Chile. In January 1970 five candiates had placed their hats in the presidential ring: Jorge Alessandri, National party (an amalgamation of the former Liberals and Conservatives); Jacques Conchol, Popular Unitary Action Movement (Movimiento de Acción Popular Unitaria, or MAPU); Radomiro Tomic, Christian Democrat; Pablo Neruda, Communist; and Salvador Allende, Socialist [the coalition was now called the Popular Union (Unión Popular, or UP)]. By March, however, the list had been narrowed to three.

The election on September 4, 1970, confirmed earlier polls. Allende led Alessandri by a narrow margin, and Tomic was a poor third. Since no candidate had a popular majority, the election was thrown into congress, which had to choose between Allende and Alessandri. In the voting on October 24, congress followed precedent and chose Senator Allende with 153 votes to 35 for Alessandri. The Popular Union (the erstwhile FRAP) had finally triumphed. Allende's large majority was composed of seventy-eight frapistas, seventy-four Christian Democrats, and one independent. The election's aftermath would be a test of Chilean democracy.

Allende had campaigned on a platform of implementing a Marxist economy in Chile—but, he emphasized, "with liberty." Immediately upon his inauguration on November 4, 1970, Allende set out on his mission of nationalization, agrarian reforms, and redistribution of income with the support of congress. He was committed to work for reform through parliamentary and legal means. But his regime was doomed to failure. By November 1972 Allende was faced with insurmountable crises that had their beginning outside the country but were reflected in internal economic paralysis. In the United States the Nixon administration was pumping money (estimated at more than $11 million between 1970 and 1973) into covert Central Intelligence Agency activities in an effort, first, to see that Allende did not reach the presidency and, second, to make it impossible for him to govern. About $3 million was used in the presidential election of 1964 to help Eduardo Frei's candidacy; another $1 million went into efforts to keep Allende out of office in 1970; approximately $5 million was used to destabilize the Chilean economy between 1971 and 1973; approximately $10 million was given to the Chilean military in 1972 and 1973 for arms purchases and for training Chilean military personnel in the United States.[2]

Meanwhile, as a result of the twenty-six–day strike of truck owners and drivers in October 1972, three military officers were brought into the Allende cabinet. This spelled the beginning of the end for the president. By March 1973

[2] *New York Times,* December 27, 1973, p. 9.

Chile had become desperately polarized; the opposition, united in one party called the Democratic Confederation (Confederación Democrática, or CODE), was encouraged by the division within the UP. CODE hoped to emerge with the two-third congressional majority needed to impeach President Allende. In the barracks, military officers began to consider their role in the political drama being unfolded. Outwardly, they refused to veer from their apolitical line that the president was freely elected and the military would remain neutral. Privately, they added " . . . except in case of a grave national crisis."

March came, and when the ballots were counted President Allende's UP coalition received 43.39 percent of the vote and CODE 56.61 percent. Instead of winning the two-thirds majority the opposition needed for impeachment, they lost three seats to the UP coalition. This was a welcome morale booster for Allende, but his enemies both at home and abroad were left with little hope that the ballot box could be counted on as a means of getting him out of office.

The situation deteriorated quickly after the March elections, with Allende walking a tightrope between the extremists in his own party. The Communists were much more sympathetic to his political tactics than his own Socialist party, which wanted more militant activism with armed activity if necessary.

The Military Presence

By summer the streets of Santiago were full of rumors about an impending coup and, indeed, two abortive coups were attempted in May and June. In July a second strike of truck owners was joined by shopkeepers and businesspeople, engineers, physicians, and more than ninety thousand professional workers; they demanded the president's removal and openly called for military intervention. The strike continued until the coup which overthrew the Allende regime.

A consensus of opinion among the highest ranking officers was that they would have to confront President Allende to avert the risk of further mini-coups by opposing colonels and captains. Another incident in August could have touched off a coup when President Allende and General Carlos Prats González, his Defense Minister, called for the resignation of General César Ruiz Danyau, the air force commander-in-chief. The leaders of all three branches urged their officers to wait until General Prats could be forced to resign from the cabinet and from his command. On August 23 General Prats was confronted and, along with two other generals, withdrew from the cabinet and resigned his command.

The military moved swiftly. Using a little known arms control law passed after the March elections, they began to control major roads in and out of Chile's leading cities, under the ruse of searching for weapons.

On Tuesday morning, September 11, 1973, military leaders went to La Moneda (the presidential palace) and demanded Allende's resignation. During the short period of resistance, the president was killed. Because of the rigid censorship immediately established by the military junta, it is still unknown exactly how he met his death. Nine days passed before foreign correspondents were allowed into Chile and, once allowed in, they were strictly warned against "false reporting."

A four-man military junta took control of the government and declared a state of siege. General Augusto Pinochet Ugarte, commander-in-chief of the army and member of the junta, was named chief of state on June 26, 1974. The junta moved quickly, returning more than two hundred businesses to their private owners, and American aid began flowing again (over $500 million was authorized during six months following the coup, with huge sums earmarked for training Chile's military).

Through a succession of decrees the junta effectively put universities under military rectors, dissolved the congress, proscribed Marxist political parties and placed parties to the right and center "in recess," imposed heavy censorship of the press, and outlawed the Central Workers' Confederation (Central Unica de Trabajadores, or CUT) along with strikes and collective bargaining.

By 1977 Chile's economic picture began to show some signs of recovery. Inflation, which had reached a staggering 500 percent in 1973, was down to 40 percent in 1979; Chile had repaid $1 billion in foreign debts during 1976 and 1977. The regime's rigid austerity program to achieve these results had bitten deep into the lower-income sector, which had previously begun to benefit from Allende's economic policies, and into middle-income groups, which had supported the military coup. By 1977, 400,000 people—13 percent of the 3.4 million labor force—were jobless, and underemployment was estimated at 25 percent.

But Chile's economic hardships pale in the light of the regime's repressive actions over the past five years. Under the command of General Manuel Contreras Sepúlveda, the Chilean secret police, known as the National Intelligence Directorate, or DINA, was created in 1973 to defend the coup, but until its dissolution and replacement in 1978, it was used to eliminate all vocal opposition to the military regime. In August 1978 retired General Contreras Sepúlveda and six other persons, including four former Cuban citizens, were indicted by a U.S. Federal grand jury for the September 1976 murder of Orlando Letelier, Chile's former Ambassador to the United States, and Ronni Moffit, his American assistant. Letelier and Mrs. Moffit were killed when a bomb exploded in Letelier's car in Washington, D.C. A fifth Cuban-American was indicted on lesser charges. Michael V. Townley, an American who worked for the Chilean intelligence agency, was charged earlier in connection with the killing. Townley was tried in the United States and was given a reduced sentence of ten years for testifying against the others. By mid-1979, of the nine men accused of involvement in the Letelier murder, four had been convicted, two were being sought, and three (General Contreras Sepúlveda and his two Chilean aides) were under "house arrest" in Chile, pending the results of U.S.-initiated extradition hearings. Relations between the United States and Chile were strained by the October 1979 decision of the Chilean Supreme Court that rejected the U.S. extradition appeal and ordered the release of the three military officers.

There is no way to tell how many thousands of people have been killed in the past five years—estimates range from five thousand to ten thousand during the first nine days of the 1973 coup alone. The Carter administration essentially denied all forms of economic and military aid to Chile and led the crusade in the United Nations for an end to repression in Chile. It was after a fourth condemnation by the United Nations General Assembly that President Pinochet held a "loaded" plebiscite on January 4, 1978, in which Chileans were required to vote approval or disapproval of the regime. The 75 percent favorable vote gave Pinochet the confidence and ostensible backing he needed to tighten his control of the government. In July 1978 with the removal of General Pinochet's major critic in the junta, General Gustavo Leigh Guzmán, commander-in-chief of the air force, President Pinochet was virtually unopposed in his plans for reforms that would keep him in power until the late 1980s.

GOVERNMENTAL AND POLITICAL STRUCTURES

The Executive Structure

In Chile, as in almost all Latin American states, the president dominated the governmental and political scene. The role of the president in Chile has fluctuated as widely and almost as systematically as anywhere in Latin America. As the office was established by the 1833 constitution, it was as powerfully consolidated, short of an extraconstitutional dictatorship, as any presidency in all Latin America. The constitution was highly realistic in granting such broad powers to the president; a strong presidency harmonized with the structure of society. Under the Pinochet government, legislative and executive power is centralized in the military. Although the judicial system continues to operate independently of the executive, it is supplemented by military courts.

The constitution of 1925 supposedly would be replaced by a completely new version. The new document, although not made public in its entirety at this writing, would give even more strength to the executive. The Pinochet government formulated three stages in implementing the new constitution, which purportedly would return Chile to constitutional rule.[3]

The first was the current "recuperation" period, which began in 1973 and would end when the new constitution was ratified. The second phase, or "transition" period, would begin immediately after the plebiscite on the new constitution. Although elections would not be held during this period, an appointed congress would perform the legislative function, and executive power would remain in the hands of the military. A statute of the role of political parties would be announced, and party activity would be allowed during the final part of the transition period. Marxist ideology and parties would be outlawed, however.

Although no timetable has been announced for this transition period, President Pinochet has mentioned 1985 or 1986 as a possibility. The third phase would be the implementation of the new constitution.

Under the 1925 constitution the executive served for six years and could not be immediately reelected. He was chosen by direct popular vote and needed a popular majority to win. If no candidate had a majority, congress in joint session decided between the two highest candidates by majority vote.

The major parties or coalitions often looked to congress, especially to the senate, for their presidential candidates. They almost never turned to the ranks of the military. Indeed, the last predictatorship time an undisguised member of the military won the presidency was the first election of Ibáñez in the highly rigged procedure in 1927. Even Ibáñez in 1952 had more the image of a civilian than of an old soldier.

The constitution carefully provided for filling any vacancy in the presidential office. If the vacancy were permanent (caused by death or resignation), the acting vice-president called a popular election to fill the office, not for the unexpired portion of the term but for a full new term.

Under the proposed constitution, the president would be popularly elected by all Chileans twenty-one years of age or older every eight years and could not be reelected. If no candidate had a majority in the first balloting, a second-round election would be held between the top two candidates.

Except for its omission of reference to those functions derived from existence of an established church, the 1925 constitution delegated to the president powers quite similar to those granted in the constitution of 1833. The contraction of the executive office in the early 1980s was a political, not a constitutional, change. The basic presidential power as stated in Article 71 was: "The administration and government of the State, and . . . all that has for its purpose the preservation of public order in the interior and the exterior security of the Republic . . . " The president had wide appointive power; in

[3] *Times of the Americas,* May 24, 1978, p. 6.

certain cases his choices were subject to senatorial approval, as was removal of many high administrative officials.

The proposed new constitution includes a provision for a security council that would consist of members of the armed forces, congress, the courts, and others who would be charged "with watching over the country's institutions so they cannot be destroyed in the future like they were in the past."[4]

Administrative Support Structures

The most important supporting executive agency under the 1925 law was the cabinet, or ministers of state. Cabinet members were usually appointed with an eye to the political support they could bring to the president. The ministry of the interior was the key portfolio, equivalent to that of minister of government in most other Latin American states.

President Pinochet gradually replaced military officers with civilians in his sixteen-member cabinet; at this writing, fourteen civilians now occupy top cabinet positions. Pinochet's civilian minister of the interior was instrumental in wiping out all legal entanglements for the holding of the plebiscite in January 1978.

The 1925 fundamental law specifically prohibited senators and deputies from serving as cabinet members. Cabinet members were free, however, to attend congressional sessions, where they might participate in debate but not vote. Much more than in most Latin American countries, ministers took advantage of this prerogative, but only at the expense of exposing themselves to occasional interpellations which sometimes became quite bitter. Such interrogations usually generated more heat than light, but at times they helped to clarify legislative policy.

The office of the comptroller general was a more powerful executive agency in Chile than any similar body elsewhere in Latin America. The comptroller was appointed by the president and confirmed by the senate but headed an autonomous office and served during good behavior. The office had broad responsibility for all fiscal accounting, for government property, for investigating any financial irregularities it discovered, and for serving, in short, as Professor Gil well states it, as "the ultimate guardian of financial legality," playing "a significant and even crucial role in all aspects of Chilean public administration."[5]

As the Chilean government expanded into the fields of social welfare and economic enterprise, many specialized autonomous agencies were established. In general, they developed without integration and in response to specific demands and legislation. These agencies were variously organized as corpora-

[4]*Ibid.*
[5]Federico G. Gil. *The Political System of Chile* (Boston: Houghton Mifflin, 1966), pp. 98–99.

tions, services, institutes, enterprises, councils, funds, societies, and so forth, but in almost all cases had autonomous boards or councils and sometimes a director general.

The oldest and best known of such agencies was the Chilean Development Corporation (Corporación de Fomento de la Producción). Corfo, as it was commonly called, dated back to 1939 and was initially established to deal with complex reconstruction problems following a severe earthquake. Though the main thrust of Corfo was to increase national production, it was also concerned with such broad objectives as coordinating industrial development with the growth of commerce, agriculture, and mining; improving Chile's international trade situation; and raising living standards, especially through the development of low-cost housing.

The Legislative Structure

Until the 1973 coup the Chilean congress enjoyed the reputation of being one of the best developed and most effective of Latin America's legislative branches. It arrived at a reasonably stable position between the relatively impotent body it was between 1833 and the 1860s and the all-powerful but irresponsible legislature of the parliamentary period.

The bicameral body included the traditional senate and chamber of deputies. As in the United States, the former carried the greater prestige. Senators were elected by direct, popular vote for eight-year terms and were eligible, as were deputies, for immediate and indefinite reelection. Senatorial terms were staggered. The senate's president and two vice-presidents collectively formed a sort of executive committee, the *mesa directiva*. The committee system remained virtually unchanged for many years. Committees played a significant part in the legislative process, comparable in importance to those in the United States Senate; most bills originated in committees.

Under the provisions of the proposed constitution, only two-thirds of the senate would be chosen through direct election. They would be elected at large for eight-year terms. The other one-third of the senate would be appointed from a pool of former presidents, supreme court justices, legislators, retired military officers, and cabinet ministers.

The chamber of deputies was chosen on a population basis. Its 147 members would increase to 150 with the new constitution. Deputies serve for four years; all are elected simultaneously with no change expected under the new constitution.

The Judicial Structure

The Chilean judiciary, like the legislature, had a far higher standing than that in most Latin American states. Most details regarding structure of the courts were found in general law, not the constitution. The system was headed by a presidentially appointed supreme court. Justices remained in office during good behavior, which was tantamount, of course, to life tenure. The supreme court was constitutionally charged with supervisory and financial control over lower judicial levels. The supreme court could recommend removal of a lower judge for improper professional conduct; his expulsion was then all but automatic.

Probably the supreme court's most significant responsibility was that of deciding, in individual cases, whether any legal provision was inapplicable "as contrary to the Constitution." This function established a qualified form of judicial review. Disqualification of a law on such grounds fell short of judicial review in the United States since no precedent was set in Chile—only the single case was affected, as is true in the operation of Mexico's celebrated writ of *amparo*.

Promotions throughout all levels of the judiciary were based largely on seniority. The whole judicial appointment and advancement process illustrated the high degree of centralization inherent in the Chilean government structure. By voluntarily confining themselves to strictly judicial functions, the Chilean courts developed a position of respect which made them almost unique among Latin American judiciaries, a far cry from what prevailed before 1925 or after 1973. Although the judicial system continued to operate under the Pinochet regime, it was supplemented by influential military courts.

Local Structures

Chile has probably the most effective and systematically centralized government of any in Latin America. In Latin America's four federal regimes, even when the federalism is in part fictitious, it is naturally not possible for the central government to dominate so systematically and undisguisedly. Centralization under those circumstances becomes political rather than constitutional. In Latin America's unitary states, historic, demographic, political, or economic factors, or some combination of these, almost always have operated to prevent centralization from moving as far or as smoothly as in Chile. Some Chileans, indeed, question whether the process may not have gone too far.

The constitution of 1925 devoted twenty articles to local government which, despite a few gestures toward decentralization, lay a foundation for the highly centralized system that has developed. The largest subdivision is the province, of which there have been twenty-five for many years. The province is primarily administrative. Its chief authority is the presidentially appointed intendant, who serves a three-year term. The intendant is far more closely connected with the president than with the province he controls. He is responsible for all provincial public works and services.

Even before 1973, Chileans have sometimes questioned whether the province as a subdivision had sufficient viability to justify its continued existence. As a unit, it had strong historic grounding, however, and in some cases manifested discontent with over-centralizing tendencies by the national government. Some provinces in the north even made slight ventures into a hazy realm of conducting their own foreign relations. The failure of the national government to activate provincial assemblies may partly be due to the fact that if established, they could provide a forum for provincial dissatisfaction with national dominance.

Below the province, in hierarchical order, are the department, the subdelegation, and the district. Until the 1973 coup, eighty-seven departments were ruled by governors, subordinate to the provincial intendants. The subdelegation was headed by a subdelegate, subordinate to and appointed by the respective governor. The district, the lowest of the hierarchical units, was ruled by an inspector. Each municipal council designated a mayor (*alcalde*) to preside over it and serve as its agent, but in cities of more than 100,000 the mayor was presidentially appointed.

The constitution delegated to municipal councils authority over such matters as elementary education, promotion of agriculture, industry, commerce, and construction and repair of roads and bridges. A national law passed in 1942 conferred on the provincial intendant broad regulatory power over municipal actions. The Chilean municipality was not a vigorous unit of government, nor did it provoke strong local political sentiment. This situation was in part intentionally created by the authors of the 1925 constitution and in part fostered by succeeding national administrations in reaction against the excessive power vested in municipalities during the parliamentary period. The rationale behind the devolution of authority was not, of course, to strengthen municipalities for their own sakes but to weaken the office of the president.

The need for official channels of local political expression is acute, especially since the province, the department, the subdelegation, and the district have no elected representative bodies. Before the 1973 coup, the municipality did have, but even the municipal council was subject to frequent higher administrative interference. A sense of Chilean nationality was not as well developed in the extreme north and south as in the central part of the country; this intensified the need for additional instrumentalities for local expression. There was much criticism that national authorities neglected local problems.

Party Dynamics

Before the military junta took control in 1973 and placed party activity in recess, party dynamics of Chile were virtually unique among Latin American states. At least two main elements of distinctiveness could be noted: First, Chile was the best Latin American example of a multiparty system; second, in Chile competing parties or families of parties occupied definite ideological positions on Right, Center, and Left.

The Right. The Chilean Right, for example, was easier to define and more monolithic and unchanging than either the Center or the Left. It was composed of the Conservative (officially, the United Conservative) and the Liberal parties. Since 1966, largely as a consequence of Frei's spectacular triumph two years earlier, Conservatives and Liberals joined as the National party (Partido Nacional, or PN) in a marriage both expedient and logical. Even yet—however natural in view of the long traditional similarity of the two groups—they tended to maintain distinct psychologies and personalities. Both were "historic" parties in the sense that they dated well back into the nineteenth century and existed continuously for many decades. The Conservative party was the older of the two. It is true that there were "Liberals" in the 1820s but, as noted earlier, the almost complete Liberal eclipse in 1830 resulted in a fifteen- to twenty-year hiatus; when the Liberal party was revived in the late 1840s and 1850s, it was almost as if a new party entered the stage.

With some qualification it may be said that the sheet anchors of the Conservative party were the wealthy landowners and the Church. Although the core of Conservative strength was traditionally the great estate owners, contemporary membership of the party was by no means limited to that group. The party included many individual prosperous businesspeople and, indeed, a scattering of membership from almost all socioeconomic levels and groups except for organized labor. In spite of the reputed radicalism of youth, university student bodies had small but active groups of affiliated members, just as Young Republican groups in the United States have university-campus units that are often quite conservative in orientation.

The attachment of the Catholic church to the Conservative party became less complete and obvious as a dichotomy arose in Catholic political thinking between the traditional conservative position (formerly all but universal) and the newer "Catholicism with a social conscience" promoted in part by Cardinal Raúl Silva, head of the Chilean hierarchy. The older wing clung to the Conservative party as virtually the only political home it could find; the newer was apt to be found in or near the camp of the Christian Democrats. Conservatives at least semiofficially oriented their party toward the Church, though of course there was no organic connection between the two.

Conservatives had, and National party members enjoyed, a theoretical advantage in that they felt they could stand in very large degree on the status quo and need not make much concession to progress. They held near sacred the traditional land tenure system.

Conservatives would in general restrict the government's role and initiative in the economic sphere—for example, in such matters as instituting exchange and price controls, taking an active direct part in industrial development. And correspondingly, they would strongly support private enterprise.

Most of the top leadership was from the elite. Party discipline was carefully maintained and authority was concentrated in the upper levels of the hierarchical party structure. Though theoretically the quadrennial national convention was sovereign, in practice it was largely a ratifying, even a rubber-stamp, body.

On the other hand, the Liberal party was primarily the party of the businessowner, the banker, the industrialist, and the professional. It represented wealth, as did the Conservative party, but not a land-based wealth. With a less monolithic composition than the Conservative party, it was subject to more internal cleavage and friction, but wealth and social position were normally a sufficient bond to keep its members together.

As has been noted earlier, the Liberal party was once truly liberal, at least in a nineteenth-century context. By the end of that century its de facto position had become almost conservative. It was the same sort of ideological shift, only greater in degree, that characterized the Radical parties in Chile and Argentina, the Colorado party in Uruguay, and others. This shift made it difficult to assign a later ideological position to the party. In the latter decades of the nineteenth century the party stressed an anticlerical and an antipresidential position. It continued to pay a slight lip service to these issues but they became largely unimportant, especially after amalgamation with the Conservatives.

The Center.   The Chilean Center was composed primarily of the Radical (Partido Radical, or PR) and Christian Democratic (Partido Demócrata Cristiano, or PDC) parties. Radical party strength was more widely dispersed throughout Chile than that of any other party. Chile's far north and south, as well as the central valley, contributed Radical members and votes; support was rural as well as urban. The socioeconomic spread was also considerable: The party had significant working-class support and in recent decades gained some industrial and business following to add to its middle-class base; the government bureaucracy was more firmly attached to the Radical party than to any other. This broad base of support was an element of strength for the party but also carried the disadvantage of making it difficult for the party to take firm policy positions.

The circumstances of the Radical party's birth in the mid-nineteenth century made it initially a party of individualism. Although anticlericalism was not an original issue with the Radical party, it became a central principle in its philosophy at a relatively early date and remained so until clerical questions were for practical purposes removed from politics by the 1925 constitution.

Since the Radical party never had close affiliations with the landed aristocracy, it was easier at least theoretically for it to favor land reform. But the party failed to practice what it preached, and in the decade and a half of its control of the presidency, it did nothing of consequence to attack one of Chile's major problems. Radicals took a more definite and detailed position regarding extension of social security benefits. They were similarly willing to see the government extend its regulatory activities, which helped account for the considerable expansion of the bureaucracy to the party. But Radical positions on such matters were vague and sometimes contradictory, and the party's indecision cost it much public confidence. Although the strongest political group in Chile before the rise of the Christian Democrats, it has been outlawed since the coup of 1973.

The Christian Democratic party (PDC) dates back to 1957 and got its real thrust with the election of Eduardo Frei to the presidency in 1964. With former President Frei as its leader, the PDC has withstood the excesses of the present military regime better than most of the regime's critics. Its party antecedents, the Falange Nacional and the Social Christian Conservative party, take it back only two decades further.

The Chilean PDC has a base of Catholic middle-class membership, but it stresses that it is not a "confessional" or clerical party. It has welcomed significant numbers of Protestants, agnostics, and even atheists. The party attracted many intellectuals and professional men, and its unofficial orientation toward neo-Catholic positions on social and economic questions made it appealing to many women. The average age level of its members is probably lower than that of Chile's other major parties. As with other parties, its electoral following greatly exceeded its formal membership.

Not until the municipal elections of 1963 did the PDC emerge as the strongest single party in the country. Then the following year it swept to an unprecedented and dramatic victory by electing Frei as president with a considerable popular majority. In congressional elections the following year it made further gains. The elections of both 1964 and 1965 showed Christian Democratic strength to be geographically widespread. But before the end of the decade it suffered serious internal schisms.

The Chilean Christian Democrats must properly be regarded as an ideological party. Its philosophy has undergone evolution, but in general it has upheld the positions taken by the famous papal social encyclicals. Thus it is positive in nature and has not seemed to be marked by the "tired blood" so characteristic of Radical ideology—if, indeed, the latter party can be said to have an ideology.

Many PDC leaders assert that the party's principles are based on Christian morality, though more conservative Catholics are wary of its reformist objectives. Most of the party does, indeed, stand relatively to the left of Christian Democratic parties in other Latin American countries. The basic principle of Chile's Christian Democratic party are belief in political democracy, advocacy of a more equitable sharing of the national wealth, and an acceptance of the pluralism of society. The Catholic coloration of the party leads it more or less officially to repudiate Marxism, and it rejects the concept of class war, but it is paradoxically sympathetic to a quite broad role for the government in the economic and social sectors. The party is much more definite and emphatic about the importance of agrarian reform than is the Radical party.

The PDC attempts to take a "third position" in world politics between that of the United States and the Soviet Union, but this has not been emphasized. Many persons both in and out of Chile now regard the Christian Democratic party under Frei's leadership as the possible spearhead—if and when civilian government is restored—of a competitive type of Latin American revolution in contrast to the style that Castro has preached. Christian Democratic *tercerismo* (the third position) applies to economic activity as well as to international politics; for example, it holds that the worker should enjoy profit sharing and should influence business and industrial management.

The Left.   Historically Chile's party Left was composed chiefly of Socialists and Communists. Although other groups cooperated with them, these two organizations comprised the bulk of leftist strength, both in membership and voter support. Since 1956 the groups on the left end of the spectrum have been associated in an effective bloc known first as the Popular Action Front (FRAP), then in a pro-Allende coalition prior to his 1970 election as the candidate of Popular Unity (UP). Since the 1973 coup they have felt the brunt of the military and secret police repression. The Radical party, which had traditionally been considered more a centrist party, moved over to the leftist coalition in 1970. This shift by the Radicals was seen by many as the turning point in the 1970 elections, due not only to their votes but also to the fractionalization of the party.

Several splinter Socialist groups existed in the early 1930s, and in 1933 they combined as the Chilean Socialist party. It took a prominent part in the organization of the Popular Front in 1936 and its presidential victory in 1938, but new Socialist schisms occurred soon thereafter and their inability to pull in harness with the Communists quickly led Socialists to withdraw from the Front. Flux and fractionation continued through the 1940s and into the 1950s, but common opposition to Ibáñez led to Socialist participation in the forming of FRAP, and soon thereafter the two major Socialist bodies—the Popular Socialist and the Chilean Socialist parties—merged to form a unified party. Because the Chilean Socialist party is less academic and doctrinaire than its counterparts in many Latin American countries, it holds greater appeal for the working classes in Chile than elsewhere.

Disavowal of the party role of shabby gentility, to which so many Latin American Socialist parties seem to be reconciled, means that the Chilean Socialist party in its various alignments and realignments consistently tended to be revolutionary and Marxian, a fact that made coalition with the Communists the easier. Basically the Socialist philosophy was orthodox: government control of all instruments of production and distribution of wealth. But it discarded the shopworn forms of nineteenth-century Socialist manifestoes and adopted a modern guise. Chilean socialism became ardently nationalistic, a stance that conventional Socialists earlier would have rejected flatly. Espousal of nationalism enabled Chilean Socialists to ride, alongside the Communists, a highly popular issue.

Socialists advocated such reforms as nationalization of Chile's mineral wealth, then largely in foreign hands; expropriation and distribution of large landed properties, accompanied by establishment of state farms and cooperatives; a general revision of the tax structure, with taxes to fall more heavily on the oligarchy; a frontal attack on illiteracy; and a broadening of the suffrage. Some Chilean Socialists were even more hostile than the Communists toward the United States and all forms of international activity and organization in which the United States has a leading role. In the international arena the Socialist party was oriented toward the fidelistas and the Chinese Communists.

Another major leftist group was the Chilean Communist party, one of the largest, oldest, and most successful Communist parties in Latin America. Its antecedents went back to 1912. The party was greatly persecuted during the Ibáñez dictatorship. In the early 1930s it was seriously split between Trotskyists and Stalinists, but it recovered prestige and power by participation in the Popular Front in 1938. When González Videla was elected president in 1946 the Communists claimed credit for having delivered the necessary votes to put him in office. Their reward was three cabinet positions, but González could stand their intransigence less than half a year before he had to reorganize his cabinet.

In 1948 congress adopted the famous Law for the Permanent Defense of Democracy, which had the effect of outlawing the Communist party. The party went underground, but not very far. The anti-Communist law was on the statute books for a decade, but nonetheless the party became increasingly active. It was a charter member of FRAP, even though still officially banned and despite the fact that FRAP had turned to the Socialists for its top candidate (Salvador Allende). Since the late 1950s it was the Communists who often gave FRAP its political coloration and tone. In the membership of Pablo Neruda, perhaps Latin America's foremost contemporary poet, Chilean Communists had, until his death in 1973, an ornament they exploited to the full.

The Communists appealed chiefly to the working class, competing with the Socialists for their support. The party also had a fringe of intellectuals and professionals, who were more important in terms of prestige than real influence. It was able to win some following among Chilean peasants. The party was extremely active, and often successful, in trying to win control of labor unions.

In basic philosophy the party was not widely different from the Socialists. As one of the more practical and realistic of Latin America's Communist parties, the Communist party was aware that it would gain nothing by advocating complete revolution immediately, and hence it tempered that pristine position by proposing successive stages of restructuring the society and economy.

The practical stance of the Communist party had a strong and conventional anti–United States tone. It opposed all those positions and operations in which the United States was interested or active. By the same token Chilean Communists have been staunch supporters of fidelismo and all it connotes. The party, for political reasons, would like to see the virtual reestablishment of a parliamentary regime.

Political Party Trends

With the military regime's ban on political party activity, it is difficult to assess the party situation in Chile. The last election before the coup showed the crystallization of parties into two coalitions: the CODE and the UP. The Right seems to support the military regime of President Pinochet who has returned land and business to its former owners. The regime's harshest critic has been the Christian Democrats. They too have suffered during President Pinochet's "recuperation" period but not to the extent that the parties to the left have.

The new constitution presumably will outlaw Marxist ideology and prevent Marxist parties from participating in Chile's political system. This will undoubtedly affect the general climate of ideological pluralism which, until recent years, has characterized Chilean politics.

The right-wing parties have been noticeably quiet during the years of military rule. The Pinochet regime's most vociferous critic continues to be the Christian Democrats. In 1977 that party drafted an answer to the proposed constitution of President Pinochet; it called for the immediate formation of a Movement of National Democratic Restoration (Movimiento Nacional de Restauración Democrática) and urged the cooperation of all political parties to work together for the return of constitutionalism.

Other Political Structures

Pressure groups hold a unique position in Chile. The pluralism of society and the relative sophistication of the economy would seem to favor extensive development of pressure groups, but the full spectrum of Chilean parties usually provided enough outlets for economic interests to keep various groups from going to great lengths to organize their own channels of political expression.

Organized labor is normally the most politicized interest group. Indeed, its political activity has frequently been more important than its economic functioning. Socialists and Communists have had the greatest influence among labor unions, with the latter seeming, until the military takeover, to have the edge. Even before that the Radical party had lost much of its influence with organized labor. Christian Democrats made a strong bid for control of certain unions. However, recent statistics indicated that more than half of Chile's almost half-million union members belonged to groups that were unaffiliated with international bodies with a Communist, anti-Communist, or Christian Democratic stamp.

In early 1979 the threat of an international transportation boycott of Chilean goods by foreign unions, including the American Federation of Labor and Congress of Industrial Organizations (AFL-CIO) shook the military government of President Pinochet, which later announced a program for normalizing the rights of organized labor in Chile. Labor leaders who opposed the Pinochet regime criticized the program as "regressive," designed to weaken the rights of unions. The major opposition labor unions in 1979 were: the Workers' Unitary Front (Frente Unitario de Trabajadores, or FUT); Confederation of Private Employees (Confederación de Empleados Particulares, or CEPTCH); the National Coordinated Syndicate (Coordinadora Nacional Sindical, or CNS); and the Group of 10. The latter union is recognized by both the American labor movement and the International Confederation of Free Trade Unions as the representative agency of democratic labor in Chilean society. These four opposition unions in Chile tried to obtain international support for those arrested as a result of the May Day demonstrations in 1979.

The Catholic church has not ceased to be politically important. Its conservative and liberal elements had entry to politics through, respectively, the National and Christian Democratic parties and seemed satisfied with such channels. Lay Catholic organizations, especially Acción Católica, espoused reformist programs. Following the military coup against Salvador Allende the Church became an obvious thorn in the side of President Pinochet. There was tension between the Church and Pinochet government over the issues of human rights and torture. Chile's Church leaders, notably Cardinal Raúl Silva Henríquez, emerged as the military junta's principal opposition. The issue of persons vanishing after arrest by security forces raised by such Church-supported groups as the Vicariate of Solidarity annoyed General Pinochet, who reportedly called the latter "solidarity with the Communists."[6] By mid-1979 the Church was still actively involved in cases of missing persons—providing legal aid where needed and using Church lawyers to represent their families before the supreme court in documented cases of missing individuals. In December 1978 Roman Catholic bishops announced the discovery of several bodies at the Lonquén kilns; sixteen members of the police (*carabineros*) were subsequently accused of involvement in the death of fifteen people whose bodies were found. The Lonquén case was as much of an embarrassment to the Pinochet government as the Letelier affair.

[6] *New York Times,* December 4, 1977, IV, p. 13.

Church-state relations seemed to worsen in 1979. In May about one hundred theological students were suspended at the Catholic University for participating in a one-day fast to protest the May Day arrest of three hundred people who defied the ban on demonstrations; the government rejected the Church's appeal against the suspension. Tensions remained high on both sides, despite the Church's mediation efforts through the Vatican since 1978 to help Chile and Argentina peacefully settle the century-old Beagle Channel dispute.

Although the large financial enterprises in banking, commerce, mining, and agriculture all have their interest associations, they have usually tended to work through the established parties, especially the Liberal and Conservative and later the National, rather than directly in the political arena.

Before the 1973 coup that brought Pinochet to power, the military had withstood the temptation to interfere in the political process. At least four factors help account for this phenomenon. First is tradition: Since the politically strong Diego Portales "put the army in its place" in the 1830s, military intervention in politics had been rare; only in 1851, 1891, and 1925 was it at all dramatic. Second, no alliance between landed oligarchy and a military caste ever developed in Chile as it did, for example, in Argentina after 1930. Third, the Chilean army had not, until recent years, become interested in promoting social change. Finally, the Chilean military was the first in Latin America to move toward professionalization; this trend, which began as early as 1885, tended to move the army away from political ventures.

What, then, made them decide to rebel against the constitutional government? The vast majority of officers of the Chilean armed forces were staunch anti-Marxists and believed that Allende deliberately set out to destroy the country's institutions. After the congressional elections in March 1973, in which the opposition did not receive the two-thirds majority needed for impeachment of Allende, the officers felt there was no other way but military intervention. A civilian solution at the ballot box had failed and if left unchecked might further increase Marxist strength in the political system.

DEVELOPMENTAL PROSPECTS

There is much speculation about the political future of Chile under military rule and especially about the prospects for a return to democracy. To the extent that the military continues to be concerned about its international image, undoubtedly some kind of democratic system (however artificial) will be introduced. An indication of the brand of democracy contemplated by the military was provided in a speech by General Pinochet in 1977. In it he made it clear that the new democracy would be "authoritarian, protected, integrative, technified, and of true social participation."[7]

[7] *La Nación,* April 10, 1978, p. 4.

What all this means is still vague. The Pinochet government has been under heavy international pressure to improve its human rights record. There is also the general attitude among such colleagues as General Gustavo Leigh (who was later dismissed) and others that governing is not the function of the military. Such developments as the proposed constitution, the granting of general amnesty to those sentenced by military tribunals since 1973, and the almost complete demilitarization of the cabinet to reflect a civilian majority in its composition all seem to signal that a new—but not necessarily democratic —system could be in the offing for Chile.

REFERENCES

ALEXANDER, ROBERT J. *The Tragedy of Chile.* Westport, Conn.: Greenwood Press, 1978.

ALLENDE GOSSENS, SALVADOR. *Chile's Road to Socialism,* ed. by Joan Garces. Baltimore: Penguin, 1973.

"Argentina-Chile: Exchange of Diplomatic Notes Concerning the Beagle Channel Arbitration." *International Legal Materials* 17:3 (May 1978), 738–753.

AYRES, ROBERT L. "Electoral Constraints and the Chilean Way to Socialism" *Studies in Comparative International Development* 8:2 (Summer 1973), 128–161.

BIZARRO, SALVATORE. "Rigidity and Restraint in Chile." *Current History* 74:434 (February 1978), 66–69.

BOORSTEIN, EDWARD. *Allende's Chile: An Inside View.* New York: International Publishers, 1977.

BRAY, DONALD W. "Chile: The Dark Side of Stability." *Studies on the Left* 4:4 (Fall 1964), 85–96.

BURNS, LAURENCE. *Chile: A Chronology and Fact Book.* Dobbs Ferry, N. Y.: Oceana, 1977.

———, ed. *The End of Chilean Democracy.* New York: Seabury Press, 1974.

BUTLAND, GILBERT J. *Chile: An Outline of Its Geography, Economy, and Politics.* 3rd ed. London: n.p., 1956.

CASSIDY, SHEILA. *Audacity to Believe.* Cleveland: Collins Publishers, 1978.

CUSACK, DAVID F. *Revolution and Reaction: the Internal Dynamics of Conflict and Confrontation in Chile.* Denver: University of Denver Graduate School of International Studies, 1977.

DEBRAY, RÉGIS. *Conversations with Allende.* New York: Random House, Vintage Books, 1971.

———. *The Chilean Revolution.* New York: Random House, 1971.

DE VYLDER, STEFAN. *Allende's Chile; The Political Economy of the Rise and Fall of Unidad Popular.* New York: Cambridge University Press, 1976.

DONOSO, RICARDO. *Las Ideas Políticas en Chile.* 2nd ed. Santiago: n.p., 1967.

DRAKE, PAUL W. *Socialism and Populism in Chile, 1932–52.* Urbana: University of Illinois Press, 1978.

EDWARDS, THOMAS. *Economic Development and Reform in Chile: Progress Under Frei 1964–1970.* East Lansing: Michigan Studies Center, 1972.

FEINBERG, RICHARD E. *The Triumph of Allende: Chile's Legal Revolution.* New York: Mentor Books, 1972.

FLEET, MICHAEL. "Chile's Democratic Road to Socialism." *Western Political Quarterly* 26:4 (December 1973), 766.

FRANCIS, MICHAEL J. *The Allende Victory: An Analysis of the 1970 Chilean Presidential Election.* Tucson: University of Arizona Press, 1973.

GIL, FEDERICO. *The Political System of Chile.* Boston: Houghton Mifflin, 1966.

GROSS, LEONARD. *The Last Best Hope: Eduardo Frei and Chilean Democracy.* New York: Random House, 1967.

HALPERIN, ERNST. *Nationalism and Communism in Chile.* Cambridge, Mass.: MIT Press, 1965.

HAMBURG, ROGER P. "The Lessons of Allende." *Problems of Communism* 27:1 (January-February 1978), 71–76.

HELLINGER, DANIEL. "Electoral Change in the Chilean Countryside: The Presidential Elections of 1958 and 1970." *Western Political Quarterly* 31:2 (June 1978), 253–273.

HIRSCHMAN, ALBERT O. *Journeys Toward Progress: Studies of Economic Policy-Making in Latin America.* New York: W.W. Norton & Co., 1973.

JOHNSON, DALE L., ed. *The Chilean Road to Socialism.* New York: Doubleday, 1973.

JOHNSON, JOHN J. *Political Change in Latin America: The Emergence of the Middle Sectors,* Chap. 5. Stanford, Calif.: Stanford University Press, 1958.

KAUFMAN, ROBERT. *The Politics of Land Reform in Chile, 1950–1970.* Cambridge, Mass.: Harvard University Press, 1972.

KAY, CRISTÓBAL. "Agrarian Reform and the Class Struggle in Chile." *Latin American Perspectives* 5:3 (Summer 1978), 117.

KERBO, HAROLD R. "Foreign Involvement in the Preconditions for Political Violence: The World System and the Case of Chile." *Journal of Conflict Resolution* 22:3 (September 1978), 363–392.

MACEVIN, GARY. *No Peaceful Way: Chile's Struggle for Dignity.* New York: Sheed and Ward, 1974.

MORAN, THEODORE. *Multinational Corporations and the Politics of Dependence: Copper in Chile.* Princeton, N. J.: Princeton University Press, 1974.

MORRIS, DAVID J. *We Must Make Haste—Slowly; The Process of Revolution in Chile.* New York: Random House, 1973.

NORTH, LISA. "The Military in Chilean Politics." *Studies in Comparative International Development* 11:2 (Summer 1976), 73–106.

PENDLE, GEORGE. *The Land and People of Chile.* New York: Macmillan, 1960.

PETRAS, JAMES F. "After the Chilean Presidential Election: Reform or Stagnation?" *Journal of Inter-American Studies* 7 (July 1965), 375–384.

———. *Politics and Social Forces in Chilean Development.* Berkeley: University of California Press, 1969.

PETRAS, JAMES F., and MORRIS MORLEY. *The United States and Chile: Imperialism and the Overthrow of the Allende Government.* New York: Monthly Review Press, 1975.

PIKE, FREDERICK P. "Chilean Local Government and Some Reflections on Dependence." *Inter-American Economic Affairs* 31:2 (Autumn 1977), 63–70.

POLLACK, BENNY. "The Chilean Socialist Party: Prolegomena to Its Ideology and Organization." *Journal of Latin American Studies* 10:1 (May 1978), 117.

ROJAS, ROBINSON. *The Murder of Allende and the End of the Chilean Way to Socialism,* trans. by Andree Conrad. New York: Harper & Row, 1977.

ROXBOROUGH, IAN, PHIL O'BRIEN, and JACKIE RODDICK. *Chile: The State and Revolution.* London: Macmillan, 1977.

SIGMUND, PAUL. "Chile: Two Years of 'Popular Unity.' " *Problems of Communism* 21 (November-December 1972), 38–50.

SILVERT, KALMAN H. *Chile: Yesterday and Today.* New York: Holt, Rinehart & Winston, 1965.

SNOW, PETER G. "The Political Party Spectrum in Chile." *South Atlantic Quarterly* 62 (Autumn 1963), 474–487.

SWEEZY, PAUL M., and HARRY MAGDOFF, eds. *Revolution and Counter-Revolution in Chile.* New York: Monthly Review Press, 1974.

TAPIA-VIDELA, JORGE. "The Chilean Presidency in a Developmental Perspective." *Journal of Inter-American Studies and World Affairs* 19:4 (November 1977), 451–482.

United States Congress, House Committee on Foreign Affairs, Sub-Committee on Inter-American Affairs. *United States and Chile During the Allende Years, 1970–1973.* 94th Congress, 1st Session, 1975, 1–677.

United States Senate, Select Committee to Study Governmental Operations with Respect to Intelligence Activities. *Covert Action in Chile 1963–1973.* 94th Congress, 1st Session. 1975, 1–62.

URIBE, ARMANDO. *The Black Book of American Invervention in Chile.* Boston: Beacon Press, 1974.

VALENZUELA, ARTURO, and J. SAMUEL VALENZUELA, eds. *Chile: Policy and Society. New Brunswick, N. J.: Transaction Books, 1976.*

———. *Chilean Socialism?* New York: Dutton, 1974.

WATERMAN, HARVEY. "Political Mobilization and the Case of Chile." *Studies in Comparative International Development* 13:1 (Spring 1978), 60–70.

WHITAKER, ARTHUR P. *The U.S. and the Southern Cone: Argentina, Chile, and Uruguay.* Cambridge, Mass.: Harvard University Press, 1976.

Part Five

THE ATLANTIC REGION

13

BRAZIL

The Politics
of Quasi-Hegemony

POLITICAL CULTURE AND ENVIRONMENT

Brazil is "the infinite country," as William L. Schurz described it. It is the large
drought-stricken area (the country's problem land) in the northeast and it is
rain forest; it is the world's mightiest river and it is the vast *sertões* or hinterland areas, a seemingly permanent frontier; it is the politically sophisticated
middle and upper classes of the cities and it is the wholly politically inarticulate
interior; it is the loveliness of much of Rio or the bold, futuristic Brasília; it
is the stark *favelas* (shantytowns) on the hillsides above the large cities; and
it is a politically resurgent army.

Perhaps the most obvious and impressive fact about Brazil is its size—
its 3,286,478 square miles make it the fifth largest country in the world.
Bordering on all but two states in South America, this single country comprises 49 percent of that continent's area and 42 percent of all Latin America.
As is true of many Latin American countries, effective Brazil is much smaller
than the whole area. Three-tenths of the land area—Minas Gerais and the
states south, plus a thin coastal strip running north to slightly beyond the
Hump—contain about nine-tenths of the population and the important economic, cultural, and political centers.

The Northeast, as the scene of recurrent droughts, some of several years'
duration, has been an economic and hence a political problem. The economic
stresses of this region provoked the development of the political actionist
movement which found its outlet in the Peasant Leagues under Francisco

Julião. Brazil's North is generally equated with Amazonia. Scores of migrants depart this section yearly, leaving still a third of the country's population living in what many feel is the "colonized" area of the politically and economically dominant South.

Brazil doubtless deserves the appellation of "melting pot" even more than the United States. The chief early components of the population were Indians, Portuguese, and blacks. Heavy immigration in the nineteenth and twentieth centuries added millions of Italians, Portuguese, Spaniards, Germans, Poles, Japanese, and many other nationalities, making the nationalistic mix, especially in the south and in the cities, extremely varied. This diversity is evident in the roster of presidents, which includes such names as Kubitschek and Geisel. Today the population is approximately 65 percent Caucasian, 30 percent mixed, and less than 0.5 percent pure Indian.

The magnitude of Brazil's area is equaled by that of its population; according to a 1977 estimate, it has more than 113 million inhabitants. This represents about half of South America's population and 33 percent of that of all Latin America. The population has grown rapidly—Brazil has one of the highest growth rates in Latin America. Brazil's population density in relation to arable land is almost one thousand per square mile. This statistical picture, added to the difficulties and inadequacies of transportation, heavily underscores the political pressures produced by growth and maldistribution of population.

Brazilian tolerance toward racial intermixture, except at the topmost social levels, has contributed to a political openness that has often helped ease tensions. The structure of Brazilian society in various periods has had a highly important conditioning effect on politics. The sugar *fazenda* (estate) was the heart of the social structure, and the *casa grande* (owner's mansion) was a symbol of social architecture as well as the physical center of plantation life and activity. Slavery was an economic cornerstone of the system. Brazil achieved independence without the slightest hint of social revolution. Breakdown of the layered society was long in coming. In broad respects the Brazilian social landscape resembled that of the planter society in the pre-Civil War United States.

Postindependence Brazilian Political Development

Political development of independent Brazil has been characterized by episodes of precarious stability and change. This continuing process has been marked by governmental experiments—sixty-seven years of empire under Pedro I and his son Pedro II, whose progressive rule laid the foundation of modern Brazil; forty years of republicanism followed by fifteen years of

Getulio Vargas's corporatist dictatorship; and then a nineteen-year interlude of constitutional normalization until military intervention in 1964.

Dom Pedro I's reign of less than a decade was an indecisive period, though certain lines of political continuity even then began to be drawn. Though he had dramatically cast in his lot with Brazil rather than Portugal, Pedro relied heavily on Portuguese favorites at the imperial court.

The first constitution, promulgated in March 1824, was in some respects more liberal than the proposed law of 1823, though the position and prerogatives of the emperor were strongly established. A combination of factors brought increasing unpopularity to Dom Pedro I, and he was forced to abdicate in 1831, passing the crown to his five-year-old son who a decade later was made Dom Pedro II. The period of the regency in the 1830s was the most erratic in Brazil's political history. It was a transitional stage—Brazil was simply trying to hold itself together until the imperial child could assume the powers constitutionally assigned the emperor and thereby provide a symbol of national unity. Finally, in 1840, when Pedro was not quite 16, he was declared of age and assumed the crown.

The reign of Dom Pedro II, just short of half a century, was a remarkable period in Brazilian political development. Pedro II was well educated and thoroughly patriotic; he was in his paternalistic way devoted to the advancement of Brazil. The emperor brought Brazil through a swaddling stage when almost all Spanish American states except Chile were undergoing the travail of *caudillismo.* He provided a symbol of national unity. His impact ranks with that of Vargas (of course in quite a different way) as the greatest in the formation of the Brazilian political character.

Brazil seemed blessed with the monarchy and rewarded by the progress made under it. But forces crystallized which increasingly demanded change. Pedro lost Church support, army support, and *fazendeiro* (landowner) support. Most important of all, from a direct political point of view, he faced the growing advocacy of republicanism. Some agitation for a republic had long existed, even though President Mitre of Argentina described Brazil as the "crowned democracy of America." The climax came in 1889, when a bloodless coup led by two ambitious generals, Manoel Deodoro da Fonseca and Floriano Peixoto, successfully established the United States of Brazil, with Deodoro as the first president. The move transferred the political center of gravity from the sugar *fazenda,* rural northern region to the coffee plantation and nascent industrial (and hence urban) south. Thus were economics and politics to be wedded under the republic.

Nonetheless the sudden change to a republic and the gradual shift of political power from north to south did not at once produce a politicized urban middle class. The growing number of immigrants did not seem especially politically minded. Brazil did not develop any counterpart of Argentina's Radical Civic Union.

The traditions of controlled elections and of irregular rotation of the presidency between the country's two most important states—São Paulo and Minas Gerais—were becoming well established before the new century was even a decade old. Indeed, from that time until after 1930, state loyalties frequently took precedence over a national allegiance.

The "revolution of 1930" was not a social upheaval. The aims of the revolution were to establish a truer political democracy and to destroy the old pattern of *rotavismo* between paulista and mineiro control of the national administration. Rio Grande do Sul was knocking at the door of the political power structure. Participation in the military action by a group of junior army officers known collectively as the *tenentes,* who had vague and amorphous ideas of social reform, gave a slight ideological tinge to the revolution, but the coup was still overwhelmingly political in nature.

Getulio Vargas is the most controversial figure in all Brazilian political life. He was a dictator during the first fifteen-year period of his rule, but it was not a dictatorship cut from the cloth of Spanish American *caudillismo.* Vargas, only a little more than five feet in height, was not physically destined to be a "man on horseback" or a saber rattler. He was genial (though less so toward the end of his rule), democratic, often easy-going. His dictatorship was mild and in many respects popular; only during the war years did it become more oppressive. Vargas personified many of the traits that are often associated with the Brazilian national character: He was energetic, somewhat cynical, astute, opportunistic, patriotic. His sense of humor prevented him from being a poseur. He was a political chameleon, even an eel. The main plank of Vargas's political platform was that Brazilian nationalism must be achieved quickly and permanently to override state loyalties.

For two years Vargas moved energetically, even drastically, to correct the more obvious ills of the preceding administration, which had been compounded by the impact of the depression. He intervened freely in state governments, abolished state tariff barriers, and moved steadily toward centralization.

The 1891 constitution had been suspended on Vargas's accession to power. A paulista rebellion in 1932 was a prod toward reestablishing constitutional government. Vargas on numerous occasions appeared to admire Fascist practice and preachment. Inspired at many points by Italian corporative models, he adopted the 1934 constitution, which gave greatly enlarged power to the national executive, established women's suffrage, and included extensive social provisions; it banned state hymns and flags. This constitution was but a preview of innovations to follow three years later.

An amenable constituent assembly elected Vargas constitutional president for the initial four-year term. By late 1935 internal politics became more disruptive, chiefly because of the activity of two recent national political organizations, Communists and Integralists. Prior to the 1930s political parties had existed, in effect, only on a state basis. State parties sometimes made loose alliances with each other, but nothing like permanent national parties had emerged.

Partly born of depression-generated stresses, both Communists and Integralists became active and threatening in the first Vargas decade. The Brazilian Communist party dated back to 1921; for some years its leader, above ground and underground, had been the capable Luiz Carlos Prestes. The Integralists were a quasi-fascist group constituting a rightist mass movement which claimed half a million members or more, though such claims were highly inflated. They borrowed heavily in political apparatus and symbolism from Mussolini's Italy, Hitler's Germany, and Salazar's Portugal. Their political philosophy was confused and fuzzy, and they spent most of their energies parading their green-shirted militia on any and all occasions. They were a rightist threat and, although Vargas appeared at times to flirt with them, he eventually broke away.

Elections were scheduled for January 1938. But Vargas's program, partly one of expediency, was incomplete. At least in his own estimation, he was becoming the indispensable man. He moved dramatically in 1937 to suspend scheduled elections, extending his own presidency for another term, replacing the 1934 constitution with one of his own devising, and dissolving the congress and the state legislatures. Thus was ushered in the Estado Novo —the New State.

Estado Novo was a venture in intense state planning and control. It was the second phase of the Vargas dictatorship. The 1937 constitution was one of the most novel among the two hundred fifty or more that Latin American states have written. It represented a long step toward centralization. Although it retained a state organization, the de facto concentration of power in national hands was so great that it is doubtful if Brazil can accurately be called a federal state from 1937 to 1945. The elaborate legislative machinery remained academic: No congressional elections were even held during the life of the Estado Novo.

Intensified propaganda, increasingly heavy censorship, and wider use of some of the symbols of totalitarianism became more and more characteristic of the regime. Vargas was such an opportunist that he felt it unnecessary to organize much of a personal political machine, whether called party or not, as other dictators in similar positions have usually done. His radio broadcasts were increasingly aimed at the working classes, which were gradually molded into a highly amorphous group of *queremistas*—"we-wanters"; what they wanted, of course, was Vargas. They later became the Labor party, on which Vargas relied considerably.

It was the increasingly heavy-handed censorship during the war that finally eroded any remaining popular support for Vargas. The military now took matters into its own hands and demanded that Vargas resign. He did so. The military coup of 1945 ended the Estado Novo and the Vargas dictatorship.

Virtually all of the Vargas bequest to Brazilian politics dates from his dictatorship. Assessing its nature and significance is not easy. Vargas has often been compared to Perón, but Vargas and his contribution were more subtle and complex than were Perón and his political legacy. Probably Vargas's greatest gift to Brazil was his stimulation of a sense of nationalism—something Argentina already had. The concept of Brazil as a unified entity was much more valid by 1945 than it had been in 1930. Elements of the change were both symbolic and substantive. Vargas, like Perón, lowered the national political center of gravity. In Argentina it was the *descamisados* (shirtless ones) who were given a political voice and status; in Brazil, Vargas more subtly shifted effective political control from partially invisible state political machines to the middle and lower classes. He always wanted to preserve his own maneuverability and hence did not become really dependent on such political mechanisms as parties, elections, and the apparatus of representative government. Vargas personified a soft-focus authoritarian trend in Brazilian politics. To a considerable degree, he molded the political Brazil of his day.

General Eurico Dutra, supported by the Social Democratic party (Partido Social Democrático, or PSD), surprised many Brazilians and foreigners by winning comfortably in December 1945. The first major task he faced was to normalize the constitutional situation. The new basic law (1945) restored a conventional federalism and limited both national and presidential powers. Much of the social legislation embodied in the 1934 and 1937 constitutions was retained.

Brazil, which by 1945 had tired of the frenetic Vargas, by 1950 had enough of the unexciting Dutra. The presidential election in 1950 was a contest primarily between the National Democratic Union (União Democrático Nacional, or UDN) candidate and a reconditioned Vargas, now running as the candidate of the Labor party. There was some apprehension among the military in 1950 when Vargas announced that he would be a candidate; yet, the military did nothing to block the former dictator from assuming office when he was easily reelected, carrying the Federal District and sixteen of Brazil's then twenty states.

But the military kept a watchful eye on his activities, and in August 1954, when political and economic discontent had reached a point similar to that of 1945, the armed forces presented an ultimatum to Vargas to withdraw. Again he chose not to resist the inevitable. On August 24, just four hours after his forced resignation, Vargas shot and killed himself.

The ensuing months were a transitional time of confusion and continued army interference in politics. Early in 1955 the PSD nominated Juscelino Kubitschek, governor of Minas Gerais, as its presidential candidate. The

Labor party concurred in the nomination of Kubitschek for president but separately nominated João Goulart for vice-president. The elections that brought Kubitschek and Goulart to power were relatively peaceful.

The new president, inaugurated at the end of January 1956, moved energetically to realize a long-neglected Brazilian dream—establishing the national capital at a point far inland in the state of Goiás. Brasília was inaugurated on April 21, 1960. That year's elections took place, in regular cycle, early in October. The system again chose a cross-party combination: Jânio Quadros (UDN) as president and João Goulart (PSD) as vice-president.

The Quadros administration began in January 1961 with actions that aroused mixed responses in and out of Brazil. On August 25, 1961, in one of the most inexplicable moves of recent Brazilian politics, Quadros suddenly resigned after less than seven months in office. Goulart, who had many enemies (including the army), was in a dilemma. The congress promptly approved a law establishing a parliamentary form of government which substantially reduced the powers of the president and created the office of prime minister, with the occupant subject to congressional confirmation. The year 1962 proved the parliamentary system weak. A national plebiscite on retention of parliamentary government was held on January 6, 1963, and the electorate overwhelmingly disapproved parliamentarism. Congress quickly passed a law restoring presidential government.

Goulart continued, however, to be highly controversial. His regime had moved increasingly leftward, toward a Vargas-style demagogic dictatorship, and the political situation rapidly deteriorated. This prompted the military and the governors of the major states to join in demanding Goulart's resignation. First denying that he would yield the presidency, he was forced to flee to Uruguay on April 2, 1964.

Authoritarianism and Corporatism

Although most Brazilians backed Goulart's ouster, few expected the military to continue in power for more than sixteen years. On April 11, 1964, the congress chose General Humberto Castelo Branco, an officer without earlier marked political activity or party alignment, as provisional president to fill out Goulart's unexpired term. A gradual hardening of attitudes took place among both the younger army men and the civilian political leaders who were eliminated from participating in the political process. Later in 1964 his authority was extended, ostensibly against his personal wishes, to March 1967. Castelo Branco suddenly converted Brazil into a dictatorship, with only a façade of congressional control. He dissolved all parties, expanded (a euphemism for *packed*) the supreme court with five additional members, substituted congressional for popular election of the next president, and took other drastic actions. He declared himself ineligible for congressional election to the presidency for the following term. Even coming from the hands of a military regime, the action was a political bombshell. Both inside Brazil and out, objection was widespread but futile.

On December 4, 1965 Castelo Branco took steps to form a National Alliance for Renovation (Aliança Renovadora Nacional, or ARENA) from progovernment elements in the old parties to provide a semblance of party backing for the regime. The step was obviously artificial.

Attention gradually focused on General Arturo da Costa e Silva, minister of war, as a successor to Castelo Branco. He resigned as minister in July 1966 to campaign for congressional election to the presidency, backed by ARENA. Manipulated elections seemed certain when, on July 5, 1966, Castelo Branco suspended for ten years the political rights of almost fifty members of the Brazilian Democratic Movement (Movimento Democrático Brasileiro, or MDB), the loose cross-party alliance opposing the regime. On October 3 congress chose Costa e Silva president to succeed Castelo Branco in March 1967. Two weeks later Castelo Branco reacted to a mild gesture of independence in congress by dissolving it and ruling by decree.

In January 1967 congress overwhelmingly approved a presidentially prepared constitution, to take effect simultaneously with the inauguration of Costa e Silva in mid-March. The new law nominally retained a federal form of government, though it dropped the words "the United States of " from the official name of the country. Executive authority was broadly increased; the president would be elected indirectly and would have the power to name state governors. Nine members of Costa e Silva's initial cabinet, named on his inauguration on March 15, 1967, were from the military; the other half were civilians. Costa e Silva never succeeded in winning broad popular support; hostility was especially manifest among students. In one incident the army demanded that congress strip legislative immunity from one of its members who had publicly attacked the military. Congress, for the first time since the 1964 revolution, challenged the military and voted 216 to 141 to refuse to bow to military pressure. The president's chief instrument was the Institutional Act No. 5 of December 13, 1968. The act gave the president power to close congress and suspend habeas corpus for those accused of subversion and authority to remove "dangerous elements from public life."[1] Over two hundred political opponents, including Carlos Lacerda and ex-president Kubitschek, were jailed. By the winter of 1968 (June-July) student unrest had become almost explosive, and in December of that year the president recessed the congress and assumed personal emergency powers.

The situation was dramatically altered when, on August 31, 1969, Presi-

[1]Rollie E. Poppino, "Brazil After a Decade of Revolution," *Current History*, 66:389 (January 1974), 3.

dent Costa e Silva was incapacitated by a stroke. Instead of allowing the office to devolve constitutionally upon civilian Vice President Pedro Aleixo, a junta of high-ranking officers in the three military services assumed executive power and on October 6 named Army General Emilio Garrastazú Médici as president; a joint session of the congress on October 25 made the action official.

President Garrastazú Médici's inauguration aroused Brazilian hopes for relaxation of political restraints. The congress had been reconvened and remained in session, prior censorship of the press had been lifted, and the new president had reiterated his own hope to leave democracy established in Brazil by the end of his term. But even as politicians and the press were becoming bolder in calling for an end to Institutional Act No. 5 and for direct elections for governors and the president, Garrastazú Médici was moving to strengthen his own power. He assumed the personal role of selecting candidates for governor and congress and decreed that political parties should not concern themselves with candidates for his successor until mid-1972; he banned all discussion of presidential succession in the press before that time.

In April 1973 he completely closed the door to any hope for a return to democracy by reinstituting censorship of newspapers and extending it to Brazilian and foreign periodicals circulated in the country. On June 15 the president announced that General Ernesto Geisel's name would be submitted for nomination at the ARENA convention in September 1973.

General Geisel's nomination met with very little dissent. His nationalist policies while president of the Brazilian Petroleum Corporation (Petróleo Brasileiro, or Petrobras) earned him much praise as an economic nationalist. Although there was no doubt about the outcome of the presidential elections, the MDB met in September 1973 to nominate its party president, Senator Ulises Guimares, to run against Geisel. A substantial number of the MDB opted to boycott the presidential campaign. However, the Garrastazú Médici administration's guarantee to give them equal television and radio time appealed to the MDB, who had complained that they were allowed to debate freely in congress but that censorship did not allow the people to read their arguments. The anticandidates, as Ulises Guimares and Barbosa Lima Sobreneo chose to call themselves since they had no possibility of winning the January 15, 1974, indirect elections, focused their criticism on civil rights issues and the government's financial and economic policies. The campaign gave the Brazilian people at least the semblance of a political contest as they watched two rival candidates discuss the issues of the day from completely different points of view.

But General Geisel's election to the presidency was a foregone conclusion inasmuch as there was no way for the MDB candidate to receive a majority vote. ARENA controlled two-thirds of both houses of congress and a majority in twenty-one of the twenty-two states. Also, it was understood that each delegate must vote for his party's choice.

President Geisel's administration started in much the same fashion as that of his predecessor: a relaxation of censorship and talk of decompression, or *distensão* (the relaxation of tension). Geisel did not enjoy the consistent support of any group during his regime but instead tried to walk a tightrope between political liberalization and the hard-line military. He faced the strongest political crisis of his government in October 1975 when massive arrests were carried out to break up the reorganization of the Brazilian Communist party. During the week of October 15, Wladimir Herzog, a well-known journalist and professor at the University of São Paulo, voluntarily appeared for questioning when notified of the military police's intention to arrest him. That same afternoon the military announced that he had committed suicide in his cell. There was little support for the suicide story, and the day after Herzog's death a storm of protest swept the city of São Paulo. Thirty thousand students at the University of São Paulo went on strike for a week; students at the Catholic University and other schools in the city joined the strike. An ecumenical memorial ceremony officiated over by Rabbi Henry Sobel, Cardinal Evaristo Arns, and Pastor James Wright attracted eight thousand persons, despite attempts by police to block the main roads into São Paulo.

Though President Geisel seemed to have come out of the 1975 turmoil with no more than a bruise to his regime, his continued oscillation from political *distensão* to censorship and repression produced a kind of political paranoia in both military and party leaders alike. In 1976 a leading Brazilian newspaper, *O Estado de São Paulo,* reported that General Golberry de Couta e Silva, chief of the president's civil household, had contacted party leaders for discussion of new political formulas which would be fully developed during the summer recess, though Justice Minister Armando Falção flatly denied that any such reforms were being considered.[2]

The Institutional Act No. 5 was used on several occasions during the Geisel regime to suspend the political rights of his critics. For the first time since 1968 President Geisel used his executive powers to close congress for ten days in April 1977. New electoral laws, proclaimed in April 1977, provided for the indirect election of the president, state governors, and a third of the senate; the requirements of a simple majority to pass constitutional amendments rather than a two-thirds majority in congress; and the continuation of the *Lei Falção* (law named after the justice minister) governing electoral publicity. These measures guaranteed that the opposition party would have no chance of coming to power in any foreseeable election and that congress would once again become a rubber stamp for the governing regime.

Many observers saw President Geisel as the most dictatorial of the four generals who have ruled the country since 1964. They cited lack of consultation with fellow military officers and cabinet members, censorship of leftist

---

[2]*Latin American Report,* 5:4 (November, 1976), 2.

publications, radio and television, literature, and plays, and the closing of congress for ten days in 1977 as justification for this description.

Geisel was also the first military president since 1964 to dismiss his army minister, Sylvio Frota. Frota had been subtly campaigning for the presidency since his appointment as army minister in 1974. But his power play in the congress in September 1977 led to his ultimate downfall when he led forty-three generals into congress where he had begun to cultivate support for the presidency.

In what was publicly spoken of as a ministerial reshuffle but was actually an aborted coup, President Geisel asked for Frota's resignation, and when Frota refused, fired him. Frota immediately convened an urgent meeting of the army high command to assess the situation. When the generals flew into the military airport for the meeting convened by Frota, they were immediately shuffled off to the presidential palace where President Geisel was waiting with the news that General Fernando Belfort Bethlem would replace Frota as army minister.

During the closing months of the Geisel administration, congress passed a constitutional amendment which repealed the Institutional Act No. 5, effective January 1, 1979. This was the first real move toward democracy, although it is still far away. Geisel has dismissed as "utopian" the hope that Brazil would become a full democracy.

In February 1978 President Geisel announced that General João Baptista de Figueiredo, the national intelligence chief, will be his successor. Although it was necessary for General Figueiredo to be "elected," this was a mere formality since the president was chosen through indirect elections of party delegates on October 15, 1978. Figueiredo took office in March 1979.

Figueiredo's power will no doubt be curtailed by the 1978 constitutional amendment. Under the change in the law the president cannot declare a "state of siege" without obtaining congressional approval within five days; congress must remain open. The new amendment also allows the president to suspend rights temporarily during a "state of emergency" without congressional approval, but he is required to justify such action before a constitutional council of congressional leaders and civilian and military cabinet ministers.

Figueiredo has promised gradual progress toward direct elections for all political posts except the presidency, which he believes should be filled through an indirect system similar to that in the United States. He has also come out against censorship as well as the Church's political activism and has promised support for labor rights that are within the law.[3] Only time will tell if General Figueiredo will bring about normalization of the political process, or if he too will continue the sixteen-year practice of making promises with no substantial change in the status quo.

[3]*New York Times,* April 23, 1978, Sec. IV, p. 1.

The organization of the Brazilian political system is largely distinguished by its federalism, which provides a backdrop for the performance of various political functions. Brazil can probably be considered the "most federal" of Latin America's four federal states, but such a generalization needs explanation and qualification.

Although some federations, such as Switzerland, are small in area, most, such as Canada, Australia, the United States, Brazil, and Argentina, are large. Their great physical expanse is likely to be characterized, at least in Latin America, by difficulties of internal transportation, considerable regional and possibly cultural dissimilarities, perhaps even linguistic variations. These considerations make political and administrative flexibility highly desirable, even necessary. If historic conditioners are also considered, the pressure for establishing federal mechanisms and relationships may become overriding. Hence, embodiment of federalism in Brazil's 1891 constitution was a logical development.

The basic issue of national-local relations remained alive in Brazil, though in a less tortured way than in Argentina. The politics of the first three decades of the twentieth century represented a high point of state freedom of action, even arrogance. São Paulo state provides the prime example; twice in the present century it revolted against the central government. On a few matters of particular interest to it, São Paulo maintained pseudodiplomatic relations with certain foreign countries. It sometimes displayed the state flag above the national emblem.

The 1934 constitution substantially downgraded the role of the states. Their hymns and flags were abolished. Control over voting and elections was more fully centralized in the national government. Several natural resources and economic functions were nationalized. Indeed, the 1937 constitution carried centralization so far that federalism became practically a fiction. Detailed provisions of this Vargas law made little difference; political considerations, not constitutional prescriptions, called the tune during the Estado Novo.

The 1946 constitution restored federalism to more respectable and conventional proportions. The distribution of powers still greatly favored the federal government but not so overwhelmingly as in the two constitutions of the 1930s. But, in effect, most of the essential centralizing powers that Vargas had arrogated for the national authority were left there. The Brazilian basic law reserved to the states powers not forbidden them by the constitution, much as the United States Constitution does, but this provision has not stayed the course of centralization.

In 1962 Governor Leonel Brizola (brother-in-law of João Goulart) of Rio Grande do Sul expropriated United States–owned utilities, to the alleged embarrassment of Brazilian national authorities, showing that significant and even dramatic areas of independent action were still open to the states. The prominent role played by certain state authorities in the events leading to the ouster of President Goulart in March–April 1964 further supported this conclusion.

Although the military-inspired 1967 and 1969 constitutions ostensibly retained federalism, centralization was once again carried forward. Powers constitutionally assigned to the federal government in Brazil are more numerous and relatively more important than in the United States. The taxing power and tax bases of the federal government are much broader than those of the states. States are hemmed in on the one side by generous grants of power to the federal government and on the other by constitutional guarantees of municipal autonomy and freedom from most state intervention.

The Executive Structure

The 1934 constitution greatly increased the power of the executive. Not only were presidential powers as such broadened, but the many provisions for enlarging the social and economic role of the national government also inevitably operated to enhance presidential authority. The zenith of presidential power vis-à-vis congress was reached in the 1937 constitution, simply because the elaborate legislative institutions provided by that curious document were never activated. The decree supplanted the statute.

The 1946 constitution restored a more nearly normal relationship. The provisions establishing free congressional elections, as much removed from presidential dominance as possible, were perhaps as effective as any in upholding some claim to legislative parity with the executive. The mystique of the presidential office is much less implied in the constitution of 1946 than in that of 1937. Nonetheless, the integrative currents of Brazilian political life force a symbolic and unifying role upon the president—at least when the office operates free of army intervention. The military presidencies following 1964 elevated executive dominance to a new high, especially when the main provisions of Castelo Branco's institutional act were incorporated into the 1967 and 1969 constitutions, which among other things abolished direct presidential elections.

Nominations for the president and vice-president, at least under normal circumstances, are closely tied to the parties. The dozen or more registered parties usually taking part in a free election do not all nominate candidates for both offices. Those with relatively little chance of winning often find it advantageous to enter into a coalition and support the candidate of a major party for one or both offices, thus gaining at least some of the prestige and spoils awarded the victor. Because parties are relatively young and lightly rooted, the element of personalism has by no means disappeared. Vargas never liked to tie himself irrevocably to a political party, even the Labor party, which he had been instrumental in founding and which nominated him in 1950. Quadros also remained relatively free from firm party connections. Ambitious politicos have to consider their own interests as well as those of their parties, and such personal considerations often lead them to avoid becoming so closely associated in the public mind with a single party that they thereafter lack maneuverability.

The 1946 constitution specified that if a vacancy occurred in the presidency during the first half of the term, new popular elections would be held; if during the second half, congress would fill the office. The constitutional amendment establishing parliamentary government in 1961 abolished the vice-presidency, but when that action was reversed two years later the vice-presidency was restored.

In his sweeping decrees of late October 1965, Castelo Branco conferred on himself virtually dictatorial powers. These powers were presumed to be only temporary, and it was assumed that the Brazilian presidency would sooner or later be restored to more normal dimensions.

The instituting of parliamentary government in 1961 considerably debased the presidency; congress elected the president, the cabinet was made responsible to the legislature, and the lower chamber was given power to approve the nomination of a cabinet head. For obvious reasons the drastically altered relationship between the president and congress was unpopular with Goulart; the country also disliked the new system, and hence it was overwhelmingly voted out, both popularly and congressionally, early in 1963. Had Goulart been more subtle and adroit, had he had greater national popularity and a better working relationship with one or more parties in congress, he probably could have restored the presidency to its customary dominance over the legislature. But he lacked those attributes, and hence the jockeying between the two branches continued until Castelo Branco foreclosed it with the power of the military behind him. It stood to reason that the new militarily inspired constitutions of 1967 and 1969 would expand the image and powers of the president.

As noted earlier, provisions in the constitutional amendment approved by the congress in 1978 have diluted presidential authority. This should affect the rule of Geisel's chosen successor, General João Baptista de Figueiredo.

The Structure of the Bureaucracy

The executive branch also includes members of the cabinet (ministers of state). Normally, they are freely appointed and removed by the president. The number and designation of portfolios is changed from time to time; in 1977 it included eighteen posts. The cabinet enjoyed much greater prestige during the brief parliamentary period but, even under presidential government, political circumstances sometimes give it a certain independence from the president. For reasons of political expediency, its members are usually appointed from various parties, which renders coordination more difficult. Most ministries are internally complex, with subcabinets and a variety of councils, institutes, and autonomous agencies attached to them.

Brazil's vast size, in both area and population, and the increasingly broad role of the government in economic and social affairs in recent decades have led to great problems of public administration and to the development of a huge civil service. Although it functions more effectively than in most Spanish American states, in some respects the Brazilian administrative mechanism is haphazard, illogical, and cumbersome. The whole federal civil service, greatly padded, is estimated to include half a million persons.

The several ministries and the multitude of independent or semiindependent agencies naturally differ greatly in degree of efficiency. At the top level, the ministry of foreign affairs has achieved an enviable reputation for excellence, continuity, and isolation from politics, and several of the subordinate agencies are respected far beyond the borders of the country.

The Legislative Structures

Brazil's legislative branch has always been bicameral. Given the vast size and complexity of the country, a unicameral legislature would be quite out of the question. Congress—again, with the qualification "normally"—is generally a more effective part of the governmental process than in most Spanish American countries.

Castelo Branco and Costa e Silva treated many constitutional provisions quite cavalierly, and after the military takeover congress did not function as freely as it had, although in some ways it was ostensibly given more power. As established in the 1946 constitution, congress consisted of the senate and the chamber of deputies. The senate was composed of three senators from each state and the Federal District, a total of sixty-nine members. The chamber of deputies was chosen on a population basis, but with certain qualifications which resulted in the intentional underrepresentation of the more populous states. The 1962 elections put 409 members in the lower chamber; state representation ranged from as few as 7 members in four of the states to as many as 59 from São Paulo. Deputies were elected for four-year terms by proportional representation. The constitution of 1967, by increasing the population base for each deputy to 300,000, reduced the size of that chamber; populous states were still penalized.

Each chamber had a number of legislative committees, filled in proportion to party strengths in the respective houses. In the past, committees played a prominent part in preparing legislation, but their importance in this role later declined. Each chamber chose its own officers, except that the vice-president, by constitutional specification, presided over the senate.

The president, as well as any member or committee of either congressional chamber, could introduce legislation. Indeed, the president became— more formally than in the United States—the chief legislator as well as chief executive.

The balance sheet of the perennial congressional contest with the executive is hard to draw. Before Castelo Branco, Costa e Silva, Geisel, and Garrastazú Médici entered the picture, the legislature held the advantage. It had gradually become more representative of the growing middle classes and of new commercial, industrial, and professional interests in the country. Electoral provisions in the 1946 constitution had considerably protected the legislature from undue presidential interference in the choice of its members. Proportional representation had theoretically made the lower chamber more democratic. But proportional representation was a two-sided coin; the chamber became unduly fragmented, internal party and chamber discipline weak, and a cohesive legislative front and program almost impossible to attain.

Legislative intransigence and confusion contributed to the frustration that led Quadros to resign the presidency. Under the resulting parliamentary system, congress should have achieved a spectacular advantage over the executive, but legislative confusion and impotence continued. Often congress could not even muster a quorum to conduct business. Its abdication of leadership made it the more willing to return to presidential government in 1963. Although, as noted above, congress became more representative, it still failed to speak directly for millions of Brazilians who, because of the continuing literacy requirement for voting, were disfranchised. Growing realization of legislative weakness, even by congress itself, probably facilitated the quasi-constitutional takeover by a military strongman in 1964.

By and large, Brazil has not been as receptive to dictatorial rule as have the majority of Spanish American states. It is true that the first years of the Vargas dictatorship were accepted with remarkably little protest; strongman leadership seemed to fit the exigencies of the time and Vargas seemed a personification of Brazilian national characteristics. As popular discontent became more acute during the Estado Novo, desire for reinstitution of the legislative machinery grew in proportion. That machinery did not measure up to demands on it, however, especially in the 1960s. The swing to exaggerated executive control under Castelo Branco and his military successors was not entirely satisfactory—the generals lacked Vargas's charm and adroitness, and the ineptness of the legislative machinery became painfully clear to the country. The nadir of the congressional role was reached following Costa e Silva's action on December 13, 1968, when he suspended congress. Congress was not dissolved, he averred, simply "sent on vacation for an undetermined period." Legislation became entirely an executive function. State legislatures, curiously, were allowed to continue.

Congress was again closed in April 1977 by President Geisel, presumably because the MDB was forming what he called a "minority dictatorship" by refusing to pass a government-sponsored judicial reform bill.[4] Although the congress was closed for only ten days, it was time enough for Geisel to make public his "April Package" of electoral reforms ratified earlier.

Judicial Structure

Like the United States and the other Latin American federal states except Venezuela, Brazil has a dual system of courts—federal and state. The Brazilian judiciary, especially the federal supreme court, has generally achieved an enviable reputation as one of the best in Latin America. The federal judiciary is composed of the supreme court, the court of appeals, and specialized military, electoral, and labor courts. The 1946 constitution set the size of the supreme court at eleven, but Castelo Branco's sweeping decrees of October 1965 padded the court with five additional members, giving him a more pliant tribunal. On January 31, 1969, Costa e Silva reduced the number to eleven. Justices are normally presidentially appointed, with senatorial approval, and have life tenure; retirement is compulsory at age seventy and optional after thirty years of service. During normal times, the most important of federal courts is probably the hierarchy of electoral tribunals, which is headed by the superior electoral court and includes regional tribunals in each state and the Federal District as well as local electoral boards and judges. The electoral courts were designed to be independent of executive domination. The military superior court heads the military court structure; congress is empowered to establish lower military tribunals. Jurisdiction of these courts extends over military crimes and military personnel, although it may be extended to civilians. In October 1965 Castelo Branco considerably broadened the functions and jurisdiction of the military courts. Courts of labor justice include the superior labor court, regional labor courts, and boards or judges of conciliation.

Although the attorney general has the approximate stature of a cabinet member, he does not sit with that body; the public ministry is the legal representative of the state. States, too, have their public ministries, roughly parallel in organization and function to that of the federal judicial structures.

[4]Robin L. Anderson, "Brazil's Military Regime under Fire," *Current History,* 74:434 (February 1978), 62.

State and Local Structures

Federal-state relations have often fluctuated. The pendulum has never swung so far as to extinguish the political viability of the states. Obviously, the degree to which a state can withstand federal or military pressures depends on its population, wealth, and traditions. The same factors condition its internal organization, operation, and general effectiveness. Brazil's larger and stronger states are generally protected by tradition from federal interference with their boundaries, their internal structure, and, to a degree, their politics. The weaker states have no such protection and at times have had border areas carved off as national territories, had them reincorporated into their own jurisdictions, been demoted *in toto* to territorial status, or returned to the dignity of statehood. Even the smallest and weakest states in the United States enjoy much more immunity from such federal interference than their opposite numbers in Brazil. Although the number has varied from time to time, Brazil now has twenty-two states, four territories, and the Federal District of Brasília.

Two circumstances in particular intensify, often abrasively, the relations between federal and state governments. One is the disparity in relative resources available respectively to the national government and to all but a few state governments; the other is the exercise of the constitutional power of intervention by federal authorities in state affairs.

Variation in income and economic strength is obviously great among states in the United States, but it is even greater among those in Brazil. A few of the wealthier states can develop well-staffed administrations, can undertake extensive public-works programs, and can provide substantial social and economic services for their populations. Other states must rely increasingly on federal financial aid to carry out even rudimentary governmental functions.

The Brazilian municipality has a tradition of self-reliance and independence extending far back into colonial times. It is now often considerably hamstrung by the limited financial resources available to it. The Brazilian *município,* like those in Spanish America, is more than just the urban area; it includes the surrounding rural territory as well, and in some ways resembles a United States county. The boundaries and number of the municipalities are subject to much reshuffling at the hands of state assemblies, often for apparently political reasons. The richer and more populous municipalities are normally fairly well protected from such state interference; smaller, poorer, more remote ones are not.

Just as in the United States, many extraconstitutional relationships between the federal government and municipal authorities and agencies are developing, increasing the direct links between top and bottom levels. Some municipalities maintain the equivalent of lobbyists to further their own interests at the national capital. Despite the efforts of national authorities, at least during periods of civilian control, to encourage and support municipal government, the bottom level of government often remains weak in services, morality, and morale. The actual effectiveness of local government often falls short of its tradition of autonomy and vigor.

The main problem of distribution of political power has involved relations between executive and legislative branches. This has been reflected on national, intermediate, and local levels but, because national agencies have arrogated to themselves the bulk of all authority, the problem is more acute and important on the federal level. In concrete terms the problem has been one of competition between president and congress, or earlier, between emperor and parliament. At lower levels it is governor versus legislature or prefect against local assembly. Although the pendulum has generally swung to favor the various executives, the disparity is by no means normally as great, as consistent, or as unchallenged as it is in the large majority of Spanish American states.

The Development of Party Structures

A growing group of writers—respectable both in numbers and qualifications—refers in recent years to the Brazilian "revolution." Use of the term requires explanation and perhaps justification. (We must necessarily exclude the abnormalities resulting from military takeover from this discussion.) Brazil has not experienced a social revolution in the sense of or to the degree that Mexico, Bolivia, and Cuba have. Furthermore, Brazilians' traditional dislike for extreme solutions would make it improbable that they would seek the violent way out of their problems.

And yet, Brazil *is* undergoing a revolution. It is a revolution that is broadening the political base, eroding the traditional seats of power, partially maturing the country's relatively young parties, realigning political forces, and changing the uncertain, sometimes reluctant, and confused role of the army even in years of military rule as an element in power politics. Because of the complexity and subtleties thus presented, the party system itself plays a lesser part than in certain Spanish American states.

Introduction of free elections in 1945 helped modernize political expression. The electorate, however, remained immature and unsophisticated, and under such circumstances machine politics almost inevitably continued for a time as it had since the beginning of any form of "democratic" expression in the country. Machine politics in the early days of independence, and, indeed, almost throughout the period of the empire, took the simple, rudimentary form of *coronelismo* (local political bossism). It served the interests of the great families, whether Liberals or Conservatives. Soon after mid-century, Conservatives began to divide into extremists and moderates. The parties had no grass roots, however, and politics remained served by unrealistic vehicles. Pedro II's manipulation of the two ostensibly competing parties at least had the advantage of accustoming the country to peaceful rotation of party control.

The first significant change in the party picture came late in the third quarter of the nineteenth century when the "Republican Manifesto" calling for abolition of the empire was issued; this event marked the birth date of the Republican party. Because of the substantive issue of empire versus republic, republicanism was at first as much a movement as a party; but the sponsors of the party quickly realized the advantages of political organization and became adept politicos.

Achievement of the republic naturally brought the Republican party to the forefront. Its mission had seemingly been accomplished, but its leaders were now professional politicians. The old parties, Conservative and Liberal, were too closely associated with the imperial regime to survive its downfall, and a potential party vacuum was avoided by the eagerness of Republican leaders to take over the role of political manipulation.

During first years of the republic, especially in view of the ineptness of the military in politics, parties were in a state of flux. Then dominant political elements in most of the states—*coronelismo* operating on a statewide level, as it were—joined with the most forceful leaders of the Republican party, borrowed its name and guise, and consolidated themselves as state political machines which were known as the Republican party of each respective state. Only a loose entente and no national organization existed among them. This was machine politics operating in a different format, but it was nonetheless realistic, and it contributed greatly to the continuance of strong state rivalries early in the twentieth century. Political oligarchies partially succeeded social oligarchies, although the two tended to overlap.

Vargas brought change; he consistently worked to supplant state loyalties and instrumentalities with national political character and agencies. A generation of backward party development was coming to an end. The partial vacuum caused by disintegration of state parties was temporarily filled in the early 1930s by the dramatic rise of Communists and Integralists. Both groups gained from at least two basic contemporary circumstances: first, Vargas's nationalistic drive, which made more logical any groups that purported to have national organizations and aims, and second, the current economic depression, for which the two extremist parties glibly offered appealing, even if unsound, panaceas. Integralists also profited from the contemporary vogue enjoyed by fascist regimes in Italy and Germany, and Communists from the brilliant leadership provided by Luiz Carlos Prestes and association with Moscow.

But Vargas was first of all a Brazilian. Although at one time or another he flirted with both Communists and Integralists, he rejected both. Immediately after the creation of the Estado Novo, he outlawed all parties, blandly explaining that, although parties were useful for representing differences of opinion, Brazil now had no significant internal differences and hence such groups were unnecessary. In contrast Perón would soon move to establish his own loyal party machinery in neighboring Argentina.

The later party pattern developed hurriedly and almost artificially in 1945 in anticipation of early free elections. They were held on schedule but only after the dramatic ouster of Vargas and the end of the Estado Novo. Two groups crystallized. The Social Democratic party (PSD) captured most of the Vargas machine, and the National Democratic Union (UDN) won the bulk of the anti-Vargas elements. They were parties of expedience; though the PSD was reputed to be rather more conservative, the philosophical differences between them were adventitious rather than inherent. The possibly greater pragmatic conservatism of the PSD is probably explained in part by its inclusion of most of the old social and political oligarchies, which considerably antedated Vargas. The unexpected victory of Dutra gave the PSD the prestige of being the party in power. The PSD is by no means an ideological party. In a vague way it favored centralized administration and tolerated federal intervention in state affairs, but it was primarily a pragmatic party—interested in getting and keeping power.

Much of the voting support of the PDS was rural, but it also had the allegiance of wealthy urban industrialists, bankers, and others who profited from its patronage and its policy of promoting the Brazilian economy.

The UDN initially tended to unite the various anti-Vargas elements and thereby assumed a negative character. The UDN, like the PSD, was oriented primarily toward the upper and middle classes; however, its voting support was concentrated among urbanites. It hence drew somewhat greater support from professional and intellectual sectors than did the PSD. Much more important was its image of opposition first to the personality and then to the memory and mystique of Vargas.

The Brazilian Labor party (Partido Trabalhista Brasileiro, or PTB) dated from 1945. Like the PSD, it could in a sense claim to have been fathered by Vargas; during the closing year of his dictatorship, he had given his blessing to its establishment, probably in order to capitalize on his considerable popularity with organized labor and with the lower classes in general. Always the chameleon, however, Vargas would not identify himself too closely with either party.

The Brazilian Labor party got off to a slower start in 1945 than did either the PSD or the UDN. It was based in considerable part on the amorphous mass of *queremistas,* and neither Vargas nor anyone else undertook to organize them as effectively as Perón organized the *descamisados* in Argentina. The PTB purported to speak for urban labor, but Brazilian labor unions are less politically oriented than those in Argentina or Mexico. As the PTB grew, it became less and less limited to an organized labor base; by 1965 it could no more be described as exclusively a party of organized labor than the British Labor party.

Vargas's more active association with the PTB, beginning in 1948, improved its position. The party thereafter became Vargas's chief instrument for directing the groundswell of support that led to his triumphant return to the presidency.

In early 1978 a rejuvenated version of the PTB—the petebistas—began to take shape. Although all party activity was still banned, the exiled Leonel Brizola was expected to be the party's leader.

Another party that might be called a major group, except for the cloud under which it has lived most of its life, was the Brazilian Communist party (Partido Comunista Brasileiro, or PCB). In 1934 Luiz Carlos Prestes joined the Communist party—perhaps the most important thing ever to happen to the PCB. He had become a living legend from his participation in the *tenente* movement in the early 1920s and his subsequent leadership of the rebel column on its five thousand-mile trek through interior Brazil. He thus brought prestige to the Communist party and, more important, he contributed unparalleled organizing ability.

Aside from the Communist party in Cuba, which has achieved a unique status in the ranks of Latin American communism since Castro has been in power, the Brazilian Communist party was, until the advent of the generals, perhaps the best organized in the New World. The party was undoubtedly active in exploiting agrarian discontent.

Despite the great prestige of Prestes, the early 1960s saw some restiveness within the PCB. Potential differences between pro-Russian and pro-Chinese blocs led to expulsion of a number of PCB members and the formation of a minuscule dissident party.

The Moscow-line PCB and the Peking-line Partido Comunista do Brasil (PC do B) agreed in supporting broad national alliances of the left with the "national bourgeoisie" to "fight imperialism." Under military rule, however, they were still illegal and would likely remain so for some time.

Party Structures under Pseudoconstitutional Military Tutelage

Many factors helped explain the disrepute into which the Brazilian party system had fallen by the time Castelo Branco abolished such organizations in 1965: the multiplicity and irresponsibility of Brazilian parties; the loose attachment of many party leaders to organizations they professed to serve; the general absence of ideological foundations; the prevalence of expediency and self-seeking as keystones of party functioning; and party failure to clarify political issues or to promote political education effectively.

The interaction among parties helped undermine the effectiveness of the party system. The three major parties customarily garnered three-fourths or more of the deputy strength in the federal chamber (a convenient yardstick of strength), even though the PSD and the UDN tended to lose ground while the PTB gained at their expense. One aspect of party maneuvering was that dissatisfied or expelled members of major parties could usually find haven in a minor party, especially if they had considerable personal voter appeal, and thus find a channel for continued political activity. The very fluidity of the system made effective discipline in the major parties almost impossible to achieve, added to the confusion of the voters, and decreased the significance of party membership and leadership because of the ease of transfer from one organization to another. A tightening of the laws governing elections and party organization and functioning would have obviated much of the difficulty, but the Brazilian congress in the early 1960s had not the discipline, will, nor wisdom to take such action.

Castelo Branco abolished political parties in October 1965. Then in December 1965 the dictator established the National Alliance for Renovation party (ARENA) and permitted the creation of an ostensible opposition group, the Brazilian Democratic Movement (MDB). The military regimes following Castelo Branco used ARENA for announcing their choice for candidates and dictated ARENA policy without fear of contradiction. ARENA was formed by Castelo Branco to give a façade of popular support to the military regime while the MDB was formed to lend an appearance of democratic opposition.

The elections on September 3, 1966, demonstrated that opposition was merely a political sham: Packed legislatures in the twelve of Brazil's twenty-two states then choosing governors confirmed ARENA candidates. Again in legislative elections of November 15, 1970, ARENA received 48 percent of the votes and MDB 22 percent (21 percent were cast in blank and 9 percent declared to be void).

The *distensão* policy of Geisel in the early years of his term gave the MDB opportunity to criticize government policies more freely, both in the congress and the press. As a result, the 1974 elections for renewal of state assemblies, the national chamber of deputies, and one-third of the senate reflected the growing support of the MDB. It received 5,470,223 of the 8,032,586 votes cast. Of the twenty-two senatorial seats up for election, it won sixteen and ARENA only six; this gave twenty seats to MDB and forty-six to ARENA in the senate. In the chamber of deputies, MDB won 43 percent of the 364 seats to 57 percent for ARENA.

Consequently, though still holding a majority in both chambers of the congress, ARENA no longer had the two-thirds majority needed for approval of constitutional amendments. Again in 1976 the MDB obtained nearly 46 percent of the popular vote in municipal elections. These victories gave the MDB enough strength to look forward to major wins in the gubernatorial and senatorial races scheduled for 1978.

Again, it should be stressed that although both present parties are artificial creations of the military government, a vote for the MDB is considered a vote against the government.

As early as 1975, when preparations were beginning for the 1978 elections of state governors, a cloud began to form over the relatively free political activity of the opposition party. Several MDB members were arrested for allegedly receiving support from the illegal Brazilian Communist party. It was during this antisubversive campaign that Wladimir Herzog's arrest and reported suicide brought a storm of protest that rocked the Geisel regime and culminated in the removal of the army commander in São Paulo.

In April 1977 President Geisel completely closed the door to any type of opposition, fabricated or otherwise, by changing the "rules of the game" through his so-called "April Package." These laws provided that various elections would be indirect and by electors primarily from the ARENA party; constitutional amendments would require a simple majority rather than a two-thirds majority in congress. He began to use the April decree freely to deprive elected MDB congressmen of their posts and to have their political rights suspended for ten years. The November 1978 congressional race gave the MDB a clear majority of votes despite the government's skillful use of the *lei Falção*. Because of the multitude of governmental reforms enacted in 1977, however, the MDB did not win a majority of seats in either the senate or chamber of deputies.

In the light of such maneuvering by the regime, many observers felt that MDB would boycott the 1979 election of General João Baptista de Figueiredo to the presidency. They were justifiably shocked to learn that the MDB would take part in the 1979 elections for president—and were further dismayed that the candidate would be retired nationalist General Euler Bentes Monteiro. Few observers had thought that the MDB would even participate in the elections.

Although Brazil continues to retain an authoritarian government, many observers feel that the tide is turning and that greater democratic participation cannot be withheld much longer. In early 1979 many of the ARENA party's political leaders began jumping the party ship and defecting to MDB; at the same time the Figueiredo government was trying to find a way of halting the growth of the "monster" the military had created only fourteen years before. The government's dilemma stemmed from the MDB's growing popularity and the realization that MDB would clearly be the victor in elections in 1982.

Seeing the writing on the wall, the Figueiredo government introduced new reform measures in mid-1979 which, if passed by congress, would have the effect of dissolving the two official parties. Many observers both within and outside the MDB saw this move as a means of weakening the opposition while the government took the position that the reforms would help "preserve the present form of government."[5] It would seem that a new party system, al-

---

[5] *Times of Americas,* July 4, 1979, p. 1.

though not necessarily in order to preserve the present form of government, is needed to reflect public opinion better and introduce new social currents, interests, and groups into Brazilian politics. The two artificial parties have thus far failed to fulfill such functions and responsibilities.

Other Political Structures

The more important channel for the expression of organized political interests has been the many pressure groups that have arisen because of the vast extent of the country and the complexity of its society. Even so, many social and economic interests are poorly organized or not organized at all (Brazil is not a nation of joiners), a fact that underscores the unintegrated and evolutionary nature of Brazilian society. In past decades the extended family was the most important and powerful social unit and its influence was almost inevitably projected into politics. Cohesiveness of the extended family has long since begun to break down; the potency of the *compadresco* (the system of godparent-kinship relationship) is not what it used to be. Whether labor union, the Church, a political party, or some other entity can become a sort of substitute *patrão,* at least for political purposes, is still very much an unanswered question.

The most important and effective pressure group is the army. Prior to 1945 the army interfered only occasionally in politics. It played a major part, of course, in bringing the empire to an end and ruled ineptly during the first few years of the republic. The army returned to center stage in the administration of Marshal Hermes da Fonseca; it was one of the most extravagant, corrupt, and bungling presidencies Brazil ever experienced, but Fonseca was more to blame than the army. Some of the *tenentes* of the 1920s were influential in the early years of the Vargas regime. It was the army that ousted Vargas from the presidency in 1945.

The few instances of military interference in politics were without bloodshed, in happy contrast to the gory experience of several Spanish American states. John J. Johnson adduces that "the peaceful nature of the Brazilian people probably helps explain why Brazil has been relatively free from violent political moves by officers while certain of its neighbors have been sub-nations dominated by their own armies."[6]

The period since 1945 has seen much more active participation by the armed forces in politics. The army found a slightly indirect and hence even more effective channel for expressing itself (when consensus could be reached, which was not always easy)—the military club, especially the predominant Clube Militar at Rio. This latter organization, founded as a private social club in 1887, soon demonstrated its political utility: Its resolutions, pronounce-

---

[6]John J. Johnson, *The Military and Society in Latin America* (Stanford, Calif.: Stanford University Press, 1964), p. 178.

ments, and manifestoes could be issued as ostensibly private and unofficial statements, although they were universally recognized by government and public as thinly veiled ultimata which could not be lightly regarded.

Before the military takeover in 1964 various cliques within the officer group contended so vigorously for control of the Rio club's policy-making function that it became a hotbed of military politics, and its collective force was thereby weakened. This difficulty brought the army closer to the ARENA of direct political participation, less "above the battle" than it formerly prided itself on being.

The involvements of Castelo Branco and his successors seem to mean more, rather than less, military influence in political life, but to what end only the military knows—if indeed it does. What appears certain is that they are of one purpose in their opposition to communism regardless of whether they identify with the idealistic castelistas (the greens) or the allegedly more realistic group called the noncastelistas (the yellows) which have comprised the two major factions within the army since Castelo Branco's presidency.

Organized labor has had less direct political influence in Brazil than in many Spanish American countries. It had almost no impact before the time of Vargas. Vargas himself gave with one hand and took away with the other. He sponsored much labor legislation that considerably improved the general lot of the worker, but at the same time the 1937 constitution prohibited strikes and lockouts as "antisocial, harmful to labor and capital, and incompatible with the supreme interests of national production." Vargas tied unions closely to his ministry of labor, and they did not succeed in freeing themselves of such subordination until long after the dictator's ouster.

The PTB attempted to spread its mantle over organized labor, but not without challenge from the Communists. The latter, indeed, were more direct, purposive, and often more successful than the PTB in winning control of labor organizations; of five national labor confederations active in Brazil in the early 1960s, three were under Communist domination. Brazilian labor is not as monolithically organized as labor in Mexico and one or two other Latin American states, which doubtless vitiates its political influence. On the other hand Brazilian working classes found more normal channels for political expression, through the PTB or even the Communist party, than did their counterparts in Argentina after 1955, who had to work in large measure through various peronista parties that operated under regular harassment from the government.

Brazil's approximately three thousand unions have found it difficult during the years since the 1964 military takeover to defend their membership's interests because of repressive measures available to the government, measures that included declaring strikes illegal, intervention of the union headquarters, and the immediate dismissal of labor leaders from their positions. A massive strike in April 1979 by two hundred thousand union workers, including bus drivers, bank and hospital workers, metal workers, and public school teachers demonstrated that a small (perhaps even minuscule) relaxation of labor policies had begun. The most widely known Brazilian labor leader, Luis Inacio da Silva, has publicly supported a single workers association. Lula, as he is known, believes that a single central union would provide better job security to workers and would give workers a united voice for negotiating collective bargaining contracts and the right to strike.

The Roman Catholic church has been a less effective pressure group than would be expected in a predominantly Catholic country. The Church is not as cohesive in Brazil as in Spanish American countries. Also, it has suffered significant competition from some of the religious groups, notably spiritualists and Protestants.

The Brazilian Church, or part of it, has had an entente with the Christian Democratic party, but it has been little more than a sympathetic relationship. Individual clerics have sponsored Catholic labor unions, student associations, and other action groups. More important, the Church has attempted to activate rural syndicates or unions in the Northeast to counteract the Peasant Leagues led by Julião and the Communists. In recent years, the military government has expressed concern about the growing political activism of the clergy, notably Cardinal Aloisio Lorscheider and Archbishop Hélder Cámara.

The heavily padded government bureaucracy serves as an interest and pressure group, if for no other reason than to protect its own padding. Efforts to reform the administrative services, especially those that would reduce personnel or stimulate greater productivity, are consistently, strenuously, and usually successfully resisted. More tightly organized and publicly identified agencies, such as the Superintendency for Development of the Northeast (Superintendência do Desenvolvimento do Nordeste, or Sudene) and Petrobras, sometimes lobby to get generous financial appropriations, salary increases, or approval of desired policies.

Financial, industrial, business, landowner, and professional interests all have their organized groups, some operating at local and state as well as national levels. All try to influence relevant government policies. Some are regulated by law, but the better financed organizations are relatively independent of administrative controls, at least when the military is not in power.

The most dramatic, though not the most effective, of the Brazilian interest groups have been the Peasant Leagues of the northeastern drought region. The Peasant Leagues (Ligas Camponesas) are in large degree the instrument of Socialist lawyer Francisco Julião, a native of Recife. He came from a family of small tenant farmers and proceeded to make a career of serving the legal and political interests of underprivileged peasants in the Northeast. Regarding politics as the channel through which improvement could be achieved, he believed that "there can be no transformation in the living standards of the

Brazilian peasants without a corresponding political changeover" and "there can be no authentic political transformation without the active pressure and participation of the Brazilian peasantry."[7]

As the Peasant Leagues grew and came more and more to resemble the fidelista movement in Cuba, they became enfants terribles in both domestic and international politics. Julião's leagues also attracted competition both from the Catholic-led rural syndicates and Communist-dominated peasant unions. Julião was reputed to be closer to the Chinese than the Russian brand of communism. He was allegedly a Brazilian counterpart of Cuba's Castro, China's Mao, and Ghana's Nkrumah. The military takeover, of course, cast a cloud over his activities and prospects.

DEVELOPMENTAL PROSPECTS

The impact of Castelo Branco and his successors—which has been much greater than that of Vargas—may be of sufficient depth and significance ultimately to merit an entire volume in Brazilian politics with their occupation of the presidency. Parties certainly will not emerge from the military interlude with the same dimensions they had previously, even if the artificial ARENA and Brazilian Democratic Movement do not continue. Laws governing organization and operation could do much to place parties on a more rational basis. Since 1945 the parties have attempted to perform a function in the total political process that their lack of experience and of acceptance by the political public ill equipped them to undertake. The laws governing party operation could easily be changed; to alter the more subtle but fundamental relationship of parties to the whole political process could be much more difficult.

Although the economic scene in Brazil has been clouded by the country's stormy politics, Brazil's efforts toward economic independence have had some success. Inflation control continues to be a top government priority. Inflation, which had topped 90 percent in 1964 when the military took power, hovered just below 40 percent in 1977 and 1978. The military continues to use tight wage controls, banning of strikes and collective bargaining, and restrictions on installment buying to control inflation.

The discovery of offshore oil deposits in 1974 gave Brazil some hope of freeing itself of dependence on oil imports, but the deposit was not as large as first thought. The new international trading company, Interbras, has taken the limelight in recent months by becoming the second fastest growing corporation in Latin America. This company was founded in 1976 to buy, insure, ship, and deliver Brazilian goods for sale abroad and to import essential materials for Brazilian consumption.

[7]Irving L. Horowitz, *Revolution in Brazil* (New York: Dutton, 1964), p. 21.

The military government can look with pride to the vast improvements in communication networks; the system of new roads, especially the three thousand-mile highway bridging the Amazon and the Andes; the 12.6 million-kilowatt hydroelectric project on the Paraná river; and Brazil's advanced technology in the field of alcohol-powered engines. Still, there are many unsettled problems to face. The nuclear program adopted between West Germany and Brazil had to be slowed down in early 1979 after the Three-Mile Island accident in the United States brought the dangers of nuclear plants to the Brazilian public's attention. Critics of nuclear energy were quick to point out the hazards in Brazil's nuclear plants, including the absence of an independent "watchdog" agency and allegations of serious construction errors.

The Brazilian working class is concerned with unemployment (it is estimated that 1.3 million new jobs are needed each year to keep up with the population explosion) and the rising cost of living. A 45.4 percent minimum wage increase announced by the government in 1979 was well below the inflation level, which had the inevitable effect of reducing the purchasing power of the cruzeiro. Enormous disparities in the economic structure continue.

The northeast sector of the country, containing a million square miles and almost one-third of Brazil's population, continues to have the greatest concentration of poverty in the entire Latin American continent. More than 33 million adult Brazilians are classified either as "underemployed" or as having no visible livelihood—they cannot be considered unemployed since they did not have jobs to lose.

Political and business leaders who supported the military takeover in 1964 are beginning to express concern that the government's "economic miracle" was achieved (if indeed it has been) at the expense of the low-wage earners and that antiinflationary policies have cut into industrial growth. Others say that a loosening of credit policies is necessary to get the economy moving again. Still others speak of the importance of less government control of the economy. The issue of human rights has been discussed by many sectors of the polity, including many military leaders who are simultaneously trying to resolve the country's political troubles.

The abolition of the Institutional Act No. 5 in January 1979 and the approval of the amnesty bill in June 1979 were seen as further signs of the liberalization policies of the military regime. Some feel that the prospects for a complete return to democracy and the scrapping of all of the military government's special powers remain within the realm of the possible but only under the leadership of a military president who may be able to sway politicized colleagues to return to the barracks. This is indeed a tall order but perhaps not for the Brazilians, who seem to have a remarkable facility for muddling through.

REFERENCES

AMOROSA LIMA, ALCEN. "Voices of Liberty and Reform in Brazil," Chap. 12 in *Freedom and Reform in Latin America,* ed. by Frederick P. Pike. Notre Dame, Ind.: University of Notre Dame Press, 1959.

ANDERSON, ROBIN L. "Brazil's Military Regime Under Fire." *Current History* 74:424 (February 1978), 61–65.

BAILEY, NORMAN A., and RONALD M. SCHNEIDER. "Brazil's Foreign Policy: A Case Study in Upward Mobility." *Inter-American Economic Affairs* 27:4 (Spring 1974), 3–26.

BAKLANOFF, ERIC N., ed. *New Perspectives of Brazil.* Nashville, Tenn.: Vanderbilt University Press, 1966.

———. *The Shaping of Modern Brazil.* Baton Rouge: Louisiana State University Press, 1969.

BELLO, JOSÉ MARÍA. *A History of Modern Brazil, 1889–1964.* Stanford, Calif.: Stanford University Press, 1966.

BRUNEAU, THOMAS C. "Power and Influence: Analysis of the Church in Latin America and the Case of Brazil." *Latin America Research Review* 8 (Summer 1973), 25–44.

BURNS, E. BRADFORD. *Nationalism in Brazil: A Historical Survey.* New York: Holt, Rinehart & Winston, 1968.

BUSEY, JAMES L. "Brazil's Reputation for Political Stability." *Western Political Quarterly* 18 (December 1965), 866–880.

CRUZ COSTA, JOÃO. *A History of Ideas in Brazil,* trans. by Suzette Macedo. Berkeley and Los Angeles: University of California Press, 1964.

DALAND, ROBERT. *Brazilian Planning.* Chapel Hill: University of North Carolina Press, 1967.

DAVIS, SHELDON H. *Victims of the Miracle: Development and the Indians of Brazil.* New York: Cambridge University Press, 1977.

DEKADT, EMANUEL J. *The Catholic Church and Social Reform in Brazil.* New York: Oxford University Press, 1970.

DELL, EDMUND. "Brazil's Partly United States." *Political Quarterly* 33 (July–September 1962), 282–293.

DULLES, JOHN W. *Unrest in Brazil; Political-Military Crisis, 1955–1964.* Austin: University of Texas Press, 1970.

ELLIS, HOWARD, ed. *The Economy of Brazil.* Berkeley, Calif.: University of California Press, 1969.

ERICKSON, KENNETH P. *The Brazilian Corporative State and Working-Class Politics.* Berkeley, Calif.: University of California Press, 1967.

FLYNN, PETER. *Brazil: A Political Analysis.* Boulder, Colo.: Westview Press, 1978.

FORMAN, SHEPARD. *The Brazilian Peasantry.* New York: Columbia University Press, 1975.

FREE, LLOYD A. *Some Implications of the Political Psychology of Brazilians.* Princeton, N.J.: Princeton University Press, 1961.

FREYRE, GILBERTO. *Brazil: An Interpretation.* New York: Knopf, 1945.

———. "Misconceptions of Brazil." *Foreign Affairs* 40 (April 1962), 453–462.

FURTADO, CELSO. "Brazil: What Kind of Revolution?" *Foreign Affairs* 41 (April 1963), 526–535.

———. *The Economic Growth of Brazil.* Berkeley, Calif.: University of California Press, 1963.

GRAHAM, LAWRENCE S. *Civil Service Reform in Brazil: Principles versus Practice.* Austin: University of Texas Press, 1968.

HOROWITZ, IRVING L. *Revolution in Brazil: Politics and Society in a Developing Nation.* New York: Dutton, 1964.

IANNI, OCTAVIO. *Crisis in Brazil.* New York: Columbia University Press, 1968.

JAGUARIBE, HELIO. *Economic and Political Development: A Theoretical Approach and a Brazilian Case Study.* Cambridge, Mass.: Harvard University Press, 1968.

JOHNSON, JOHN J. *Political Change in Latin America: The Emergence of the Middle Sectors,* Chap. 8. Stanford, Calif.: Stanford University Press, 1958.

KEITH, HENRY, and ROBERT HAYES, eds. *Perspectives on Armed Politics in Brazil.* Tempe: Arizona State University, Latin American Studies, 1976.

LEFF, NATHANIEL H. *Economic Policy-Making and Development in Brazil, 1947–1964.* New York: John Wiley, 1968.

NICHOLS, WILLIAM H., and RUY MILLER PAIVA. *Ninety-Nine Fazendas: The Structure and Productivity of Brazilian Agriculture, 1963.* Nashville: Graduate Center for Latin American Studies, Vanderbilt University, 1966.

POPPINO, ROLLIE E. *Brazil: The Land and the People.* 2nd ed. New York: Oxford University Press, 1968,

QUARTIM, JOÃO. *Dictatorship and Armed Struggle in Brazil,* trans. by David Fernbach. New York: Monthly Review Press, 1972.

RAINE, PHILIP. *Brazil, Awakening Giant.* Washington, D.C.: Public Affairs Press, 1974.

ROETT, RIORDAN. *Brazil: Politics in a Patrimonial Society.* Rev. ed. New York: Holt, Rinehart & Winston, 1978.

———, ed. *Brazil in the 1970s.* Washington, D.C.: American Enterprise Institute for Foreign Policy Research, 1976.

ROWE, JAMES W. "Revolution or Counterrevolution in Brazil." *American Universities Field Staff Reports* (East Coast South America) 11 (June 1964), 649–665.

SCHMITTER, PHILIPPE C. *Interest Conflict and Political Change in Brazil.* Stanford, Calif.: Stanford University Press, 1971.

SCHNEIDER, RONALD M. *The Political System of Brazil: Emergence of a "Modernizing" Authoritarian Regime, 1964–1979.* New York: Columbia University Press, 1971.

———. *Brazil, Foreign Policy of a Future World Power.* Boulder, Colo.: Westview Press, 1976.

SIEGEL, GILBERT B. *The Vicissitudes of Governmental Reform in Brazil: A Study of the DASP.* Washington, D.C.: University Press of America, 1978.

SKIDMORE, THOMAS E. *Politics in Brazil, 1930–1964: An Experiment in Democracy.* New York: Oxford University Press, 1967.

SMITH, T. LYNN. *Brazil: People and Institutions,* Chap. 21. Baton Rouge: Louisiana State University Press, 1963.

STEPAN, ALFRED. *The Military in Politics: Changing Patterns in Brazil.* Princeton, N.J.: Princeton University Press, 1971.

———. *Authoritarian Brazil: Origins, Policies and Future.* New Haven: Yale University Press, 1973.

SYVRUD, DONALD. *Foundations of Brazilian Economic Growth.* Stanford, Calif.: Hoover Institution, 1974.

WAGLEY, CHARLES. *An Introduction to Brazil.* Rev. ed. New York: Columbia University Press, 1971.

WEFFORT, FRANCISCO C. "State and Mass in Brazil." *Studies in Comparative International Development* 2:12 (1966), 187–196.

WIRTH, JOHN D. *The Politics of Brazilian Development: 1930–1954.* Stanford, Calif.: Stanford University Press, 1970.

YOUNG, JORDON M. *The Brazilian Revolution of 1930 and the Aftermath.* New Brunswick, N.J.: Rutgers University Press, 1967.

———. "Some Permanent Political Characteristics of Contemporary Brazil." *Journal of Inter-American Studies* 6 (July 1964), 287–301.

14

ARGENTINA
The Politics of Alienation

POLITICAL CULTURE AND ENVIRONMENT

Argentina, a proud and progressive South American state, was traditionally regarded as the foremost of the score of Latin American republics, and for good reason. Its primacy was not in area (Brazil is more than three times as large) or population (1977 estimates indicated that Brazil exceeded it by more than 87 million and Mexico by over 35 million people) but rather in long-range political stability and advancement, cultural and economic development, and general prestige. Many consider Brazil to have a greater potential, but Argentina has tenaciously claimed leadership.

Effective Argentina is a well-defined and vastly favored area which comprises the great fan-shaped region forming the hinterland for Buenos Aires and known as the pampas. Through much of the colonial and early independent periods the pampas were a little-exploited, unimportant area, despite early recognition of Buenos Aires's great potential value as a port. Around the middle of the nineteenth century, industrial Europe began to grow rapidly, requiring more food, to the consequent advantage of the pampas, Argentina's natural granary. This area's importance was intensified later in the century with the development of the beef industry in the same broad area.

Since the middle of the nineteenth century, then, the pampas have progressively gained importance in Argentina. This is especially true of Buenos Aires province, which overwhelms Argentina far more than any single state dominates the United States. The city of Buenos Aires dominates the province.

Other major geographic portions of the country include (1) the north, divided broadly between Mesopotamia (the area between the Paraná and Uruguay rivers) and the Argentine Chaco, (2) the Andean region, including the piedmont, and (3) Patagonia, the vast cone-shaped area of dry and wind-swept plateaus stretching southward toward Antarctica which is important for sheep raising but for little else.

Argentina has traditionally been known as a "white" country. The proportion of Indians now stands considerably below 1 percent, and the number of blacks and others of non-European descent is negligible. An important factor in the progressive "whitening" of Argentina was the large-scale immigration from Europe in the late nineteenth and early twentieth centuries, after the successful conclusion of Argentina's Indian Wars in the 1870s had opened up large areas to settlement and agricultural exploitation, with significant social, economic, and political consequences. Hundreds of thousands of Italians and Spaniards and smaller numbers of many other nationalities poured into the country. Argentina probably has a larger percentage of persons of foreign birth or with recent foreign ancestry than any other country in the Western Hemisphere.

More significant than the country's ethnic pattern is its social organization. By the 1560s interior cities such as Tucumán, Córdoba, and San Juan became important in their own right. In the sixteenth and seventeenth centuries immigration to Argentina was from the northwest, especially Lima, from an area and at a time in which Spanish control was firmly cemented. Buenos Aires was not then a port of legal entry, and smuggling quickly developed. The interior cities were of far greater importance than Buenos Aires in the early generations, and they grudgingly yielded that primacy to Buenos Aires after it became the viceregal capital in 1776. The psychological, economic, and political disparity that consequently developed between the provinces and Buenos Aires explains in large measure the inland conservatism—even the psychological feudalism or pathological backwardness—which, in contrast to Buenos Aires's political sophistication, accounts for the differences that had developed by the nineteenth and twentieth centuries. Thus arose "the two Argentinas," the hinterland or the provinces and the metropolis of Buenos Aires. The interior has been subtly walled off from access to the outside world while Buenos Aires profited fully from such access.

After creation of the viceroyalty, the port of Buenos Aires was legally opened to trade with Spain, which at once gave a fillip to the city. British occupation of Buenos Aires in 1806 brought further opportunity for freer trade because of the heavy commercial expansion, and on May 25, 1810 (since celebrated as independence day), a *cabildo abierto* (roughly translated as a town meeting) established a governing junta of nine creoles, ostensibly ruling the colony in the name of King Ferdinand VII but in effect governing independently. The subsequent political history of Argentina can be conveniently divided into seven periods: (1) bickering and near-chaos, 1810–1829; (2) the "era of Rosas," 1829–1852; (3) the decades of national maturation, 1852–1916; (4) Radical party control, 1916–1930; (5) domination by the oligarchy, 1930–1943; (6) the "era of Perón," 1943–1955; and (7) the post-Perón years, 1955 to the present.

The early nineteenth century was a time of confusion. Creoles (persons of full Spanish blood born in the Americas) in Buenos Aires—the *porteños*—sought to establish their hegemony over the whole country; the provinces resisted. Two so-called parties soon began to form—the Unitarians, based in the capital city and favoring a centralized government, and the Federalists, advocating a more decentralized organization, which in effect meant a loose alliance of provincial *caudillos.*

The principal figure to emerge from the confusion of the second decade of the century was the great military leader, General José de San Martín, but he stubbornly refused to become embroiled in the civil strife that centered on Buenos Aires.

The Agents of Development

Anarchy existed for two years after 1827. Then a figure destined to dominate the country for more than two decades came onto the political stage, Juan Manuel de Rosas. Rosas was the archetype of Latin American *caudillos.* He was heavy-handed, xenophobic, charismatic, opportunistic. Although Rosas came from a prominent family, his formative education was that of a gaucho on the plains.

After some field campaigns on behalf of the Federalists, Rosas was named governor of Buenos Aires province in 1829 at the age of thirty-six. Ostensibly he was a Federalist, but his rule was purely personal, and he exercised his influence beyond his own province through a loose alliance of regional *caudillos* whom he clearly dominated in personality and forcefulness. From the beginning of his reign, he mercilessly harried the Unitarians of Buenos Aires. He used, probably instinctively, many of the propaganda techniques of a twentieth-century dictator, such as the reiteration of slogans, the near compulsory display of his picture (even in churches), the imputation of all sorts of crimes to his opponents, the stimulation of laudatory processions, and the promotion of a partly synthetic but highly political adulation.

Finally, other *caudillos* rose against him and decisively defeated him early in 1852. An era had ended. It is not simple to assess Rosas's political balance sheet. The debits are numerous, obvious, and weighty, but certain credits are there as well. Despite Rosas's theoretical adherence to federalism, he ruled Argentina with more of an iron hand than any Unitarian had ever aspired to impose. His tight control probably prevented the divisive tendencies which had already resulted in the separation of Uruguay and Paraguay from the former viceroyalty of La Plata and might well have led to the secession of additional regions. He can probably also be credited with stimulating a degree of nascent nationalism, part of it a negative reaction to him, which laid a foundation for a solid nationalistic development in the decades to follow. Beyond that, his political record is inscribed principally in red ink. He, along with Perón, another strongman, left as great an impression on Argentine politics as anyone in the country's history.

The withdrawal of Rosas left a political and constitutional vacuum. Late in 1852 a constituent assembly met at Santa Fe and proceeded to draft a new constitution, one of America's most notable basic laws. It was a very practical document, which accounts in considerable measure for its long life. It drew heavily on the United States Constitution.

For several years the province of Buenos Aires, or essentially the city, petulantly remained aloof from the new government, but in 1859–1860 political compromise produced several constitutional amendments that gave more favorable treatment to Buenos Aires. The national capital was soon thereafter returned to the port city. But the question of where the capital would be located was not yet permanently solved.

Bartolomé Mitre (1862–1868) was followed for six years by one of the greatest figures Argentina has produced, Domingo Faustino Sarmiento, "the schoolmaster-president." Cultural and economic progress continued, and the habit of following constitutional political processes became more deeply rooted. At the end of the 1870s, Colonel Julio A. Roca led a successful campaign against obstreperous Indian tribes in the south. The aborigines were nearly wiped out, and vast new areas of good agricultural land were opened for exploitation, not by homesteading as had been done in the United States a few years earlier but rather by grants to already big *estancieros.* The economic, social, and political consequences of these grants to large landholders were subtle but considerable: The *oligarquía* became entrenched as the dominant group in Argentine life and continued so, even politically, until 1916.

Roca demonstrated the political advantage of a spectacularly successful military campaign by riding it into the presidency in 1880. Nor was it without considerable political effect that Roca successfully organized and long operated one of the first "machines" known in Argentine politics. One of his early accomplishments as president was the final settlement, at least formally, of the long-standing capital question. He federalized the city of Buenos Aires and made it directly subordinate to the national government, somewhat as the United States had done with the District of Columbia.

In the meantime new political forces were emerging. The periodicity that frequently marks Latin American politics was again illustrated. The exit of Rosas and the advent of constitutionalism in 1852–1853 had ushered in a new political generation, but by the late 1880s it was giving way to yet another. The long period of peace and prosperity had stimulated European immigration, especially in the 1880s and 1890s. Buenos Aires in particular grew rapidly. Many immigrants arrived with some capital and a reasonably good education; almost all arrived with no disposition to immerse themselves in the traditional political rivalries of Argentine public life. Furthermore, the tightly knit socio-economic oligarchy, now more powerful and prestigious than ever as a result of the Indian wars and the consequent distribution of lands, was unwilling to accept the newcomers. The *estancieros* became natural allies of the wealthy *porteño* families. Most of the new immigration became an element that was politically unattached but potentially receptive to political organization and direction. The capital had traditionally been more sympathetic to political and social ideas and stimuli from abroad—from France, England, the United States. Even though its growing cosmopolitan population afforded room for a degree of aristocratic conservatism, Buenos Aires contained far more ferment than the interior.

The primary leadership of the new current came from a middle-aged, middle-class lawyer of Basque ancestry, Leandro Alem. In 1889 he organized the Civic Union of Youth, which soon became the Radical Civic Union (Unión Cívica Radical, or UCR), although it was popularly referred to simply as the Radical party. As the years passed, the name became a label and not a description. Earlier parties of a sort had characterized Argentine politics, but the period between 1853 and 1890 had been essentially one of personal politics. The unrealistic and personalistic groupings within the oligarchy had no grass roots and could not be thought of as parties in any modern sense. The Radical party provided something new under the Argentine political sun. The UCR reflected the political yearning of the unrepresented potential middle classes. It grew in numbers and assertiveness, even though disrupted by internal feuding. Alem's suicide in 1896 made way for his nephew, the enigmatic Hipólito Irigoyen (or Yrigoyen), to assume leadership of the rising movement. Irigoyen —arrogant, austere, mystical, and thoroughly honest—brooked no competition in exercising control over the Radicals.

In the two decades between 1890 and 1910 the oligarchy continued in power. In 1910 it again elected a president, Roque Sáenz Peña, son of a part-term president of the 1890s. Sáenz Peña, a man of integrity, campaigned on a platform of electoral reform and effective suffrage. Conservatives casually dismissed his pledges as campaign oratory but once elected—not without the customary fraud—Sáenz Peña moved to carry out his campaign promises. The result was the passage, in early 1912 after bitter Conservative opposition, of Law No. 8871, the famous "Sáenz Peña law," which provided for secret and compulsory voting, more effective registration of voters, and minority representation. Sáenz Peña died in August 1914, but by that time the Radicals, protected by the honestly applied law, had already won spectacular municipal and provincial elections.

Irigoyen had no competition for the Radical party nomination in 1916. He narrowly won the election. For the first time in more than sixty years the Argentine ship of state was not being steered by a member of the oligarchy. Irigoyen's election essentially represented a triumph of the middle class in national politics. As a sociopolitical shift of power to a lower level, it had points in common with the similarly significant election of Andrew Jackson almost ninety years earlier in the United States. Argentina had not experienced a social revolution, but its aristocracy was being successfully challenged by more popular segments of the newly enlarged electorate. But Irigoyen was so erratically and unpredictably personalist that his reflection of a trend in Argentine politics must be correspondingly qualified.

His control over the Radical party was complete and highly individualistic. Personally honest, he nonetheless undertook or permitted many interventions in provincial affairs, some of which were doubtless to further his own or his followers' political interests. Without question, a considerable amount of graft occurred behind his back.

In the 1928 elections Irigoyen, by now obviously senile, decided to run for a second term. So considerable was the continuing magic of his name that he was easily reelected. His second term was a dismal failure. Finally, in September 1930 the army took matters into its own hands and pushed over the tottering regime. Irigoyen was kept in detention on the island of Martín García for about a year and a half and died soon after his release.

The short period of Radical party impact was at an end. Basically, the party had missed its opportunity. It had not forged middle-class sentiment into an effective and enduring political weapon; it had not broken the political or economic back of the oligarchy; it had made no appeal or even gesture to the slowly waking proletarian elements in the capital. The failure was in large part due to the shortcomings of its two outstanding leaders: the erratically personalistic and ultimately senile Irigoyen and the dull Marcelo de Alvear. But also it could not withstand the effects of the depression. It did not answer its call to glory, or at least constructiveness.

The military regime quickly won support and alliance from the oligarchy. The army and the aristocracy were hence in control and in the thirteen years following 1930 paved the way for Juan Domingo Perón. Under increasing public pressure, the government held elections for a new full presidential term. The country chose another military man, General Agustín P. Justo.

General Justo and his fellow oligarchs chose as his successor a well-known lawyer and businessman, Roberto M. Ortiz. In a fraudulent election in 1937 the moderate Ortiz easily triumphed. After his death in 1940 he was succeeded by his vice-president, Ramón S. Castillo, a law-school dean and archconservative who had been nominated in 1937 to balance the ticket.

Castillo, in power first as acting and then as constitutional president, made little attempt to conceal his sympathies with the Axis powers in World War II. Late in 1941 Castillo declared a state of siege.

The Perón Mystique

The climax came on June 4, 1943, when the army intervened and in an almost bloodless revolt forced Castillo out, just as it had ousted Irigoyen thirteen years earlier. The people celebrated wildly, though they had no clear idea of what they were celebrating.

The dominant officers were members of the famous "colonels clique" (an army group obviously not composed exclusively of colonels) that for the past dozen years or so had endeavored to bring about a neonationalistic revival of Argentine hegemony internationally and a dominance of military leadership within the country. It was known more formally as the GOU, and had apparently been founded formally in 1941. The initials stood for *Grupo de Oficiales Unidos* (Group of United Officers) but were also conveniently assigned to the words of its motto: Gobierno, Orden, Unidad (Government, Order, Unity). Its appallingly cynical and frank goals became apparent with the publication of a bombastic manifesto its leaders had secretly distributed among Argentine army officers, allegedly some three months before the June 1943 coup. It was soon wryly realized, both at home and abroad, that the secret manifesto was as good a road map of the regime's course as Hitler's *Mein Kampf* had been for his bloody pathway.

A considerable behind-the-scenes power struggle went on within the government, but a bald military dictatorship quickly emerged. Democratic organizations and activity were suppressed, provincial and municipal governments were "intervened," and civilian officials supplanted by military officers. Economic life was subjected to much regimentation, universities purged of liberals, organized labor remodeled to standards of compliance, the press (with a few exceptions) cowed into servility. "Government, Order, Unity" obviously represented rules, not rhetoric.

In the meantime Colonel Juan Domingo Perón, an officer with a vibrant personality and remarkable qualities of leadership, shunted aside potential military rivals. As secretary of labor and welfare, he could maneuver the powerful ranks of organized labor into a solid backing for his ambitions. For nine chaotic days in October 1945, Perón was forced from power by a poorly planned coup. In the meantime, "the colonel's lady," Eva Duarte, was busy. A third-rate bit actress and radio performer, she had become Perón's mistress. Later she would be his wife and, as "la Presidenta," the most powerful woman in Latin American history. Perón was brought back to Buenos Aires ostensibly for medical treatment. Eva rallied organized labor to stage a great mass demonstration for Perón in the Plaza del Mayo. Perón addressed the rally,

President Fárrell embraced him, and the pathetically mismanaged coup promptly collapsed.

Perón was now more solidly than ever in the center of the political picture. Two months later he became the government candidate in presidential elections set for February 1946. By this time the *descamisados* ("the shirtless ones") had become a rudely disciplined but enthusiastic and loyal band of shock troops, ready to be led wherever Perón willed. Perón was proclaimed victor by a virtual landslide.

"The New Argentina," now to be implemented, was built around the grandiose Five-Year Plan, an ambitious scheme to move Argentina forward industrially. The regime quickly took on an elaborate and expensive political-administrative apparatus. It revolved especially around two mechanisms, the Eva Perón Foundation (Fundación Eva Perón) and the Argentine Institute for Promotion of Exchange (Instituto Argentino de Promoción de Intercambio, or IAPI). The former was a gigantic government welfare agency which promptly, ruthlessly, and flamboyantly took over the sedate charitable activities of the women of the *oligarquía*. The Argentine Institute for Promotion of Exchange was an equally grandiose agency designed to "buy cheap" from the Argentine wheat producer and "sell dear" to the hungry foreign consumer. Its profits were intended to finance the costs of industrialization.

This emphasis on the more glamorous industrialization meant that agriculture, long the backbone of the Argentine economy, was allowed to languish. Many farm laborers went to the cities, especially Buenos Aires, where they swelled the ranks of the *descamisados* and existed on the Argentine equivalent of bread and circuses.

Perón's manipulation of the instruments of power in Argentina was shrewd and unscrupulous. His initial reliance was understandably on the army, but he fully realized the danger of relying on it exclusively and quickly began developing the ranks of organized labor as a counterpoise. This necessitated his intervening in the major labor organizations, chief of which was the General Confederation of Workers (Confederación General de Trabajo, or CGT). It became a staunch support of the regime and was repaid by many concessions, though their real economic advantage was substantially reduced by inflation. Probably the greatest gain for the laboring classes (or for the lower classes generally) was their improvement in status, their gain in face. In that respect Argentine history could never be reversed; the change constituted the most basic aspect of the peronista revolution.

A 1949 action which substituted a "new" constitution for that of 1853 paved the way for the presidential election of 1951. The new document was largely a carry-over from the old, but it also included a considerable admixture of Peronist economics, philosophy, and moralizing. The raison d'etre of the new basic law was the laconic statement that the president "is eligible for reelection"; Argentina thus abandoned its long-standing ban on immediate return of the president to office.

Adoption of the new constitution was followed by the consolidation of the Peronista party, one of the very few Latin American political parties officially named for an individual. The presidential campaign of 1951 was frenetic, even though its result was completely predictable. The balloting in November gave Perón about 60 percent of the vote, a larger fraction than he had received in 1946.

Perón's second term in office saw the flowering of *justicialismo,* the dialectic with which he sought to undergird his regime. The expositors of *justicialismo* (freely translated as *social justice*) emphasized four allegedly conflicting social forces—idealism and materialism, individualism and collectivism—and sought to provide a rationale, soon filled with slogans and platitudes, that would reconcile them. Peronista *justicialismo* furnishes the only instance, or at least the only full-blown example, of a Latin American dictatorship's bolstering itself with a consciously devised dialectic.

Eva Perón died of cancer in July 1952. Speculation immediately began (and still continues) regarding her true role in the Perón era, the effect of her death on Perón's political fortunes, and her ultimate place in political history. Without doubt she had been a shrewd political operator. She unquestionably had enormous influence with the *descamisados* and with organized labor. On the other hand, her name was anathema to large parts of the army officer corps, to the oligarchy, and perhaps to the Church. She had provided the regime with glamor and applied her considerable ability to such agencies as the Eva Perón Foundation and the Women's Peronist party (Partido Peronista Feminino).

It cannot be denied that Perón's fortunes progressively deteriorated after Evita's death. Some reorganization in the power structure was of course necessary. Agriculture fell on progressively harder times. Industrialism did not prove the "open sesame" to prosperity that the government had hoped. The army became increasingly disenchanted with the regime. By 1954 the Church and Perón had come to an unpublicized parting of the ways.

Unrest and violence grew in mid-1955, and an army and navy uprising on September 16 forced Perón's resignation three days later. An era was at an end, but political peace was not just around the corner. Perón was allowed to leave Argentina. General Pedro E. Aramburu, as provisional president, led the government until a civilian regime took over in May 1958.

Proper assessment of the epoch of Perón is even yet difficult. The dictator was *muy macho* ("very virile"), heavy-handed to the point of ruthlessness, and dynamic. At the cost of fiscal and economic prudence, he undertook changes in Argentine life that shook the country profoundly. Perhaps the most significant contribution of the years of Perón (1943–1955) was the political consciousness and articulateness he gave to the lower classes. Even the Radicals had had little awareness of the masses; the oligarchy was of course blind to them. Perón, for reasons of expediency, employed his considerable charisma to awake them, raise their status, and weld them into an effective political force. For better or worse, from Perón's time on the lower classes, still conveniently labeled the *descamisados,* had to be reckoned with.

Perón, even from exile across the Atlantic, continued to wield great political influence. Although the Peronista party was banned, in more than one post-Perón election large numbers of blank ballots were cast, probably the response of a disciplined group of followers to his directives from Spain that loyal peronistas should register a protest in such fashion. A subtle but important question was raised: Did Perón remain to some extent an absentee directing force in Argentine politics, or was he transmuted into a living legend, becoming simply a symbol under whose name dissident elements within Argentina, to some extent manipulated by labor unions, could rally to express their opposition to successive regimes?

Immobilism and Stagnation

President Aramburu followed a hard anti-Perón line. In 1956 the constitution of 1853 was restored. The government's announcement that elections would be held in 1957 was immediately a catalyst for party activity. The Radical party had been poorly knit since the days of Irigoyen and Alvear, and the prospect of resuming power was more than its feeble cohesion could stand. By July 1957 it had split into the Intransigent Radical party (Unión Cívica Radical Intransigente, or UCRI) and the People's Radical party (Unión Cívica Radical del Pueblo, or UCRP). In an election for a constituent assembly, the UCRP led by a comfortable plurality, although the peculiarities of the electoral system gave the Intransigent Radicals slightly more representation in the assembly. The number of blank ballots substantially and ominously exceeded those for any single party.

The election of February 23, 1958, saw Arturo Frondizi, UCRI presidential candidate, win easily; he was said to be beholden to the Peronistas, whose support he had cultivated. Frondizi's partial term in office was a record of crisis piled upon crisis. One of them, politically fatal for Frondizi, was brought on by his decision to allow Peronista candidates on the ballot in the provincial and congressional elections scheduled for mid-March 1962. Peronista candidates won handsomely. The military then moved quickly and on March 29 forced Frondizi from office. José María Guido, president of the senate, became president and held the office for a little over a troubled year at the sufferance of the army. The March elections were annulled, the congress was recessed, parties were dissolved, and provincial governments were replaced.

New presidential elections were held in early July. Under army pressure, the government refused to permit Peronista candidates on the ballot. The election gave Dr. Arturo Illia (UCRP) 169 electoral votes, a strong plurality but 70 votes short of the majority needed. The electoral college, however, confirmed Illia on July 31 by a comfortable margin. Because of the adoption of a new system of proportional representation, the new chamber of deputies included representatives of twenty-five political parties instead of the four groups that had previously had membership.

With the choice of a civilian as president in a reasonably democratic election (though Peronistas were still excluded from direct participation), Argentina breathed a collective sigh of relief and hoped to settle down to a period of relative calm and stability. Analysts were uncertain about the significance of the considerably smaller number of blank ballots in the 1963 election (only 1,827,464); the hopeful interpretation was that Peronista impact had declined sharply. Illia's administration was a moderate one, quite lacking in flamboyance. Both the army and organized labor remained enmeshed in politics.

Peronists ran congressional candidates in March 1965 under the label of the Popular Union party (Unión Popular, or UP) (the supreme court had partially barred the neo-Peronist Justicialist party from participation). Peronista candidates won fifty-two seats as deputies when congress convened in May. Peronists, now the second-largest political bloc, claimed that the congressional elections must be interpreted as a clear mandate for the return of Perón.

Perón remained in exile, but in the latter part of 1965 his second wife, Isabel (Isabelita), did return to Buenos Aires and immediately became the focus of speculation and political intrigue. President Illia's downfall in 1966 was brought about not only by the resurgence of peronismo but also by a break between military and the civilian government. It was no surprise, then, when a military ax fell on Illia's regime on June 28, 1966. An army coup led by General Juan Carlos Onganía ousted him, removed all governors, dissolved congress, provincial legislatures, and all political parties, and dismissed the supreme court.

Onganía became provisional president on June 29, 1966. He began ruling dynamically, but he immediately struck sparks. Despite an outward appearance of unity, the military was divided. Onganía had to walk a tightrope between the liberals, who wanted a return to an economic policy of austerity and an end to military rule once the economy was back in order and the more conservative nationalists, who were also for reorganizing the economy but were not inclined to return the government to civilian rule quite so readily.

By 1968 Onganía's austerity program had begun to show some results: Exchange reserves were at their highest level in twenty years and inflation had dropped from over 40 percent in 1966 to less than 5 percent in 1968. Onganía had made some progress in slowing down price increases and opening up the mining industry to foreign as well as domestic capital. His problems began when the liberal faction of the military, under the direction of General Alejandro Lanusse, thought it time to loosen the reins and return to democracy. Onganía responded to their request by relieving Lanusse of his command. He stated that there would be no elections or return to "politics as usual" for perhaps ten years.

In May 1969 students and police clashed over the Onganía regime's decision to deprive universities of their traditional autonomy. Labor workers joined in antigovernment riots throughout Argentina. Urban terrorism began to grip the country with the assassination in 1969 of Augusto Vandor, a prominent labor leader and the kidnapping in early 1970 of ex-President Pedro Aramburu; Aramburu was killed, presumably by his abductors. Divisions among the military and a number of shifts in control followed. General Lanusse assumed the presidency in March 1971.

The Peronist Revival

Upon taking office, General Lanusse claimed his main concern was the "full reestablishment of democratic institutions in a climate of liberty, progress and justice." He also pledged that elections would be held in March 1973.

In November 1972 the seventy-seven-year-old Juan Perón returned to Buenos Aires from his exile in Madrid to be nominated as the Justicialist Front's candidate for president. The Lanusse government had made it clear, however, that Perón was not eligible to run as a candidate in the 1973 elections. After trying without success to gather enough support to challenge the Lanusse decision, Perón declined the nomination and returned to Madrid in December 1972. Many Argentines seemed disappointed that the man who returned from Madrid was not the charismatic "man on horseback" that they remembered or had heard about from their parents and grandparents. They felt that the spark was gone; they saw only a tired old man. The Justicialist Front subsequently nominated Héctor Cámpora as its candidate for president.

The country faced still other problems at this time. The continuing wave of violence that erupted during the latter part of the Onganía regime continued rampant. The Lanusse government imposed a state of siege until after the 1973 election. The government also barred Perón from returning to Argentina until after the elections and began legal action against him for his remark that "if he were fifty years younger, he would be in Argentina throwing bombs and taking justice into his own hands."[1]

Héctor Cámpora's decisive victory on March 11, 1973 shocked almost everyone, especially the Lanusse government: It was so sure that none of the nine contenders would receive a majority that a runoff had been scheduled. On May 25, 1973, Cámpora became the first civilian president in Argen-

[1] *Times of the Americas,* February 21, 1973, p. 1.

tina since 1966. Many Argentines felt that once Cámpora assumed office, much of the guerrilla activity would cease. Instead, terrorist attacks intensified.

In June Cámpora brought Juan Perón back to Argentina to help restore order to the divided Peronist movement. His arrival at Ezeiza Airport caused still more disorder.

The following night Perón went on national television, proclaiming that, "We have a revolution to carry out, and to succeed it must be peaceful." Perón then went into seclusion for twenty-three days in what he described as a state of "difficulty and introspection."

On July 13, 1973, President Cámpora and Vice-President Lima resigned so that Perón might be duly elected. By this time business and labor groups and even the military were united in their belief that it was time for Perón to return to restore peace in the country. The Argentine congress named Raúl Lastiri, president of the chamber of deputies, interim president and called for new elections.

The Peronist convention met on August 4 and named Perón's wife, Isabel Martínez de Perón, as its vice-presidential candidate. Following the nomination, most of the campaigning was relegated to Isabel because of Perón's poor health.

On September 23, 1973, the eighteenth anniversary of the day of his overthrow, the husband and wife team of Juan and Isabel Perón swept the country with 61.8 percent of the 12,200,000 votes; on October 12, Perón, in full general's attire, took the oath of office in an emotion-filled ceremony at the Casa Rosada.

Perón's third tenure as president of Argentina was plagued with factionalism from within his own Peronist movement and by terrorist attacks and kidnappings. The violence was seen as an effort to scare away foreign capital and to discredit the Perón government, which had vowed to bring terrorism under control. Perón suffered a mild heart attack in November 1973 and Isabel began to take over more and more of his duties. He died on July 1, 1974, at the age of seventy-eight, and his vice-president and widow, Isabel, was inaugurated as president of the Republic.

Isabel Perón's term in office was marked by runaway inflation and hundreds of political kidnappings and assassinations. By December 1, 1975, more than six hundred persons had lost their lives in the terrorist conflict that continued unabated. Inflation, running at about 10 percent per year when she assumed office, increased to well over 200 percent.

While the body of Perón was still lying in state, Peronist factions began to jockey for power. Strife continued throughout Isabel Perón's term, complicated by her policy of favoring the right-wing group over the leftist faction. In September 1975 she took a leave of absence to recover from exhaustion and ill health, delegating presidential powers to Italo Argentino Luder, president of the senate and her constitutional successor. Much to the dismay of many

Argentines both within and outside the Peronist movement, Isabel Perón returned after a five-week leave of absence, stating that she would continue as president and called for solidarity with the armed forces in their battle against subversion.

The political situation continued to deteriorate. In November 1975 the Radical Civic Union (Unión Cívica Radical, or UCR), the major political opposition party, asked for a committee of inquiry to investigate charges of corruption in the administration. President Perón meanwhile tried desperately to retain the slippery reins of power by offering to hold new presidential elections before the end of 1976, a suggestion made earlier in the year by Ricardo Balbín, leader of the Radical party. Her turbulent reign ended on March 24, 1976, when a three-man military junta overthrew and imprisoned her. The junta proclaimed martial law and dismissed congress. On March 26 Lt. General Jorge Rafael Videla of the junta was sworn in as Argentina's thirty-ninth president.

Videlismo

Videla's first priority was to end leftist terrorist activities that had caused more than fourteen hundred deaths. The government was so successful that by the end of 1976 over five thousand persons had been arrested, many others killed, and scores held in what was called "executive detention." General Videla announced at the end of that year that his government was "very close to final victory" over left-wing terrorism.

Videla next began a program to revive the economy, emphasizing free enterprise and encouraging foreign investments. The economic life of Argentine businesspeople, workers, and consumers underwent drastic changes. Unions were brought under military control and workers forbidden to strike —a ban that proved only partially successful. The economic situation did improve but at the cost of a recession in 1978. Still, inflation was running at 170 percent and 1979 workers' wages were at their lowest level of purchasing power since 1970.

The mandate of the junta was scheduled to end in March 1979 as agreed in 1976 when it came to power. At a meeting of the armed forces high command in May 1978, however, it was agreed that the military would stay in power at least through the second three-year stage of the military process. It was also agreed that General Videla would continue as president. The navy agreed for the time being to a new term for Videla on the condition that the junta retain supreme power over policy and key appointments. Videla's success over navy opposition stemmed from a number of factors. Both Videla and Economy Minister Martínez de Hoz enjoyed considerable support domestically and abroad, including Washington. Still others felt that Videla's success rested on his ability to cripple left-wing terrorism. He continued to point out that it was necessary to suppress leftist subversives before power could be transferred.

In March 1978 Videla announced that the armed forces wanted a "dialogue with representative civilians with the aim of working out a political plan to restore democratic rule." But implementation and agreement on details ran into many difficulties. For one thing, Videla's relatively broad view of who should take part in the discussions was narrowed considerably by powerful military leaders who disqualified the Radical and Peronist parties. The disagreement among the military made it impossible for General Videla to make headway toward a return to democratic rule. In his July 1978 farewell address before retiring as commander-in-chief of the army, General Videla stressed to his military colleagues that the final objective of his "process of national reorganization" would be "no other than to restore in due time a democracy that is authentic, strong, stable, and modern."[2] Observers of Argentine politics await the realization of that goal.

GOVERNMENTAL AND POLITICAL STRUCTURES

It is possible that when constitutional norms and civilian control are reestablished in Argentina, it will be along lines similar to those prevailing before the military takeovers. Hence, it seems justifiable and even desirable to deal with the structures and forms that have influenced Argentine political culture and development in the light of situations that prevailed during earlier and more normal times.

Any treatment of Argentine government organization should of course first take into account the federalism and interventionism that have imbued the political culture in which the government operates.

The federal system adopted in 1853 was designed in frank imitation of that in the United States, but the grant of powers made to the Argentine central government was substantially broader. Central authority normally erodes the authority of subdivisions, wherever the country and whatever the system; Argentina and the United States were no exceptions. In the United States the instruments of the erosion were primarily those of financial subsidy and federal control over interstate commerce. In Argentina increased central authority was achieved more baldly by direct federal intervention in the government of provinces, cities, universities, and other entities.

Ironically, both the United States and Argentina use very similar constitutional springboards in dealing with federal-state (or federal-provincial) relations. The United States Constitution says that the federal government "shall

[2]*La Nación,* July 17, 1978, p. 1.

guarantee to every State . . . a republican form of government, and shall protect each of them against invasion, and . . . against domestic violence." In imitation, the Argentine basic law says "The Federal Government may intervene in the territory of a Province in order to guarantee the republican form of government or to repel foreign invasions, and at the request of its constituted authorities, to support or reestablish them, should they have been deposed by sedition or invasion from another Province."

From these almost identical starting points, the provision in the United States constitution has become almost a dead letter; that in the Argentine constitution has been made the basis for more than 200 federal interventions in provincial affairs since 1853. From 1853 to 1860, when the first federal-provincial compromise occurred, 20 interventions took place; in the 70 years between 1860 and the downfall of Irigoyen in 1930, the number jumped to 101; in the 13 years from 1930 until the advent of the GOU, the number was 145; during the dozen years of the military regime the number was high enough to make intervention almost continuous; and after the middle 1960s the administrations of Generals Onganía, Levingston, Lanusse, and Videla continued such actions.

The Executive Structure

In a situation such as exists in Argentina, it is inevitable that the president will become the central figure of politics and government. Obviously, a personalist such as Irigoyen would make himself the pole around which all else revolved, but so, almost equally, did such constitutionalists as Mitre, Sarmiento, and Ortiz. The Argentine president is not a "republican king" as the Mexican chief executive is, but there is no denying his central role. This needs only one important qualification: When a civilian was president, at least in the second and third quarters of the twentieth century, he was likely to find the army breathing down his neck. In 1930, 1943, 1962, 1966, and 1974 this military interposition in the operation of the government went to the length of pushing aside a civilian regime to make way for a military government.

Constitutional provisions governing the presidency were drafted in 1853. While keeping the long tyranny of Rosas in mind, the *constituyentes* at the same time agreed with Alberdi that a strong presidency should be established. As a result they established a limited term (six years), provided for indirect election, prohibited immediate reelection, restricted the presidency and vice-presidency to Catholics, authorized legislative impeachment of the executive, and so forth. (Perón rewrote the constitution in 1949 primarily, of course, to remove the ban on immediate reelection.) In the 1853 constitution (even more so in the 1949 constitution) the president was given a broad range of powers.

In normal times the avenue to the presidency is through long activity in one of the major parties. Argentina's party system has important differences from those of other outstanding Latin American states; the chief difference in selection of a president is that no single person controls a party to the extent that he can assure his own nomination or that of a handpicked friend. In some instances a high appointive or elective government position, such as cabinet member or senator, has served as a stepping stone to a presidential nomination, but no firm political pattern emerged. The nominee is also usually a *porteño*.

The constitution lists many specific presidential powers. They are conventional but broad. They fail, however, to delimit completely the dimensions of the presidential office. The president "has in his charge the general administration of the country" and is responsible "for the execution of the laws of the Nation, being careful not to alter their spirit by exceptions in the regulations." This latter restraint is only a pious hope; few if any presidents have felt conscientiously bound by it.

The executive branch in Argentina is supposedly delimited constitutionally; in effect, it becomes little more than a projection of the presidency. Hence, the personality, background, and inclinations of the individual president are key factors in determining the dimensions of the whole executive branch. Of the twenty-four persons who have occupied the presidency since Irigoyen, fourteen were army officers. Before 1930 Argentina had seemed to be firmly turned along a civilian pathway of political development; since then, civilian presidents have been in a minority and have ruled less than half of the time. The principal dichotomy does indeed seem to be between civilians and military officers in the presidency itself, with the differences projected into almost every other aspect of government. Even with such rulers as General Aramburu, firmly and honorably determined to return the government to civilian control, and perhaps even with General Justo, a military tone cannot help but pervade the administration and politics in general.

At an earlier time this strong military coloration of more than a third of a century might have been written off as simply an unfortunate interlude in the nation's politics. Its continued recurrence, however, would seem to suggest that it reflects the tortured nature of the country's political organization and operation and is much more than a superficial canker.

In this context it can be argued that such political-administrative structures as the cabinet, legislature, judiciary, and provincial and municipal entities play a relatively marginal role vis-à-vis the executive in the overall business of governance.

The Argentine cabinet has formally existed for more than a century, but its effectiveness does not equal its longevity. The 1853 constitution rigidified the cabinet pattern by specifying five ministries, a provision adapted from the French constitution of 1791. An amendment in 1898 increased the number of portfolios to eight but omitted any designations, thus adding flexibility to the organization. Even with the increased number, it became necessary to combine functions in several instances, and the device of adding secretariats within ministries was adopted. The 1949 constitution did not limit the number of portfolios and Perón quickly increased the size of the cabinet to more than twenty. Return to the former constitution again restored the limited number of posts. With the reimposition of military control and suspension of the constitution in 1976, the cabinet was reduced to nine posts.

In the ministry of foreign relations and worship, a significant consequence often results from what was orginally a wholly arbitary combination of the two unrelated responsibilities. Because duties connected with worship (*culto*) are included in the post, in most instances a member of an old, established, staunchly Catholic family is selected as minister. This in turn frequently results in a conservative orientation of foreign policy; when the minister is able and dynamic, as was true of Luis Drago or Carlos Saavedra Lamas, the resulting policy inclination can be of real consequence. The ministry of economy enjoys a great deal of authority in the Videla regime, though the ministry's austerity program came under a great deal of opposition from political parties, labor groups, and the navy.

The cabinet's relation to congress, when the latter exists, is in theory relatively close—cabinet members have the right to attend congressional sessions and to debate (but not to vote); they have the responsibility to provide congress with explanations and information. In practice, however, this close relationship has never developed. Ministers are politically and administratively attached to the president.

The political nature of the cabinet implies a rapid turnover in its composition and a consequent lack of continuity in administration. Various presidents attempted to alleviate such a difficulty by establishing permanent undersecretariats, as in Britain and France, but the device fell short of expectations because of the tendency to appoint to such posts promising young politicos rather than experienced apolitical technicians.

The Argentine civil service is in considerable measure a political spoils system. Unlike Brazil, Argentina has done little to study and scientifically develop the civil service. The situation was especially bad under Perón, when the chief qualification for government service was unquestioning allegiance to the regime.

Legislative and Judicial Structures

The structure of the Argentine congress—when it exists—resembles that of the United States. Before its dissolution in 1976, the congress consisted of a senate and a chamber of deputies. The senate was composed of three senators from each province and the Federal District, for a total of sixty-nine seats.

The "popular" (but not the more powerful) branch, the chamber of deputies, has grown progressively at irregular intervals from an original size of 50 deputies in 1853 to a membership of 243 before the 1976 military takeover. In both houses, members are chosen, of course, as party representatives, and according to a 1972 constitutional amendment, by direct election for renewable four-year terms.

Internal organization and operation of the chambers parallels that found in the United States. There is the same reliance on committees, the same tendency to fritter away the early weeks of a session. Days and hours of meeting are often severely limited, and much of the regular five-month session usually passes before any serious work is accomplished. Filibustering and excessive demands for roll calls are not normal, but the bloc absence of party minorities is a device that at times successfully stymies disliked legislative action and may blackmail the majority into concessions. Disorder in debate is common; violence is not unknown.

Viability of the legislative branch is, of course, directly related to the balance and vigor of the party system. Existence of a de facto one-party system, as in Mexico, will inevitably debilitate the effectiveness of a legislature vis-à-vis an executive, as Argentina bitterly discovered during the regime of Perón and the Peronista party. But all cannot be blamed on the absence of genuine party competition in the legislature. Such a monopoly will almost inevitably be accompanied by distortion in the political process, and this broader and more intangible phenomenon must bear a considerable share of the blame for any existing imbalance. The military junta dissolved both houses of the national congress in March 1976, together with all provincial legislatures and municipal councils.

The judiciary, on the other hand, enjoys considerably greater prestige than the legislature in Argentina, at least in normal times. Only when Perón had supreme court members impeached and removed in order to get a pliant judiciary was that branch of the government reduced to the state of undignified puppetry. Normally, the Argentine judiciary, particularly in its uppermost levels, enjoys a reputation as one of the best in Latin America.

Argentina, like Brazil and Mexico, has a dual court system, with both federal and provincial tribunals. The structure of the judiciary is largely borrowed from the United States; the system of jurisprudence was taken primarily from France, Spain, and Italy, with one exception: In the field of constitutional law Argentina largely relies on precedents and commentaries from the United States. Of course, because of the differences between the Roman, or civil-law, foundation of Argentine jurisprudence and the English common-law basis used in the United States, precedent as such receives far less emphasis in Argentina and other Latin American countries.

As was accomplished in the United States by *Marbury* v. *Madison,* the supreme court in Argentina early assumed the extraconstitutional function of judicial review, the first such court action dating back to 1864. Nonetheless the supreme court has been reluctant to use this power, and the consequent development of judicial review in Argentina has lagged far behind the practice in the United States. Yet, it was action by the Argentine high tribunal in April and May of 1945 in declaring unconstitutional a number of decrees of the military regime that began the executive-judicial breach that culminated two years later in the spectacular impeachment and removal of the entire supreme court.

In the aftermath of the 1976 military takeover, all supreme court and provincial court justices were dismissed, and five high court justices were appointed by the military junta.

Local Structures

In the absence of military rule the powers and operation of provincial legislatures are in general pale reflections of those of the federal congress. Much of the legislative function in the provinces disintegrates into feuding with the respective governors. Only in Buenos Aires province is the legislature even a reasonably effective counterpoise to the governor. The legislature's control over the appropriation of the greater financial resources of that province tends to balance the governor's power. Each province has a popularly elected governor; prior to 1966 they served three- or four-year terms and in most provinces were ineligible for immediate reelection. Onganía appointed provincial executives but he continued to call them governors, not interventors; they served at the pleasure of the president. Under Videla, all leading officials involved in provincial administration are designated by the military junta.

The pattern of municipal governmental organization is reasonably consistent. In most instances the municipality has a gubernatorially appointed intendant and a popularly elected unicameral council. Rivalry and friction between the two agencies are almost inevitable. Councils usually feel professionally obligated to protect what they consider to be true local interests from interference by the intendant or the provincial government behind him.

The lack of adequate financial resources makes many cities almost chronically dependent on provincial or federal government financing for various local services and improvements. This further reduces any feeling of grassroots control or civic self-confidence. With the return of military rule in 1976, the military also intervened in municipal governmental structures.

It is generally agreed that as such formal governmental structures in Argentina lack the pragmatic-instrumental quality associated with more developmentally stable political systems. In them the political process permits relatively uninterrupted performance of governmental functions by civilian personnel. Even the aggregative function of party structures through which political interests are translated into policy alternatives has been lacking in Argentina in the sense that political parties have failed to integrate the diverse interests of the masses and to legitimize public policy.

Party Structures

The most that can be said for any systematization of the Argentine party scene is that the many groups tend to fall into four broad categories: conservative, radical, Peronist, and extreme leftist (such as Socialist and Communist). The multiplication of parties is in itself a sorry commentary on the disintegration that has taken place in the Argentine political environment. In addition the lack of political consensus and of reconciliation of even superficial party differences is symptomatic of the grave deterioration of the political culture. In fact the divisiveness which characterizes the party scene is without a credible rationale; there is no general movement except toward disintegration. (It is of interest that Argentine party names, unlike Mexican ones, seldom contain the word *revolutionary.*) Until the major problems of political divisiveness are removed from the general party network, one can expect a continuing high level of citizen alienation from the political culture.

Diagnosis of the party problem, however tentative, must take into account the importance of the Argentine middle class. Evolution of political parties and general articulation of political opinion in Argentina are probably more closely tied to the fortunes of the middle class than in any other Latin American country.

In broad outline, development of the middle class in Argentina paralleled that in Chile and Uruguay. Perhaps even more than in the other two countries, in Argentina the middle class was based on European immigration. Immigrants became tradespeople, professionals, small entrepreneurs, and tenant farmers. Some of the wealthier Englishmen became *estancieros,* but most of the immigrants contributed to a stable, prosperous, urban-oriented, and ultimately politically hungry middle class. That hunger was increased by the fact that inflation tended to cut into their prosperity and a government of, by, and for the oligarchy was quite unconcerned with their plight.

The frustration of the middle class resulted in the creation of the Radical party, to serve as the political reflection and avenue of the middle class. The Radical party, or UCR, was not Argentina's first party. But in the days of the Unitarians and Federalists, parties had not been divided by genuine political issues of importance; the Radical party was the first that represented the plea of a new socioeconomic group for admission to the body politic. Although its platform was reasonably detailed, it boiled down to a demand for free suffrage and honest elections. In its early years the party was rent by schisms caused by nominating deals and also by the feuds between Leandro Alem, father of the party, and his intransigent nephew, Hipólito Irigoyen. For the thirty-five years after Alem's suicide in 1896, Irigoyen was either the undisputed leader of the party or its dominant personality. Irigoyen's personalism succeeded in driving from the party such influential figures as Juan B. Justo and Lisandro de la Torre, each of whom founded an independent party.

For half a dozen years or more around the turn of the century, the UCR was virtually moribund because of Irigoyen's refusal to accept compromises or alliances. He worked assiduously at rebuilding the party's strength. The election of Roque Sáenz Peña as president in 1910 was a significant event for the UCR because of Sáenz Peña's conviction that electoral reform was necessary. Irigoyen probably had a direct hand in the shaping of the famous Sáenz Peña law of 1912. Honest enforcement of the reform law brought Irigoyen and the Radicals to power in 1916. It was the first time the party had advanced a presidential candidate and only the third time it had run congressional nominees.

The charismatic *caudillo* Irigoyen gave the Radicals a positive though personally tailored program. He favored extending education, improving the lot of the lower classes (though he savagely suppressed a stevedores' strike in 1919), widening public health services, and increasing the government's role in regulating the national economy. He was also, if not xenophobic, at least very nationalistic.

The Radicals by no means brought social revolution to Argentina. The party failed to organize those elements of the economy that might have provided a counterpoise to the highly unified oligarchy; it failed to arrive at an accommodation with the military, which would be its Achilles' heel in 1930; and it failed to achieve a genuine rapprochement with organized labor, which would increasingly follow the Socialists and Communists and later the Peronists. Torn by internal splits of all sorts, the Radicals no longer represented dynamic or economic interests.

Although the UCR as a whole reached its nadir early in 1955, the ouster of Perón gave it a needed shot in the arm. The party split into two factions, the Intransigent Radical party (UCRI) and the People's Radical Party (UCRP).

The UCRI had organizational and strategic advantages not enjoyed by the Popular Radicals. The Intransigents were built almost wholly around the personality of Frondizi, who made the party almost as much a personal vehicle as Irigoyen had done with the UCR early in the century, though Frondizi was not as erratic as his prototype. Hence, the party's program was Frondizi's program. Like Irigoyen, he was inclined to be messianic in his approach to politics, but he was also opportunistic. He was nationalist, anti-imperialist, semi-Marxist.

The UCRP was composed of heterogeneous elements united only by their opposition to Frondizi. Thus they could not easily agree on either plat-form or leader. A negatively organized party found it more difficult to choose candidates, make political deals, and wage an aggressive campaign. Parts of the UCRP were so conservative that they could almost belong to the party of that name, although others inherited the Movement of Intransigence and Renovation (Movimiento de Intransigencia y Renovación, or MIR) liberal or even leftist tradition of a decade earlier and could, except for personal reasons, have made common cause with the UCRI.

By the latter part of 1962, the UCRI, like the UCRP, was becoming badly split. Three well-recognized factions existed. The dominant one soon became that headed by Oscar Alende, former governor of Buenos Aires prov-ince, who would be the UCRI candidate for president in 1963.

The party situation at the time of the 1963 election was legalized confu-sion such as Argentina had seldom if ever known before the provisional Guido regime had decreed, in mid-1962, a new statute of political parties and a law of elections. The statute governing parties attempted both to restrict the major neoperonista parties that had been so active and successful the year before and also to limit the number of parties. The number of legally recognized parties was reduced from sixty-three to twenty-three, though amendments later per-mitted activity by many more. The parties' statute also made a distinction between national and provincial parties and provided that only the former could nominate presidential and vice-presidential candidates. At the time this decree was issued it would have limited nominations to the UCRP, UCRI, Christian Democrats, and Conservatives. Liberalization of the statute by amendment permitted many more parties to become active and ultimately more than one hundred were registered, with thirty-nine of them nominating presidential electors.

As the 1963 elections approached, party activity, maneuvering, and deals were confusion compounded. The UCRP managed to pull itself together—it was generally conceded to have the most widespread and effective grass-roots structure of any Argentine party—but the Intransigents concerned themselves with trying to organize a broad bloc including Peronists, Christian Democrats (PDC), and several smaller parties. The coalition was known as the National and Popular Front (Frente Nacional Popular, or FNP), but the PDC soon withdrew from it and the alliance ended by being composed primarily of Intransigent Radicals and Peronists.

The UCRP tactic of eschewing alliances paid off: The party, which had been third in the election of 1962, now led all others. But its standard-bearer, Arturo Illia (1963–1966), like his predecessor, found it difficult to govern effectively in an atmosphere fraught with bitter party factionalism. The mili-tary stepped in to rule the country for a period of seven years under the leadership of Generals Onganía, Levingston, and Lanusse until 1973 when Perón was permitted to reenter national politics.

The Peronist View of Party Politics

In his political prime, Juan Domingo Perón's attitude toward parties developed slowly. In fact his whole political style continues to intrigue political analysts. Perón bulldozed through a marriage of convenience between collaborationist Radicals and Laboristas under the Single Party of the Revolution (Partido Unico de la Revolución). Objections were made to the name and organization by Perón's own advisers; as a result, after careful planning in the first half of 1949, the Peronista party was formally organized to supplant the Single Party of the Revolution. One day later, under the aegis of Evita Perón, the Peronista Feminino party was born. Next to Mexico's PRI and its predecessors, the Peronista party was undoubtedly Latin America's most monolithic and effectively organized political group.

The Peronista party had many of the characteristics of an elitist fascist party: a dialectic *(justicialismo)*; restricted and screened membership; the requirement of demonstrated loyalty to the leader as inside track to nearly all government positions; and issuance of membership cards. It made use of mass rallies, with the *descamisados* (who were not members of the party) as a ready-made but synthetic source of sheer numbers when the party needed to impress Argentina with the presumed mass support of the regime.

But if the Peronista party did not live, the movement did. Perón had given a political voice and the vote to a new social group, one that was in many ways more cohesive than the middle class. Whether the lower class remained personally attached to Perón, even in the absence of the Peronista party and various neoperonista groups that were usually under a ban, or whether the amorphous peronista masses were simply manipulated by demagogic and partly anonymous politicians exploiting the mystique of an exiled Perón, the Perón-entranced millions still remained a potent force in Argentine politics.

The continued appeal of *peronismo* is perhaps partly due to the deep social cleavages that remain in Argentina and the consequent fact that the "underdogism" reflected by the movement combines a defensive-aggressive approach to politics. The fuzzy dialectic of *justicialismo* seemed to have something for everyone and hence it was easy for Perón in Spain and his agents in Argentina to manipulate his following. The tactical question of greatest importance was whether to accept the system and put on a cloak of at least partial respectability or to maintain an attitude of intransigence and martyrdom and take advantage of continuing confusion and disintegration in Argentine politics in the hope that continued national instability would provide an opportunity to return to power.

Such political strategy did work for Lanusse. Unable to resolve the country's social and economic problems, he called the first general elections since 1965, hoping either to explode the myth of the superman or win his collaboration.

Argentine citizens of all political views participated in the 1973 elections. Lanusse revised the electoral rules to permit full Peronist participation, the introduction of the ballotage (or runoff) system, the replacement of proportional representation with single-member districts requiring a majority vote, and use of direct popular vote for electing the president, vice-president, and provincial governors. As noted in Table 14–1, changes in the electoral rules had little impact on the number of parties represented in the 1973 elections. Thirteen political parties were represented in the chamber of deputies after the election; nine (two more than in 1963) contested the presidential race, in which Héctor Cámpora won the largest victory since Juan Perón's landslide in 1951. Cámpora shortly thereafter resigned the presidency to make way for Perón who, in a special election of September 1973, won an overwhelming victory with his running mate, Isabelita, for vice-president.

TABLE 14–1   Party Representation in the Chamber of Deputies (1973)

Party	Seats
Frente Justicialista de Liberación	145
Unión Cívica Radical	51
Alianza Popular Federalista	20
Alianza Popular Revolucionaria	12
Partido Bloquista	3
Partido Autonomista-Liberal	3
Movimiento Popular Neuquino	2
Partido Demócrata de Mendoza	2
Cruzada Renovadora de San Juan	1
Movimiento Popular Provincial de San Luis	1
Movimiento Popular Salteño	1
Partido Acción Chubutense	1
Partido Provincial de Río Negro	1
Total	243

Source: *La Nación*, April 2, 1973

The political maelstrom worsened during the *caudillo's* short term as president. On July 1, 1974 the seventy-eight-year-old *líder* died of a heart attack and his widow became president of the republic. The administration of both Juan and Isabel Perón did little indeed to restore the military's confidence in constitutional government and political activity. Rampant terrorism plagued the country, and the economy was in a state of sharp decline. In March 1976 the military reimposed its control of the government. Under the Videla administration political activity was curtailed and party activity ultimately banned.

TABLE 14-2   Presidential Election Results (March 1973)

Party	Candidate	Percent of Vote
Frente Justicialista de Liberación	Campora	49.56
Unión Cívica Radical	Balbín	21.29
Alianza Popular Federalista	Manrique	14.90
Alianza Popular Revolucionaria	Alende	7.43
Alianza Republicana Federal	Martínez	2.91
Nueva Fuerza	Chamizo	1.97
Partido Socialista Democrático	Ghioldi	.91
Partido Socialista de los Trabajadores	Coral	.62
Frente de Izquierda Popular	Ramos	.41

Source: *La Nación*, April 2, 1973.

TABLE 14-3   Special Presidential Election Results (September 1973)

Party	Candidate	Percent of Vote
Frente Justicialista de Liberación	Perón	61.86
Unión Cívica Radical	Balbín	24.35
Alianza Popular Federalista	Manrique	12.12
Partido Socialista de los Trabajadores	Coral	1.57

Source: *La Nación*, October 1, 1973.

Speculation has arisen about the formation of a Movement of National Opinion (Movimiento de Opinión Nacional, or MON) intended to facilitate the military's democratization process. It would have the characteristics of a suprapartisan, suprasectoral structure, with the possibility of becoming a true civil-military political party. It is theorized that such a political party would guarantee the institutionalization of military input in any kind of proposed democratic arrangement. There is also speculation that the Argentine military may opt to shape the political future according to the model of development that emerged from the 1964 Brazilian revolution to include the formation of an Argentine political party along the lines of the Brazilian ARENA. It is difficult to predict the outcome of the political transition at this time.

Assessment of the Military Structure

In most Latin American countries that purport to be constitutional republics or in which an out-and-out military regime does not rule, the army may be considered a pressure group, usually the most effective one if sufficiently organized, because it has the weaponry with which to enforce its will.

In Argentina, however, the military must be considered in a different context. In that state the armed services are more than a pressure group—they constitute a vital, and perhaps preeminent, part of the decision-making process in the government, even when not in full power, as they have been since mid-1966. The situation is full of subtleties and is almost impossible to consider diagrammatically, but it is probably accurate to say that in no other comparable Latin American state does the military play so intimate a role in the government.

Ironically, the indecision and counterbalancing divisions that the military charge are so characteristic and self-defeating in the civilian sector are revealed time after time among the military themselves. In part this may be due to the political mindedness of and rivalries within the upper echelons of the officer corps.

Argentina has tried little governmental experimentation. It has never established a monarchy (as did Brazil), attempted parliamentary government (as did Chile), or undertaken a bifurcated executive or collegiate government or "half-and-half" senate (as did Uruguay). It has never legally provided for a one-party state (as did Trujillo's Dominican Republic), or constitutionally established biparty parity (as did Colombia), or even experimented much with *fomento* corporations (as did Chile, Venezuela, and other states). Nor has it constitutionally empedestaled the military (as did Honduras). But Argentina does illustrate extreme involvement of the military in the whole structure and functioning of government. That is perhaps as significant a phenomenon as is to be found in the Argentine government.

The Interest Group Spectrum

Argentina has its full quota of interest groups. If the military were to be considered a pressure group, it would by all odds be the most powerful. But as noted earlier, it is so intimately a part of the fabric of government that it cannot be considered a conventional interest organization. Among true interest groups, organized labor is the most politically minded and effective. Removal of Perón's strong paternalistic hand brought a consequent lessening of discipline and unity within organized labor. The chief post-Perón groupings became the Thirty-Two, the Sixty-Two, and the Nineteen. These blocs of unions of the indicated numbers had respectively a prodemocratic stance, a strongly peronista position, and a Communist orientation. The numbers themselves became inaccurate after a short time but because they were politically familiar they were kept as colloquial labels. The unions have been shamelessly manipulated for political ends, often to the personal advantage of their leaders.

Effectiveness of the Church as an interest group has been lessened by the dichotomy between the traditional conservative segments and the newer and more adaptable portions of both hierarchy and membership, between the literalism of the interior and the liberalism of the capital. This uncertainty in the Church's political stance has weakened the potential impact of the Christian Democratic party. The various branches of Catholic Action have introduced a degree of dynamism into lay Catholic policy, especially since mid-century.

Big business, big industry, and big agriculture are all organized in Argentina and usually operate in a relatively sophisticated fashion. Bankers, manufacturers, wool and beef producers, exporters, and others all have their business associations and chambers and all attempt, as far as they may, to exert political influence. Professional associations of physicians, lawyers, engineers, architects, and others are also well organized and politically active.

DEVELOPMENTAL PROSPECTS

Neither Juan nor Isabel Perón could quell the violent terrorist attacks begun in 1970 with the assassination of former President Aramburu. The military junta that seized power from Isabel Perón in 1976 virtually eliminated the violence which had spread between left-wing and right-wing groups in the Peronist movement, causing more deaths in a single year than in a decade of violence in Northern Ireland.

The junta, however, did not eliminate the right-wing paramilitary terrorists. This group, called the Argentine Anti-Communist Alliance, had close ties with the military and police organizations and used police department credentials to abduct their targets. Right-wing extremists were seldom arrested. It is estimated that in 1979 there were more than thirty-five hundred people in the jails of Argentina for security reasons and several hundred more held without charge.[3]

Although some gains were made in the fight against inflation in 1979, inflation was still running at approximately 170 percent. The Videla government found it increasingly difficult to strike a balance between measures to fight inflation and the risk of a damaging recession. It has been estimated that it could take a decade for workers to regain the purchasing power they had in 1973.

The Peronist movement is still divided, but its strength in the labor unions continues. Union leaders continue to insist that their organizations be returned to the control of their elected officials and that collective bargaining be restored. Without Perón, their attention has turned from *el líder* to more basic issues of wages and employment. The military has made life in the labor

---

[3]The Videla government released a statistical breakdown in July 1979 which stated that 1,723 persons were being detained without charges. See *Times of Americas,* July 18, 1979, p. 13.

unions extremely difficult, and labor is the most serious opposition to the military government. Strikes, although illegal, continue to be called to dramatize the disparity between wages and the rising cost of living. Though the military has made some concessions to avoid widespread discontent, many labor leaders considered subversive have been "detained" or, in some cases, executed by paramilitary groups.

It has been theorized that one reason why the military allowed Juan Perón to return after eighteen years in exile and why it hesitated to return to power in 1976 was its desire to watch the Perón regime spread the seeds of its own destruction, thus putting to rest the myth of Perón.[4] The military now seems reluctant to return Argentina to democratic rule because it might encourage a return to the conditions which brought the military to power in 1976.

The military's process of national reorganization is aimed at national unity based on the revitalization of institutions, but it is not necessarily aimed at the restoration of full partisan activity. To be sure the military does not discount the importance of a republican, representative, and federal form of government. For now *diálogo* (dialogue) and not *apertura política* (political openness) is the name of the political game. But there is a great deal of guessing about how long this will last. Some feel that the government is waiting for the younger generation who have developed under the military's control to become political leaders before restoring democratic rule. Others speculate that the *proyecto nacional* (National Plan) or blueprint for government is flexible enough to permit the military to realize the objectives of its short- and medium-range plans, which cover a time span lasting until 1982 and would lead to cooperation between military and civilians and the transfer of power to elected leaders.[5]

The military government seems reluctant to fix timetables for realizing its broad objectives. On the third anniversary of his coming to power in March 1979, President Videla announced that the military would "stay in power until all the structures of the nation are reorganized and the country achieves political maturity."[6] It seems likely that the process of rebuilding republican institutions will be slow and that military rule may exist indefinitely.

REFERENCES

ALEXANDER, ROBERT. *The Perón Era.* New York: Columbia University Press, 1971.

"Argentina-Chile: Exchange of Diplomatic Notes Concerning the Beagle Channel Arbitration." *International Legal Materials* 17:3 (May 1978), 738–753.

[4]Julio A. Fernández, "Political Immobility in Argentina." *Current History,* 70:413 (February 1976), 87.

[5]Cf. *Hispano Americano,* 121:1844 (September 5, 1977), 39.

[6]*New York Times,* March 25, 1979, Sec. IV, p. 3.

BAILEY, SAMUEL. *Labor, Nationalism and Politics in Argentina.* New Brunswick, N.J.: Rutgers University Press, 1967.

BLANKSTEN, GEORGE I. *Perón's Argentina.* Chicago: University of Chicago Press, 1953.

CIRIA, ALBERTO. *Parties and Power in Modern Argentina (1930–1946),* trans. by Carlos A. Astiz with Mary F. McCarthy. Albany: State University of New York Press, 1974.

DIAZ ALEJANDRO, CARLOS F. *Essays on the Economic History of the Argentine Republic.* New Haven: Yale University Press, 1970.

EASUM, DONALD B. "Justicialismo in Retrospect: Failure of the Peronista Timetable." *Inter-American Economic Affairs* 6:3 Winter 1952, 32–50.

FERNÁNDEZ, JULIO A. "The Nationalism Syndrome in Argentina." *Journal of Inter-American Studies* 8 (October 1966), 551–564.

———. *The Political Elite in Argentina.* New York: New York University Press, 1970.

FALCOFF, MARK, and RONALD DOKART, eds. *Prelude to Perón.* Berkeley: University of California Press, 1975.

FILLOL, TOMAS ROBERTO. *Social Factors in Economic Development; The Argentine Case.* Cambridge: MIT Press, 1961.

FITZGIBBON, RUSSELL H. *Argentina: A Chronology and Factbook.* Dobbs Ferry, N.Y.: Oceana, 1974.

———. "Argentina after Eva Perón." *Yale Review* 42 (Autumn 1952), 32–45.

GERMANI, GINO. *Política y Sociedad en una Epoca de Transición.* Buenos Aires: Paidós, 1962.

INGENIEROS, JOSÉ. *La Evolución de las Ideas Argentinas.* 2nd ed. Buenos Aires: n.p., 1951.

JOHNSON, JOHN J. *Political Change in Latin America: The Emergence of the Middle Sectors,* Chap. 6. Stanford, Calif.: Stanford University Press, 1958.

KENNEDY, JOHN J. *Catholicism, Nationalism, and Democracy in Argentina.* Notre Dame, Ind.: University of Notre Dame Press, 1958.

McGANN, THOMAS F. *Argentina: The Divided Land.* Princeton, N.J.: D. Van Nostrand, 1966.

MALLON, R. D., and J. V. SOURROUILLE. *Economic Policymaking in a Conflict Society: The Argentine Case.* Cambridge, Mass.: Harvard University Press, 1975.

O'DONNELL, GUILLERMO. *Modernization and Bureaucratic-Authoritarianism in Latin American Politics.* Politics of Modernization Series, No. 9. Berkeley: University of California Institute of International Studies, 1973.

OWEN, FRANK. *Perón: His Rise and Fall.* London: Cresset Press, 1957.

PALACIOS, ALFREDO. *Los Partidos Políticos: Su Organización y Funcionamiento.* Buenos Aires: n.p., 1938.

PENDLE, GEORGE. *Argentina.* New York: Gordon Press, 1976.

PERÓN, JUAN D. *The Speeches of Juan Domingo Perón.* New York: Gordon Press, 1973.

POTASH, ROBERT A. *The Army and Politics in Argentina, 1928–1945: Irigoyen to Perón.* Stanford, Calif.: Stanford University Press, 1970.

RANIS, PETER. "Peronismo without Perón, Ten Years after the Fall (1955–65)." *Journal of Inter-American Studies* 8 (January 1966), 112–128.

ROMERO, JOSÉ LUIS. *A History of Argentine Political Thought,* trans. by Thomas F. McGann. Stanford, Calif.: Stanford University Press, 1963.

ROWE, JAMES W. "Argentina: An Election Retrospect." *American Universities Field Staff Report* (East Coast South America) 11 (February 1964), 161–174.

———. "Argentina's Restless Military." *American Universities Field Staff Report* (East Coast South America) 11 (May 1964), 439–463.

SANTOS GOLLÁN, JOSÉ. "Argentine Interregnum." *Foreign Affairs* 35 (October 1956), 84–94.

SCHOULTZ, LARS. "The Socioeconomic Determinants of Popular-Authoritarian Electoral Behavior: The Case of Peronism." *American Political Science Review* 71:4 (December 1977), 1423–1446.

SCOBIE, JAMES R. *Argentina: A City and a Nation.* New York: Oxford University Press, 1964.

SCOTT, ROBERT E. "Argentina's New Constitution: Social Democracy or Social Authoritarianism?" *Western Political Quarterly* 4 (December 1951), 467–576.

SILVERT, KALMAN H. "The Annual Political Cycle in Argentina." *American Universities Field Staff Report* (East Coast South America) 8:6 (December 12, 1961), 1–12.

———. "The Costs of Anti-Nationalism: Argentina." Pp. 347–372 in *Expectant Peoples: Nationalism and Development,* ed. by K. H. Silvert. New York: Random House (Vintage Books), 1963.

SMITH, PETER. *Argentina and the Failure of Democracy: Conflict Among Political Elites, 1904–1955.* Madison: University of Wisconsin, 1974.

———. *The Politics of Beef in Argentina.* New York: Columbia University Press, 1969.

SNOW, PETER. *Political Forces in Argentina.* Boston: Allyn & Bacon, 1971.

WELLHOFER, E. SPENCER. "Peronism in Argentina: The Social Base of the First Regime, 1946–1955." *Journal of Developing Areas* 11:3 (April 1977), 335–356.

WHITAKER, ARTHUR P. *Argentina.* Englewood Cliffs, N.J.: Prentice-Hall, 1964.

———. "The Argentine Paradox." *Annals of the American Academy* 334 (March 1961), 103–112.

———. *Argentine Upheaval: Perón's Fall and the New Regime.* New York: Holt, Rinehart & Winston 1956.

———. *The United States and the Southern Cone: Argentina, Chile, and Uruguay.* Cambridge, Mass.: Harvard University Press, 1976.

WYNIA, GARY W. *Argentina in the Postwar Era.* Albuquerque: University of New Mexico Press, 1978.

15

PARAGUAY

Institutionalized Authoritarianism

POLITICAL CULTURE AND DEVELOPMENT

Writers in the colonial and early independent periods rhapsodized over that portion of Paraguay east of the Paraguay River, or effective Paraguay. They called it idyllic, a paradise, an Eden, an Arcadia, and a land of perpetual spring. In physical terms these characterizations are still largely valid. Even the people have been described as "gentle" and as "anything but warlike and belligerent." Yet it has been Paraguay's lot to suffer some of Latin America's most notorious dictators, to have been a victim of Latin America's most disastrous two wars, and to have been placed at the bottom in four successive surveys of Latin American democratic development over a fifteen-year period.[1]

Effective Paraguay is a plateau of moderate elevation, well watered and fertile, and divided between luxuriant forests and pleasant meadows. The contrast with the immense Chaco (or more strictly speaking, Chaco Boreal, the northern Chaco) across the Paraguay River is extreme. "Nowhere else in the world, perhaps," says George Pendle, an authority on the country, "does a river divide so abruptly two such different lands." Maps of Paraguay designed to show different characteristics of the land are startlingly and oppressively uniform with regard to the large pear-shaped Chaco area, which is

[1]Russell H. Fitzgibbon and Kenneth F. Johnson, "Measurement of Latin American Political Change." *American Political Science Review,* 55 (September 1961), 515–526. Recent surveys in 1965 and 1975, respectively, put Paraguay in next to last position.

characterized almost entirely by plains and scrub forest with almost no significant land use or population.

The population of Paraguay, estimated in 1980 at 3,062,000, is overwhelmingly mestizo. Probably twenty-nine out of every thirty persons are descendants of the original Guaraní inhabitants and the invading Spaniards. The Spanish found the Guaranís so attractive, in both appearance and temperament, that the early, large-scale miscegenation that resulted is now reflected in the considerable uniformity of the general population. European immigration since the close of the Paraguayan War has added a small extraneous element to the population, but it is an element greater in economic and cultural influence that its numbers would indicate.

The population is primarily rural; only about one-third is considered urban. Asunción, the capital, with an estimated metropolitan population of 425,000 in 1972, is the only city of more than 40,000. In most indices of development, Paraguay ranks low among Latin American countries. The political superstructure is built on this foundation.

Political Development

Paraguay's political history has been almost unrelievedly tragic. Independence was won bloodlessly under the leadership of José Gaspar Rodríguez de Francia, who swiftly transformed his regime into one of the most absolute dictatorships ever experienced by a Latin American state. He soon made Paraguay a hermit nation, almost completely isolated—culturally, economically, and politically—from the outside world. The Church, reduced to subservience, was in effect nationalized. Francia's high-handed rule did spare Paraguay from the anarchy so frequently characteristic of the austere years of the fledgling Latin American republics; his determined isolationism compelled the development and diversification of the internal economy and laid the foundations for a rude and rudimentary sense of nationalism.

After a few months of disorder following Francia's death in 1840, another dictator seized power and held onto it for two decades. He was Carlos Antonio López—less cruel and isolationalist than Francia, perhaps equally capricious, and probably more intelligent. In 1845 he appointed his son, Francisco Solano, then nineteen, commander-in-chief of the army, for even at that early date disputes with Rosas and other neighboring rulers led to a disproportionate development of the Paraguayan military.

Francisco Solano López had to wait sixteen years, until his father's death in 1862, to assume political prominence. The megalomaniacal younger López was proud, ambitious, and tyrannical. Told he resembled Napoleon, he promptly began dressing and posturing like him, and perhaps it was from Napoleon that he gained the delusions of conquest and grandeur that precipitated the Paraguayan War (or War of the Triple Alliance). His buildup of his country's army had been so elaborate that for a time he successfully stood off the combined forces of Argentina, Brazil, and Uruguay. The overwhelming strength of the Brazilian and Argentine forces gradually won out, however, and López himself was killed in northern Paraguay in 1870. Paraguay had all but committed suicide; the prewar estimated population of 525,000 had declined to 221,079 by 1871, and of these only 28,746 were men.

Paraguay's recovery was slow and painful. In the six decades following the war of 1864–1870 Paraguay had more than thirty presidents; many were petty dictators, two were assassinated. It underwent three successful and eight unsuccessful revolutions. Its "party" activity would have been ludicrous were it not so pathetic, but it had only one constitution, a basic law adopted in 1870 and continued until 1940. Conservatives and Liberals contested with each other, but force alone determined the occupancy of the presidential palace; not until 1912 was a president elected (Eduardo Schaerer, of German ancestry) who served out his four-year constitutional term.

In 1932 Paraguay was plunged into a major war with Bolivia over the long-disputed Chaco Boreal. Three years and 250,000 casualties later a truce was arranged, and three years after that, in October 1938, a definitive settlement of the boundary controversy gave Paraguay almost nine-tenths of the disputed area. Relatively speaking, the war was not as serious for Paraguay as for Bolivia. Paraguay gained territory, and the major casualties along with the territorial and psychological defeat were Bolivia's. Nonetheless, a conflict of such proportions could not avoid having political consequences for Paraguay.

The chief result of the Chaco War was the revolt of February 1936, which placed Colonel Rafael Franco in power as dictator for a troubled year and a half. Franco's was not the ordinary sort of palace or barracks revolt. He announced in bold terms that he would establish a totalitarian state and that far-reaching social reforms would be undertaken.

The war had intensified the latent nationalism and xenophobia; they were coupled with the vague idealism and socialism produced by the ferment of the times. Franco's movement—it was not yet a party—thus possessed an ideological basis, even though it was not carefully and rationally conceived. Chaotic internal political conditions, added to the potential opposition of Argentine and other foreign interests to such Franquista proposals as distribution of land (partly Argentine-owned) led to the ultimate downfall of the regime.

Within a short time the movement, led by Franco, had become a party, even though most of its leaders were in exile. First called the Franquista party, it later became known as the Febrerista party (from the month in which Franco's revolt had taken place). It was the first political party in Paraguay to have anything resembling an ideological foundation. Its predecessors had included the Liberals and Conservatives; the latter were more commonly known as the National Republicans by the 1930s. The Liberals, who were in power from 1904 to 1936 and again from 1937 to 1940, were liberal only in a vague and academic nineteenth-century fashion. They had neither genuine roots nor identification with the problems of the mass of the Paraguayan people. The National Republicans—later more commonly known as Colorados—were an out-and-out conservative group who opposed, purely and simply, any change. It was not surprising, then, that the unrealistic party approach to the actual political scene which prevailed at the end of the Chaco War should invite the rise of a new party.

But Paraguay was not yet ready for a genuine party reflection of issues and problems. Franco's ouster resulted in assumption of the national presidency by the university president for two troubled years. He was succeeded by a general who gave some promise of a moderate but progressive administration, but he was killed in a plane accident a year after he took office. The next president, General Higinio Morínigo, soon established himself as a dictator and remained in power for eight years, during which Paraguayan history was little more than his lengthened shadow. Morínigo had to contend with roused Febrerista sentiments and ambitions, as well as with a turbulent and undisciplined party situation. Leading Liberals were forced into exile, conservative sentiment became resurgent through the channel of the Colorado party, and rumblings of Communist agitation were occasionally heard.

Morínigo's control assumed an increasingly military cast. In 1943 he was the sole candidate for reelection to the presidency. His position was further strengthened by the war-created opportunity to arrogate additional "emergency" powers to himself, an opportunity of which more than one Latin American dictator of that period availed himself.

Morínigo was finally forced out by a military coup in 1948. In the following year and a half, six changes of government occurred. Upon ousting President Federico Chaves (who had been a "benevolent" dictator for five years) in May 1954, General Alfredo Stroessner quickly became a less benevolent dictator. His ability to hold on probably illustrated the political backwardness of Paraguay.

After years in power, Stroessner seemed to want to give an appearance of mellowing. In elections for a constituent assembly, he permitted four parties to campaign, and the Radical Liberals received more than 20 percent of the vote. The new basic law, effective in 1967, appeared to point toward a more relaxed political process—it established a senate and was relatively permissive with regard to political parties. It also approved *continuismo,* authorizing the immediate reelection of an incumbent president, but stipulated that no person may occupy the presidency for more than five terms. Presidential elections were held February 11, 1968, and the results were not surprising: Stroessner was returned for a third term, winning 70 percent of the vote.

A constitutional convention in March 1977 amended the 1967 constitution to provide for a lifetime presidency; on February 11, 1978, President Stroessner was reelected for a sixth consecutive term. Two presidential candidates from the opposition Liberal and Liberal Radical parties campaigned in this election, albeit in the shadow of the president.

GOVERNMENTAL AND POLITICAL STRUCTURES

As is true in most Latin American states, the Paraguayan governmental structure revolves around the president. But to an almost unique extent, the Paraguayan presidency must be considered in relation to the army. The president and the military are halves of what seems an almost indivisible whole, an analogy that loses only a little of its essential validity when a civilian is chief executive. Civilians, usually *pensadores,* occasionally occupy the presidency, but usually only by sufferance. The customary coloration of the executive branch is militaristic, and there is normally little competition between president and army. It is not, as in Perón's Argentina, a situation in which the dictator and the military engage in a power struggle; nor is it, as in Trujillo's Dominican Republic, one in which a *caudillo* maintains contemptuous and complete control over a military machine; nor, as in Odría's Peru or Rojas Pinilla's Colombia, one in which a military president becomes somewhat detached from the environment which raised him to prominence to develop a partially independent political personality of his own.

The Paraguayan presidency (and hence the Paraguayan government) is archaic. With the possible exception of Haiti under Duvalier, contemporary Paraguay represents the sole surviving classic nineteenth-century dictatorship.

In one respect the 1967 Paraguayan constitution is less realistic than its predecessor about a quarter of a century earlier. The 1940 basic law had dealt with the executive branch of government before turning to the legislative; of some two-hundred-fifty Latin American constitutions it was one of the few to recognize political reality and establish executive priority over the other branches of government. The vast majority of Latin American constitutions, including the new one in Paraguay, gave lip service to the late eighteenth-century concept that representative branches of government should be given formal priority over the executive.

The president is chosen by direct, popular election and is limited to two terms by constitutional prescription. General Stroessner's reelection as president in 1963 (with more than 90 percent of the vote) was achieved through a tortured and specious interpretation of the constitutional restriction. His reelection in 1968 took advantage of the 1967 constitution's tacit authorization of *continuismo.* The 1977 constitutional amendment provided for Stroessner's lifetime presidency. A minimum age of forty and membership in the Catholic church are prescribed as qualifications.

The president is given broad powers, some formal and others substantive, but all stated briefly in the constitution. The main limitations on presidential powers are the thin and flexible ones imposed by tradition. An interesting instance of realism in the definition of presidential powers is the provision that bills submitted by the executive to the congress must be acted upon during the session in progress, and that if they are not thus disposed of, they will become law. In addition the president exercises wide decree authority.

The cabinet is wholly responsible to the president and does not even constitute a common proving ground for future presidential possibilities. A more interesting, though not necessarily more important, agency is the council of state. This quasi-executive body includes the cabinet, the rector of the national university, the archbishop of Asunción, three retired military officers, and others, all chosen on a functional basis. Duties of the council include advising the president on decree laws and other matters, approving nomination of the attorney general, and other functions.

Until 1967 Paraguay was unique in having South America's only unicameral legislature, an innovation of the 1940 constitution. The new constitution reverted to a more conventional organization by reestablishing a senate. Both the senate and the chamber of representatives are chosen on a population basis; they have thirty and sixty members respectively. Members serve five-year terms and are all elected concurrently with the president. If the executive required control over the legislature in addition to that which the general political picture already guarantees—which the executive does not—this concurrence of terms would help to provide it. The actual operation of the congress is perfunctory. From the late 1940s onward, the entire membership of the legislature belonged to the Colorado party.

The 1967 constitution guarantees two-thirds of the legislative seats to the party winning the majority of the seats. Elections in 1978 gave twenty senate seats and forty deputy seats to the Colorados as usual, with the remaining one-third allocated to the Liberal Radical party (Partido Liberal Radical, or PLR) and the Liberal party (Partido Liberal, or PL) in proportion to the votes cast for them.

The organization of the Paraguayan judiciary is among the simplest in Latin America. The supreme court is composed of five members who are appointed by the president with the approval of the senate. Lower levels of the judiciary include courts of appeal, judges of first instance, and justices of the peace. A tribunal of accounts has constitutional authority over problems involving taxation. Operation of the Paraguayan judiciary is, to say the least, undistinguished.

Local government is also uncomplicated. The constitution of 1940 was silent about it, and that of 1967 said relatively little. In practice it is almost wholly dominated by the president and in certain areas strongly colored by military administration. For administrative purposes, Paraguay is divided into two regions, the eastern and the western, the latter comprising the Chaco Boreal. The eastern region is subdivided into thirteen departments and the western into three; each department is headed by a presidentially appointed delegate.

Departments are in turn subdivided into districts and these into municipalities. Two departments in the Chaco are still run as military territories. Rural districts are known as *partidos.* Asunción is established as an independently administered district. No tradition of effective local control or of challenge to higher authority exists. The general administrative system is highly centralized and presidentially controlled.

In Paraguay the marriage of the presidency and the military is a relationship of long standing. The constitution of 1844 gave the president the title of Supreme Chief and declared that he was to "wear the uniform and enjoy all the attributes and prerogatives of a Captain-General." From that time on the military has almost uniformly been prominent in the governmental process, if indeed it did not completely dominate it. What Edwin Lieuwen aptly calls "predatory praetorianism" has become as pronounced in Paraguay as anywhere in Latin America, and the army remains by far the most important interest group in the country.

The dominion of the military is not strictly a matter of its size: All Paraguayan regular armed forces, including navy and air force, total fewer than thirteen thousand men. Nor is it entirely a matter of budgetary treatment, though the proportion of the total budget allotted to the military is often more than a fourth of the total and after the coup of 1954 rose to 50 percent. Rather, the influence of the military is related to the enormity of its general impact on politics.

When Morínigo became president in 1940 he found he had to placate ambitious officers who had come through the testing of the Chaco War. He did so willingly and generously with positions and power. Stroessner continued both the process and the attitude. Colorados were quite willing to arrive at an understanding with the army because that provided them with a sure and easy way of blocking the political aspirations of both the Febreristas and the Liberals. The 1967 constitution provides that Chaco War veterans "shall enjoy powers and privileges; pensions that will permit them to live in dignity; preferential, free and complete health care," and other benefits. Not even the American Legion or the Canadian Legion has such favored constitutional status!

As matters now stand there is simply no civilian potential, organized or unorganized, for an effective political challenge to the Paraguayan military.

Party Structures

Neither at the local nor at the national level does Paraguay have any significant popular participation in the political process. All citizens over eighteen have the vote, including women; Paraguay, which extended the vote to women in 1961, was the last Latin American state to adopt women's suffrage. Ostensibly, the party system provides an opportunity for democratic expression, but actually the government party furnishes only window dressing, and the opposition provides only sound and fury—and precious little of that. The Colorados are officially the National Republican Association; both they and the Liberals are elite-oriented and give not the slightest impression of having grass roots.

The Colorado party, undisguisedly conservative despite its name, which means "red," originated in the nineteenth century. Along with the Dominican party in the republic of that name, the Colorados have in recent years been one of the few Latin American parties to receive a legal monopoly of the political state in their respective countries. This situation was so unrealistic that few were surprised when splinters began to break off from the central group.

The Colorado Popular Movement came into being, composed of dissidents who could not accept the dictates of the monopolistic party. An insubstantial Christian Democratic Social Movement was organized as recently as 1960, but it, like the Colorado Popular Movement, has had no real impact or vitality. Paraguay's presidency has alternated irregularly between *caudillos* and *pensadores,* and very few rulers combined the strong hand of the one with the idealistic mind of the other.

The old Liberal party has split into two wings: the Radical Liberal party (PLR), a conservative group which, in line with Liberal party tradition in Paraguay, maintains an entente with the oligarchy, and the Liberal party (PL), a component of the original group which split from the PLR in 1961. In 1977 dissident members of both the PL and PLR formed the Unified Liberal party (Partido Liberal Unificado, or PLU) in an effort to revitalize conservative liberalism. The party joined the Febreristas in boycotting the 1977 constitutional convention election. After a court ruling in July 1977 declared the party illegal, it was forced to watch the 1978 presidential elections from the sidelines.

Government action in 1964 restored the Febreristas to good standing, but their new status did not transform them into an effective opposition. Febreristas maintain a loose affiliation with parties of the democratic Left in other Latin American states, but they are poorly organized in Paraguay itself. The Febreristas refused to participate in the 1973 legislative election, the 1977 choice of constitutional convention delegates, and the 1978 presidential election.

A Christian Democratic Movement was established in 1959; it has remained small and unimportant, even after its rechristening as the Christian Democratic party in 1965. It is intellectualized and partially reformist.

Communist activity dates back to 1928. The 1940 constitution provided political oppositionists with the choice of exile as an alternative to detention, and many availed themselves of this ironic privilege. The small Paraguayan Communist party (Partido Comunista Paraguayo, or PCP) is divided into three exiled groups: the Buenos Aires-based faction, reportedly aligned with the Soviet party; the Montevideo-based group, a Chinese-oriented party; and the Obdulio Barthe faction, a Leninist-leaning faction composed of Montevideo dissidents.

Other Political Structures

Paraguayan economic development is so rudimentary that interest groups with economic rooting are essentially weightless. Organized labor has little significant pressure potential within Paraguay. The Paraguayan Confederation of Workers (Confederación Paraguaya de Trabajadores, or CPT), under government control since 1958, was suspended from the European-based International Confederation of Free Trade Unions for its subservience to the Stroessner regime. Only as recently as 1978 did the CPT show opposition to the Stroessner regime over the arrest of nineteen labor leaders accused of revitalizing the Organización Político-Militar, or OPM. The administration used the alleged discovery of the organization of the guerrilla group as a means of stirring up anti-Communist sentiment.

Industrial, commercial, banking, and agricultural interests are similarly without effectiveness in the political arena. The 1940 constitution was pristinely free of any significant material of social or economic purport. The 1967 constitution devotes more wordage—but perhaps it is only wordage—to the same subjects.

From time to time the government has made gestures toward solving the problems of underdevelopment by setting up institutes, or *cajas,* to deal with social insurance, labor disputes, and other such matters, but their record has been notably unimpressive. Only lip service has been paid to land reform; most government-owned lands were alienated in the 1880s and 1890s for a pittance. Allegedly, eleven holdings recently embraced more than a third of the land in the eastern region.

In a country as little affected by contemporary currents of change as Paraguay, it stands to reason that the face of the Church would be conservative. Indeed, the Church normally works closely and cooperatively with a heavy-handed and conservative government. The constitution recognizes Roman Catholicism as the "state religion" (although ostensibly "without prejudice to religious freedom"), the president is required to be a Catholic, and the archbishop is an ex officio member of the council of state. Occasionally, religiously motivated voices are heard advocating better treatment of Paraguay's underprivileged classes, but normally the Church is content with maintaining the status quo.

DEVELOPMENTAL PROSPECTS

Paraguayan government and politics are most accurately described as primitive. In this regard the country may be said to resemble Haiti. The two situations have points of difference as well as of similarity. Paraguay's educational level is certainly higher than Haiti's, although Paraguay's published statistics on this score are open to question. The people of Paraguay are certainly better integrated, ethnically and psychologically, than those of Haiti. Democracy has virtually no foothold in either state, and dictatorship is the normal pattern of political organization in both.

Raw power, largely with military and even praetorian overtones, is the essence of the political progress in Paraguay, despite an ostensible relaxation in recent years. After an occasional successful revolution, a power source may be displaced but only by another, competing source of raw power. Paraguay still provides Latin America's best example of irregular rotation between the *caudillo* and the *pensador,* and it is significant that an adequate bridge between the two stereotypes has not yet been found.

The mass of the people, in any event, remain aloof from the contest, either because they instinctively realize that discretion is the better part of political valor or because they are characterized by a servile willingness to submit to authority. Such apathy, of course, is made to order for dictators. Isolation is a function not merely of geography, but also of political mentality.

On the credit side of the ledger, ethnic amalgamation has been accompanied by a relative absence of class friction and class consciousness, and this social equality should be good soil in which to nurture the growth of political democracy. An intangible asset which Paraguay took into the Chaco War with Bolivia in the 1930s was its highly developed sense of nationalism. Nationalism can of course be perverted and prostituted, but the lack of it can be a serious retarding factor in a nation's political development.

President Stroessner claimed to run the most successful government in Paraguay's history. He has led the country through a gradual economic development phase and future prospects for greater wealth are seen. The two mammoth dams on the Paraná river, one at Itaipú (the world's largest) and another at Yacyretá near Argentina, will make Paraguay a major exporter of electricity. This economic potential has brought about a gradual breaking of Paraguay's isolationist policies but has caused a simultaneous worsening of relations with the country's two neighbors, Brazil and Argentina.

Politically, speculators have mused over the possibility of the president announcing some sort of "democratic opening" or "decentralization of power" in the near future. Perhaps the ouster of the Somoza dynasty in Nicaragua and the Carter administration's constant concern for human rights will kindle the idea.

REFERENCES

ALBERTO, CARLOS. *El Coloradismo: su Unidad Ideológica y Moral.* Asunción: n.p., 1951.

GIMÉNEZ CABALLERO, ERNESTO. *Revelación del Paraguay.* Madrid: Espasa-Calpe, 1958.

GONZÁLEZ, JUAN N. *El Estado, Servidor del Hombre Libre.* Mexico: n.p., 1960.

LEWIS, PAUL H. *The Politics of Exile: Paraguay's Febrerista Party.* Chapel Hill: University of North Carolina Press, 1965.

PENDLE, GEORGE. *Paraguay: A Riverside Nation.* New York: Gordon Press, 1976.

PHELPS, GILBERT. *The Tragedy of Paraguay.* New York: St. Martin's Press, 1975.

RAINE, PHILIP. *Paraguay,* Chap. 7. New Brunswick, N.J.: Rutgers University Press, 1956.

VELÁZQUEZ, RAFAEL ELADIO. *Breve historia de la Cultura en el Paraguay.* 2nd ed. Asunción: n.p., 1968.

WARREN, HARRIS G. "Political Aspects of the Paraguayan Revolution, 1930–1940." *Hispanic American Historical Review* 30 (February 1950), 2–26.

———. *Paraguay, an Informal History.* Norman: University of Oklahoma Press, 1949.

16

URUGUAY

The Politics of Coercive
Political Mobilization

POLITICAL CULTURE AND ENVIRONMENT

The "purple land" of Uruguay, as W. H. Hudson fondly described it, is in many ways Latin America's most distinctive republic. It is South America's smallest country (68,536 square miles) and, at the same time, the one which has the least waste land; 78 percent of its land surface is utilizable. Its climatic and geographic factors are highly favorable. The rainfall is usually sufficient. Soils are thinner than in the Argentine pampas; therefore, only a relatively small portion of the entire country is really suitable for cropping, which means that cattle and sheep raising is far more important economically than crop production. This agricultural orientation also accounts for certain political repercussions and attitudes.

Along with Argentina and Costa Rica, Uruguay is one of the three essentially "white" countries of Latin America. There are no Indians and the mestizo population is negligible. By the time of independence, the population was almost entirely Spanish, in large part creole. A few blacks and mulattoes are found near the Brazilian border. Turbulent political conditions during most of the nineteenth century retarded large-scale European immigration, but by the 1890s Uruguay began to receive considerable numbers of Europeans, especially Italians, with the result that a significant proportion of the population, particularly in the major cities, is now Italian by either birth or ancestry. In addition large numbers of Germans, English, Swiss, French, Near Easterners, and other peoples have emigrated to Uruguay.

Economic activity is largely agricultural and mainly pastoral. Particularly since 1946, when government subsidies were instituted, wheat raising has increased in importance, and wheat is now a significant export commodity. Mining is significant. Manufacturing is important in Montevideo, but it is largely a byproduct of the pastoral industries and consists of meat processing, weaving, shoe manufacturing, and similar industries.

Political Development

During most of the nineteenth century, the course of Uruguayan political development was at best undistinguished. Independence, nominally achieved in 1828, was followed by years of serious meddling by both Argentina and Brazil, which had used Uruguay as a staging ground for attacks on each other even during the colonial period. Uruguay's internal politics was in considerable measure a reflection of this foreign involvement. The only significant development of this early period was the emergence in the latter half of the 1830s of two competing groups which, because of the distinguishing colors that they respectively adopted for identification, quickly came to be called the Colorados (Reds) and the Blancos (Whites). Ultimately, these groups were transformed into definite parties. The legal foundation for Uruguayan government during this period was the basic law of 1830. It was an orthodox and relatively short constitution. Its longevity was definitely exceptional: It lasted eighty-nine years, making it the third longest-lived of all Latin American constitutions.

The kaleidoscopic changes of government, which saw frequent shifts in power between Blancos and Colorados, brought the Colorados to power in 1865, and for ninety-three years they remained in control of the executive branch of government. It was the longest uninterrupted hold on power ever maintained by a single Latin American party.

In the ensuing decades, the social, economic, and political face of Uruguay began maturing. Population growth, which was reversed by strife in the middle years of the century, began again after 1852 and, especially in the 1870s, involved the immigration of large numbers of Europeans, who settled largely in Montevideo and were a potent force for order and stability. The two major parties worked out a financial "accommodation," which was cheaper and less upsetting than recurrent revolutions.

Professional soldiers dominated Uruguayan politics for about two decades; one resigned the presidency in 1880, stating in disillusionment that he was "dejected to the point of thinking that our country is an ungovernable country." By the 1890s the Colorados and the Blancos, who initially had had few ideological differences between them, had gravitated into more easily recognizable political postures: The Colorados became urban-centered (especially focusing on Montevideo) and in a vague way more progressive and liberal. The Blancos found their strength in the great rural *estancias,* were more conservative, and had a slight orientation towards the Church. The great philosophical demarcation between the two, however, had to await the coming of the twentieth century.

In the 1890s José Batlle y Ordóñez, son of a former president, emerged as the most influential figure in Uruguayan politics. He was a Colorado leader who believed his party could and should be purged of its venality and given a definite reform program; in the next third of a century he had a remarkable impact on the shaping of Uruguayan life. Batlle was elected president for the term from 1903 to 1907, and then reelected for a second term, 1911 to 1915. He introduced many economic, social, cultural, and political reforms. It can indeed be said that Uruguay was thus the first Latin American country to experience a genuine modern social revolution, antedating (but in peaceful and largely unnoticed fashion) the much more spectacular movement which began in Mexico in 1910.

Clearly the most publicized and perhaps the most significant reform put forward by Batlle was his proposal that the Uruguayan executive branch be reorganized essentially on the Swiss model by abolishing the presidency and substituting a national council. The political infighting between the Colorados and the Blancos resulted in some defections from Batlle's own Colorado party. The necessary constitutional changes could have been pushed through the Colorado-controlled congress, but Batlle deemed it more democratic to accomplish his reform by means of a constituent assembly. An assembly compromise had to be worked out, and the plan finally written into the relatively short new constitution of 1917 (which took effect in 1919) provided for the retention of the presidency, now to be filled by popular instead of legislative election and the simultaneous selection by popular vote of an independent nine-member National Council of Administration. This bifurcated executive branch was one of the most unusual constitutional experiments ever attempted in Latin America.

The 1920s saw Batlle standing largely in the background of politics, though he remained until his death in 1929 a potent political force. Opinion varied as to the success of the national council, which the Blancos dominated for short periods; certainly it was not an unmixed success. The depression which arrived with the end of the decade brought a severe strain to Uruguay's economy and, inevitably, to its politics as well.

Gabriel Terra, a batllista, was elected president in 1930 and was immediately forced to cope with a variety of depression-born political problems. He regarded the gravest of these as the malfunctioning of the national council. On March 31, 1933, he precipitated a climax (not without some forewarning) by means of a coup, in which he dissolved the national council of administration and the congress, suspended the 1917 constitution, and installed a de facto dictatorship. A constituent assembly—composed (because of opposition boy-cotting) only of terristas from both major parties—completed work on a new constitution early in 1934.

The new basic law, which was largely a reflection of Terra's own ideas, naturally made no provision for a bifurcated executive. The presidency was hence restored to a more traditional Latin American position. The price Terra had to pay for Blanco support in the constituent assembly was guaranteed minority-party representation in both the cabinet and the senate. In the latter body the party with the second largest number of popular votes—which was then and for almost a quarter of a century continued to be the Blancos—was given half the seats, thus establishing the so-called half-and-half senate, an open invitation to tie votes and frequent impasses.

The two leading candidates in the election of 1938 were Terra's brother-in-law and son-in-law. The former, General Alfredo Baldomir, won the election, and governed democratically for most of his four-year term. The coming of the war rendered Baldomir's democratic position almost untenable. In February 1942 he announced postponement of the imminent quadrennial elections; subsequently, he replaced the Blanco members of his cabinet, dissolved the congress, and proposed constitutional amendments, including one to abolish the half-and-half senate. These changes were approved, and another Colorado was elected president in the November 1942 balloting.

Andrés Martínez Trueba, a Colorado, won the presidency in November 1950 and early the following year proposed anew the abolition of the presidency and the substitution of the old nine-member council. An extensive revision of the constitution, tantamount to a new basic law, was voted on in a national plebiscite in mid-December 1951 and with the support of the two major political groups in the country, batllista Colorados and herrerista Blancos (named for its leader and six-time presidential candidate, Luis Alberto de Herrera), it was adopted.

The new *colegiado*, or collegiate executive, this time in undiluted form with no president to share executive responsibility, took effect on March 1, 1952. After an initial cooperative period between the major parties, which now shared control of the executive branch, party rivalry and recrimination were renewed even more bitterly. This, coupled with economic dislocation and strain, was responsible for a deteriorating political situation. Each major party was seriously divided internally, and by 1958 the entire political scene reflected a degree of political defeatism and disillusion unusual in Uruguay. Hence, in the elections of November 1958 the Partido Nacional (Blancos) displaced the Colorados from majority control of the executive branch for the first time in ninety-three years. It was a peaceful revolution of genuine significance. For a portion of the people, the plural executive soon lost much of its earlier charm.

Discontent with the *colegiado* continued to grow, and by 1966 this discontent had produced four proposals for reform, all of which would restore the single presidency. Although collegiate government was the major issue in the election of November 27, it was complicated by the fact that a full complement of senators and representatives, plus 891 departmental and a large number of local officials, had to be chosen. Almost complete returns—which indicated that 1,129,020 voters had cast ballots, with 675,109 favoring abolition of the national council of government—provided the necessary constitutional margin to effect the change. Since the *colegiado* had been rejected, a president had to be chosen. The winner was Oscar D. Gestido, a Colorado. The Communists increased their vote by almost 50 percent over 1962. Christian Democrats and Socialists both lost.

Not only would a single president supplant the national council and the Colorado party replace the Blanco as controller of the executive branch, but the presidential term would be extended to five years and congressional terms lengthened by a year to make them coincide with that of the president. A vice-presidency was restored and its occupant made eligible for immediate reelection, although the president would have to wait out an intervening term before he could be returned to office.

President Gestido, who was inaugurated on March 1, 1967, immediately faced a sorry bequest of economic and political problems. Inflation was rampant and strikes were numerous. Gestido undertook an unpalatable austerity program. He died within a year of his inauguration and was succeeded in December 1967 by Jorge Pacheco Areco, his vice-president. Pacheco's political-economic diet was as indigestible as that of his predecessor, and the strikes and the slowdowns became almost chronic. Reports in 1969 attributed some of the disorders in Montevideo to the activity of a secret band of urban guerrillas, the Tupamaros (a corruption of the name of the eighteenth-century Incan leader, Túpac Amarú), who allegedly had affiliates even within the civil service. Tupamaro activity reached a dramatic climax in August 1970 with the kidnapping of a Brazilian diplomat and two United States advisers in Montevideo. One of the United States advisers was "executed" a short time later. President Pacheco tried desperately to halt the rising violence but finally conceded to the armed forces the handling of the guerrilla attacks.

In 1971 Pacheco's hand-picked successor, Juan M. Bordaberry, was elected president but only after charges of electoral fraud and a seventy-nine–day recount. In June 1973 Bordaberry ended Uruguay's forty years of democratic government by suspending the constitution, banning political activity, and agreeing to share power with the military. By April 1973 the armed forces had virtually eliminated the Tupamaro strength, but the military was unwilling to give up its newly acquired power. President Bordaberry reluctantly accepted the military's nineteen-point program to reduce corruption, advance economic reforms, and add greater military participation to Uruguay's political life. A new national security council (consejo de seguridad nacional) was established, leaving Bordaberry with little but his title. He seemed content with his titular role and even had visions of suspending political parties indefinitely and becoming Uruguay's permanent president.

Bordaberry's longevity stemmed less from his own political prowess than from the military's lack of agreement on who should succeed him if scheduled elections were held in November 1976. Bordaberry was overthrown on June 12, 1976, and temporarily replaced by Alberto Demicheli, the president of the national security council.

There was some speculation that the military might take a cue from the Argentine military's experience in 1976 and return politics to the politicians. Yet, within a month the generals dominating the newly organized council of the nation (incorporating the three heads of the armed services and the members of the former security council) "elected" seventy-two-year-old Aparicio Méndez as president for a five-year term. Upon taking office on September 1, 1976, President Méndez suspended the political rights of all Uruguayans who had held public office in the past ten years. According to Méndez, the restriction, which had the support of the military, would "end the inertia of political parties."[1] The military also announced that a new constitution would be drafted by 1980 and that a general election would be held in 1981. Although political parties would not be permitted to resume normal functions until 1986, the military promised that the Colorado and Blanco parties would be permitted to participate in selecting the president in 1981.

GOVERNMENTAL AND POLITICAL STRUCTURES

The most novel feature in recent Uruguayan constitutions was the establishment of a pluripersonal executive branch, the national council of government, which was amended out of the constitution in 1966. In considerable degree the *colegiado* resembled the national council of administration created by the constitution of 1917.

The collegiate executive was abolished in 1966 and a more conventional unipersonal presidency was returned. As defined, presidential powers were similar to those in effect prior to the institution of the *colegiado* in 1952, except that the president enjoyed increased authority to enact emergency legislation.

In 1973 the military government revised the 1966 constitution with its own version, which stipulated that the executive would be selected and assisted by a national security council comprising the president, the ministers of defense, foreign affairs, interior, economy, and planning as well as the leaders of the three armed services. The security council was responsible for the administration of the country; the council of the state had legislative control.

[1] *New York Times,* September 5, 1976, Sec. IV, p. 3.

Although the bicameral congress was suspended in 1973, under normal parliamentary conditions members of this body were almost on a par with the executive branch of the government, a relationship unique among Latin American states. The home of the legislative branch is symbolic of its status on the Uruguayan political scene. Indeed, the $12 million legislative palace is one of the few grandiose showplaces of Montevideo, far more elaborate, more costly, and more impressively situated than the executive palace.

The organization and operation of the Uruguayan judiciary departs less from the conventional Latin American pattern than either of the other two branches. The court system is composed of a symmetrically organized group of units, staffed by dignified, professionally trained, able officials.

On taking office in 1977 President Méndez placed the supreme court under the ministry of justice; he subsequently put it directly under executive control. Before the suspension of constitutional rule, the five members of the supreme court were elected by two chambers of the congress.

In Uruguay the field of intermediate-level and local government had traditionally been a product partly of politics and partly of administration. Uruguay was never influenced by federalism as a principle of internal political organization.

As in several other Latin American countries the principal Uruguayan subdivision is the department, of which there are nineteen. A department's closest United States counterpart, in both size and functions, is a county.

The constitutional changes of 1966 continued an elective legislative junta or board and reinstated the former elected *intendente*. Since 1973 the military government has appointed these officials. In towns other than those constituting departmental capitals—there are not many—local boards may be established with members appointed insofar as is possible by a scheme of proportional representation. Members of local and departmental boards receive no salary; for that reason, as well as because of a strong centripetal tradition, local government suffers from lack of substance and vitality.

The Party Scene

Nowhere else in Latin America do parties have the deep roots, the weight, the vigor, the pervasiveness, or the overall impact that they have had in normal times in Uruguay. Uruguay provided the most significant Latin American example of the development of political parties as a viable force in public affairs. Political parties were as significant a phenomenon in Uruguay as in the United States or Great Britain; they may even have exercised more influence in Uruguay than in either of the other two countries.

The parties may be traced historically to the trivial differentiation between two groups of followers of rival *caudillos* in the crude political life of early independent Uruguay. Ideological differences between the two groups, Blancos and Colorados, were not sharp during most of the nineteenth century. By the later decades of that century the Colorados came to be more closely identified with Montevideo and the Blancos with the great *estancias*. It was Batlle who revitalized the Colorado party, purged it of its cynicism, gave it an idealistic program and a moral tone which no Uruguayan party had previously had, and in general remolded the role of the party in Uruguay. So great was his charisma that the Colorado party was transformed into a fanatically loyal personal following; not until his proposal of a collegiate executive was there any serious defection in his party following.

By the laws of political physics the Blanco party was forced into an opposition stance, although for some years it had gradually been moving toward a more conservative orientation. A curious consequence of this realignment was that, although the Colorado party become definitely anticlerical, the Blancos did not become equally pro-Church; that orientation was reserved for the minor Unión Cívica.

Colorados.   Only the operation of the election law, which stated that the accumulation of votes of the various *sublemas* (election tickets) within a single party, all to be given to the *sublema* with the most votes, enabled the Colorado party to maintain itself in power for so long. So great was the friction between party wings—it was also true of the Blancos—that some persons believed that a single Colorado party and a single Blanco party no longer existed and that the Uruguayan biparty pattern had disappeared. That was probably not a justifiable conclusion, but it is still difficult to overestimate the depths and rancor of the intraparty schisms.

Blancos.   The Blancos, also a mass party, usually wore their ideology less professionally than the Colorados. A qualification needs to be made, however, regarding the impact on the party of its long-dominant reactionary leader (and six-time presidential candidate), Luis Alberto de Herrera. Until his death in 1959 he ruled his party, or at least its dominant herrerista wing, with an iron discipline that not even Batlle was able to impose on the Colorados. The nature of Blanco psychology was still determined to a considerable degree by the *campo,* or the rural areas, which represent, insofar as *estanciero* opinion is concerned, social and economic conservatism, just as the party stood at least formally for political conservatism. The Blancos, especially the herreristas, often were regarded as more cultured and substantial than the Colorados and as representing a "better class of society."

A moderate and enlightened group of Blancos was for many years forced to operate as a legally distinct party, the Independent Nationalists (or Blancos), because the Blanco party refused to allow the dissidents to use the party *lema,* or name, over which it had legal control. In 1958 the Independent

Nationalists were officially reunited with the Blanco party, although they continued to maintain their identity as a separate list (*sublema*) within that party.

A more significant schism in the Blanco party was the development of the Unión Blanca, an urban-oriented wing of the party, in the late 1950s. Agreement among the three Blanco factions to use the same *lema* permitted them to win over the Colorados by about 120,000 votes in 1958. This did not presage harmony, however, and almost constant squabbling characterized later intra-Blanco politics. By 1978 the Blancos were divided into the Herristas, the Rocha Movement, the Unión Blancos, and the Herrerista Ortodoxos.

Other Parties. Parties with more strongly ideological bases included Unión Cívica, the Socialists, and the Communists. Unión Cívica, called the Christian Democratic party since 1962, has consistently followed a Catholic position and has attracted only a Catholic membership. Many Catholics belong to other parties, although they are confined mainly to the Blanco and its offshoots because of the traditional batllista tenet of anticlericalism. As might be expected, the establishment of women's suffrage in the late 1930s benefited Unión Cívica. Although the vote of Unión Cívica was small, its leadership was capable and respected.

The Socialist party, which was in existence for about half a century, never had wide appeal for Uruguayan voters; its maximum voting percentage strength was reached in 1958, but even then it was only 3.5 percent. For a long time its guiding genius was the eminent and highly respected Dr. Emilio Frugoni. The party gave a slight impression of shabby gentility. Its orientation, like that of the Colorados and Communists, was working class, but those classes were so thoroughly the preserve of the Colorados that the Socialists were left with little distinctive ground on which to stand. In 1962 the party merged with other small groups under the rubric of Unión Popular. Later in the 1960s the Socialists split into the Socialist Movement, headed by the patriarchal Frugoni, and a much more radical Socialist party.

The Communist party has followed an unapologetically erratic Communist line since it was organized in the 1920s. Its greatest voting strength was in the 1946 election, in which it received one vote out of every twenty cast. Ironically, the party was forced to print its ballots in black ink, since the Colorados held a legal monopoly on red-ink ballots. The party affected a professional proletarianism, but its chief importance was as a focal point of intrigue and invective against the United States. For the 1962 elections the Communists renamed themseves the Leftist Liberation Front (Frente Izquierda de Liberación, the initials of which with the insertion of the "de" form an obviously Castro-inspired acronym, FIDEL). It was later superseded by the Frente Amplio, or Broad Front coalition. The Broad Front was organized in 1971 as an alliance of left-wing parties including FIDEL to put forward the candidacy of Líber Seregni Mosquera.

The National Liberation Front (Movimiento de Liberación Nacional, or MLN, the Tupamaros) flourished during the late 1960s and early 1970s as an urban guerrilla group. The young men and women making up this group were largely from the middle class and used violence as a means of weakening and discrediting the Uruguayan government. The full weight of the military was used by President Bordaberry to put down the violence, and by 1973 the Tupamaro organization was in disarray; those members not in prison or dead were in exile or underground.

Upon his installation on September 1, 1976, President Aparicio Méndez banned all political parties in existence before congress was closed in 1973 and denied for ten years the political rights of all political leaders, including former Presidents Bordaberry and Pacheco Areco; Walter Ferreira Aldunate, the National party presidential candidate against Bordaberry; General Líber Seregni of the Broad Front; and Jorge Batlle of the Colorado party faction.

The schedule for the return of democratic rule to Uruguay calls for a pro forma election in 1981 in which a single presidential candidate would be presented by the two major parties, Colorado and Blanco. A free election for members of congress would be held in 1986 with the lifting of the ban on political parties and their leaders.

Other Political Structures

Uruguay had not known a military takeover in its history, but in 1972 the Uruguayan military left its barracks and by the end of the decade had not returned. Rather than staging a sharp, bloody coup d'etat, the military gradually grasped the governmental reins. Military leaders ruled jointly with President Bordaberry for over a year before finally making the decision to take full control.

Although most political observers in the early 1970s felt that the military's role would be temporary, once out of the barracks to wage war against the Tupamaros, the military found it difficult to return. When Bordaberry called on the military to control guerrilla activity in the country, the army set a condition: The government was to declare a "state of war" which would cancel all constitutional guarantees and leave the armed forces free from accountability.[2]

After the declaration of war against the Tupamaros in 1972, thousands of Uruguayans were brought to trial; the size of the armed forces increased from approximately twelve thousand men for the three services to an estimated twenty-five thousand, plus an additional twenty thousand in the police force. The military considered its actions necessary for the suppression of leftist subversion. More recently it became involved in educational planning and economic policies as well as political decision making.

[2]See Arturo C. Porzecanski, "Authoritarian Uruguay." *Current History,* 72:424 (February 1977), 74.

Although the military gave every outward indication of keeping its promise of a return to democratic rule in 1981, many observers felt the friction between the two military factions could be the main stumbling block to a return of democratic rule. One faction consisted of those officers who were committed to the return of democratic rule in 1981 and favored present commander-in-chief of the army, General Gregorio Alvarez, as the single candidate; the other consisted of the extreme right-wing elements who were loyal to General Amaury Prantl and tried to block the presidential aspirations of Alvarez.

The exalted position which the Catholic church enjoys or has enjoyed in many Latin American countries has been reduced to a far more modest level in Uruguay. Batlle, who was strongly anticlerical, succeeded in imparting to Uruguay a seemingly permanent orientation of the same kind. Education has been almost completely laicized, religious ceremonies are held to modest proportions, and there has been a general dilution of religiosity. Yet, none of the persecution which characterized the government attitude toward the Church in Mexico has taken place in Uruguay.

DEVELOPMENTAL PROSPECTS

Uruguay, which had once been called the most democratic state in Latin America, the "Switzerland of South America," and "South America's first welfare state," is now under a military dictatorship. The end of Uruguayan democracy came as a result of many things, not the least of which were the reform programs inaugurated by President Batlle.

The Batlle government began to exhibit concern for the welfare of the underpriviliged classes at an early date. Early in the century pensions for governmental employees were instituted. Divorce was legalized; women were granted the right to hold title to and bequeath property; and illegitimate children were given legal status. Uruguay was the first Latin American state to adopt the eight-hour work day. Labor organization was encouraged and an advanced plan of social security was enforced. Compulsory liability insurance and vacations with pay were established. Medical services for the poor were free, and education was entirely free for everyone at all levels. Conciliation and arbitration tribunals were provided.

These extensive social welfare services were inevitably very expensive. As the social and economic programs of the government expanded through the decades, one new tax after another was added to finance them, with relatively little thought given to a systematization and rationalization of the entire tax structure.

During the years of military dominance, thousands of people have left

Uruguay for either political or economic reasons. Political parties and their leaders were banned from political activity for ten years in order to encourage a new generation of political leaders. Congress was replaced by a twenty-five–member council of state which answers to the military. All union activity was outlawed and labor leaders imprisoned; opposition newspapers were shut down. The average wage was reduced to a subsistence level, while inflation (at 45 percent in 1978) continued to increase prices. Despite the drastic economic measures imposed by the military government, Uruguay continued to have a high unemployment rate in 1978, with 13 percent of the labor force out of work.

Although the military has returned the country to a semblance of order in these past few years, the price has been the elimination of individual freedoms and a democratic political life not found anywhere else in Latin America. As one Uruguayan said: "We don't even have economic progress to show for our political repression."[3]

REFERENCES

ALISKY, MARVIN. *Uruguay: A Contemporary Survey.* New York: Holt, Rinehart & Winston, 1969.

FITZGIBBON, RUSSELL H. "Adoption of a Collegiate Executive in Uruguay." *Journal of Politics* 14 (November 1952), 616–642.

JOHNSON, JOHN J. *Political Change in Latin America: The Emergence of the Middle Sectors*, Chap. 4. Stanford, Calif.: Stanford University Press, 1958.

KAUFMAN, EDY. *Uruguay in Transition: From Civilian to Military Rule.* New Brunswick, N. J.: Transaction Books, 1978.

LINDAHL, GÖRAN G. *Uruguay's New Path: A Study in Politics during the First Colegiado, 1919–1933.* Stockholm: n.p., 1962.

PACHECO SERÉ, ALVARO, and JULIO M. SANGUINETTI. *La Nueva Constitucíon.* Montevideo: Alfa, 1967.

PENDLE, GEORGE. *Uruguay.* London: Oxford University Press, 1963.

PIKE, FREDERICK. *Uruguay: Portrait of a Democracy.* New Brunswick, N. J.: Transaction Books, 1954.

TAYLOR, PHILIP B., JR. *Government and Politics of Uruguay.* New Orleans: Tulane University Press, 1962.

———. "Interests and Institutional Dysfunction in Uruguay." *American Political Science Review* 57 (March 1963), 62–74.

VANGER, MILTON I. *José Batlle y Ordóñez of Uruguay: Creator of His Times, 1902–1907,* Vol. 1. Cambridge, Mass.: Harvard University Press, 1963.

WEINSTEIN, MARTIN. *Uruguay: The Politics of Failure.* Westport, Conn.: Greenwood, 1975.

WHITAKER, ARTHUR P. *The United States and the Southern Cone: Argentina, Chile, and Uruguay.* Cambridge, Mass.: Harvard University Press, 1976.

[3] *New York Times,* July 2, 1978, Sec. IV, p. 3.

Part Six

CONCLUSION

17

CONCLUSION

This book has focused on the diversity of contemporary Latin American politics. Individually, each system operates within the network of a political culture which has produced a people with a peculiar set of orientations to their governments and the overall decision-making process. Collectively, the political culture in Latin America essentially represents a variety of factors which bear on the entire prospects for stable development in the area.

The general characteristics of Latin American political experience and the important factors that have exerted a formative influence on the politics of the region must be taken into account in any attempt to ascertain the prospects for democracy or totalitarianism in the area. The plan for democracy in Latin America, to the extent that one exists, is a political design, but its achievement depends considerably on the ability of policy makers to deal with the disruptive complexities that attend the Latin American family of nations. Indeed, a design for democracy in Latin America is a large order and proceeds on the assumption that a homogeneous consensual political culture or set of attitudes can be produced to preclude or minimize the obstacles blocking the way to democratic social aspirations.

Realistically, however, it is known that the political culture—a dynamic, transitional culture reflecting various political shortcomings—is hardly homogeneous or consensual; this underscores the importance of continued study to ascertain the direction in which Latin American democratization, as a form of development, may be headed.

What can be gleaned from the overall analysis of specific Latin American systems? Essentially, political culture in Latin America represents a conglomeration of factors which deserve the careful attention of students. A willingness to face squarely some of the hardcore problems which, though they will vary with a nation's circumstances at various times, may provide clues to why a politics of democracy has remained in limbo.

One might justify evaluation of the prospects for democracy in Latin America as a whole, notwithstanding the diversities to be found in the area. There is sufficient evidence to show that Latin Americans do have a broad denominator—their interest in or aspiration for modernization, progress, and the overall rapid development of political, social, and economic structures. The countries in Latin America are striving to move up to or even surpass the material achievements attained in North America and Europe.

Most would agree that the road to successful development of Latin America will be difficult. Approaches to development borrowed from the more advanced European countries, for example, cannot be expected to succeed when applied in the Latin American context. Nor is it easy to accept the thesis that imported political ideologies, if indeed they work at all in the contemporary Latin American milieu, will create the necessary popular responsiveness to the demands of social and economic change.

In a balanced look at the problems of political democracy in Latin America, one cannot be satisfied with explanations that focus only on the transitional character of the Latin American society—the conditioning factors of political violence, the cult of *machismo, caudillismo,* or for that matter, the weakness of the middle class, or the *patrón-peón* mentality—although all are indeed strategic variables in the dynamic changing culture we know as Latin America. Much as these factors help us analyze the forces impeding democratic development in Latin America, they do not altogether represent the entire picture.

We must pay attention to the way of life of the Latin people as well as to their ethic, social fabric, and organization. We must carefully study the rapid population growth, increased urbanization, revolutionary, agricultural, and industrial developments, national efforts against illiteracy, the growth of organized labor, the social role of the Church, the acculturation of various ethnic elements, governmental complexity, and statism.

Social and economic problems bear a strong political connotation for Latin America. Economically Latin America is well known as a producer of raw materials. Such republics as Brazil, Argentina, Venezuela, and Mexico, dissatisfied with this situation, are diligently striving to bring maximum industrialization to their countries.

The monocultural, or one-product, character of Latin American economies cannot be overlooked. Chile, for example, derives its major revenues from copper production and must use a substantial portion of this income to pay for its imported foodstuffs. Colombia depends on sugar and coffee for revenue; Venezuela on petroleum; Cuba and the Dominican Republic on sugar; the Central American republics of Honduras, Costa Rica, and Nicaragua on bananas; Ecuador on sugar, bananas, and tobacco. Quite simply, all these countries appear to be captives of a global economic arrangement manipulated in such large cities as London, New York, and Hamburg. This particular line of thinking is reflected in the politicization of the *dependencia* argument, which explains Latin American underdevelopment as a result of expanded capitalism from major capitalist powers. The usefulness of the *dependencia* concept, together with such other developmental ideas of the cooperatist-authoritarian, collectivist-monocratic, pluralist-democratic variety, is being debated in academic circles.[1]

The latter three ideas form the core of Professor Schmitter's "lattice model of political development," which is readily applicable to Latin America's transitional politics. This model suggests the heterogeneous character of development in Latin America. It assures us that the Latin American states are not peas in a pod and can develop in a variety of ways. We are reminded that these polities may not necessarily choose the same developmental path, as any survey of Latin American countries would indicate. Despite the variety of available options, however, many Latin American political systems seem to be leaning toward the corporatist-authoritarian alternative, which leaves them easy prey to foreign and domestic power elites.

The question most often asked in academic circles is whether Latin America's external dependence on such benefactors as the United States is responsible for, or perhaps associated with, patterns of authoritarian-corporatist development in the area. It has become fashionable among the so-called *dependistas* to associate Latin American underdevelopment or delayed development with the region's subordinate relationship to the colossus of the north. The dependency literature suggests various factors which characterize a Latin American external dependency—including export dependence, U.S. private investments, market dependence, trade orientation, and external debt.

It has been hypothesized that levels of dependency correlate with levels of authoritarianism in Latin America. But a study designed to find a plausible relationship between these two variables revealed a mere 0.05 rank-order correlation.[2]

The burgeoning literature suggests that there is no relationship between dependency—whether based on U.S. capital, commerce, or massive economic

[1]Philippe C. Schmitter, "Paths to Political Development in Latin America," in *Changing Latin America: New Interpretations of Its Politics and Society,* Douglas A. Chalmers, ed., *Proceedings of the Academy of Political Science,* 30:4 (1972), 83–105.

[2]David Scott Palmer, "The Politics of Authoritarianism in Spanish America," in *Authoritarianism and Corporatism in Latin America,* James M. Malloy, ed. (Pittsburgh: University of Pittsburgh Press, 1977), p. 386.

aid—and the general modes of democratic pluralism or political participation in Latin America.

Cursory analysis of the political systems covered in this book would lead one to conclude that the countries of Latin America are probably not developing along a democratic-participant cultural path. Nor is there any universally accepted political development formula available that could be used to predict whether democracy, totalitarianism, corporatist authoritarianism, or some other variant will be the eventual outcome of the dynamic change process in the area.

In 1978 political analysts noticed the political virus of change spreading throughout the entire Latin American body politic. Both in military and civilian-controlled regimes, elections of one kind or another were scheduled and held. There was much speculation in the media, press, and professional journals as to why the democratic alternative became so fashionable in such die-hard militarily controlled countries as Peru, Bolivia, Ecuador, Chile, Uruguay, and Argentina. Two of the more popular theories were (1) that the military had simply become disenchanted with existing structures of power and wanted to change them through the ballot box; and (2) that the armed forces, beset with divisions within their ranks, recurring economic crises, border disputes, and a general sense of frustration at not being able to resolve these problems satisfactorily, were predisposed to move towards elections or some qualified form of democracy. Others interpreted the 1978 military swing towards some sort of quasi-democracy as a tactical move by military regimes to legitimize their rule through some type of controlled representative system, hoping to ease the pressure from Washington for a genuine democratic process.

Whatever the intentions of the armed forces the widespread election fever in 1978, especially in the then military-ruled states, has been heralded as a significant development in the volatile politics of these countries. It would be foolhardy to use the 1978 rush to elections alone as a reliable indicator of commitment to political development in Latin America. The overall picture in the region is far too complicated for sweeping generalizations. Aside from Colombia, Costa Rica, and Venezuela, which continue on their regular democratic paths, the remaining countries discussed in this volume are merely flirting with democratic forms and procedures of government. For reasons that defy simplistic answers, none of the countries that resorted to democratic experimentation through the ballot box in 1978 seemed satisfied with their political performance or development record.

Both Ecuador and Peru, for example, staunchly committed to military alternatives, appeared willing to play out their constitutional options. Both countries have made progress toward elections, but it remains to be seen whether the military will abide by the electoral results. In the praetorian stronghold of Bolivia elections were held and a provisional government installed. Through indirect presidential elections in Brazil another military man came to power. It will be interesting to observe how this Brazilian will govern without the benefit of Institutional Act No. 5, which empowered the president to deprive citizens of their rights and to suspend an unruly congress whose majority might well be controlled by the opposition MDB party. What might happen in the foreseeable future in military-controlled Chile, Argentina, and Uruguay is anyone's guess. In these three countries the military governments are thinking of phasing in some kind of democracy which would be compatible with traditional military prejudices. Although lip service is being paid to the virtues of political participation and democratic pluralism, it is doubtful that the military in these countries will tolerate anything less than a qualified, controlled form of democracy. This is perhaps to be expected in a region where the political culture is generally based on a politics of power, violence, and paternalism.

It is understandable that the notion of "democracy through militarism" would be anathema to many whose conception of political democracy is premised on the Anglo-American model. Lest we become bogged down in the continuing debate on what is "pure" or "impure" democracy, suffice it that we acknowledge that Latin American democratic weathervanes are still undergoing refinement, which dictates even more reliance on understanding the overall political culture to explain the relative prevalence or absence of democratic development.

Over the years specialists in Latin America have been trying to deal with the problems of assessing democracy in a changing Latin American environment. Professor Kenneth Johnson's study of scholary images of Latin American political democracy in 1975 is based on five select criteria (freedom of press, speech, and so on; free elections; freedom of political organization; independent judiciary; degree of civilian supremacy). It reveals the following rank orderings according to a country's status of political democracy: (1) Costa Rica, (2) Venezuela, (3) Colombia, (4) Mexico, (5) Argentina, (6) Dominican Republic, (7) Uruguay, (8) El Salvador, (9) Guatemala, (10) Ecuador, (11) Panama, (12) Honduras, (13) Peru, (14) Cuba, (15) Bolivia, (16) Brazil, (17) Nicaragua, (18) Chile, (19) Paraguay, and (20) Haiti.[3]

Another 1975 assessment using a different set of criteria (individual rights and freedom of choice; security under the rule of law; and meaningful participation in decision making for the greatest allowable period) indicates four broad categories, going from the most to the least democratic, into which the Latin American republics fall: In the first category, labeled "Stable Democracies," are Costa Rica, Venezuela, and Colombia; in the second category, labeled "Democratic with Authoritarian Features," are Guatemala, Mexico,

[3]Kenneth F. Johnson, "Scholarly Images of Latin American Political Democracy in 1975," *Latin American Research Review,* 11:2 (1976), 129 and 140.

and El Salvador; in the third category, labeled "Authoritarian with Democratic Features," are Argentina, Dominican Republic, and Brazil; and in the fourth category, labeled "Tyrannical or High Authoritarian," are Nicaragua, Honduras, Paraguay, Ecuador, Peru, Bolivia, Panama, Cuba, Chile, Uruguay, and Haiti.[4]

It should be emphasized that any assessment of Latin American political democracy must of course be tentative, given the emotive (to say nothing of the conceptual) difficulties surrounding the concept itself. What should also be kept in mind is that "the question of democracy will be affected in each country by the norms, styles, skills, and arenas that most prominently characterize the nation's share in the overall political culture"[5] What this suggests is that the level of democracy will largely be determined by the regimes' predisposition to allow citizen participation in the sharing of political ends and means.

Several of the Latin American republics now seem to be moving in the direction of democracy. In those countries generally described as authoritarian because of their sharp curtailment of freedom (Argentina, Bolivia, Chile, Cuba, Haiti, Honduras, Nicaragua, and Paraguay), presidential elections were held in Paraguay in 1978 and Bolivia in 1979; elections were promised for Honduras in 1980. Following Nicaraguan President Somoza Debayle's resignation in 1979, a new Government of National Reconstruction was installed which pledged to hold elections. A plebiscite on the new constitution to return to civilian rule and democracy in Chile will be submitted to the electorate, and a format for a return to democracy is being considered in Argentina.

Among those countries that generally fall in the quasi-authoritarian category (that is, countries moving toward more democratic practice—Brazil, Ecuador, El Salvador, Guatemala, Panama, and Peru), presidential elections were held in Brazil, Ecuador, and Guatemala; also parliamentary elections were held in Panama, constitutional assembly elections in Peru, and municipal elections in El Salvador. There were no surprises in those countries customarily described as democratic (those which rely on free elections for the selection of their leadership): Colombia, Costa Rica, Dominican Republic, Mexico, and Venezuela. Presidential elections were held on schedule in an open and free manner. The most exciting of the contests in these democratic or semidemocratic systems was in the Dominican Republic, where former president Joaquín Balaguer lost and the military had to be restrained from intervening.

The tendency to reestablish democratic forms, albeit slowly and hesitatingly in many of the countries under military rule, has constituted the major

---

[4]James L. Busey, *Latin American Political Guide* 16th ed. (Manitou Springs, Col.: Juniper Editions, 1975), p. 2.
[5]Johnson, "Scholarly Images," p. 132.

development of the late 1970s in the volatile politics of Latin America. Among average Latin Americans, the general mood seems to be one of apathy if not skepticism about the meaningfulness of any kind of democracy that is encouraged by military governments. In the absence of strong political parties in countries long controlled by military rule, many voters have felt alienated and disillusioned with the value of the ballot box. Their political atomization is further exacerbated by the death or relative impotence of such personalities as a Velasco Ibarra, Haya de la Torre, Arnulfo Arias, or Paz Estenssoro in a militarily engineered democratic process.

Cynically, many Latin Americans view democracy as a self-serving alternative used by the military to dismount gracefully from the presidential saddle when they are unable to ride out the political and economic storm. It has become almost a principle of Latin American politics that an elected civilian rules only by the grace of the military.

Thus, whether the type of democracy is called authoritarian, viable, organic, or tutelary, as one might be inclined to name the several versions of democracy now being practiced or contemplated in countries subjected to military rule, none of these democratic versions would endure without military imprimatur. Over the years the military has emerged as one of the most important power elite structures in Latin America. Indeed, the political influence of the other classic interest structures in Latin American society has vastly diminished, or at least been modified, by the deliberate penetration of the military into the politics of the region. The military has become a surrogate *caudillo* for the alienated masses in Latin America.

A century ago armies, in virtually every case, were repositories of raw force. Air forces were nonexistent and navies almost so; hence, comment can be confined to armies. They completely lacked modern professionalization; they were led by *caudillos* in most instances, and to achieve political power, they rode roughshod over all opposition. Finesse was introduced into the operation of even military *caudillos* in the latter part of the nineteenth century and even more so in the twentieth century. Professionalization of Latin American armies began with Chile and Argentina and continued to spread into other Latin American republics. But such professionalism undoubtedly became a two-edged sword, for the conviction began to grow among the military, particularly after economic breakdowns demonstrated frequent civilian inability to cope with governmental impasses, that the armed forces were both equipped and morally bound to step into political crises and to try to resolve them. More often the military hurled itself in the thick of the political battle with the conviction of a political mission and obligation partly born of a new pride and confidence felt by the army as it became increasingly professionalized. The pride and confidence were admirable as long as they led the armed forces down a strictly military path, but when they began serving as guide posts to political activity and intervention, they became unfortunate.

Viewing the contemporary Latin American political picture, one would be inclined to say that the trend toward civil rule is indefinite. There is always the possibility, of course, of the pendulum swinging in the other direction, although the prospects at this writing seem rather bleak. Increasing political anomie and economic stagnation in many parts of Latin America could, if accompanied by general insensitivity toward the basic causes of political alienation, result in blind military insistence on retaining power indefinitely. To the extent that military or tutelary-type designs of political rule continue, however, popular resistance of the guerrilla variety should be expected. Outbreaks of guerrilla violence have been known to reappear with intensity in Latin America.

Despite Castro's involvement in the African continent, his views about "exporting revolution" not only to Africa but to other parts of Latin America are too well known to be dismissed lightly. It is difficult to assert that guerrillas would not be maintaining some kind of organization in countries such as Uruguay, Argentina, Chile, Bolivia, and Brazil, where it would seem clear that repressive measures have eliminated this type of activity. Nor can it be assumed that such democratically ruled countries as Colombia, Venezuela, and Mexico have remained free of insurgent or subversive action. Subversive activity has persisted in Mexico but with less importance than in times past, due to the successful campaigns waged thus far by Mexican security forces. On the other hand, in Venezuela, which until the end of 1977 seemed relatively protected from such activity, a reappearance of insurgency has been closely monitored by Venezuelan authorities.

There have also been isolated eruptions of anomic activity in Central America which have precipitated an increase in official repression. Notably in Nicaragua we noticed what some political observers have called the "state terrorism" of Somoza against the Sandinista forces.

The political scapegoat for the upsurge of peasant unrest and leftist guerrilla activity in the region has noticeably become the Catholic church. In the absence of effective opposition structures, the Church has been deeply involved in spearheading the offensive against the dominant military and civilian groups which have not been in step with the tenets of the reform-minded second Vatican Council of the 1960s and the Latin American Bishops' Conferences (especially the 1968 CELAM session at Medellín, Colombia). This has resulted in a marked radicalization of the Catholic church not only in Central America but also in the rest of Latin America, where their Catholic progressive social-action efforts have incurred the wrath of conservative military regimes.

It is obvious that the Church has lost much of its former impact on Latin American politics. No one, not even the most devoted Catholic, now maintains that Latin America is so staunchly Catholic that communism could make no headway there. Communism is making headway; so is Protestantism, especially with the redirection of missionary thrust which came about when many Asian regions were blocked off; and so are spiritualism and other marginal cults. Emphasis on economic development tends to provide more fertile soil for a "Protestant ethic," however defined, than was the case when it was regarded as only a counterweight in Latin American fields. It is apparent that in many parts of Latin America the Church is on the defensive and not in a position to take an aggressive role in politics. Because of the close ties between the oligarchy and military regimes, Church involvement in matters of political repression and social and economic justice is being monitored very closely and discouraged where necessary.

Granting that the political influence of the classic institutions in Latin American society has vastly diminished, a question then arises concerning the optimal approach for the economic and political development of Latin America. To the best of our knowledge, there is no single or foolproof approach to development. Even a casual examination of the economic picture in Latin America reveals the tremendous extremes in distribution of wealth. Although gross national product is not a perfect index of growth or lack of it, variation in GNP from one Latin American country to the next does demonstrate the giant economic strides which still must be taken to overcome a relative economic stagnation. With a majority of the people in Latin America outside the money economy and living on a bare subsistence level, it is understandable that there is often little if any interest in political matters aimed at improving the general lot of the inhabitants of the area.

To the dismay of many, there is often endemic apathy which, as is to be expected, is the concomitant of low literacy, poor health, and inadequate housing. Given this overall circumstance, it is hardly possible for the millions of Latin Americans who are laboring under such conditions to take a positive, activist role in improving the political fabric of their nations. Often these unsung *olvidados*, or "forgotten people," do not even know the country to which they belong. One might suspect that they are prime targets for any ideology that preaches quick change for the better, such as *fidelismo*, or the Castro-Communist doctrine of salvation for downtrodden masses. It would seem, therefore, that the first step toward any amelioration of this situation would be economic modernization with a view toward the reshaping of archaic structures to meet the present demands of the modern economy and the polity.

As far as the sovereign states comprising the Latin American system are concerned, there seems to be one common denominator which binds them together—the general aspiration for development. But like everything else about Latin America, a development plan for realizing this hope is neither here nor there. The 1967 Punta del Este "Action Program" was perhaps the closest that the Latin American states have ever come toward an approach for accelerating the process of modernization in the entire region. The program pledged the Latin American presidents to take the necessary steps to accomplish such important objectives as the full establishment of a Latin American common market by 1985 based on the Latin American Free Trade Association (LAFTA) and Central American Common Market (CACM) and the commitment to encourage the incorporation of other countries of the Latin American region into the existing integration systems.

Since the program began, political analysts have been baffled as to whether its goals are realistic in view of the modernization differentials that exist between the Central American Common Market group and the LAFTA group of countries. The problem of economic modernization in the sense of fusing several differentiated countries into a single economic community appears overwhelmingly difficult when one considers the vast development gaps within the major bloc of countries comprising the Latin American Free Trade Association. In Latin American circles there are those who feel that LAFTA is a farce and needs to be revitalized.

In 1978 more attention was being paid to such subregional organizations as the Caribbean Group for Cooperation in Economic Development and the Andean bloc whose increasing influence might be helpful to such organizations as LAFTA and the Latin American Economic System (SELA). The Latin American Economic System, which comprises twenty-three Latin American nations (including Cuba and other Caribbean countries), was established in 1975 with the general goal of promoting multicountry economic projects and formulating unified Latin American positions for the international arena. It was hoped that SELA would be able to coordinate the economic activities of the varied and complex Latin American integration programs.

Lack of a unified regional policy in Latin America has proved to be costly in both developmental trade and aid. There is evidence that U.S. bilateral development aid to Latin America is gradually being discontinued, and no longer is Latin America considered by such international lending institutions as the World Bank as the most favored third-world region for development assistance. The World Bank's cumulative lending ratios to Latin America vis-à-vis Africa and Asia have sharply declined in recent years—partly because of the bank's displeasure with Latin America's brand of capitalism. Even the resources of the Inter-American Development Bank, whose assets increased as the result of a 1976 Venezuelan loan to help "poor Latin American states," are expected to grow relatively more slowly, which could greatly curtail its ability to make loans to Latin America.

Latin America also finds itself in the awkward position of no longer having the good offices of such strong personalities as Felipe Herrera, Raúl Prebisch, and Carlos Sanz de Santa María to lobby in favor of their trade and aid interests in high international circles. The recently elected president of the United Nations General Assembly, Colombian foreign minister Indalecio Liévano, has tried to renew the North-South dialogue emphasizing the problem of economic inequalities between nations, but the prospect for success is not encouraging. Many political analysts have characterized the North-South dialogue as simply another one of those "get-rich-quick schemes" which, like the Latin American common market, the new international economic order, and the Latin American Economic System, looked good on the drawing board but have hardly provided a cure-all for Latin American underdevelopment. For that matter, third worldism has provided neither the answer nor the solution to the development crisis in Latin America. As a third-world region, Latin America has demonstrated greater interest in economic than the political concerns of other third-world members. This does not mean that as a voting bloc Latin America has tended to break ranks on the latter with its third-world colleagues in the international forums.

Among the strongest third-world advocates in Latin America were to be found such political notables as Salvador Allende of Chile, Luis Echeverría of Mexico, General Velasco Alvarado of Peru, Andrés Pérez of Venezuela, and Fidel Castro of Cuba, who has exercised special influence in tricontinental circles. Despite ideological differences, in some cases more severe than others, these leaders entertained third worldism as a viable option for development in Latin America. Third-world–style economic planning has generally produced more problems than solutions, however, especially in such countries as Mexico, Chile, and Peru.

Many of the Latin American countries that entered into the crucial stage of full industrialization and urbanization were not prepared for the OPEC-induced world recession and high oil prices, which created balance-of-payments problems for their developing economies. Beyond the shared sense of pride with the prosperity of Venezuela and Ecuador (OPEC members), the Latin American nonpetroleum nations have derived little in the way of tangible benefits for their economies. With spiraling inflation and the depressed price of commodity exports, the prospect for establishing other Latin American commodity cartels as another third-world trade wedge is rather bleak.

At this point Latin America seems to realize that cooperation instead of confrontation might prove to be the best strategy to follow toward the industrialized nations. Instead of relying on third-world attachments or Washington-approved policies, Latin America might find it profitable to experiment with the capitalist policies of contemporary European societies, which would be compatible with Latin America's political culture. To the extent that Latin America is interested in maintaining its Western values without strings to Washington, the establishment of a close partnership with Europe might be mutually beneficial.

It is debatable how the United States might react to a renewed Latin American kinship to Europe. OAS Secretary General Alejandro Orfila has taken note of the fact that Latin America is exploring the European alternatives "not only to expand its economic relationships, especially in the area of trade, but also to determine whether the contemporary political and economic experience of Europe does not offer special insights and solutions that could aid development in this hemisphere."[6] The implication here is that European capitalism might be better for Latin America than its United States counterpart.

At the beginning of the 1980s Latin American anxiety was at a dangerous level because of the scheduled reduction in bilateral and multinational assistance and plans to erect significant protectionist barriers, which would probably inflict heavy economic damage on the area. Latin America's anxiety was further exacerbated by the sterile results of the North-South dialogue, third-world–style economic planning, the Latin American common market, and the OAS failure to produce concrete proposals for cooperation in economic and trade development. There was also suspicion about the Carter administration's approach to Latin America. Many people felt that, despite President Carter's human-rights emphasis but with sufficient flexibility to reestablish limited relations with Communist Cuba and to sign new Canal treaties with an authoritarian Panamanian government, the Carter administration had demonstrated itself to be no more liberal on economic issues than had its Republican predecessors. Both military and democratic regimes in Latin America have expressed concern that other inter-American problems might be ignored because of the administration's militant human-rights initiative.

Growing concern has been expressed, for example, about the increasing volatility of Latin American territorial disputes and the spiraling arms sales in Latin America. It is noteworthy that at the 1978 General Assembly of the Organization of American States held in Washington, President Carter called for "peaceful and just solutions" of Latin American border disputes, specifically mentioning Belize/Guatemala and El Salvador/Honduras as well as Bolivia's demand for access to the sea. There are, of course, several other pressing claims which were not mentioned, such as the question of the Guantánamo naval base in Cuba, the Caribbean islands that the United States promised in a 1972 treaty to turn over to Colombia, the Beagle Channel issue between Chile and Argentina, and the mineral-rich Atacama desert between Peru and Chile. Other potentially disruptive territorial disputes simmer between Peru and Ecuador and between Venezuela and both Guyana and Colombia.

Over the years Latin America has become an armed camp, thus increasing the potential for war between and even among nations on the continent for the settlement of hopelessly tangled disputes. The major powers were doing very little to defuse this explosive situation. According to a study released by the Stockholm Institute for Peace Studies, the three major suppliers of arms to South America for the 1970–1976 period were the United States, Great

[6]*The Vision Letter: A Political and Economic Report on Latin America,* 29:13 (July 15, 1978), 2.

Britain, and France; their military exports to the region were valued at more than $2,070 million. According to the study the arms sales were distributed among eleven countries in the region with Brazil, Chile, and Venezuela heading the list of purchasers. Many observers view these vast Latin American expenditures on arms as a waste of valuable resources which could be used to bolster their underdeveloped economies.

Some indications surfaced that the Latin American countries were considering limiting weapons purchases. In 1974 eight governments (Argentina, Bolivia, Chile, Colombia, Ecuador, Panama, Peru, and Venezuela) signed the declaration of Ayacucho in which they pledged cooperation in controlling the acquisition of arms. In 1978 the Ayacucho nations also considered a broader regionwide conventional arms limitation agreement. A similar proposal was presented by Mexico in the Organization of American States. In October 1978 the Soviet Union and the United States agreed to initiate negotiations designed to regulate the supply of conventional arms to Latin America. This has been viewed as an important step by the major powers to contain the arms race among the developing nations. Generally, Latin American countries tend to give priority to economic development over arms purchases. Their need to maintain modernized, independent military forces is often explained as a manifestation of national sovereignty.

As Latin America moves further into the twentieth century—and some states are doing it only slowly and seemingly reluctantly—it must inevitably respond more or less as those states did that were pressured into the political arena around the turn of the century. This means that the dead hand of the past can be expected to lose some of its hold over the present. Quite likely, Latin Americans will gradually learn that national sovereignty, or *dignidad*, has a higher price tag than compromise. Many in Latin America are disinclined to look favorably upon conciliation and compromise which may involve a risk to *dignidad* or *honor.*

By the same token complete reliance on the ballot box as the implement for solving political problems is the exception rather than the rule, with good historical reason—the integrity of elections has too often been open to question. The Latin American states are advancing from the stage of mere aspiration to deliberate action to achieve development, possibly in the direction of democracy. Still, it cannot be overemphasized that the contemporary problems are difficult and numerous and will require much understanding by all those concerned with the problems of establishing a permanent beachhead for the full implementation of representative democracy and human rights. It is also essential that the forces of militarism, nationalism, modernization, overpopulation, and the psychology of alienation, which relate to the structural problems of Latin American development, be kept in mind. The inescapable fact of Latin American political life is change—alteration, innovation, transition, conversion, or revolution. And, Latin America does need a second revolution, a humanistic revolution of being in which genuine participation and national independence become the paramount goals of the political culture.[7]

REFERENCES

BARBER, WILLARD R., and C. NEALE RONNING. *Internal Security and Military Power: Counterinsurgency and Civic Action in Latin America.* Columbus: Ohio State University Press, 1966.

BERGER, PETER. *Pyramids of Sacrifice: Political Ethics and Social Change.* New York: Basic Books, 1974.

CARDOSO, FERNANDO HENRIQUE. "Associated-Dependent Development: Theoretical and Practical Implications." In *Authoritarian Brazil: Origins, Policies and Future,* pp. 142–178, ed. by Alfred Stepan. New Haven: Yale University Press, 1973.

CHILCOTE, RONALD. "A Critical Synthesis of the Dependency Literature." *Latin American Perspectives* 1:1 (Spring 1974), 4–29.

CORBETT, CHARLES D. "Politics and Professionalism: The South American Military." *Orbis* 16 (Winter 1973), 927–951.

DAHL, ROBERT. *Polyarchy: Participation and Opposition.* New Haven: Yale University Press, 1971.

DICKSON, THOMAS I., JR. "Approach to the Study of the Latin American Military." *Journal of Inter-American Studies and International Affairs* 14 (November 1972), 455–468.

DREKONJA, GERHARD. "Religion and Social Change in Latin America." *Latin American Research Review* 6 (Spring 1972), 53–72.

DUFF, ERNEST, and JOHN MCCAMANT. "Measuring Social and Political Requirements of System Stability in Latin America." *American Political Science Review* 62:5 (December 1968), 1125–1143.

EINAUDI, LUIGI R., and ALFRED C. STEPAN. *Latin American Institutional Development: Changing Military Perspectives in Peru and Brazil.* Santa Monica, Calif.: RAND, 1971.

EINAUDI, LUIGI R., RICHARD MAULLIN, ALFRED STEPAN, and MICHAEL FLEET. *Latin American Institutional Development: The Changing Catholic Church.* Santa Monica, Calif.: RAND Corporation, 1969.

FRANK, ANDRE GUNDER. *Latin America: Underdevelopment or Revolution.* New York: Monthly Review Press, 1969.

——. *Lumpen-Bourgeoisie and Lumpen-Development: Dependence, Class and Politics in Latin America.* New York: Monthly Review Press, 1972.

GANNON, FRANCIS X. "Catholicism, Revolution and Violence in Latin America." *Orbis* 12 (Winter 1969), 1204–1225.

HEEGER, GERALD A. *The Politics of Underdevelopment.* London: Macmillan, 1974.

HOROWITZ, IRVING LOUIS, JOSUÉ DE CASTRO, and JOHN GERASSI, eds. *Latin American Radicalism.* New York: Vintage Books, 1969.

HIRSCHMAN, ALBERT O. *Latin American Issues: Essays and Comments.* New York: Twentieth Century Fund, 1961.

——. *A Bias for Hope.* New Haven: Yale University Press, 1974.

HUNTINGTON, SAMUEL. *Political Order in Changing Societies,* Chap. 4. New Haven: Yale University Press, 1968.

[7] See Gustavo Lagos and Horacio H. Godoy, *Revolution of Being: A Latin American View of the Future* (New York: Free Press, 1977), pp. 58–59. See also Eduardo Frei Montalvo, "The Second Latin American Revolution," *Foreign Affairs,* 50:1 (October 1971), 83–96.

HYMAN, ELIZABETH. "Soldiers in Politics: New Insights on Latin American Armed Forces." *Political Science Quarterly* 89 (September 1972), 401–418.

JACKMAN, ROBERT. "Politicians in Uniform: Military Government and Social Change in the Third World." *American Political Science Review* 70:4 (December 1976), 1078–1097.

JANOWITZ, MORRIS. *The Military in the Political Development of New Nations: An Essay in Comparative Analysis.* Chicago: University of Chicago Press, 1964.

JOHNSON, JOHN. *The Military and Society in Latin America.* Stanford, Calif.: Stanford University Press, 1964.

KOHL, JAMES, and JOHN LIN. *Urban Guerrilla Warfare in Latin America.* Cambridge, Mass.: MIT Press, 1974.

KOSOK, MANFRED. "Armed Forces in Latin America: Potential for Changes in Political and Social Functions." *Journal of Inter-American Studies and International Affairs* 14 (November 1972), 375–398.

LIEUWIN, EDWIN. *Arms and Politics in Latin America.* New York: Holt, Rinehart & Winston 1961.

———. *Generals vs. Presidents: Neo-Militarism in Latin America.* New York: Holt, Rinehart & Winston, 1964.

LOWENTHAL, ABRAHAM F., ed. *Armies and Politics in Latin America.* New York: Holmes & Meier, 1976.

McALISTER, LYLE N. "Civil-Military Relations in Latin America." *Journal of Inter-American Studies* 3 (July 1961), 341–350.

McALISTER, LYLE N., ANTHONY P. MAINGOT, and ROBERT A. POTASH. *The Military in Latin American Sociopolitical Evolution: Four Case Studies.* Washington, D.C.: Center for Research in Social Systems, 1970.

McCOY, TERRY L., ed. *The Dynamics of Population Policy in Latin America.* Cambridge, Mass.: Ballinger, 1975.

MALLOY, JAMES M., ed. *Authoritarianism and Corporatism in Latin America.* Pittsburgh: University of Pittsburgh Press, 1977.

MUTCHLER, DAVID E. *The Church as a Political Actor in Latin America.* New York: Holt, Rinehart & Winston, 1971.

NEEDLER, MARTIN. "Political Development and Military Intervention in Latin America." *American Political Science Review* 60:3 (September 1966), 616–626.

NORDLINGER, ERIC A. "Soldiers in Mufti: The Impact of Military Rule upon Economic and Social Change in the Non-Western States." *American Political Science Review* 64:4 (December 1970), 1131–1148.

NUN, JOSÉ. "A Latin American Phenomenon: The Middle Class Military Coup." In *Latin America: Reform or Revolution?* pp. 145–185, ed. by James Petras and Maurice Zeitlin, New York, Fawcett Books Group—CBS Publications, 1968.

O'DONNELL, GUILLERMO A. *Modernization and Bureaucratic-Authoritarianism: Studies in South American Politics.* Berkeley: Institute of International Studies, University of California, 1973.

PUTNAM, ROBERT D. "Toward Explaining Military Intervention in Latin American Politics." *World Politics* 20:1 (October 1967), 83–110.

PETRAS, JAMES, and ROBERT LaPORTE. *Cultivating Revolution: The United States and Agrarian Reform in Latin America.* New York: Random House, 1971.

RANKIN, RICHARD. "The Expanding Institutional Concerns of the Latin American Military Establishments: A Review Article." *Latin American Research Review* 9 (Spring 1974), 81–108.

SOLAÚN, MAURICIO, and MICHAEL A. QUINN. *Sinners and Heretics: The Politics of Military Intervention in Latin America.* Illinois Studies in the Social Sciences, No. 58, Urbana: University of Illinois Press, 1973.

TANCER, SHOSHANA BARON. *Economic Nationalism in Latin America: The Quest for Economic Independence.* New York: Holt, Rinehart & Winston, 1976.

TULLIS, F. LAMOND. *Politics and Social Change in Third World Countries.* New York: John Wiley, 1973.

WIARDA, HOWARD J. "Corporatism and Development in the Iberic-Latin World: Persistent Strains and New Variations," in *The New Corporatism Social-Political Structures in the Iberian World,* ed. by Frederick B. Pike and Thomas Stritch. Notre Dame: University of Notre Dame Press, 1974.

BIBLIOGRAPHY

This bibliography, like those following the various chapters, is selective. The several bibliographies include those published references that have been considered significant and relevant for the general purposes of the volume. Many additional materials have been examined and omitted. For some countries, such as Ecuador and Paraguay, the number of useful references is woefully small. Recency of publication has not, of itself, been a key to inclusion of items, nor has a relatively old publication date been an automatic reason for omission.

The problem of good current materials is always a plaguing one. For general coverage, the *New York Times* and *Washington Post* are still the best sources. A few other newspapers, among them the *Christian Science Monitor* and the *Los Angeles Times,* are worth consultation. Among foreign language publications *Hispanoamericano* (Mexico City), *Latinoamérica al Mes* (Lima), *Visão* (São Paulo), and *La Nación* (Buenos Aires) are useful. English language periodicals to be recommended include *Latin America Political Report* (London), *Times of the Americas* (Washington, D.C.), and *Latin America Economic Report* (London). Also to be recommended are James L. Busey, *Latin American Political Guide* (Manitou Springs, Colorado), Arthur S. Banks, *Political Handbook of the World* (New York), *Latin American Annual Review & the Caribbean* (Essex, England), and *Statistical Abstract of Latin America* (Los Angeles). Aside from the titles mentioned above, and perhaps a few others— *caveat lector.*

ADAMS, MILDRED, ed. *Latin America: Evolution or Explosion?* New York: Dodd, Mead, 1964.

ADAMS, RICHARD N., JOHN P. GILLIN, ALLAN R. HOLMBERG, OSCAR LEWIS, RICHARD W. PATCH, and CHARLES WAGLEY. *Social Change in Latin America Today.* New York: Random House, 1960.

AGEE, PHILIP. *Inside the Company: CIA Diary.* New York: Stonehill, 1975.

AGOR, WESTON H., ed. *Latin American Legislatures: Their Roles and Influence.* New York: Holt, Rinehart & Winston, 1971.

AGUILAR, LUIS E., ed. *Marxism in Latin America.* New York: Knopf, 1968.

ALBA, VÍCTOR. *Alliance Without Allies: The Mythology of Progress in Latin America.* New York: Holt, Rinehart & Winston, 1966.

———. "Communism and Nationalism in Latin America." *Problems of Communism* 7:5 (September–October 1958), 24–31.

———. *Politics and the Labor Movement in Latin America.* Stanford, Calif.: Stanford University Press, 1968.

ALEXANDER, ROBERT J. *Communism in Latin America.* New Brunswick, N.J.: Rutgers University Press, 1957.

———. *Latin American Politics and Government.* New York: Harper & Row, 1965.

———. *Organized Labor in Latin America.* New York: Free Press, 1965.

———. *Prophets of the Revolution.* New York: Macmillan, 1962.

———. "The Emergence of Modern Political Parties in Latin America." Chapter 5 in *Politics of Change in Latin America,* ed. by Joseph Maier and Richard W. Weatherhead. New York: Holt, Rinehart & Winston, 1964.

ASTIZ, CARLOS A. *Latin American International Politics: Ambitions, Capabilities, and the National Interest of Mexico, Brazil, and Argentina.* Notre Dame, Ind.: University of Notre Dame Press, 1969.

ATKINS, G. POPE. *Latin America in the International Political System.* New York: Free Press, 1977.

BAILEY, HELEN MILLER, and ABRAHAM P. NASATIR. *Latin America: The Development of Its Civilization* 3rd ed. Englewood Cliffs, N.J.: Prentice-Hall, 1973.

BAILEY, SAMUEL L. *Nationalism in Latin America.* New York: Knopf, 1971.

BAKLANOFF, ERICK N. *Expropriation of U.S. Investments in Cuba, Mexico and Chile.* New York: Holt, Rinehart & Winston, 1975.

BARAN, PAUL. *The Political Economy of Growth.* New York: Monthly Review Press, 1957.

BARNET, RICHARD, and RONALD MULLER. *Global Reach: The Power of the Multinational Corporations.* New York: Simon & Schuster, 1974.

BARRACLOUGH, SOLON LOVETT. *Agrarian Structures in Latin America: A Resume of the CIDA Land Tenure Studies of Argentina, Brazil, Chile, Colombia, Ecuador, Guatemala, Peru.* Lexington, Mass.: Lexington Books, 1972.

BERNARD, JEAN PIERRE, SILAS CERQUEIRA, HUGO NEIRA, HELEN GRAILLOT, LESLIE F. MANIGAT, and PIERRE GILHODES. *Guide to the Political Parties of South America.* Baltimore: Penguin, 1973.

BLAKEMORE, HAROLD. *Latin America.* London: Oxford University Press, 1973.

BLANKSTEN, GEORGE I. "Caudillismo in Northwestern South America." *South Atlantic Quarterly* 51 (October 1952), 493–503.

———. "Political Groups in Latin America." *American Political Science Review* 53 (March 1959), 106–127.

BRANDENBURG, FRANK R. "Communism and Security in Latin America." *Yale Review* 46 (Spring 1957), 413–424.

BURR, ROBERT. *Our Troubled Hemisphere; Perspectives on U.S. Latin American Relations.* Washington, D.C.: Brookings Institution, 1967.

————, ed. "Latin America's Nationalistic Revolutions." *Annals of the American Academy* 334 (March 1961), v–vi.

BUSEY, JAMES L. *Latin America: Political Institutions and Processes.* New York: Random House, 1965.

————. "Observations on Latin American Constitutionalism." *Americas* 24 (July 1967), 46–66.

BRYANT, JOHN. *Health and the Developing World.* Ithaca, N.Y.: Cornell University Press, 1969.

CHILCOTE, RONALD, and JOEL C. EDELSTEIN. *Latin America: The Struggle with Dependency and Beyond.* New York: Halsted Press, 1974.

CLISSOLD, STEPHEN. *Latin America, New World, Third World.* New York: Holt, Rinehart & Winston, 1972.

COLE, J. P. *Latin America: An Economic and Social Geography.* London: Butterworth, 1965.

Commission on U.S.–Latin America Relations. *The Americas in a Changing World.* New York: Quadrangle/The New York Times Book Co. 1975.

COSÍO VILLEGAS, DANIEL. *Change in Latin America: The Mexican and Cuban Revolutions.* Lincoln: University of Nebraska Press, 1961.

COTLER, JULIO, and RICHARD FAGEN, eds. *Latin America and the United States.* Stanford, Calif.: Stanford University Press, 1974.

CRAWFORD, WILLIAM R. *A Century of Latin American Thought.* New York: Holt, Rinehart & Winston, 1966.

DAVIS, HAROLD E., ed. *Government and Politics of Latin America.* New York: Ronald, 1956.

————. *History of Latin America.* New York: Ronald Press, 1968.

————. *Latin American Thought.* Baton Rouge: Louisiana State University Press, 1972.

DAVIS, HAROLD E, and LARMON C. WILSON, eds. *Latin American Foreign Policies.* Baltimore: Johns Hopkins University Press, 1975.

DAVIS, STANLEY M., and LOUIS WOLF GOODMAN, eds. *Workers and Managers in Latin America.* Lexington, Mass.: Heath, 1972.

DITELLA, GUIDO. "Regional Cohesion and Incoherence in Latin America." *World Today* 30:12 (December 1974), 522.

DOUGLAS, WILLIAM O. *Holocaust or Hemispheric Co-operation: Cross Currents in Latin America.* New York: Vintage Books, 1971.

EDELMANN, ALEXANDER T. *Latin American Government and Politics.* 2nd ed. Homewood, Ill.: Dorsey Press, 1969.

EINAUDI, LUIGI R., ed. *Beyond Cuba: Latin America Takes Charge of Its Future.* New York: Crane, Russak, 1969.

FAGG, JOHN E. *Latin America: A General History.* Toronto: Collier-Macmillan, 1969.

FANN, K. T., and DONALD HODGES, eds. *Readings in United States Imperialism.* Boston: Porter Sargent, 1971.

FERGUSON, YALE H., ed. *Contemporary Inter-American Relations.* Englewood Cliffs, N.J.: Prentice-Hall, 1972.

FIGUERES, JOSÉ. "The Problems of Democracy in Latin America." *Journal of International Affairs* 9 (1955), 11–23.

FINER, SAMUEL E. *The Man on Horseback.* 2nd ed. New York: Holt, Rinehart & Winston, 1974.

FITZGIBBON, RUSSELL H. "Constitutional Development in Latin America: A Synthesis." *American Political Science Review* 39 (June 1945), 511–522.

————, "Seven Dilemmas of Latin America's National Revolutionary Parties." *Orbis* 14 (Summer 1970), 443–462.

————. "The Party Potpourri in Latin America." *Western Political Quarterly* 10 (March 1957), 3–22.

————. "Revolutions: Western Hemisphere." *South Atlantic Quarterly.* 55 (July 1956), 263–279.

FREI MONTALVO, EDUARDO. *Latin America: The Hopeful Option.* London: Orbis, 1978.

GERMANI, GINO. *Política y sociedad en una época de transición.* Buenos Aires: Editorial Paidos, 1964.

————. *Sociologiá de la modernización.* Buenos Aires: Editorial Paidos, 1969.

GIL, FEDERICO G. *Latin American–United States Relations.* Englewood Cliffs, N.J.: Prentice-Hall, 1971.

————. "Responsible Political Parties in Latin America." *Journal of Politics* 15 (August 1953), 333–348.

GOLDHAMER, HERBERT. *The Foreign Powers in Latin America.* Princeton, N.J.: Princeton University Press, 1972.

GLADE, WILLIAM P. *The Latin American Economies.* New York: Van Nostrand Reinhold, 1969.

GORDON, WENDELL C. *The Economy of Latin America.* New York: Columbia University Press, 1950.

————. *The Political Economy of Latin America.* New York: Columbia University Press, 1965.

GOTT, RICHARD. *Guerrilla Movements in Latin America.* New York: Doubleday, 1971.

GRIGORYAN, Y. "Latin America: A New Form of Dependence." *International Affairs (USSR)* 7 (July 1978), 103–107.

GUNNEMAN, JON, ed. *The Nation-State and Transnational Corporations in Conflict: With Special Reference to Latin America.* New York: Holt, Rinehart & Winston, 1975.

HALPER, STEFAN A., and JOHN R. STERLING. *Latin America: The Dynamics of Social Change.* New York: St. Martin's Press, 1975.

HALPERIN, ERNEST. *Proletarian Class Parties in Europe and America: A Comparison.* Cambridge, Mass.: MIT Monograph, Center for International Studies, August 1967.

HARRIS, WALTER D., Jr. *The Growth of Latin American Cities.* Athens: Ohio University Press, 1971.

HAYTER, TERESA. *Aid as Imperialism.* Baltimore: Penguin, 1971.

HERMENS, FERDINAND A. "Constitutionalism, Freedom and Reform in Latin America." Chap. 5 in *Freedom and Reform in Latin America,* ed. by Frederick B. Pike. Notre Dame, Ind.: University of Notre Dame Press, 1959.

HERRING, HUBERT. *A History of Latin America: From the Beginnings to the Present.* New York: Knopf, 1962.

HOPKINS, JACK. "Contemporary Research on Public Administration and Bureaucracies in Latin America." *Latin American Research Review* 9 (Spring 1974), 109–114.

HOROWITZ, MICHAEL M. *Peoples and Cultures of the Caribbean.* Garden City, N.Y.: National History Press, 1971.

HIRSCHMAN, ALBERT O. *Journeys Toward Progress: Studies of Economic Policy-Making in Latin America.* New York: Twentieth Century Fund, 1963.

HUMPHREYS, ROBIN A. "Latin America: The Caudillo Tradition." Chap. 8 in *Soldiers and Governments: Nine Studies in Civil-Military Relations,* ed. by Michael Howard. Bloomington: Indiana University Press, 1959.

INGRAM, GEORGE M. *Expropriation of U.S. Property in South America: Nationalization of Oil and Copper Companies in Peru, Bolivia and Chile.* New York: Holt, Rinehart & Winston, 1975.

INKELES, ALEX. "Participant Citizenship in Six Developing Countries." *The American Political Science Review* 63 (December 1969), 1120–1141.

JACKSON, D. BRUCE. *Castro, the Kremlin, and Communism in Latin America.* Baltimore: Johns Hopkins University Press, 1968.

JAMES, PRESTON E. *Introduction to Latin America; The Geographic Background of Economic and Political Problems.* New York: Odyssey Press, 1964.

———. *Latin America.* New York: Odyssey Press, 1969.

JOHNSON, JOHN J., ed. *Continuity and Change in Latin America.* Stanford, Calif.: Stanford University Press, 1964.

———. *Political Change in Latin America: The Emergence of the Middle Sectors.* Stanford, Calif.: Stanford University Press, 1958.

———. "The Latin American Military as a Politically Competing Group in Transitional Society." pp.91–129 in *The Role of the Military in Underdeveloped Countries,* ed. by John J. Johnson. Princeton, N.J.: Princeton University Press, 1962.

JOHNSON, KENNETH F., and MARIA FUENTES. *Política de poder y participación política en América Latina.* Buenos Aires: Ediciones IDELA, 1973.

JORRIN, MIGUEL, and JOHN D. MARTZ. *Latin American Political Thought and Ideology.* Chapel Hill: University of North Carolina Press, 1970.

LANDSBERGER, HENRY A., ed. *The Church and Social Change in Latin America.* Notre Dame, Ind.: Notre Dame University Press, 1970.

LANGGUTH, A. J. *Hidden Terrors.* New York: Atheneum, 1978.

LA PALOMBARA, JOSEPH, ed. *Bureaucracy and Political Development.* Princeton: Princeton University Press, 1963.

LEVINSON, JEROME, and JUAN de ONIS. *The Alliance that Lost Its Way.* New York: Quadrangle/The New York Times Book Co. 1970.

LEWIS, PAUL H. *The Governments of Argentina, Brazil, and Mexico.* New York: Thomas Y. Crowell, 1975.

LINDQVIST, SVEN. *The Shadow: Latin America Faces the Seventies.* Baltimore: Penguin, 1972.

LINOWITZ, SOL, ed. *The Americas in a Changing World.* New York: Quadrangle/The New York Times Book Co. 1975.

LIPSET, SEYMOUR MARTIN, and ALDO SOLARI. *Elites in Latin America.* New York: Oxford University Press, 1967.

McDONALD, RONALD H. "Electoral Fraud and Regime Control in Latin America." *Political Quarterly* 25 (March 1972), 81–93.

———. *Party Systems and Elections in Latin America.* Chicago: Markham, 1971.

MAGDOTT, HARRY. *The Age of Imperialism.* New York: Monthly Review Press, 1969.

MAIER, JOSEPH, and RICHARD W. WEATHERHEAD, eds. *Politics of Change in Latin America.* New York: Holt, Rinehart & Winston, 1964.

MANDER, JOHN. *The Unrevolutionary Society: The Power of Latin American Conservatism in a Changing World.* New York: Knopf, 1969.

MARTIN, JOHN B. *Overtaken by Events: The Dominican Crisis from the Fall of Trujillo to the Civil War.* New York: Doubleday, 1966.

MARTZ, JOHN D. "The Place of Latin America in the Study of Comparative Politics." *Journal of Politics* 28 (February 1966), 57–80.

MECHAM, J. LLOYD. *Church and State in Latin America.* Rev. ed. Chapel Hill: University of North Carolina Press, 1966.

MERCIER VEGA, LUIS. *Roads to Power in Latin America.* London: Pall Mall Press, 1969.

MORNER, MAGNUS. *Race Mixture in the History of Latin America.* Boston: Little, Brown, 1967.

NADRA, FERNANDO. "The October Revolutionary Awakening in Latin America." *International Affairs (USSR)* No. 12 (December 1977), 49–56.

NEEDLER, MARTIN C. "Detente; Impetus for Change in Latin America?" *Journal of International Affairs* 28:2 (1974), 219.

————. "Putting Latin American Politics in Perspective." *Inter-American Economic Affairs* 16:2 (Autumn 1962), 41–50.

OJEDA GÓMEZ, NARIO. "The U.S.–L.A. Relationship Since 1960." *World Today* 30:12 (December 1974), 513–521.

PARKINSON, F. *Latin America, the Cold War and the World Powers, 1945–1973.* Beverly Hills, Calif.: Sage Publications, 1974.

PETRAS, JAMES. *Latin America: From Dependence to Revolution.* New York: John Wiley, 1973.

PETRAS, JAMES, and MAURICE ZEITLIN, eds. *Latin America: Reform or Revolution? A Reader.* New York: Fawcett Books Group–CBS Publications, 1968.

PETRAS, JAMES. *Politics and Social Structure in Latin America.* New York: Monthly Review Press, 1970.

PIKE, FREDERICK P. "Corporatism and Latin American–U.S. Relations." *Review of Politics* 36:1 (January 1974), 132.

————, ed. *Freedom and Reform in Latin America.* Notre Dame, Ind.: Notre Dame University Press, 1959.

————. *The Conflict between Church and State in Latin America.* New York: Knopf, 1964.

PITT-RIVERS, JULIAN. "Race, Color, and Class in Central America and the Andes." *Daedalus* 94 (Spring 1967), 542–559.

POBLETE TRONCOSO, MOISÉS, and BEN G. BURNETT. *The Rise of the Latin American Labor Movement.* New York: Bookman Associates, 1960.

POPPINO, ROLLIE. *International Communism in Latin America: A History of the Movement, 1917–1963.* New York: Free Press, 1964.

POWELL, JOHN D. "Peasant Society and Clientelist Politics." *American Political Science Review* 64 (June 1970), 275–284.

POWELSON, JOHN. *Institutions of Economic Growth: A Theory of Conflict Management in Developing Countries.* Princeton: Princeton University Press, 1972.

RANIS, PETER. "A Two-Dimensional Typology of Latin American Political Parties." *Journal of Politics* 30 (August 1968), 798–832.

————. *Five Latin American Nations.* New York: Macmillan, 1971.

RATLIFF, WILLIAM E. *1971 Yearbook on Latin American Communist Affairs.* Stanford, Calif.: Hoover Institution Press, 1971.

RONNING, C. NEALE. *Law and Politics in Inter-American Diplomacy.* New York: John Wiley, 1963.

ROTHCHILD, JOHN, ed. *Latin America, Yesterday and Today.* Toronto: Bantam Books, 1973.

SANTOS, EDUARDO. "Latin American Realities." *Foreign Affairs* 34 (January 1956), 247–257.

SCHMITT, KARL M., ed. *The Roman Catholic Church in Modern Latin America.* New York: Knopf, 1972.

SCHMITT, KARL M., and DAVID D. BURKS. *Evolution or Chaos: Dynamics of Latin American Government and Politics.* New York: Holt, Rinehart & Winston, 1963.

SCOTT, ROBERT E. "Government Bureaucrats and Political Change in Latin America." *Journal of International Affairs* 20 (1966), 318–331.

————. *Latin American Modernization Problems.* Urbana: University of Illinois Press, 1973.

SHAFER, R. J. *A History of Latin America.* Lexington, Mass.: Heath, 1978.

SILVERT, K. A. *Essays in Understanding Latin America.* Philadelphia: Institute for the Study of Human Issues, 1977.

SMITH, DONALD E. *Religion and Political Development.* Boston: Little, Brown, 1970.

STAVENHAGEN, RODOLFO. *Agrarian Problems and Peasant Movements in Latin America.* New York: Doubleday, 1970.

STOKES, WILLIAM S. "Parliamentary Government in Latin America." *American Political Science Review* 39 (June 1945), 522–536

———. "Violence as a Power Factor in Latin American Politics." *Western Political Quarterly* 5 (September 1952), 445–468.

SZULC, TAD. *Twilight of the Tyrants.* New York: Holt, Rinehart & Winston, 1959.

———. *The Winds of Revolution.* New York: Holt, Rinehart & Winston, 1963.

THEBERGE, JAMES D. *The Soviet Presence in Latin America.* New York: Crane, Russak, 1974.

THURBER, CLARENCE E., and LAWRENCE S. GRAHAM. *Development Administration in Latin America.* Durham, N.C.: Duke University Press, 1973.

TOMASEK, ROBERT D., ed. *Latin American Politics: Twenty-four Studies of the Contemporary Scene.* New York: Doubleday/Anchor Books, 1966.

TURNER, FREDERICK C. *Catholicism and Political Development in Latin America.* Chapel Hill: University of North Carolina Press, 1971.

VALLIER, IVAN. *Catholicism, Social Control, and Modernization in Latin America.* Englewood Cliffs, N.J.: Prentice-Hall, 1970.

VELIZ, CLAUDIO, ed. *Obstacles to Change in Latin America.* London: Oxford University Press, 1965.

———, ed. *Politics of Conformity in Latin America.* London: Oxford University Press, 1970.

VON LAZAR, ARPAD, and ROBERT R. KAUFMAN. *Reform and Revolution.* Boston: Allyn & Bacon, 1969.

WAGNER, R. HARRISON. *U.S. Policy Toward Latin America.* Stanford, Calif.: Stanford University Press, 1970.

WEAVER, JERRY L. "Value Patterns of a Latin American Bureaucracy." *Human Relations* 23 (June 1970), 225–234.

WEBB, KEMPTON E. *Geography of Latin America.* Englewood Cliffs, N.J.: Prentice-Hall, 1972.

WEST, ROBERT C., and JOHN P. AUGELLI. *Middle America: Its Lands and Peoples.* 2nd ed. Englewood Cliffs, N.J.: Prentice-Hall, 1976.

WELTY, PAUL T. *Latin American Cultures.* Philadelphia: Lippincott, 1974.

WHITAKER, ARTHUR P., ed. *Latin America and the Enlightenment.* Ithaca, N.Y.: Cornell University Press, 1961.

———. "Nationalism and Social Change in Latin America." Chap. 4 in *Politics of Change in Latin America,* ed. by Joseph Maier and Richard W. Weatherhead. New York: Holt, Rinehart & Winston, 1964.

WILKIE, JAMES W., and KENNETH RUDDLE, eds. *Quantitative Latin American Studies: Methods and Findings.* Los Angeles: UCLA Latin American Center, 1977.

WILLIAMS, EDWARD J. *Latin American Christian Democratic Parties.* Knoxville: University of Tennessee Press, 1976.

———. "The Emergence of the Secular Nation-State and Latin American Catholicism." *Comparative Politics* 5 (January 1973), 261–277.

WILLIAMSON, ROBERT, WILLIAM GLADE, and KARL SCHMITT, eds. *Latin America–United States Economic Interactions: Conflict Accommodation and Policies for the Future.* Washington, D.C.: American Enterprise Institute, 1974.

WOOD, BRYCE. *The United States and Latin American Wars.* New York: Columbia University Press, 1966.

WYCKOFF, THEODORE. "The Role of the Military in Contemporary Latin American Politics." *Western Political Quarterly* 13 (September 1963), 745–763.

WYNIA, GARY W. *Politics and Planners: Economic Development Policy in Central America.* Madison: University of Wisconsin Press, 1972.

"Y." "On a Certain Impatience with Latin America." *Foreign Affairs* 28 (July 1950), 565–579.

Index

A

ABC group, 228
Agrarian Reform Law, 107, 110
Alcalde, defined, 169
Alienation, politics of, 290–318
Alienation phenomenon, 6–7
Alternación, defined, 164
Ancien régime, 26
Apertura democrática, 30, 48
Aprismo, defined, 8
Argentina
  cabildo abierto, 291
  developmental prospects, 317–18
  governmental and political structures, 304–17
    executive, 305–7
    interest groups, 316–17
    legislative and judicial, 307–9
    local, 309–10
    military, 315–16
    parties, 310–15
  political culture and environment, 290–304
    agents of development, 292–96
    caudillos, 292
    immobilism, 299–301
    stagnation, 299–301
  presidential election results, 1973, 315
Artificiality, politics of, 89–96
Authoritarianism, institutionalized, 321–30

B

"Banana republics," 85
Barriadas, 5
Batista, Fulgencio, 8, 104–6
Bolivar, Simon, 4, 15, 193
Bolivia
  campesinos, 213
  Chaco War, 212
  composition of population, 210–11
  developmental prospects, 225–26
  geographic plan, 210
  governmental and political structures, 218–25
    campesino syndicates, 220
    executive, 218–19
    legislative and judicial, 219
    local, 219–20
    military, 224–25
    military *caudillos,* 220
    miners, 224
    parties, 220–22
  political culture and environment, 210–18
  political development, 211–18
    caudillos, 211
  pressure groups, 219
  War of the Pacific, 211
Botellas, defined, 107
Brazil
  communication network, 287
  democracy, 269
  developmental prospects, 286–87
  economic independence, 286
  geographic plan
    favelas, 259
    sertões, 259
  governmental and political structures, 270–86
    bureaucratic, 272–73
    coronelismo, 277–78
    descamisados, 279
    executive, 271–72
    judicial, 275
    legislative, 273–75
    party development, 277
    political pressure groups, 283–86
    pseudoconstitutional military tutelage, 280–83
    queremistas, 279
    state and local, 276–77
  political culture and environment, 259–69
    authoritarianism, 265–69
    caudillismo, 261–62
    corporatism, 265–69
    descamisãdos, 264
    distensao, 268
    postindependence period, 260–65
    queremistas, 263
    rotavismo, 262
    tenentes, 262
  population, 260
  racial tolerance, 260
  slavery, 260
  social structure
    casa grande, 260
    fazenda, 260
Buitre Justiciero (Vulture of Justice), 60

C

Callampas, 5
Calles, Plutarco Elias, 26–27
Capoulards, defined, 123
Cárdenas, Lázaro, 27–29
Castro, Fidel, 8, 105–8
  and communism, 111–13
  success, 106–8
Catholic Church, impact on Latin American
    politics, 354–55
Caudillismo, 127, 128
Caudillo(s), 14, 15, 24, 27, 40, 173, 353
  defined, 11
Caudillo-pensador dichotomy, 15
*Caudillo-*type leader, 3
Central America, 54–86 *See also individual*
    country.
Central American Common Market (CACM), 58
Central American Federation, 54–86
Central American five, assessment of, 85–86
Chile
  audiencia, 229
  Catholic Church, impact of, 230, 252–53
  developmental prospects, 253–54
  geographical features, 228–29
  governmental and political structures, 240–51
    administrative support, 242–43
    executive, 240–42
    judicial, 243–44
    legislative, 243
    local, 244–45
    party dynamics, 245–51
    political party trends, 251
  immigration, 229
  island possessions, 228
  mestizo, 229
  political culture and development, 228–40
    colonial period, 229
    conservative period, 230–31
    liberal period, 231
    Marxist period, 237–38
    military presence, 238–40
    parliamentary period, 231–34
    postindependence period, 229–30
    postparliamentary period, 234–36